The Political Thought of
Benjamin Franklin

THE AMERICAN HERITAGE SERIES

THE AMERICAN HERITAGE SERIES

The Political Thought of Benjamin Franklin

Edited by

RALPH L. KETCHAM

Syracuse University

Hackett Publishing Company, Inc.
Indianapolis/Cambridge

This book was originally published as a volume in the American Heritage Series under the general editorship of Leonard W. Levy and Alfred Young.

Copyright © 1965 by Bobbs-Merrill.

Reprinted 2003 by Hackett Publishing Company, Inc. All rights reserved

Printed in the United States of America

09 08 07 06 05 04 03   1 2 3 4 5 6 7

For further information, please address:

    Hackett Publishing Company, Inc.
    P.O. Box 44937
    Indianapolis, IN 46244-0937

    www.hackettpublishing.com

Cover design by Rick Todhunter and Abigail Coyle
Printed at Sheridan Books, Inc.

Library of Congress Cataloging-in-Publication Data

Franklin, Benjamin, 1706–1790.
    The political thought of Benjamin Franklin / edited by Ralph L. Ketcham.
    p. cm.
    Originally published: Indianapolis: Bobbs-Merrill, c1965 (The American heritage series).
    Includes bibliographical references and index.
    ISBN 0-87220-684-X (alk. paper)—ISBN 0-87220-683-1 (pbk.: alk. paper)
    1. United States—Politics and government, 1775–1783. 2. United States—Politics and government—1783–1789. 3. United States Foreign relations—To 1865. 4. Political science—Early works to 1800. 5. Political science—Untited States—History—18th century. I. Ketcham, Ralph Louis, 1927– II. American heritage series (New York, N.Y.)

E302.F82 2003
973.3'092—dc22

                                            2003054420

The paper used in this publication meets the minimum requirements of American National Standard for Information Sciences—Permanence of Paper for Printed Library Materials, ANSI Z39.48-1984

The Political Thought

of Benjamin Franklin

Foreword

There is an old tale that Ben Franklin was not trusted with the responsibility of framing the Declaration of Independence because some thought that he might plant a sly jape in the midst of the solemn statement. Franklin doubtlessly regarded human events with a certain skepticism, amusement, and tolerance, which is probably why he was a sage rather than a philosopher. A spokesman and practitioner of robust utilitarianism, he could not abandon himself to the perfervid support of any fixed set of principles, whether in politics or diplomacy. His mind was too complex, too subtle, too versatile, and above all too practical to engage in the kind of systematic philosophizing about politics that passes for political theory in the grand and formal manner. Yet there never was a political theory that more closely abutted the public interest and political issues of consequence than Ben Franklin's. To regard him as one of the least philosophic of all American statesmen is to misunderstand the *ad hoc*, pragmatic character of American political thought. To dismiss his thought as a simplistic philosophy of common virtues and common sense is to miss the fact that his conclusions were the result of an extraordinarily enlightened, secularistic, and critical mind that had cut away abstractions and pretentiousness. To pass over his letters, essays, and fugitive papers is to ignore the reflections of one who lived and learned from a lifetime of politics. To categorize him as the representative colonial democrat is to ignore his complexities and inconsistencies — his condemnation, for example, of seditious scribblers who inflamed the people against authority and order; or, his criticism of protest literature for stirring up the poor and leading to insurrection.

The virtue of this anthology, which has been compiled with commentary by an editor of the monumental *Franklin Papers*, is that it gives Franklin's achievements and expressions as a political theorist appropriate recognition. There have been several anthologies of Franklin's writings, and some are excellent; but they stress the biographical or the literary. This is the first collection that focuses on Franklin as a political theorist.

This book is part of a series that provides the essential primary sources of the American experience, especially of American thought, from the colonial period to the present. The series, when completed, will constitute a documentary library of American history. These volumes will fill a need among scholars, students, libraries, and even general readers, for authoritative collections of original materials that illuminate the thought of significant individuals, such as James Madison or Louis Brandeis; or of groups, such as Puritan political theorists, or American Catholic leaders on social policy; or of movements, such as the Antifederalists or the Populists. There are a surprising number of subjects traditionally studied in American history for which there are no documentary anthologies. This series will be by far the most comprehensive and authoritative of its kind. It will also have the distinction of presenting representative pieces of substantial length that have not been butchered into snippets.

Leonard W. Levy
Alfred Young

Contents

Foreword

VII

Introduction

XXVII

Chronology

LVII

Selected Bibliography

LXI

Editor's Note and Acknowledgments

LXVII

An Analytical Table of Contents, indicating the documents in which Franklin expressed his major ideas, appears on pages 433–440.

PART ONE

Business, Civic, and Political Leader, 1722–1757

Contents

[ESSAYS IN *The New-England Courant, 1722–1723*]
Silence Dogood, Number Three
2
Silence Dogood, Number Nine
3
An Editorial
7
On Titles of Honor
9

[1729]
The Busy-Body, Number Three
12
The Nature and Necessity of a Paper-Currency
14

[1731]
Observations on Reading History
18
An Apology for Printers
20

[1732]
Junto Queries
24

[1735]
Natural Religion and Freedom of Thought
27

[1740]

Freedom of the Press

33

[1741]

The Character of Andrew Hamilton

35

[1742]

On Lawful Process

37

[1745]

The Evils of Taverns

37

[1747]

Speech of Miss Polly Baker

39

Plain Truth

43

Proposals for a Volunteer and Republican Military Force

46

[1748]

Advice to a Young Tradesman

51

[1749]

Education and the Public Good:
pamphlet and letter to Samuel Johnson

54

[1751]

Hospitals, Charity, and the Public Good

57

Criminals and Citizenship

60

Observations Concerning the Increase of Mankind

62

[1753]

Poverty and the Effects of German Immigration
to Pennsylvania: letter to Peter Collinson

72

The Social Value of a Religion of Good Works:
letter to Joseph Huey

80

The Evils of the Indian Trade

82

[1754]

The Albany Plan of Union

83

Reasons and Motives for the Albany Plan of Union

88

Letters to William Shirley on the Place
of the Colonies in the British Empire

97

Contents   xiii

Plan for Establishing English Colonies
in the Ohio Valley

105

[1755]

Humility and the Search for Truth:
letter to John Lining

109

A Parable Against Persecution

109

The Rights of a Colonial Assembly

111

A Militia Act Protecting Conscientious Objectors

126

[1756]

A Rebuke to Cowards and Idlers:
letter to Augustus Spangenberg

133

Franklin's Political Principles

134

Popular Support and Resisting the Proprietors:
letter to Peter Collinson

138

xiv *Contents*

PART TWO

Spokesman for America in England, 1757–177

[1757]

Conversation with a Noble Lord
on Legislation for the Colonies

141

The Social Value of Religion

142

[1758]

The Vices of British Government and the Virtues
of William Pitt: letter to Joseph Galloway

144

[1759]

Friends and Foes of America in England:
letter to Isaac Norris

146

[1760]

The Future of the British Empire in North America:
letter to Lord Kames

149

The Interest of Great Britain Considered with Regard
to Her Colonies and the Acquisition
of Canada and Guadaloupe

150

[1764]

The Barbarism and Injustice of "White Savages"

158

Royal Government Better than Proprietary Rule

162

The Foolishness of British Commercial Restrictions:
letter to Peter Collinson

167

[1765]

On Passage of the Stamp Act:
letters to Charles Thomson and to John Hughes

169

Repeal of the Stamp Act:
letters in the London *Gazetteer*
and the *Public Advertiser*, 1765–1766

171

[1766]

An Examination Before the House of Commons

182

The American Interest in Parliament:
letter to Joseph Galloway

191

On a Common Parliament for the British Empire:
letter to Cadwallader Evans

192

Contents

[1767]

The Uses of Paper Currency

193

The Nature of the British Empire:
letter to Lord Kames

197

America and British Politics:
letter to Joseph Galloway

202

On Smuggling

204

[1768]

Causes of the American Discontents Before 1768

209

The British Constitution

216

Corruption in Parliamentary Elections:
letters to Joseph Galloway

217

On the Labouring Poor

219

Riots in London over "Wilkes and Liberty":
letters to John Ross and to Joseph Galloway

224

[1769]

Positions to Be Examined, Concerning National Wealth

226

A Strategy for Resisting British Oppression:
letter to Samuel Cooper

229

[1770]

Fables on the Mother Country and Her Colonies

232

The Right to Vote

233

An Evil Parliament and a Good King:
letter to Samuel Cooper

235

On Office-Holding: letter to Jane Mecom

237

[1771]

The Seeds of a "Total Disunion"
Between Great Britain and America:
letter to the Committee
of Correspondence in Massachusetts

239

A Realistic Appraisal of the British Empire:
letter to Thomas Cushing

241

[1772]

The Farmers of Great Britain
and New England Compared:
letter to Joshua Babcock

244

xviii *Contents*

Toleration in Old England and New England

245

[1773]

Advice to the Colonies: Union, Moderation,
and Firmness; letter to Thomas Cushing

251

Rules by which a Great Empire May Be Reduced
to a Small One and An Edict by the King of Prussia

254

The Natural Right of Emigration

270

[1774]

Defense of Franklin's Career as Agent
and the Loss of His Offices: The Hutchinson Letters;
tract and letter to Thomas Cushing

275

The Boston Tea Party: letter to the Committee
of Correspondence in Massachusetts

278

A Final Plea to Preserve the British Empire:
letter to Thomas Cushing

279

Some Good Whig Principles

280

[1775]

On Corruption in England: letter to Joseph Galloway

282

Great Britain and Europe at the Beginning
of the American Revolution

282

PART THREE

Revolutionist in America, 1775–1776

[1775]

British Vices and American Virtues:
letter to Joseph Priestley

287

Articles of Confederation and Perpetual Union

288

[1776]

First Proposals for Peace with Great Britain

294

PART FOUR

Minister to France, 1776–1785

[1777]

Comparison of Great Britain
and the United States

297

xx Contents

Franklin's Candid View of His Mission in France:
letter to Jan Ingenhousz

301

The American Revolution in Europe:
letter to Samuel Cooper

302

[1778]

The Alliance with France: letters to David Hartley,
to Thomas Cushing, and to William Pulteney

303

Diplomacy in Paris: letter to James Lovell

307

[1779]

Parable Against English Proposals
that America Break the French Alliance:
letter to David Hartley

309

Passport for Captain Cook

310

The Morals of Chess and Diplomacy

312

[1780]

Washington's Fame in Europe and America's Future:
letter to George Washington

314

Franklin and John Adams on Franco-American Relations:
letter to Samuel Huntington

315

On State Support for Religion:
letter to Richard Price

317

Spain, The United States, and the Mississippi River:
letters to John Jay

318

[1781]

Franklin's Diplomatic Service:
Attack and Vindication; letters to Samuel Huntington
and to William Carmichael

319

[1782]

On Betraying France to Secure Peace
with Great Britain: letters to David Hartley

322

British Barbarity during
the American Revolution

324

Human Depravity in War: letter to Joseph Priestley

330

On Reconciliation between Great Britain
and The United States

331

xxii *Contents*

Progress, Prosperity, and Peace:
letters to Sir Joseph Banks

334

Information to Those Who Would Remove to America

336

The Art of Diplomacy: letter to Comte de Vergennes

346

[1 7 8 3]

Proposals to Make Wars Less Likely
and Less Destructive

347

The Advantages of a Free Trade:
letters to Comte de Vergennes
and to Robert R. Livingston

351

Dispute with John Adams over Gratitude Toward France:
letter to Robert R. Livingston

352

The Foundations of American Foreign Policy:
letters to Thomas Mifflin, to Samuel Mather,
and to Charles Thomson

354

The Obligation to Pay Taxes:
letter to Robert Morris

357

[1 7 8 4]

On Hereditary Societies and the Eagle

as an American Symbol: letter to Sarah Franklin Bache

358

On Dueling: letter to Thomas Percival

362

Selfish Interests, Commerce, Necessities,
and Luxuries: letter to Benjamin Vaughan

363

Remarks Concerning the Savages of North America

368

[1785]

Crime and Punishment: letter to Benjamin Vaughan

373

The Legitimate Powers of Elected Assemblies:
letter to George Whateley

375

American Loyalty to the Ancient English Liberties:
letter to Francis Maseres

376

PART FIVE

Sage at Home, 1785–1790

[1786]

The Progress of Government and Prosperity
in The United States: letters to Jonathan Shipley
and to William Hunter

379

The Internal State of America
381
[1787]
Speeches at the Constitutional Convention
387
The Constitutional Convention
and the Foolishness of War: letter to Jane Mecom
403
[1788]
On the Abuse of the Press: letter to the editors
of *The Pennsylvania Gazette*
404
A Comparison of the Conduct of the Ancient Jews
and of the Anti-Federalists
in The United States of America
408
On the New Constitution and Prospects
for Government Under It:
letters to friends in France
413
[1789]
On Abuses of Freedom of the Press
417
A Unicameral Legislature
and Extension of the Suffrage
421

Education for Emancipated Slaves

426

On The French Revolution: letters
to Jean-Baptiste LeRoy and to David Hartley

427

[1790]

The Evils of the Slave Trade

428

Analytical Table of Contents

433

Index

441

Introduction

Benjamin Franklin never wrote a treatise on political philosophy. It is not possible even to find in his extant writings explicit statements on fundamental questions of political theory; nowhere does he explain systematically his concepts of the nature of man, the purpose of government, or the meaning of justice in society. He would have denied that he was a political philosopher, or that he had any understanding of their inquiries. In the fashion of his day he disdained any particular interest in government or public affairs, preferring instead to pose as a scientist, printer, or moralist.

Franklin's political thought is embodied in his long career as a public servant and is embedded in the thousands of letters and essays he wrote about the events and issues of that service. Furthermore, his mind was mature and well-disciplined long before he had to take public affairs seriously. When that time did come, he simply applied to politics principles he already considered well-tested from use in his personal and business affairs. Thus, the foundations of Franklin's political thought are found in the precepts and habits of mind formed many years before he first took a leading role in public life when past age forty.

VIRTUE, CIVIC IMPROVEMENT, AND POLITICAL OBLIGATION

Franklin records among the memorable exploits of his youth the story of leading a group of boys in building a fishing wharf on the mill pond in Boston, a worthy enterprise, Franklin thought, except that they had taken the stones from a nearby building site. Caught in the act, he sought to persuade his father that the project was useful, but the elder Franklin admonished his son that "nothing was useful which was not honest." Had Franklin missed the point of this lesson he could not easily have avoided it elsewhere. His child's catechism, for example, explained that "thou shalt not steal" meant men were forbidden "to take away another man's goods without his leave: or to spend our own without benefit to ourselves or others," and required them to "get our goods honestly, to keep them safely, and to spend them thriftily." In hundreds of instances he learned, like other Puritan youths, that before a person could be useful in the world at large he had first to be trained in the personal virtues; it was chimerical to think a bad person could be a good politician.

The character of Franklin's father illustrates the point. He was a devout, humble man, engrossed in the task of raising a large family, and would doubtless have been forgotten had not his famous son described him so vividly. Among other things, the elder Franklin took his social responsibilities seriously, beginning with the rearing of his children. He took care that his sons learned a useful trade, and he insisted that the family use its hours together to some good purpose; he often had interesting guests at the dinner table whose instructive conversation "improved," he thought, the assembled children. His prudence, honesty, and good judgment soon made him an arbitrator in neighborhood disputes, and he took a modest role in the affairs of his church and town. Though Benjamin Franklin soon rejected his father's theology, he never ceased to honor and respect his parents. His political thought has no underlying principle or purpose beyond the assumption that the personal virtues taught in *Pilgrim's Progress* and personified in the most admirable relatives and counselors of his youth were necessary to effective statecraft and were the qualities of life that social institutions, including government, existed to encourage. The practical, perhaps even mundane aspect of much of Franklin's political thought and action has its root in his conviction that no social act (or scientific discovery) had value unless it promised to nurture in some way the virtues and habits of life he had learned to admire in his father's house.

Clinton Rossiter has suggested that the three foundations of colonial political thought were natural rights, Whig constitutionalism, and virtue, linked in a way that Franklin must have heard and read hundreds of times before he entered public life: the great principles (natural rights) were best protected by the English system of government (Whig constitutionalism) which required for its effective conduct and administration that virtuous men be in the seats of power. Later, Franklin forsook his allegiance to England, when he was convinced that her rulers no longer possessed virtue. To him, in a very fundamental sense, government was a matter of ethics; if men did not possess the requisite personal qualities they could not be good governors. Consequently, the purpose of any government was to create conditions that would encourage the virtues essential to a society worthy of preservation.

Franklin expressed his belief in the prime importance of personal virtue in many ways. He wrote his *Autobiography* to display the simple habits and attitudes that had enabled him to serve mankind; he assumed that to instruct by precept and example in the art of virtue was to build the good society. In preaching thrift and prudence as Poor Richard he sought, he said, to relieve men of burdens much heavier than government taxes: "We are taxed twice as much by our *Idleness*, three times as much by our *Pride*, and four times as much by our *Folly*." He said over and over again that the colonists could best secure their rights and even their independence through their industrious habits and belief in the strength derived from union. These were matters, of course, over which the colonists themselves had complete control and to which the virtue of every individual made an indispensable contribution. Franklin the politician is inexplicable apart from Franklin the moralist, a connection upon which he himself always insisted and of which his colleagues in statecraft were always aware. To honor America's first Minister to France John Paul Jones named his ship the *Bonhomme Richard*.

Between Franklin's youthful education in virtue and his election to public office when forty-two years old, he had a notable career as a civic leader. Displaying a talent for organizing in the public interest reminiscent of Daniel Defoe's *Essay upon Projects*, and accepting a hint from Cotton Mather's *Essays to do Good* on forming clubs to nourish social responsibility, Franklin set about making Philadelphia a better place to live. His "Junto" of fellow tradesmen, all ambitious for personal improvement and civic welfare, expressed the essence of his social outlook: men of good will acting together *could* make a difference, both in their individual self-discipline and in the well-being of the community. Franklin seems never to have despaired of being able to *do something* about the ills of mankind. It required only that men organize, work together, and apply their hearts and minds and energy to the problem at hand. In this spirit he founded a library, a college, and a hospital, organized fire and insurance companies, and saw to it that the streets of Philadelphia were paved, cleaned, lighted, and safe.

In every promotion he meant simply to "write large" the personal virtues to which he was devoted. He sought personally to help care for the sick, to make books widely available, and to keep his shop clean, but his genius was to see that by combining talents and resources a hospital, for example, could go far beyond the ability of any one individual, however able or well-intended, to alleviate human suffering. Likewise a library open at a modest cost to all with a zeal to learn multiplied one-hundredfold the skimpy knowledge otherwise available to those who could afford to buy but a few books. By organizing to have the streets swept regularly Franklin proposed to save shoppers and shopkeepers alike from the countless petty vexations of having dirt soiling goods and blowing in people's eyes. Just as Franklin's insistence on the personal virtues is the moral basis of his political thought, his instinct for molding men and ideas into institutions for human improvement is its operational basis.

When he took his seat in the Philadelphia City Council in 1748 and in the Pennsylvania Assembly in 1751, he knew perfectly well *what* he wanted and *how* he would seek his ends. He sought to enhance the quality of the life of the people in the province by extending to the political sphere habits of action he had found effective as a civic leader. He did not accept office as part of any "revolution" in the affairs of the province. Rather he entered the Assembly with the blessing of its long-dominant Quaker leaders who had spotted Franklin as a useful fellow now ready for a larger arena. He accepted the service as an opportunity to act at large on behalf of community projects he had long supported as a businessman and citizen.

Thus, as Franklin began his long career as a politician and diplomat, he had an already mature public philosophy which sought to extend personal convictions to ever wider horizons. Though some students have argued that his private habits and his public life were discordant, in fact they were in close harmony. He believed, as Cato had in ancient Rome, that free government could not long survive the corruption and degeneracy of its constituents. Wise laws could not preserve the liberty and happiness of a depraved people. Franklin's practical mind then turned to means: how could virtue be maintained and enlarged? In addition to supporting churches and other value-conserving institutions, Franklin, as Poor Richard, instructed the masses, and as a good citizen he formed the Junto to discipline his habits and those of his friends in ways useful to the commonweal. Next he reached out to express this sense of virtue and discipline in the civic promotions for which he is to this day most honored in his adopted city. In reaching further, to the colonial legislature, he did not conceive, as many are inclined to do today, that he had crossed a momentous gulf between private and public action. Government to him was simply the ultimate and potentially the most effective agency for acting in the public interest. His skilful persuasion of the legislature to support the privately-founded academy and hospital is evidence of his faith in the beneficence of political power whenever used with integrity. His subsequent careers as a builder of a dynamic, freedom-extending British Empire, as an organizer of colonial union, and finally as a founder of an independent nation were but further enlargements of his zeal to make political institutions enrich and enhance the lives of the citizens. Franklin accepted as truisms, in short, political concepts that more formal or legalistic minds have seen fit to debate and define endlessly. To him the obligation of the body politic was a seamless robe: virtuous citizens should act together exercising such political power as seemed useful in seeking the good of all. Though many political philosophers popular in Franklin's day, Locke foremost among them, would have endorsed this view, Franklin did not cull it from books; by the time he was fifty he had learned it emphatically and indelibly from his extraordinarily active life.

Introduction xxxiii

FREEDOM OF EXPRESSION AND RELIGION

In assuming a more active role in politics Franklin further explained his understanding of freedom of expression and of the social importance of religion. As a newspaper publisher he had long sought to educate and uplift the public. Furthermore, following the conventional view of his day, he accepted the doctrine of seditious libel, which, according to English common law in the eighteenth century, held that merely to express or print an opinion bringing government into contempt might be unlawful. He once wrote approvingly of applying a coat of tar and feathers to printers who "affronted" the public by defaming the honor and dignity of government. He wrote in his *Autobiography* that he could not as a responsible newspaper publisher fill his columns with "Libelling and Personal Abuse . . . [or] scurrilious Reflections on the Government." He asserted rather that newspapers should be vehicles of public instruction and edification. Franklin had the same objective as a publisher as he had as a civic leader: to promote consciously and directly the public good. He never accepted the libertarian concept that the only antidote to defaming and scandalous charges against government was the test of truth in open and unlimited discussion.

Yet Franklin nearly always shrank from penalizing a printer or anyone else for circulating sensational charges. In 1758 he defended the right of his publishing partner, David Hall, to print a libelous assault on the Pennsylvania Assembly (though he thought in so doing Hall might have been imprudent). At the same time he made clear his own objection to high-handed contempt proceedings by the Assembly against the author of the libel, but he reversed the reasoning he had given to Hall: he upheld the right of the Assembly to defend itself regardless of the rights of free expression, but he objected that it was unwise for it to have acted as it did in the case at hand. The defense of Hall's rights as a printer and of the Assembly's contempt rights cannot be wholly reconciled. Nevertheless, in each instance Franklin in effect opposed restraint on freedom of expression. His New World faith in an open society had, perhaps without his realizing it, undermined the formal concepts of legitimacy which for centuries had nourished the doctrine of seditious libel in England. His keen sense of constructive action in the public interest kept him from espousing the libertarian ideas later given classic expression by John Stuart Mill, but at the same time he did not really believe that in a free country mere words could be dangerous, nor did he have any real sympathy for the oppressive purposes which had long supported license and censorship of the press.

Franklin rejected the widely-held view that attacks on religion, its ministers, or its doctrines could be so dangerous to public order and morality as to require suppression by law. His Addisonian abhorrence of the fanatical sects and overbearing establishments that so often used the doctrine of blasphemous libel to persecute rival groups made him a ready foe of any form of religious intolerance. Moreover, his experience with religious pluralism in Pennsylvania convinced him that toleration was the only practical course there. He wrote in his *Autobiography* of the friendly support he gave all the churches in Philadelphia, and in his first years as a newspaper publisher he defended courageously a Presbyterian minister whose fellow clergymen sought to bar him from the pulpit for his alleged heresy. "Nothing, in all Probability," Franklin wrote, "can prevent our being a very flourishing and happy People, but our suffering the Clergy to get upon our Backs, and ride us, as they do their Horses, where they please." In 1755 he wrote his famous "Parable against

Persecution" pretending to show in a scriptural incident that God himself had scolded Abraham for persecuting one of a different religion. Though he never defended freedom of conscience in the absolute terms of James Madison's "Memorial and Remonstrance" (1785), persecution or intolerance instantly and instinctively repelled Franklin.

He failed to stand for complete separation of church and state because he believed strongly that organized religion provided important, probably indispensable support for public morality and virtue. He had no objection therefore to established churches that neither restrained dissenters nor compelled them to support a form of worship abhorrent to them. He accepted the Lockean concept of religious toleration. Again and again he chastised religious men so obsessed with polemics and sectarian doctrines that they neglected to teach morality, good will, and Christian forebearance. For the same reason in 1757 he advised the author of a deistical tract not to publish it because it "struck at the Foundation of all Religion." It might, Franklin wrote, undermine the faith of "weak and ignorant Men and Women, and of inexperienc'd and inconsiderate Youth" who needed religion "to restrain them from Vice, to support their Virtue, and retain them in the Practice of it till it becomes *habitual*." Franklin believed religion served a crucial public function, but he agreed with liberal opinion in his day that persecution undercut rather than reinforced its social utility.

THE RIGHTS OF REPRESENTATIVE ASSEMBLIES

In 1747, before Franklin entered the Pennsylvania Assembly and thus became an important politician, he played a leading role as a private citizen in persuading its Quaker leaders that the province might defend itself in war in spite of its pacifist principles. Franklin saw that most men on both sides of the pacifism issue were not in irreconcilable conflict. Moderate Quakers in government asked only that they be spared having to make laws that would coerce their strict pacifist brethren to pay war taxes or march in the militia, while moderate non-Quakers asked only that *they* be permitted to defend themselves and the province. Franklin wrote a pamphlet, *Plain Truth,* proposing on the one hand that the Quaker Assembly continue its indirect war appropriations and not impede private defense measures, and on the other, that those who favored action form themselves into a voluntary militia and raise money to build a fort. The plan received enthusiastic acceptance, armed men marched for the first time in the streets of Philadelphia, and Franklin became, as the uneasy Proprietor, Thomas Penn, remarked, "a Sort of Tribune of the People [who] must be treated with regard." Franklin thus perceived that his instinct for accommodation and his sense of the general welfare could be effective on the largest questions of public policy, and entered the Assembly in 1751 confident of his course.

He believed that the Quakers had been on the whole "good and useful" rulers in Pennsylvania, that they had developed modes of government suited to the free society of the province, and that they ought not to be excluded from the Assembly because some of them (a minority Franklin thought as a result of his experience in 1747) were strict pacifists. Moreover, he shared wholeheartedly their insistence that Pennsylvania be governed by the Assembly and executive officials in the province for its general welfare rather than by the Proprietors in England for their private enrichment. The dispute erupted bitterly when Thomas Penn insisted that his vast lands be exempt from taxation. Franklin served as penman for the Assembly in a long debate in which he laid down the basic principles of self-government for America: that as freemen enjoying the privileges of Englishmen, Pennsylvanians were entitled to decide their own modes of taxation, that under their Charter of Liberties and the natural rights of man they had the right to regulate their own internal affairs, that a Proprietor in a remote country could not in justice or practicality rule Pennsylvania, and that only the elected representatives of the people would govern consistently in their interest. In working out this stand Franklin experienced for the first time bitter political animosities. When he left for England in 1757 to plead the Assembly cause, he had in six years of controversy turned his general concern for the public welfare into political precepts that no longer permitted him to agree with men of all parties. Franklin the politician, eager for accommodation but willing to accept a challenge or fight if necessary to maintain essential principles, was a product of the Pennsylvania party strife of the 1750's.

Franklin's prescription for the ills of proprietary rule in Pennsylvania, royal government, shows that he had no elaborate, systematic natural rights theory in mind in opposing the Proprietors. He began with a practical judgment, based on twenty-five years of deep involvement in the affairs of the province. Because an increase in proprietary power would inhibit the capacity of Pennsylvanians to deal with their problems in ways best suited to them, he exalted the authority of an assembly that had long discharged faithfully its public trust, resisted proprietary privilege, and in annual elections kept in close touch with the people. These were but the simple precepts of Poor Richard—common sense, fair play, and concern for the commonweal—applied to government. Franklin doubtless knew that the precepts agreed with the doctrines of John Locke and other natural rights' theorists, just as he knew that his readers were well-versed in those theories. But nothing is plainer in Franklin's ever-growing commitment to public life than his inductive approach: he sought laws that would account for and deal with the circumstances and conditions he knew existed among his friends and neighbors.

Franklin's understanding of the rights of a colonial legislature was similar to that of dozens of men from Massachusetts to Georgia. The quest for power, a phrase used recently by Jack P. Greene to describe the guiding objective of southern legislatures from 1689 to 1776, was for Franklin and many others a quest for the right of the people of a particular province to direct their own destinies. By the mid 1750's, when Franklin developed his concept of assembly rights, he was utterly certain that just governments could exist only with the consent of the governed, and that the rights to life, liberty, and the pursuit of happiness were self-evident and inalienable. He had supposed all his life that these rights were integral parts of the British constitution, applicable in all parts of the Empire. When English rulers denied this, Franklin was ready to accept, expound, and expand the doctrines of liberty and constitutional government, which were the theoretical foundations of the American Revolution. His career in the Pennsylvania Assembly, then, was both a fulfillment of things past and a forecast of things to come.

**FEDERATION AND UNION:
FROM EMPIRE TO INDEPENDENCE**

In asserting Assembly rights against the Proprietors Franklin showed no sign of disloyalty to Great Britain. Rather, he wrote and acted zealously for the growth and glory of the Empire from the year of his first election to the Assembly. In 1751, in "Observations concerning the Increase of Mankind, Peopling of Countries. . ." he argued

Introduction xxxix

that the open lands of North America, settled by Englishmen and increasing rapidly in population and wealth as they were sure to do if left unrestrained, would make the British Empire the largest, most powerful, most glorious, and freest state the world had ever known. Rightly understood, the interests of Britain and her colonies were in perfect harmony: American farms would be a profitable market for British manufactures and commerce for ages to come. England had only to rule as "a wise and good Mother," seeking to strengthen, not weaken, her dynamic and intensely loyal colonies, to assure this great future. Franklin restated the argument in 1760 in a pamphlet urging Great Britain to retain possession of conquered Canada. By expelling France from North America England had an opportunity to extend her benign rule to millions of square miles of virgin land. Though he did not say so directly in these pamphlets, Franklin's thesis implied that should England foolishly pursue policies of restraint and oppression, she would fail. Franklin never doubted that North American expansion in freedom and prosperity was irresistible. His confidence in 1776 that the new United States could "go it alone" if necessary, his calm insistence that France rode the wave of the future in sponsoring American independence, and his limitless faith in the prospects for government under the Constitution of 1787 were all founded in his belief that America was destined to be, in Jefferson's apt phrase, "an empire of liberty"; under what flag was a matter of less significance.

In seeking North American expansion Franklin returned many times to the theme of union. Under the motto "Join or Die" he sought at Albany in 1754 to persuade colonists and English officials alike that a "Plan of Union" was the obvious way to resist French encroachments, to deal with the Indians, and to regulate such general matters as settling new colonies and deciding defense levies. He there-

xl *Introduction*

fore proposed that an assembly elected by the colonial legislatures roughly according to the population of each colony, with a president general appointed by the king, share the government. When a royal official suggested eliminating the legislatures from any part in the Plan, Franklin responded with his famous "Letters to Governor William Shirley" (December 1754) setting forth for the colonies as a whole the doctrine he had already proclaimed for Pennsylvania: the colonists had far too long laid their own taxes through their elected assemblies to submit to a plan of union which denied them that power. In fact, the colonial assemblies would not even accept the coordinate legislative voice of the president general provided for in Franklin's Plan. In looking back nearly forty years later at its rejection, Franklin observed that if it "or something like it, had been adopted and carried into Execution, the subsequent Separation of the Colonies from the Mother Country might not so soon have happened . . . the Crown disapproved, as having plac'd too much Weight in the democratic Part of the Constitution; and every Assembly as having allow'd too much to Prerogative."

Franklin's Albany Plan of Union embodied the federal principle of divided sovereignty between the general and local governments, a notion common to many of the proposals for union that culminated in the Constitution of 1787. Franklin gave power over Indian affairs, western lands, defense, and taxation to the general government, but he denied it power to interfere with provincial constitutions. By implication, powers not granted to the general government were reserved to the provinces. In this plan Franklin set down what in nearly 150 years of experience had come to be regarded as the legitimate concerns of central and of local government, but he also proposed a division of power that seemed to him to be completely practical. The powers granted the general government were

Introduction xli

obviously those it could exercise most advantageously and efficiently. Moreover, the English colonies could not survive, in Franklin's view, without the strength afforded by union. Finally, acceptance of the Plan of Union would eliminate potentially explosive sources of friction between mother country and colonies by making clearer the relationship between them and by providing a process for resolving differences.

Franklin's 1775 "Articles of Confederation and Perpetual Union" are further evidence of his skill in devising ways to solve the difficult "one in many" riddle. He proposed that the union have all the powers given it under his Albany Plan, and in a prophetic article he proposed as well that the federal congress "make such general ordinances as, tho' necessary to the General Welfare, particular Assemblies cannot be competent to, viz. those that may relate to our general Commerce, or general Currency; the establishment of Posts; and Regulation of our common Forces." Franklin also suggested representation according to population, ratification of the Articles by "Provincial Assemblies or Conventions," and an easy mode of amendment since "all new Institutions may have Imperfections, which only Time and Experience can discover." In this plan, as in his later effective participation in the Federal Convention of 1787, he showed a master hand in projecting improvements and devising means of cooperation of which his father, Daniel Defoe, and the Philadelphia Junto would all have been proud. In fact, the sometimes miraculous increment in power to do good arising from social accord seems to have made urging and planning for union the most congenial of Franklin's political tasks.

Looking back on his long career, after he had become the foremost enemy to George III, Franklin would have noted the irony of his first diplomatic mission in England:

xlii Introduction

to exchange Pennsylvania's proprietary charter for royal government. In fact, though, Franklin's loyalty, like that of many liberal Whigs on both sides of the Atlantic, was to the *idea* of the British constitution developed by the theorists and spokesmen of the Revolution of 1688. The corruption of this ideal by unregenerate Tory autocrats, the spoilsmen of the Duke of Newcastle, or the intrigues of Lord North and George III, disgusted Franklin and Edmund Burke alike, and made each in his own way turn on those he thought had betrayed the constitution. Before Franklin had been in England a month in 1757, he tasted aristocratic disdain. Lord Granville, President of the Privy Council, told him that "you Americans have the wrong Ideas of the Nature of your Constitution; you contend that the King's Instructions to his Governors are not Laws, and think yourselves at Liberty to regard or disregard them at your Discretion. . . . They are . . . the *Law of the Land,* for the KING IS THE LEGISLATOR OF THE COLONIES." Franklin replied that "this was new Doctrine to me. I had always understood from our Charters, that our Laws were to be made by our Assemblies . . . [and] as the Assemblies could not make permanent Laws without [the King's] Assent, so neither could he make a law for them without theirs." Franklin's first intent in Great Britain, then, was to join with William Pitt, Lord Camden, and other likeminded Englishmen to preserve good Whig principles "at home," as Americans still called England, and then to secure these same privileges for the colonies.

Cooperation with William Pitt and his counselors was especially easy for Franklin because he already agreed with their concept of the British Empire: a commercial and political federation under the king that because of its natural dynamism would soon extend to the four corners of the earth. Franklin wrote incessantly on this theme during the fifteen years he spent in England (1757–1762, 1764–

1775), seeking always to point out the economic advantages of a prosperous, expanding Empire, which as it trained seamen, encouraged manufacturing, and otherwise nourished the means of war, would soon be invulnerable to the envy of its enemies. Until the experiences of 1770-1775 disillusioned him, Franklin's residence in England served to heighten his regard for the mother country and its people and made him more alert than ever to the advantages of union with England.

At the same time, though, the increasingly apparent gulf between the Whig ideals and the actual conduct of government, and the contrast more and more noted by Franklin between the open, prosperous society of America and the oppressive poverty of so many people in the British Isles, made him determined to resist at all costs a lasting connection with the worst aspects of the mother country. The House of Commons, for example, was supposed to represent the people of the realm and be a counterweight to the power of the lords and the king. Franklin thought this was in some measure the fact when he arrived in England, and he therefore looked upon the cause of the Commons as his own and sought to find support among its members for the rights of colonial assemblies. When, however, after the Stamp Act and during the Grenville, Townshend, and North ministries it became apparent that Parliament had been bought and corrupted, that most of its members were no more than paid agents of King George III, Franklin had nothing but contempt for the trumpeted representative government of Great Britain. Likewise, when it became obvious that rather than being the dupe of his ministers, George III was, in fact, the prime mover of repressive measures against his subjects in the colonies, Franklin responded with the anger of a spurned and betrayed man. Finally, as he acquired firsthand knowledge of the wretched conditions in the British countryside oppressed by absentee landlords, Franklin wrote in wondrous amazement at the contrast with the sturdy well-being of the New England farmer who worked his own farm and enjoyed the fruits of his labor.

Franklin had a firm though perhaps largely unconscious pride in the conditions of American life and government while he lived in Philadelphia. After a good look at English society his attitude became one of outspoken admiration for the "new man" of the New World. He was firm for independence and republicanism in 1776, not because he had imbibed any intoxicating ideology, but because he had experienced the effect of different principles and had no doubt as to which he preferred. He ceased to speak of the rights of Englishmen, not because *he* abandoned those rights, but because he found *them* mocked and abandoned in England. He approved enthusiastically of the sentiments Jefferson expressed in the Declaration of Independence, because in becoming a citizen of the world Franklin had learned that since no nation had a monopoly on political virtue, the only sure foundation for a free society was the pattern of rights so many of his colleagues in revolution called "natural."

During Franklin's long residence in England, there was no marked change in his political principles to explain why his fervent loyalty to the British monarchy had by 1776 disappeared. He merely revised his estimate of the kinds of political institutions most likely to support the self-government and abounding opportunity in which he had always believed, and he came to a more mature understanding of the novel society and "personality" that had come into being in the colonies. When he began in 1771 to write his *Autobiography*, telling of his rise from obscure poverty to success in business and then to world fame as moralist, scientist, and politician, he put in it the essence of his political philosophy: men were by nature full of

Introduction xlv

potential requiring only sound training, a sense of social responsibility, and liberal government to bring into being a just and prosperous society. The person Franklin created in the *Autobiography was* the responsible, reasonable citizen required by the philosophy of the Declaration of Independence.

INTERNATIONAL RELATIONS

When Franklin went to France in 1776 he faced the intricate task of relating a new nation, founded on elevated principles but not yet strong enough to protect them alone, to the dangers and cynicisms of the real world. Though the United States needed help in her war against England, American leaders, including Franklin, saw clearly that she had no real interest in the dynastic intrigues of Europe. How, therefore, could she get aid and still remain true to her dreams of freedom and independence? Many Americans, especially Arthur Lee, Samuel Adams, and the faction in the Continental Congress named after their families, thought genuine friendship with Catholic, despotic, corrupt France impossible. Fearful of sly courtiers and suspicious of alliances and commercial agreements, they envisioned simple, republican America preserving her virtue by having as little as possible to do with Europe.

Franklin, on the other hand, had a serene confidence that the contagious dynamism of his new country would be more than a match for the established powers of the Old World. Moreover, he retained his vision that all mankind, not just North Americans, had a destiny in freedom; therefore he saw no virtue in weakening the bonds of the great Atlantic community of which he already felt himself a citizen. The task and opportunity were in his mind harmonious rather than antagonistic: French help was needed to win the war, but the bonds forged through aid could also encourage economic and cultural ties useful to prosperity and freedom on both sides of the ocean. In diplomacy as in civic improvement Franklin had faith that action and power could have useful ends. He had no patience with paranoids so obsessed with possible abuses and corruptions that they feared to *do* anything or engage in any enterprises of cooperation, alliance, or union. He went to France, then, confident of his power to do good and anxious that the United States play a leading role in the progress of mankind toward freedom.

Franklin's hopeful view of international relations found characteristic expression in his attitude toward trade, war, and "natural" boundaries. He accepted the free trade doctrines of Adam Smith, though his own observation of flourishing trade in America and of the disastrous effects of the British restrictive system rather than *The Wealth of Nations* or other books were the sources of his ideas. Franklin argued that a free exchange of goods would lead to the most efficient production and the widest possible prosperity; any nation that restricted its trade in any way succeeded only in increasing the cost of what it bought and diminishing the price of what it sold. Years of listening to the pleas of special interest groups for trade barriers in their favor and observing that some other group, or the nation as a whole, always bore the burden of the favors, convinced him that free trade was an essential part of the worldwide open society of which he dreamed. One suspects, too, that Franklin's speculative mind, saturated with Newtonian ideas of a harmonious universe, welcomed the thought that an "invisible hand" guided the exchange of goods for the benefit of all, if only men would abhor artificial restraints and let trade alone.

Even more destructive and foolish than trade barriers were the absolute, barbaric barriers nations thrust against each other in war. Though Franklin never doubted the need for defense against aggression, he scorned the idea that war could be a useful instrument of national policy. Over and over again he argued that territories conquered by armies and navies could have been purchased for a fraction of the cost of the war. He applied the doctrine to England's conquest of Canada in the Seven Years' War, to Great Britain's war against her former colonies, and to suggestions that the United States fight Spain for control of the Mississippi. In each case, Franklin held, not only was the war itself more costly than a purchase or an acquiescence in the policies the war was meant to resist, but the legacy of the war in suffering, degradation, and animosity almost always led to more bloodshed and destruction. Franklin wrote many times that "there never was a good war, or a bad peace." He believed furthermore that the agricultural pursuits that occupied nearly all Americans, and the absorption of the United States in internal expansion, would make the nations of the Old World see that America was not predatory and thus set for them a new example in international politics: a nation becoming great and prosperous without seeking to conquer or oppress its neighbors. Franklin had no illusions about the hard, cynical nature of world affairs, but at the same time he hoped that the spread of reason and the good conduct of enlightened nations eventually would convince all that war was as foolish and self-defeating as it was costly and barbaric. He extended to the international sphere his boundless faith in the virtues of union and cooperative enterprise.

Like many Americans before and since, Franklin's sense of the "manifest destiny" of the English settlements in North America both defined his view of the "natural" boundaries of the United States and imparted a certain overbearing aspect to his attitude toward nations and peoples that seemed to block that destiny. He argued repeatedly that possession of Canada and the Mississippi Valley by any power other than that in control of the thirteen seaboard settlements would be an endless source of war. Thus he urged first that France relinquish Canada to England, and after 1776 that the United States acquire Canada, or at the very least control the Northwest Territory. Similarly, he stood firm for American rights to navigate the Mississippi and to fish in the waters off Newfoundland. In each case he pointed out both the injustice of shutting off activities which to him were the rightful bounty of people whose livelihood depended on them, and the impracticality of such unnatural restraints.

Though Franklin never advocated aggressive war in pursuit of "manifest destiny," he seems not to have considered whether the French or the Spanish, to say nothing of the Indians, had other and conflicting notions of *their* "destiny" in the open lands of the New World. Whether he considered himself a Briton or an American, Franklin believed that the steady growth of agricultural settlement, spreading plenty and orderly cultivation as it went, which characterized the colonies from Massachusetts to Georgia, was the most fruitful and beneficent way to develop North America. Thus, he assumed, the nation that fostered such growth should guide the settlement of the continent. In Franklin's view, opposing French and Spanish feudalism and autocracy, or teaching stable agriculture to Indian savages, was to bring a civilized freedom to a new land. Franklin shared the ethnocentrism of his compatriots and took part at least by acquiescence in the often high-handed intrusion of the people of the English settlements into lands claimed or occupied by the French, the Spanish, or the Indians, but he thought armed conquest unnecessary and never supported it because he had supreme confidence that natural forces — the energy of free men reaching out to settle and fulfill the earth — would prevail.

Even this sense of destiny did not blind Franklin, as it did many of his contemporaries, to the injustices done to the Indians and to their frequent moral superiority over more self-righteous white men. He deplored and sought repeatedly to correct the abuses of the Indian trade which he saw corrupted their natural virtues, and he wrote scathingly of cruel, barbaric wars carried on by supposedly civilized and Christian Europeans.

To protect the new United States in pursuit of this expansive destiny during its period of relative weakness in world politics, Franklin outlined a realistic policy toward Europe. Though he did not live to see the great wars of the Napoleonic era, he knew that the fate of the United States depended upon its skill in balancing between the ambitions of England and France. He thus sought enough conciliation with Great Britain to dampen French hopes, and to maintain the French alliance as long as English pride and power threatened American independence. As an object lesson to each nation he urged that the United States retain some of its armed forces, but he proposed ultimately to rest the nation's security on its rapidly growing economic strength and on its reputation for just and honest dealings with other countries. He believed that such virtuous conduct was not only good in itself but would at the same time bring the United States the trade, investment, and sympathy she needed, and, by helping to spread prosperity and good will in the world, would diminish the tensions and hostilities that caused the worst of all human scourges, war. Even in the eighteenth century he knew that war anywhere in the world threatened peace and prosperity everywhere. Like realists in all ages Franklin understood the necessities of power in an imperfect world, but he also affirmed the realism of high hopes and idealism. As tough and resourceful in war as Winston Churchill, Franklin stands at the beginning of the persistent tradition

1 *Introduction*

in American foreign policy, espoused in the twentieth century by Woodrow Wilson and Franklin Roosevelt, that the pursuit of virtue in international affairs *is* practical, and that men *can* build institutions like the United Nations which however haltingly *do* strengthen the forces of light in the world.

PUBLIC PHILOSOPHY

When Franklin returned to America in 1785, in his eightieth year, he had a unique opportunity to apply his wisdom and political skills to the forming of a more effective constitution for the new United States. In a way his greatest service at the Constitutional Convention of 1787 was simply to be there. His universal fame and legendary sagacity made failure seem much less likely; he seemed to give his colleagues courage to have great expectations. Furthermore, his was a respected voice able over and over again to soothe heated tempers and suggest constructive compromises. He seldom did more than lay his own proposals before the Convention, admitting that his opinion might be changed by the debate, that useful amendments might be made to his suggestions, and that he would acquiesce in some measures with which even after debate he disagreed. He pled repeatedly for reason and light rather than "warmth and discord." During the bitter fight over representation he cooled tempers by making his famous proposal that the sessions be opened with prayer, and a few days later, upon his motion, the Convention adopted the "Great Compromise" that the states be represented equally in the Senate and the people equally in the House.

On the final working day of the Convention, in a speech which has become a revered part of the American political tradition, he urged each member to "doubt a little of his own Infallibility" and despite reservations sign the Constitution to give maximum force to its submission to the people. Indeed, Franklin himself disagreed with many of the provisions of the Constitution, but in accepting it and in asking others to do the same he bespoke an essential quality of government by consent, recognition of which had by this time become the distinguishing feature of his own political career: in assemblies of free men there are bound to be conflicting views which must be accommodated by compromise if not by persuasion. Only by understanding this, Franklin felt, could men learn to take the next short step toward a little bit better today or tomorrow. At the same time they had to eschew plans for perfection and inclinations to demand everything at the expense of others having nothing. In teaching the habit of accommodation and the value of accord Franklin placed indispensable *principles* at the foundation of the union of free states.

While working for agreement, though, Franklin sought diligently to adhere to the principle of government by consent. He had conventional views for his day about the dangers of democracy and the turmoil of mob rule, but he nevertheless believed that the people, properly educated, properly led, and under wise institutions of government, could be good and effective rulers. He insisted, as did his admiring fellow republicans Jefferson and Madison, that the dignity and responsibility with which enlightened ideas and the open society of the New World had come to surround men admitted of no ultimate authority in government other than that of the people being governed. Thus, since "those who feel, can best judge . . . money affairs [should] be confined to the immediate representatives of the people." Thus it was no disgrace to make an officer ineligible for reelection because to return to a private station was merely to resume a seat among the real governors. Thus the suffrage should not be restricted because to

lii *Introduction*

do so would "depress the virtue and public spirit of our common people," and in any case the Convention had no right to limit the privileges of the people. Thus, since representatives were inclined to act as agents for particular regions or interests, justice required that "the number of Representatives should bear some proportion to the number Represented, and that decisions should be by the majority of members, not by the majority of States." In these opinions, rather than in his support of a unicameral legislature (which merely reflected his experience with such a system in colonial Pennsylvania and his zeal for simple, efficient procedures), Franklin displayed his deep, unequivocal faith in the cardinal principle of the American Revolution, the right of self-government.

To Franklin, as to most of the other men who gathered at Independence Hall in the summer of 1787 to draft the new constitution, a spirit of compromise and the representative principle were not the only necessary qualities of good government. He knew very well that compromise could be cynical and corrupting, and that the representatives of the people could enact grossly unjust measures. He had little more faith than John Adams that majority rule would always be *good* rule, though Franklin had more hope than Adams that majority rule *might*, under some circumstances, be just and responsible. To this modest optimism about the possibility of deriving virtue from the people Franklin added a firm belief in the right and capacity of republican government to exercise broad powers on behalf of the public welfare. Just as compromise and the representative principle stood at the center of Franklin's theory of the *process* of government, so an insistence on the possibility of deriving just and virtuous measures from the people and a willingness to give *their* government almost unlimited power to act on *their* behalf stood at the center of his understanding of the *purpose* of government. He scorned the analogy that government was like a joint stock company where each shareholder (citizen) had a right to a voice commensurate with his stake in the company (society), and where the direction of the company (government) simply reflected the interaction of the selfish interests of the shareholders. He believed that government was a uniquely significant social force requiring of the sovereign (the people in the case of republican governments) a reasoned, disinterested pursuit of the public good. Thus, the virtuous principles of the people and their capacity to engage in forum-like discussions of the *general* welfare, not the tenacious cupidity of individuals and groups each defending its own interest, had to be the ultimate resource of self-governing societies.

Franklin adhered as passionately as Samuel Adams to the right of free men to oppose the oppressions of rulers, and he shared Jefferson's conviction that an easy, permissive, frugal government was often the best for men schooled in responsible self-reliance. Furthermore, Franklin did not doubt that social progress had no other solid foundation than the energy, hard work, and initiative of men like the earnest tradesmen among whom he had been reared in Boston and with whom he worked in Philadelphia. But he also understood that even men of good will often needed to act *together* to accomplish useful social ends, and that in fact the possession of property and other social advantages depended upon the existence of government which could therefore demand a portion of that advantage to preserve the community and promote its welfare.

Remembering Franklin's lifelong, many-sided support of value-conserving and virtue-promoting institutions and enterprises, the core of his public philosophy appears. He respected the religious ways, if not the theology, of his father's house because he believed those ways helped make men good citizens. He admired the evangelist George Whitefield because his sermons improved men's conduct. He wrote and spread abroad the adages of Poor Richard because he thought they would encourage the habits necessary to make men useful members of society. He founded and supported a dozen community enterprises in Philadelphia because he felt they gave force and effect to important social virtues. Franklin believed in freedom *from* oppression, the value of unfettered initiative, and the justice of self-government, but he believed as well that without the personal virtue and good will of individuals good government was impossible, that cooperation and accord yielded immense social benefit, and that the power of a republican state could be used in whatever measure deemed appropriate by its governors (the people) to seek and give effect to that benefit. Franklin abhorred both chaotic license and stifling legalism. He was almost as far from Tom Paine in his public philosophy as he would have been from John C. Calhoun. To him personal virtue, civic cooperation, and governmental power served together, each indispensably, to enhance the public good.

Franklin's political thought, then, is in the final analysis a product of his active life and finds its best expression in the deeds of his long public service. Even more than most American political thinkers who have combined philosophy with public life (and this includes a great many of the important ones), his most significant writings on government are occasional, piecemeal, and implicit. Indeed he can have standing as an important figure in American political thought only in terms of his public career and the writings inspired by it. Thus, like politics, his political thought lacks a systematic, or even rigidly consistent pattern. At the same time, though, Franklin's ceaseless connection of deed and doctrine stamps his political thought with relevance and practicality, thus making him one of the most "usable" and pertinent of American "public philosophers." He ranks, therefore, as one of the authentic, perennially significant sages of the American political tradition.

Ralph L. Ketcham

Syracuse University
August 1964

Chronology

1683	Franklin's father, Josiah, emigrates to New England.
1706	Franklin born in Boston; baptized at Old South Church.
1722	"Silence Dogood" published in *New England Courant*.
1723	Runs away to Philadelphia.
1724–1726	In England; works at printer's trade.
1727	Forms the Junto.
1729	Begins publishing the *Pennsylvania Gazette*. Publishes pamphlet on paper currency.
1730	Marries Deborah Read. Appointed printer to the Pennsylvania Assembly.
1731	Founds the Library Company of Philadelphia.
1732	Begins publishing *Poor Richard: An Almanack;* continued annually until 1758.
1735	Defends Reverend Samuel Hemphill.
1736	Forms Union Fire Company. Appointed clerk of the Assembly.
1737	Appointed postmaster of Philadelphia.
1743	Publishes *Proposal for Promoting Useful Knowledge*.
1747	Writes *Plain Truth;* organizes first militia in Pennsylvania.

1748 Retires from active business.
Elected to the Philadelphia Common Council.
1749 Publishes *Proposals Relating to the Education of Youth in Pennsylvania;* active in founding the Academy of Philadelphia.
1751 His *Experiments and Observations on Electricity* first published in London.
Pennsylvania Hospital chartered.
Begins service in Pennsylvania Assembly; elected annually until 1764.
Writes *Observations Concerning the Increase of Mankind.*
1753 Receives honorary M.A. degrees from Harvard and from Yale.
Appointed deputy postmaster general of North America.
1754 Proposes Albany Plan of Union; writes letters to Governor Shirley.
1755 Active aiding General Braddock, defending Pennsylvania against Indian attacks, and in writing antiproprietary messages for the Assembly.
Writes "A Parable Against Persecution."
1756 Elected Fellow of the Royal Society.
1757 Goes to England as Assembly agent.
Composes preface to *Poor Richard* for 1758, later known as "The Way to Wealth."
1759 Receives honorary LL.D. degree from University of St. Andrews.
Meets David Hume and Lord Kames.
1760 Writes *Interest of Great Britain Considered* (Canada pamphlet).
Secures Privy Council approval of taxation of proprietary estates in Pennsylvania.
1762 Receives honorary D.C.L. degree from Oxford University.

Returns to Philadelphia.
1764 Writes series of pamphlets on Pennsylvania politics.
After a scurrilous campaign defeated for reelection to the Assembly.
Returns to England.
1765 Opposes Stamp Act and then works for its repeal; writes many anonymous pieces for the London press.
1766 Examined before the House of Commons on the Stamp Act.
1768 Writes "Causes of American Discontents before 1768."
Appointed agent for Georgia.
1769 Elected president of the American Philosophical Society; reelected annually during his life.
1770 Intense newspaper propaganda campaign against Townshend duties; repealed, except that on tea.
Appointed agent for Massachusetts.
1771 Begins autobiography.
1773 Writes famous satires attacking British imperial policy.
1774 Hears of Boston Tea Party; attacked before the Privy Council; dismissed as deputy postmaster general.
Coercive Acts passed; begins final negotiations with Lord Chatham and others to preserve the British Empire.
1775 Returns to America; elected to the Continental Congress and to the Pennsylvania Committee of Safety; active in support of war measures.
Submits Articles of Confederation for United Colonies.
1776 Helps draft and signs Declaration of Independence.

Presides at Pennsylvania Constitutional Convention.

Sails for France as an American Commissioner; has first audiences with French Foreign Minister Vergennes.

1777 Lionized by Parisian society and French intellectuals.

Obtains first subsidies (secret) from French government.

1778 Negotiates and signs French alliance.
1779 Receives appointment as Minister to France.
1780 Harassed by onerous duties and plagued by quarrels with Arthur Lee and others, but retains and broadens French support of the American cause.
1781 Appointed a commissioner to negotiate peace; hears of American victory at Yorktown.
1782 With John Adams and John Jay negotiates treaty of peace with Great Britain.

Writes *Information to Those Who Would Remove to America*.

1784 Negotiates treaties of commerce with Prussia and other European nations.

Resumes autobiography; writes *Remarks Concerning the Savages of North America*.

1785 Returns to Philadelphia.

Elected President of Pennsylvania; reelected annually until 1788.

1787 Elected President of Pennsylvania Society for Promoting the Abolition of Slavery.

Delegate to the Federal Constitutional Convention.

1789 Finishes last long section of his autobiography.
1790 April 17; dies quietly at his home, aged 84 years, 3 months.

Selected Bibliography

ORIGINAL SOURCES

Leonard W. Labaree and others, eds., *The Papers of Benjamin Franklin*, New Haven: Yale University Press, 1959–, 7 vols. (1706–1758) to date. The standard edition which, when complete, will supercede all others. Includes all of Franklin's writings and, so far, all letters written to him. Fully annotated.

Albert H. Smyth, ed., *The Writings of Benjamin Franklin*, New York: The Macmillan Company, 1905–1907, 10 vols. The best completed edition of Franklin's writings, still necessary for documents not yet printed in *The Papers of Benjamin Franklin*.

Leonard W. Labaree and others, eds., *The Autobiography of Benjamin Franklin*, New Haven: Yale University Press, 1964. The standard edition, richly annotated, placing the famous autobiography for the first time in the full context of what is known of Franklin's life from other sources.

Verner W. Crane, Ed., *Benjamin Franklin's Letters to the Press, 1758–1775*, Chapel Hill: University of North Carolina Press, 1950. Valuable for Franklin's political writings in England.

Carl Van Doren, ed., *The Letters of Benjamin Franklin and Jane Mecom*, Princeton: Princeton University Press, 1950. An important series of letters between Franklin and his sister covering the sixty-five years of their adult lives.

Carl Van Doren, ed., *Letters and Papers of Benjamin*

Franklin and Richard Jackson, Philadelphia: The American Philosophical Society, 1947. Contains important papers on Franklin's agency in England.

Francis Wharton, ed., *The Revolutionary Diplomatic Correspondence of the United States*, Washington: U.S. Government Printing Office, 1889, 6 vols. Contains many letters on Franklin's diplomatic service in France not printed elsewhere.

Selected Bibliography lxiii

Collateral Reading

Alfred O. Aldridge, *Franklin and His French Contemporaries*, New York: New York University Press, 1957. Authoritative account of Franklin's association with French intellectuals.

Carl L. Becker, *Benjamin Franklin, A Biographical Sketch*, Ithaca, N. Y.: Cornell University Press, 1946, first printed in the *Dictionary of American Biography*. An excellent brief study especially useful in assessing Franklin's place in eighteenth-century thought.

Carl L. Becker, *The Declaration of Independence*, New York: Harcourt, Brace, and Co., 1922. Excellent summary of the political theory of the American Revolution.

Samuel F. Bemis, *The Diplomacy of the American Revolution*, New York: Appleton Century and Co., 1935. The standard work on the subject.

Carl and Jessica Bridenbaugh, *Rebels and Gentlemen: Philadelphia in the Age of Franklin*, New York: Reynal and Hitchcock, 1942. The best account of life in Franklin's adopted city in his day.

Verner W. Crane, *Benjamin Franklin and a Rising People*, Boston: Little, Brown and Co., 1954. A good study emphasizing politics and diplomacy by a distinguished Franklin scholar.

[The Franklin Institute], *Meet Dr. Franklin*, Philadelphia: The Franklin Institute, 1943. Essays by leading authorities, including Carl Van Doren and Robert E. Spiller, assessing various aspects of Franklin's career.

William S. Hanna, *Benjamin Franklin and Pennsylvania Politics*, Palo Alto, Calif.: Stanford University Press, 1964. An analysis of Franklin's political career, 1750–1776, emphasizing his connection with the dominant Quaker oligarchy.

Selected Bibliography

Ralph L. Ketcham, *Benjamin Franklin:* Great American thinkers series, New York: Washington Square Press, 1965. A brief summary and criticism of Franklin's thought, emphasizing its origins and development.

Ralph L. Ketcham, "Conscience, War, and Politics in Pennsylvania, 1755–1757," *William and Mary Quarterly,* 3rd ser., XX, No. 3, July, 1963, pp. 416–439. A detailed account of an important crisis in Franklin's political career.

Adrienne Koch, "Franklin and Pragmatic Wisdom," *Power, Morals, and the Founding Fathers,* Ithaca, N. Y.: Cornell University Press, 1961. Sees Franklin as a "pragmatic humanist."

F. L. Lucas, *The Art of Living, Four Eighteenth-Century Minds; Hume, Horace Walpole, Burke, and Benjamin Franklin,* New York: The Macmillan Co., 1959. An interesting comparative study.

Frank L. Mott and Chester E. Jorgenson, "Introduction," *Benjamin Franklin: Representative Selections. . . ,* New York: American Book Company, 1936, pp. xiii–cxli. Emphasizes Franklin's standing as an Enlightenment thinker.

Robert R. Palmer, *The Age of Democratic Revolution,* Princeton: Princeton University Press, 1959. An excellent study of the cross-currents of politics and ideas in Europe and America, 1760–1790.

Vernon L. Parrington, "Benjamin Franklin: Our First Ambassador," *Main Currents in American Thought: The Colonial Mind, 1620–1800,* New York: Harcourt, Brace, and Co. (1927), 1954, pp. 166–181. Pictures Franklin, somewhat inaccurately, as an early American democrat.

Caroline Robbins, *The Eighteenth-Century Commonwealthman,* Cambridge: Harvard University Press, 1959.

Excellent study of the English radical Whig and dissenting traditions upon which Franklin drew heavily.
Clinton Rossiter, *Seedtime of the Republic*, New York: Harcourt, Brace, and Co., 1953. The best study of "The Origin of the American Tradition of Political Liberty." Includes a good summary of Franklin's political thought, pp. 281–312.
Charles L. Sanford, ed., *Benjamin Franklin and the American Character*, Boston: D. C. Heath and Co., 1955. Reprints a judicious selection of comments on Franklin, including the famous assault by D. H. Lawrence in *Studies in Classic American Literature* (1923).
William R. Shepherd, *History of Proprietary Government in Pennsylvania*, New York: Columbia University Press, 1896. A sympathetic account of the government under which Franklin lived for most of his adult life; a useful antidote to Franklin's anti-proprietary bias.
Gerald Stourzh, *Benjamin Franklin and American Foreign Policy*, Chicago: University of Chicago Press, 1954. An excellent, well-informed, analytic study.
Theodore Thayer, *Pennsylvania Politics and the Growth of Democracy, 1740–1776*, Harrisburg: Pennsylvania Historical and Museum Commission, 1953. A useful survey of Franklin's political context despite its over-ambitious attempt to make Franklin and his associates early American "democrats."
Carl Van Doren, *Benjamin Franklin*, New York: The Viking Press, 1938. A superb, full-length biography indispensable to any serious study of Franklin's life and thought.
Max Weber, *The Protestant Ethic and the Spirit of Capitalism*, trans. by Talcott Parsons, New York: Scribner's, 1930; pp. 47–78. Evaluates Franklin's place in the evolution of the Protestant ethic.

Editor's Note and Acknowledgments

The documents reprinted in this volume are arranged chronologically; the date of writing, or first known publication, is indicated in the source note for each. When necessary, further information on the nature of the document is given in the headnote. Franklin's title for a document is used when he assigned one; in cases where he had none, as in letters, a brief, descriptive title has been supplied by the editor. Franklin's spelling, capitalization, and punctuation are retained according to the usage in the works or original source from which the document is quoted. Except for the source footnote for each document, all footnotes are Franklin's own, unless designated thus: [Ed.]. Editorial insertions in the text are enclosed in brackets. Deletions in the text are indicated by ellipses. Information necessary for an understanding of each document is included, whenever possible, in the headnote rather than in footnotes.

The editor is pleased to make the following acknowledgments:

1. All selections from Franklin's writings, 1706–1758, are from Leonard W. Labaree and others, eds., *The Papers of Benjamin Franklin* (New Haven, Yale University Press, 1959—), vols. I–VII, and are included with the kind permission of the Yale University Press. The editors have been exceedingly scrupulous in following Franklin's own usage in spelling, punctuation, and capitalization. Cited in the footnotes as *Papers*.

2. The standard source for Franklin's writings not as yet included in the above work (those dated after March 1758) is Albert H. Smyth, ed., *The Writings of Benjamin Franklin* (10 vols., New York: The Macmillan Co., 1905–1907). Though an older work not conforming in every respect to the high standards of contemporary documentary publication, this edition is based in most instances on the original documents and generally follows Franklin's usage. Cited in the footnotes as *Writings*.

3. Selections from Verner W. Crane, ed., *Benjamin Franklin's Letters to the Press, 1758–1775* (Chapel Hill, The University of North Carolina Press, 1950) are included with the kind permission of The University of North Carolina Press. Mr. Crane has followed meticulously the style of the newspaper in which each document was first printed. Cited in the footnotes as Crane, *Franklin's Letters to the Press*.

4. Franklin's speeches at the Federal Constitutional Convention are taken from the comprehensive and highly accurate standard source: Max Farrand, ed., *The Records of the Federal Convention of 1787* (4 vols., New Haven, Yale University Press, 1937).

Since Franklin's famous *Autobiography* has been printed hundreds of times and is currently available in a dozen or more editions, selections from it have not been included in this work. Readers are reminded, however, that in spite of occasional inaccuracies and the too-bland account of politics in the *Autobiography*, it is nevertheless an exceedingly important source for understanding Franklin's concept of political obligation. Those who would know Franklin the political thinker must know Franklin the man and those who would know Franklin the man must know his self-told story.

Selections dated before 1752, when Great Britain adopted the Gregorian calendar, nevertheless carry the

Editor's Note and Acknowledgments lxix

"New Style" year rather than retaining the "Old Style" form of beginning the new year on March 25; e.g., the "Old Style" date February 11, 1722, sometimes written February 11, 1722/23, is written in this work simply as February 11, 1723, to conform with the Gregorian calendar which begins each new year on January 1.

PART ONE

Business, Civic and Political Leader
1722–1757

ESSAYS IN *The New-England Courant*

Benjamin Franklin first wrote for the press in 1722 when as a lad of sixteen he served as an apprentice to his brother James, then printer of *The New-England Courant,* a newspaper printed in Boston. Fearing the ridicule of his brother's literary friends whom he admired and in some measure sought to emulate, Franklin wrote and submitted anonymously to the newspaper a series of fourteen essays signed "Silence Dogood." After their publication he had the "exquisite pleasure," he relates in his autobiography, to hear them praised by the literary circle. The Dogood essays were part of a campaign in the *Courant* to satirize and ridicule the reigning Boston orthodoxy, then presided over by Cotton Mather. Franklin's *non de plume,* "Silence Dogood," is a thrust at Mather, author of *Essays to do Good,* to be silent. The Dogood essays Numbers 3 and 9, and the two pieces following them also printed in the *Courant,* are significant for their clear revelation of Franklin's place in the literary tradition of the *Spectator,* and as evidence that he took a stand at the beginning of his "public life" in opposition to a stifling Establishment and in defense of a dynamic, open society.

"Silence Dogood, Number Three," *Papers,* I, 13–14; first printed in *The New-England Courant,* April 30, 1722.

2 *The Political Thought of Benjamin Franklin*

SILENCE DOGOOD, NUMBER THREE

This essay is so close in tone and style to the *Spectator* papers of Joseph Addison, especially such early ones as Number 10, as to make it clear that Franklin had in mind encouraging good will, moderation, and a zeal for the public welfare in Boston as Addison had done ten years before in London. Franklin believed, as did Addison, that virtue and sanity in the politics of a constitutional monarchy depended on spreading good habits and a constructive attitude among the citizens.

It is undoubtedly the Duty of all Persons to serve the Country they live in, according to their Abilities; yet I sincerely acknowledge, that I have hitherto been very deficient in this Particular; whether it was for want of Will or Opportunity, I will not at present stand to determine: Let it suffice, that I now take up a Resolution, to do for the future all that *lies in my Way* for the Service of my Countrymen.

I have from my Youth been indefatigably studious to gain and treasure up in my Mind all useful and desireable Knowledge, especially such as tends to improve the Mind, and enlarge the Understanding: And as I have found it very beneficial to me, I am not without Hopes, that communicating my small Stock in this Manner, by Peace-meal to the Publick, may be at least in some Measure useful.

I am very sensible that it is impossible for me, or indeed any *one* Writer to please *all* Readers at once. Various Persons have different Sentiments; and that which is pleasant and delightful to one, gives another a Disgust. He that would (in this Way of Writing) please all, is under a Necessity to make his Themes almost as numerous as his Letters. He must one while be merry and diverting, then more solid and serious; one while sharp and satyrical, then (to mollify that) be sober and religious; at one Time let the Subject be Politicks, then let the next Theme be Love: Thus will every one Fancy, and in his Turn be delighted.

According to this Method I intend to proceed, bestowing now and then a few gentle Reproofs on those who deserve them, not forgetting at the same time to applaud those whose Actions merit Commendation. And here I must not forget to invite the ingenious Part of your Readers, particularly those of my own Sex to enter into a Correspondence with me, assuring them, that their Condescension in this Particular shall be received as a Favour, and accordingly acknowledged.

I think I have now finish'd the Foundation, and I intend in my next to begin to raise the Building. Having nothing more to write at present, I must make the usual excuse in such Cases, of *being in haste*, assuring you that I speak from my Heart when I call my self, The most humble and obedient of all the Servants your Merits have acquir'd,

Silence Dogood

SILENCE DOGOOD, NUMBER NINE

On June 12, 1722 the General Court of Massachusetts ordered James Franklin imprisoned for his insinuation that the Court had not taken proper exertions against pirates off the coast. Benjamin Franklin managed the *Courant* during his brother's confinement and printed two Dogood essays aimed at the ruling oligarchy. The first, Number 8, reprinted from a London newspaper an eloquent plea for freedom of speech, and the second, reprinted here, was Franklin's sharpest stricture on his brother's tormen-

---

Papers, I, 30–32; first printed in *The New-England Courant*, July 23, 1722.

tors. Though the attack on the theocratic aspects of Massachusetts government derived mainly from circumstances in the colony, the two paragraphs quoted to conclude the essay, from the famous "Cato" letters of Thomas Gordon and John Trenchard, link Franklin importantly early in his life to the English "radical Whig" tradition that Gordon and Trenchard represented.

It has been for some Time a Question with me, Whether a Commonwealth suffers more by hypocritical Pretenders to Religion, or by the openly Profane? But some late Thoughts of this Nature, have inclined me to think, that the Hypocrite is the most dangerous Person of the Two, especially if he sustains a Post in the Government, and we consider his Conduct as it regards the Publick. The first Artifice of a *State Hypocrite* is, by a few savoury Expressions which cost him Nothing, to betray the best Men in his Country into an Opinion of his Goodness; and if the Country wherein he lives is noted for the Purity of Religion, he the more easily gains his End, and consequently may more justly be expos'd and detested. A notoriously profane Person in a private Capacity, ruins himself, and perhaps forwards the Destruction of a few of his Equals; but a publick Hypocrite every day deceives his betters, and makes them the Ignorant Trumpeters of his supposed Godliness: They take him for a Saint, and pass him for one, without considering that they are (as it were) the Instruments of publick Mischief out of Conscience, and ruin their Country for God's sake.

This Political Description of a Hypocrite, may (for ought I know) be taken for a new Doctrine by some of your Readers; but let them consider, that *a little Religion, and a little Honesty, goes a great way in Courts.* 'Tis not inconsistent with Charity to distrust a Religious Man in Power, tho' he may be a good Man; he has many Temptations "to propagate *publick Destruction* for *Personal Advantages and Security*": And if his Natural Temper be covetous, and his Actions often contradict his pious Discourse, we may with great Reason conclude, that he has some other Design in his Religion besides barely getting to Heaven. But the most dangerous Hypocrite in a Common-Wealth, is one who *leaves the Gospel for the sake of the Law:* A Man compounded of Law and Gospel, is able to cheat a whole Country with his Religion, and then destroy them under *Colour of Law:* And here the Clergy are in great Danger of being deceiv'd, and the People of being deceiv'd by the Clergy, until the Monster arrives to such Power and Wealth, that he is out of the reach of both, and can oppress the People without their own blind Assistance. And it is a sad Observation, that when the People too late see their Error, yet the Clergy still persist in their Encomiums on the Hypocrite; and when he happens to die *for the Good of his Country,* without leaving behind him the Memory of *one good Action,* he shall be sure to have his Funeral Sermon stuff'd with *Pious Expressions* which he dropt at such a Time, and at such a Place, and on such an Occasion; than which nothing can be more prejudicial to the Interest of Religion, nor indeed to the Memory of the Person deceas'd. The Reason of this Blindness in the Clergy is, because they are honourably supported (as they ought to be) by their People, and see nor feel nothing of the Oppression which is obvious and burdensome to every one else.

But this Subject raises in me an Indignation not to be born; and if we have had, or are like to have any Instances of this Nature in New England, we cannot better manifest our Love to Religion and the Country, than by setting the Deceivers in a true Light, and undeceiving the Deceived, however such Discoveries may be represented by the ignorant or designing Enemies of our Peace and Safety.

I shall conclude with a Paragraph or two from an ingenious Political Writer in the *London Journal*, the better to convince your Readers, that Publick Destruction may be easily carry'd on by *hypocritical Pretenders to Religion.*

"A raging Passion for immoderate Gain had made Men universally and intensely hard-hearted: They were every where devouring one another. And yet the Dirctors and their Accomplices, who were the acting Instruments of all this outrageous Madness and Mischief, set up for wonderful pious Persons, while they were defying Almighty God, and plundering Men; and they set apart a Fund of Subscriptions for charitable Uses; that is, they mercilessly made a whole People Beggars, and charitably supported a few *necessitous* and *worthless* FAVOURITES. I doubt not, but if the Villany had gone on with Success, they would have had their Names handed down to Posterity with Encomiums; as the Names of other *publick Robbers* have been! We have *Historians* and ODE MAKERS now living, very proper for such a Task. It is certain, that most People did, at one Time, believe the *Directors* to be *great and worthy Persons.* And an honest Country Clergyman told me last Summer, upon the Road, that Sir John was an excellent publick-spirited Person, for that he had beautified his Chancel.

"Upon the whole we must not judge of one another by their best Actions; since the worst Men do some Good, and all Men make fine Professions: But we must judge of Men by the whole of their Conduct, and the Effects of it. Thorough Honesty requires great and long Proof, since many a Man, long thought honest, has at length proved a Knave. And it is from judging without Proof, or false Proof, that Mankind continue Unhappy." I am, Sir, Your humble Servant,

Silence Dogood

AN EDITORIAL

Imprisonment did not deter James Franklin from his attacks on the rulers of Massachusetts. He continued to print satires on them, causing the General Court to bar him from further publication "except it be first Supervised by the Secretary of this Province." To circumvent this order James decided to have the *Courant* published under his brother's name. The "editorial" printed here, probably written jointly by the Franklins, appeared in the first paper carrying the name "Benjamin Franklin." Efforts to punish James Franklin came to an end in May 1723 when a grand jury refused to indict him.

The late Publisher of this Paper, finding so many Inconveniencies would arise by his carrying the Manuscripts and publick News to be supervis'd by the Secretary, as to render his carrying it on unprofitable, has intirely dropt the Undertaking. The present Publisher having receiv'd the following Piece, desires the Readers to accept of it as a Preface to what they may hereafter meet with in this Paper. . . .

Long has the Press groaned in bringing forth an hateful, but numerous Brood of Party Pamphlets, malicious Scribbles, and Billingsgate Ribaldry. The Rancour and bitterness it has unhappily infused into Mens minds, and to what a Degree it has sowred and leaven'd the Tempers of Persons formerly esteemed some of the most sweet and affable, is too well known here, to need any further Proof or Representation of the Matter.

No generous and impartial Person then can blame the present Undertaking, which is designed purely for the

---

Papers, I, 48–50; first printed in *The New-England Courant*, February 11, 1723.

Diversion and Merriment of the Reader. Pieces of Pleasancy and Mirth have a secret Charm in them to allay the Heats and Tumors of our Spirits, and to make a Man forget his restless Resentments. They have a strange Power to tune the harsh Disorders of the Soul, and reduce us to a serene and placid State of Mind.

The main Design of this Weekly Paper will be to entertain the Town with the most comical and diverting Incidents of Humane Life, which in so large a Place as Boston, will not fail of a universal Exemplification: Nor shall we be wanting to fill up these Papers with a grateful Interspersion of more serious Morals, which may be drawn from the most ludicrous and odd Parts of Life.

As for the Author, that is the next Question. But tho' we profess our selves ready to oblige the ingenious and courteous Reader with most Sorts of Intelligence, yet here we beg a Reserve. Nor will it be of any Manner of Advantage either to them or to the Writers, that their Names should be published; and therefore in this Matter we desire the Favour of you to suffer us to hold our Tongues: Which tho' at this Time of Day it may sound like a very uncommon Request, yet it proceeds from the very Hearts of your Humble Servants.

By this Time the Reader perceives that more than one are engaged in the present Undertaking. Yet is there one Person, an Inhabitant of this Town of Boston, whom we honour as a Doctor in the Chair, or a perpetual Dictator.

The Society had design'd to present the Publick with his Effigies, but that the Limner, to whom he was presented for a Draught of his Countenance, descryed (and this he is ready to offer upon Oath) Nineteen Features in his Face, more than ever he beheld in any Humane Visage before; which so raised the Price of his Picture, that our Master himself forbid the Extravagance of coming up to it. And then besides, the Limner objected a Schism in his Face, which splits it from his Forehead in a strait Line down to

Business, Civic and Political Leader 9

his Chin, in such sort, that Mr. Painter protests it is a double Face, and he'll have *Four Pounds* for the Pourtraiture. However, tho' this double Face has spoilt us of a pretty Picture, yet we all rejoiced to see old Janus in our Company.

There is no Man in Boston better qualified than old Janus for a *Couranteer*, of if you please, an *Observator*, being a Man of such remarkable *Opticks*, as to look two ways at once.

As for his Morals, he is a chearly Christian, as the Country Phrase expresses it. A Man of good Temper, courteous Deportment, sound Judgment; a mortal Hater of Nonsense, Foppery, Formality, and endless Ceremony.

As for his Club, they aim at no greater Happiness or Honour, than the Publick be made to know, that it is the utmost of their Ambition to attend upon and do all imaginable good Offices to good Old Janus the Couranteer, who is and always will be the Readers humble Servant.

P.S. Gentle Readers, we design never to let a Paper pass without a Latin Motto if we can possible pick one up, which carries a Charm in it to the Vulgar, and the learned admire the pleasure of Construing. We should have obliged the World with a Greek scrap or two, but the Printer has no Types, and therefore we intreat the candid Reader not to impute the defect to our Ignorance, for our Doctor can say all the Greek Letters by heart.

ON TITLES OF HONOR

One important legacy of Franklin's humble New England background was his lifelong disdain for pomp, ceremony, and titles of honor. The quoted material in this essay is a parody of

---

Papers, I, 51–52; first printed in *The New-England Courant*, February 18, 1723.

part of William Penn's *No Cross, No Crown: Or several Sober Reasons Against Hat-Honour, Titular-Respects. . .* , first published in London in 1669.

There is nothing in which Mankind reproach themselves more than in their Diversity of Opinions. Every Man sets himself above another in his own Opinion, and there are not two Men in the World whose Sentiments are alike in every thing. Hence it comes to pass, that the same Passages in the Holy Scriptures or the Works of the Learned, are wrested to the meaning of two opposite Parties, of contrary Opinions, as if the Passages they recite were like our Master Janus, looking *two ways at once,* or like Lawyers, who with equal Force of Argument, can plead either for the *Plaintiff or Defendant.*

The most absurd and ridiculous Opinions, are sometimes spread by the least colour of Argument: But if they stop at the first Broachers, *they* have still the Pleasure of being wiser (in their own Conceits) than the rest of the World, and can with the greatest Confidence pass a Sentence of Condemnation upon the Reason of all Mankind, who dissent from the Whims of their troubled Brains.

We were easily led into these Reflections at the last Meeting of our Club, when one of the Company read to us some Passages from a zealous Author against *Hatt-Honour, Titular Respects,* &c. which we will communicate to the Reader for the Diversion of this Week, if he is dispos'd to be merry with the Folly of his Fellow-Creature.

"*Honour*, Friend, *says he*, properly ascends, and not descends; yet the Hat, when the Head is uncover'd, *descends*, and therefore there can be no Honour in it. Besides, Honour was from the *Beginning*, but Hats are an Invention of a *late Time*, and consequently true Honour standeth not therein.

"In old Time it was no disrespect for Men and Women to be call'd by their own Names: Adam, was never called *Master* Adam; we never read of Noah *Esquire*, Lot *Knight* and *Baronet*, nor the *Right Honourable* Abraham, *Viscount Mesopotamia, Baron of Carran;* no, no, they were plain Men, honest Country Grasiers, that took Care of their Families and their Flocks. Moses was a great Prophet, and Aaron a Priest of the Lord; but we never read of the *Reverend* Moses, nor the *Right Reverend Father in God,* Aaron, by Divine Providence, *Lord Arch-Bishop of Israel:* Thou never sawest *Madam* Rebecca in the Bible, my *Lady* Rachel, nor Mary, tho' a Princess of the Blood after the Death of Joseph, call'd the *Princess Dowager of Nazareth;* no, plain Rebecca, Rachel, Mary, or the *Widow* Mary, or the like: It was no Incivility then to mention their naked Names as they were expressed."

If common civility, and a generous Deportment among Mankind, be not put out of Countenance by the profound Reasoning of this Author, we hope they will continue to treat one another handsomely to the end of the World. We will not pretend an Answer to these Arguments against *modern Decency* and *Titles of Honour;* yet one of our Club will undertake to prove, that tho' Abraham was not styl'd *Right Honourable,* yet he had the Title of *Lord* given him by his Wife Sarah, which he thinks entitles her to the Honour of *My Lady* Sarah; and Rachel being married into the same Family, he concludes she may deserve the Title of *My Lady* Rachel. But this is but the Opinion of one Man; it was never put to Vote in the Society.

P.S. At the last Meeting of our Club, it was unanimously agreed, That all Letters to be inserted in this Paper, should come directed to old Janus; whereof our Correspondents are to take Notice, and conform themselves accordingly.

THE BUSY-BODY, NUMBER THREE

When Franklin undertook to found a newspaper of his own in Philadelphia, his rival printer and former master, Samuel Keimer, learned of the plan and to undercut it immediately started a paper himself. To combat this Franklin and his friend Joseph Breintnall wrote a series of essays under the title "The Busy-Body" for Andrew Bradford's newspaper, hoping to attract readers to it and thus drive Keimer out of business. "The Busy-Body" enlivened Bradford's paper, and in less than a year Keimer sold out to Franklin, thereby affording him his first chance to publish his own newspaper, the soon-to-be-famous *Pennsylvania Gazette*. This portion of one of Franklin's essays, Busy-Body Number 3, shows his faith that the good society has as its indispensible foundation plain, virtuous, and wise citizens such as the fanciful "Cato" here depicted.

> *Non vultus instantis Tyranni*
> *Mente quatit solida—neque Auster*
> *Dux inquieti turbidus Adriae,*
> *Nec fulminantis magna Jovis manus.* Hor. [1]

It is said that the Persians in their ancient Constitution, had publick Schools in which Virtue was taught as a Liberal Art or Science; and it is certainly of more Consequence to a Man that he has learnt to govern his Passions; in spite of Temptation to be just in his Dealings, to be Temperate in his Pleasures, to support himself with Fortitude under his Misfortunes, to behave with Prudence in

---

Papers, I, 118–120; first printed in *The American Weekly Mercury*, February 18, 1729.

[1] Horace, *Odes*, III, iii, 3–6, John Conington Translation [Ed.].
No tyrant's brow, whose frown may kill,
Can shake the strength that makes him strong:
Not winds that chafe the sea they sway,
Nor Jove's right hand, with lightning red:

all Affairs and in every Circumstance of Life; I say, it is of much more real Advantage to him to be thus qualified, than to be a Master of all the Arts and Sciences in the World beside.

Virtue alone is sufficient to make a Man Great, Glorious and Happy. He that is acquainted with Cato, as I am, cannot help thinking as I do now, and will acknowledge he deserves the Name without being honour'd by it. Cato is a Man whom Fortune has plac'd in the most obscure Part of the Country. His Circumstances are such as only put him above Necessity, without affording him many Superfluities; Yet who is greater than Cato? I happened but the other Day to be at a House in Town, where among others were met Men of the most Note in this Place: Cato had Business with some of them, and knock'd at the Door. The most trifling Actions of a Man, in my Opinion, as well as the smallest Features and Lineaments of the Face, give a nice Observer some Notion of his Mind. Methought he rapp'd in such a peculiar Manner, as seem'd of itself to express, there was One who deserv'd as well as desir'd Admission. He appear'd in the plainest Country Garb; his Great Coat was coarse and looked old and thread-bare; his Linnen was homespun; his Beard perhaps of Seven Days Growth, his Shoes thick and heavy, and every Part of his Dress corresponding. Why was this Man receiv'd with such concurring Respect from every Person in the Room, even from those who had never known him or seen him before? It was not an exquisite Form of Person, or Grandeur of Dress that struck us with Admiration. I believe long Habits of Virtue have a sensible Effect on the Countenance: There was something in the Air of his Face that manifested the true Greatness of his Mind; which likewise appear'd in all he said, and in every Part of his Behaviour, obliging us to regard him with a Kind of Veneration. His Aspect is sweetned with Humanity and Benevolence, and at the same Time emboldned with Resolution, equally free

14   *The Political Thought of Benjamin Franklin*

from a diffident Bashfulness and an unbecoming Assurance. The Consciousness of his own innate Worth and unshaken Integrity renders him calm and undaunted in the Presence of the most Great and Powerful, and upon the most extraordinary Occasions. His strict Justice and known Impartiality make him the Arbitrator and Decider of all Differences that arise for many Miles around him, without putting his Neighbours to the Charge, Perplexity and Uncertainty of Law-Suits. He always speaks the Thing he means, which he is never afraid or asham'd to do, because he knows he always means well; and therefore is never oblig'd to blush and feel the Confusion of finding himself detected in the Meanness of a Falshood. He never contrives Ill against his Neighbour, and therefore is never seen with a lowring suspicious Aspect. A mixture of Innocence and Wisdom makes him ever seriously chearful. His generous Hospitality to Strangers according to his Ability, his Goodness, his Charity, his Courage in the Cause of the Oppressed, his Fidelity in Friendship, his Humility, his Honesty and Sincerity, his Moderation and his Loyalty to the Government, his Piety, his Temperance, his Love to Mankind, his Magnanimity, his Publick-spiritedness, and in fine, his *Consummate Virtue,* make him justly deserve to be esteem'd the Glory of his Country. . . .

THE NATURE AND NECESSITY
OF A PAPER-CURRENCY

In England's rapidly growing North American colonies, trade was often restricted by a tight money supply when the only circulating media were specie and the "hard currencies" of

Papers, I, 146–147, 156–157; first printed as a pamphlet in Philadelphia, April 3, 1729.

Business, Civic and Political Leader 15

Western Europe. In 1729 this condition was especially acute in Pennsylvania, inspiring Franklin to write and distribute a pamphlet recommending a substantial issue of paper currency. In between explaining why the additional currency would increase prosperity, and a lengthy discourse (following the writings of Sir William Petty) on why inflation would not ensue, Franklin characterized persons who would oppose and those who would favor paper currency. He concluded with a plea for rational public discussion of the matter. The list of likely friends and foes and the plea for debate show Franklin's conviction that an expanding economy was good for the common people and that intelligent discussion would lead to wise decisions in public affairs.

1. Since Men will always be powerfully influenced in their Opinions and Actions by what appears to be their particular Interest: Therefore all those, who wanting Courage to venture in Trade, now practise Lending Money on Security for exorbitant Interest, which in a Scarcity of Money will be done notwithstanding the Law, I say all such will probably be against a large Addition to our present Stock of Paper-Money; because a plentiful Currency will lower Interest, and make it common to lend on less Security.

2. All those who are Possessors of large Sums of Money, and are disposed to purchase Land, which is attended with a great and sure Advantage in a growing Country as this is; I say, the Interest of all such Men will encline them to oppose a large Addition to our Money. Because their Wealth is now continually increasing by the large Interest they receive, which will enable them (if they can keep Land from rising) to purchase More some time hence than they can at present; and in the mean time all Trade being discouraged, not only those who borrow of them, but the Common people in general will be impoverished, and

consequently obliged to sell More Land for less Money than they will do at present. And yet, after such Men are possessed of as much Land as they can purchase, it will then be their Interest to have Money made Plentiful, because that will immediately make Land rise in Value in *their* Hands. Now it ought not to be wonder'd at, if People from the Knowledge of a Man's Interest do sometimes make a true Guess at his Designs; for, *Interest,* they say, *will not Lie.*

3. Lawyers, and others concerned in Court Business, will probably many of them be against a plentiful Currency; because People in that Case will have less Occasion to run in Debt, and consequently less Occasion to go to Law and Sue one another for their Debts. Tho' I know some even among these Gentlemen, that regard the Publick Good before their own apparent private Interest.

4. All those who are any way Dependants on such Persons as are above mentioned, whether as holding Offices, as Tenants, or as Debtors, must at least *appear* to be against a large Addition; because if they do not, they must sensibly feel their present Interest hurt. And besides these, there are, doubtless, many well-meaning Gentlemen and Others, who, without any immediate private Interest of their own in View, are against making such an Addition, thro' an Opinion they may have of the Honesty and sound Judgment of some of their Friends that oppose it, (perhaps for the Ends aforesaid) without having given it any thorough Consideration themselves. And thus it is no Wonder if there is a *powerful* Party on that Side.

On the other Hand, Those who are Lovers of Trade, and delight to see Manufactures encouraged, will be for having a large Addition to our Currency: For they very well know, that People will have little Heart to advance Money in Trade, when what they can get is scarce sufficient to purchase Necessaries, and supply their Families with Provision. Much less will they lay it out in advancing new

Manufactures; nor is it possible new Manufactures should turn to any Account, where there is not Money to pay the Workmen, who are discouraged by being paid in Goods, because it is a great Disadvantage to them.

Again, Those who are truly for the Proprietor's Interest (and have no separate Views of their own that are predominant) will be heartily for a large Addition: Because, as I have shewn above, Plenty of Money will for several Reasons make Land rise in Value exceedingly: And I appeal to those immediately concerned for the Proprietor in the Sale of his Lands, whether Land has not risen very much since the first Emission of what Paper Currency we now have, and even by its Means. Now we all know the Proprietary has great Quantities to sell.

And since a Plentiful Currency will be so great a Cause of advancing this Province in Trade and Riches, and increasing the Number of its People; which, tho' it will not sensibly lessen the Inhabitants of Great Britain, will occasion a much greater Vent and Demand for their Commodities here; and allowing that the Crown is the more powerful for its Subjects increasing in Wealth and Number, I cannot think it the Interest of England to oppose us in making as great a Sum of Paper Money here, as we, who are the best Judges of our own Necessities, find convenient. And if I were not sensible that the Gentlemen of Trade in England, to whom we have already parted with our Silver and Gold, are misinformed of our Circumstances, and therefore endeavour to have our Currency stinted to what it now is, I should think the Government at Home had some Reasons for discouraging and impoverishing this Province, which we are not acquainted with. . . .

. . . As this Essay is wrote and published in Haste, and the Subject in it self intricate, I hope I shall be censured with Candour, if, for want of Time carefully to revise what I have written, in some Places I should appear to have express'd my self too obscurely, and in others am liable to

18 *The Political Thought of Benjamin Franklin*

Objections I did not foresee. I sincerely desire to be acquainted with the Truth, and on that Account shall think my self obliged to any one, who will take the Pains to shew me, or the Publick, where I am mistaken in my Conclusions, And as we all know there are among us several Gentlemen of acute Parts and profound Learning, who are very much against any Addition to our Money, it were to be wished that they would favour the Country with their Sentiments on this Head in Print; which, supported with Truth and good Reasoning, may probably be very convincing. And this is to be desired the rather, because many People knowing the Abilities of those Gentlemen to manage a good Cause, are apt to construe their Silence in This, as an Argument of a bad One. Had any Thing of that Kind ever yet appeared, perhaps I should not have given the Publick this Trouble: But as those ingenious Gentlemen have not yet (and I doubt never will) think it worth their Concern to enlighten the Minds of their erring Countrymen in this Particular, I think it would be highly commendable in every one of us, more fully to bend our Minds to the Study of *What is the true Interest of* PENNSYLVANIA; whereby we may be enabled, not only to reason pertinently with one another; but, if Occasion requires, to transmit Home such clear Representations, as must inevitably convince our Superiors of the Reasonableness and Integrity of our Designs.

OBSERVATIONS ON READING HISTORY

These somewhat cynical observations on human history and Franklin's conclusion that good men needed zeal and organization to improve society were inserted by Franklin at the begin-

---

Papers, I, 192–193; from a paper dated May 9, 1731, inserted in a part of the *Autobiography* written in August 1788.

ning of Part III of the *Autobiography* where he told of how he proposed to increase in every way he could the sway of virtue in the world.

That the great Affairs of the World, the Wars, Revolutions, &c. are carried on and effected by Parties.

That the View of these Parties is their present general Interest, or what they take to be such.

That the different Views of these different Parties, occasion all Confusion.

That while a Party is carrying on a general Design, each Man has his particular private Interest in View.

That as soon as a Party has gain'd its general Point, each Member becomes intent upon his particular Interest, which thwarting others, breaks that Party into Divisions, and occasions more Confusion.

That few in Public Affairs act from a meer View of the Good of their Country, whatever they may pretend; and tho' their Actings bring real Good to their Country, yet Men primarily consider'd that their own and their Country's Interest was united, and did not act from a Principle of Benevolence.

That fewer still in public Affairs act with a View to the Good of Mankind.

There seems to me at present to be great Occasion for raising an united Party for Virtue, by forming the Virtuous and good Men of all Nations into a regular Body, to be govern'd by suitable good and wise Rules, which good and wise Men may probably be more unanimous in their Obedience to, than common People are to common Laws.

I at present think, that whoever attempts this aright, and is well qualified, cannot fail of pleasing God, and of meeting with Success.

AN APOLOGY FOR PRINTERS

After two years as a newspaper publisher, Franklin had had enough complaints about his editorial practices to elicit this explanation of them.

Being frequently censur'd and condemn'd by different Persons for printing Things which they say ought not to be printed, I have sometimes thought it might be necessary to make a standing Apology for my self, and publish it once a Year, to be read upon all Occasions of that Nature. Much Business has hitherto hindered the execution of this Design; but having very lately given extraordinary Offence by printing an Advertisement with a certain *N.B.* at the End of it, I find an Apology more particularly requisite at this Juncture, tho' it happens when I have not yet Leisure to write such a thing in the proper Form, and can only in a loose manner throw those Considerations together which should have been the Substance of it.

I request all who are angry with me on the Account of printing things they don't like, calmly to consider these following Particulars

1. That the Opinions of Men are almost as various as their Faces; an Observation general enough to become a common Proverb, *So many Men so many Minds.*

2. That the Business of Printing has chiefly to do with Mens Opinions; most things that are printed tending to promote some, or oppose others.

3. That hence arises the peculiar Unhappiness of that Business, which other Callings are no way liable to; they who follow Printing being scarce able to do any thing in

---

Papers, I, 194–196, 199; first printed in *The Pennsylvania Gazette*, June 10, 1731.

Business, Civic and Political Leader 21

their way of getting a Living, which shall not probably give Offence to some, and perhaps to many; whereas the Smith, the Shoemaker, the Carpenter, or the Man of any other Trade, may work indifferently for People of all Persuasions, without offending any of them: and the Merchant may buy and sell with Jews, Turks, Hereticks, and Infidels of all sorts, and get Money by every one of them, without giving Offence to the most orthodox, of any sort; or suffering the least Censure or Ill-will on the Account from any Man whatever.

4. That it is as unreasonable in any one Man or Set of Men to expect to be pleas'd with every thing that is printed, as to think that nobody ought to be pleas'd but themselves.

5. Printers are educated in the Belief, that when Men differ in Opinion, both Sides ought equally to have the Advantage of being heard by the Publick; and that when Truth and Error have fair Play, the former is always an overmatch for the latter: Hence they chearfully serve all contending Writers that pay them well, without regarding on which side they are of the Question in Dispute.

6. Being thus continually employ'd in serving all Parties, Printers naturally acquire a vast Unconcernedness as to the right or wrong Opinions contain'd in what they print; regarding it only as the Matter of their daily labour: They print things full of Spleen and Animosity, with the utmost Calmness and Indifference, and without the least Ill-will to the Persons reflected on; who nevertheless unjustly think the Printer as much their Enemy as the Author, and join both together in their Resentment.

7. That it is unreasonable to imagine Printers approve of every thing they print, and to censure them on any particular thing accordingly; since in the way of their Business they print such great variety of things opposite and contradictory. It is likewise as unreasonable what some assert, *That Printers ought not to print any Thing*

but what they approve; since if all of that Business should make such a Resolution, and abide by it, an End would thereby be put to Free Writing, and the World would afterwards have nothing to read but what happen'd to be the Opinions of Printers.

8. That if all Printers were determin'd not to print any thing till they were sure it would offend no body, there would be very little printed.

9. That if they sometimes print vicious or silly things not worth reading, it may not be because they approve such things themselves, but because the People are so viciously and corruptly educated that good things are not encouraged. I have known a very numerous Impression of *Robin Hood's Songs* go off in this Province at 2s. per Book, in less than a Twelvemonth; when a small Quantity of *David's Psalms* (an excellent Version) have lain upon my Hands above twice the Time.

10. That notwithstanding what might be urg'd in behalf of a Man's being allow'd to do in the Way of his Business whatever he is paid for, yet Printers do continually discourage the Printing of great Numbers of bad things, and stifle them in the Birth. I my self have constantly refused to print any thing that might countenance Vice, or promote Immorality; tho' by complying in such Cases with the corrupt Taste of the Majority, I might have got much Money. I have also always refus'd to print such things as might do real Injury to any Person, how much soever I have been solicited, and tempted with Offers of great Pay; and how much soever I have by refusing got the Ill-will of those who would have employ'd me. I have heretofore fallen under the Resentment of large Bodies of Men, for refusing absolutely to print any of their Party or Personal Reflections. In this Manner I have made my self many Enemies, and the constant Fatigue of denying is almost insupportable. But the Publick being unacquainted with

all this, whenever the poor Printer happens either through Ignorance or much Persuasion, to do any thing that is generally thought worthy of Blame, he meets with no more Friendship or Favour on the above Account, than if there were no Merit in't at all. Thus, as Waller says,
> *Poets loose half the Praise they would have got*
> *Were it but known what they discreetly blot;*

Yet are censur'd for every bad Line found in their Works with the utmost Severity. . . .

[Franklin then explained that in printing an advertisement for passengers on a ship bound for the West Indies which concluded "No Sea Hens nor Black Gowns will be admitted on any Terms," he intended no insult to clergymen ("Black Gowns") by coupling them with the noisy birds or croaking fish sometimes called Sea Hens. He had, Franklin asserted, been very careful in public and in private to cast no aspersion on any religion or any believers therein.]

. . . I take leave to conclude with an old Fable, which some of my Readers have heard before, and some have not.

"A certain well-meaning Man and his Son, were travelling towards a Market Town, with an Ass which they had to sell. The Road was bad; and the old Man therefore rid, but the Son went a-foot. The first Passenger they met, asked the Father if he was not ashamed to ride by himself, and suffer the poor Lad to wade along thro' the Mire; this induced him to take up his Son behind him: He had not travelled far, when he met others, who said, they were two unmerciful Lubbers to get both on the Back of that poor Ass, in such a deep Road. Upon this the old Man gets off, and let his Son ride alone. The next they met called the Lad a graceless, rascally young Jackanapes, to ride in that Manner thro' the Dirt, while his aged Father trudged along on Foot; and they said the old Man was a Fool, for suffering it. He then bid his Son come down, and walk with him, and they travell'd on leading the Ass by the Halter; 'till they met another Company, who called them a Couple of sensless Blockheads, for going both on Foot in such a dirty Way, when they had an empty Ass with them, which they might ride upon. The old Man could bear no longer; My Son, said he, it grieves me much that we cannot please all these People: Let us throw the Ass over the next Bridge, and be no farther troubled with him."

Had the old Man been seen acting this last Resolution, he would probably have been call'd a Fool for troubling himself about the different Opinions of all that were pleas'd to find Fault with him: Therefore, tho' I have a Temper almost as complying as his, I intend not to imitate him in this last Particular. I consider the Variety of Humours among Men, and despair of pleasing every Body; yet I shall not therefore leave off Printing. I shall continue my Business. I shall not burn my Press and melt my Letters.

JUNTO QUERIES

Of Franklin's projects for civic- and self-improvement in Philadelphia, the Junto (founded in 1727) was the first and most fundamental. Franklin met regularly with a group of young men, mostly ambitious tradesmen like himself, to enhance mutually their personal virtue and prosperity, and to explore ways of making their city a better place in which to live. In demonstrating an earnest concern for the public welfare and in encouraging the personal virtues as the only sure foundation for that

---

Papers, I, 257–258; probably drawn by Franklin and used at Junto meetings from 1732 on.

Business, Civic and Political Leader 25

welfare, Franklin laid the cornerstone on which his public career rested. The queries here reprinted were the standing ones asked at the regular Friday meetings to test the steadiness of every member.

. . . 1. Have you met with any thing in the author you last read, remarkable, or suitable to be communicated to the Junto? particularly in history, morality, poetry, physic, travels, mechanic arts, or other parts of knowledge.

2. What new story have you lately heard agreeable for telling in conversation?

3. Hath any citizen in your knowledge failed in his business lately, and what have you heard of the cause?

4. Have you lately heard of any citizen's thriving well, and by what means?

5. Have you lately heard how any present rich man, here or elsewhere, got his estate?

6. Do you know of any fellow citizen, who has lately done a worthy action, deserving praise and imitation? or who has committed an error proper for us to be warned against and avoid?

7. What unhappy effects of intemperance have you lately observed or heard? of imprudence? of passion? or of any other vice or folly?

8. What happy effects of temperance? of prudence? of moderation? or of any other virtue?

9. Have you or any of your acquaintance been lately sick or wounded? If so, what remedies were used, and what were their effects?

10. Who do you know that are shortly going voyages or journies, if one should have occasion to send by them?

11. Do you think of any thing at present, in which the Junto may be serviceable to *mankind?* to their country, to their friends, or to themselves?

12. Hath any deserving stranger arrived in town since last meeting, that you heard of? and what have you heard or observed of his character or merits? and whether think you, it lies in the power of the Junto to oblige him, or encourage him as he deserves?

13. Do you know of any deserving young beginner lately set up, whom it lies in the power of the Junto any way to encourage?

14. Have you lately observed any defect in the laws of your *country*, [of] which it would be proper to move the legislature for an amendment? Or do you know of any beneficial law that is wanting?

15. Have you lately observed any encroachment on the just liberties of the people?

16. Hath any body attacked your reputation lately? and what can the Junto do towards securing it?

17. Is there any man whose friendship you want, and which the Junto or any of them, can procure for you?

18. Have you lately heard any member's character attacked, and how have you defended it?

19. Hath any man injured you, from whom it is in the power of the Junto to procure redress?

20. In what manner can the Junto, or any of them, assist you in any of your honourable designs?

21. Have you any weighty affair in hand, in which you think the advice of the Junto may be of service?

22. What benefits have you lately received from any man not present?

23. Is there any difficulty in matters of opinion, of justice, and injustice, which you would gladly have discussed at this time?

24. Do you see any thing amiss in the present customs or proceedings of the Junto, which might be amended? . . .

NATURAL RELIGION
AND FREEDOM OF THOUGHT

In 1735 an eloquent young minister, Reverend Samuel Hemphill, earned Franklin's admiration by urging from the pulpit of the Presbyterian Church in Philadelphia that Christians exhibit virtue in their daily lives and charity toward their neighbors. Hemphill's predecessor, Reverend Jedediah Andrews, was in Franklin's opinion not worth listening to because he said nothing to encourage virtue and morality but instead preached sermons that "were chiefly either polemic Arguments, or Explications of the peculiar Doctrines of our Sect . . . dry, uninteresting and unedifying." When Andrews sought to have the Synod bar Hemphill from further preaching, Franklin came to Hemphill's defense by writing and publishing a series of articles and pamphlets on his behalf. Initially, as the first of these three selections shows, Franklin pleaded moderation. More aroused, in the second selection he called upon all Christian laymen to uphold their rights of conscience, and in the final selection Franklin abandoned restraint and bitterly denounced Hemphill's clerical persecutors. The incident shows Franklin's devotion to free inquiry and his lifelong struggle to enlist religious energies on behalf of socially constructive goals.

Franklin first sought support for Hemphill by printing a clever dialogue in which, after presenting the conventional arguments that religion should concern itself mainly with teaching morality, he pleaded for religious toleration.

. . . T. *If Mr. H. is a Presbyterian Teacher, he ought to preach as Presbyterians use to preach; or else he may*

Papers, II, 31–33, 66–67, 125; from *The Pennsylvania Gazette*, April 10, 1735, and two pamphlets printed later that year.

justly be condemn'd and silenc'd by our Church Authority. We ought to abide by the Westminister Confession of Faith; and he that does not, ought not to preach in our Meetings.

S. The Apostacy of the Church from the primitive Simplicity of the Gospel, came on by Degrees; and do you think that the Reformation was of a sudden perfect, and that the first Reformers knew at once all that was right or wrong in Religion? Did not Luther at first preach only against selling of Pardons, allowing all the other Practices of the Romish Church for good? He afterwards went further, and Calvin, some think, yet further. The Church of England made a Stop, and fix'd her Faith and Doctrine by 39 Articles; with which the Presbyterians not satisfied, went yet farther; but being too self-confident to think, that as their Fathers were mistaken in some Things, they also might be in some others; and fancying themselves infallible in *their* Interpretations, they also ty'd themselves down by the Westminster Confession. But has not a Synod that meets in King George the Second's Reign, as much Right to interpret Scripture, as one that met in Oliver's Time? And if any Doctrine then maintain'd is, or shall hereafter be found not altogether orthodox, why must we be for ever confin'd to that, or to any, Confession?

T. *But if the Majority of the Synod be against any Innovation, they may justly hinder the Innovator from Preaching.*

S. That is as much as to say, if the Majority of the Preachers be in the wrong, they may justly hinder any Man from setting the People right; for a *Majority* may be in the wrong as well as the *Minority*, and frequently are. In the beginning of the Reformation, the *Majority* was vastly against the Reformers, and continues so to this Day; and, if, according to your Opinion, they had a Right to silence the *Minority*, I am sure the *Minority* ought to have been silent. But tell me, if the Presbyterians in this Country, being charitably enclin'd, should send a Missionary into Turky, to propagate the Gospel, would it not be unreasonable in the Turks to prohibit his Preaching?

T. *It would, to be sure, because he comes to them for their good.*

S. And if the Turks, believing us in the wrong, as we think them, should out of the same charitable Disposition, send a Missionary to preach Mahometanism to us, ought we not in the same manner to give him free Liberty of preaching his Doctrine?

T. *It may be so; but what would you infer from that?*

S. I would only infer, that if it would be thought reasonable to suffer a Turk to preach among us a Doctrine diametrically opposite to Christianity, it cannot be reasonable to silence one of our own Preachers, for preaching a Doctrine exactly agreeable to Christianity, only because he does not perhaps zealously propagate all the Doctrines of an old Confession. And upon the whole, though the *Majority* of the Synod should not in all respects approve of Mr. H.'s Doctrine, I do not however think they will find it proper to condemn him. We have justly deny'd the Infallibility of the Pope and his Councils and Synods in their Interpretations of Scripture, and can we modestly claim *Infallibility* for our selves or our Synods in our way of Interpreting? Peace, Unity and Virtue in any Church are more to be regarded than Orthodoxy. In the present weak State of humane Nature, surrounded as we are on all sides with Ignorance and Error, it little becomes poor fallible Man to be positive and dogmatical in his Opinions. No Point of Faith is so plain, as that *Morality* is our Duty, for all Sides agree in that. A virtuous Heretick shall be saved before a wicked Christian: for there is no such Thing as voluntary Error. Therefore, since 'tis an Uncertainty till we get to Heaven what true Orthodoxy in all points is, and since our Congregation is rather too small to be divided, I hope this Misunderstanding will soon be got over, and that we shall as heretofore unite again in mutual *Christian Charity*.

T. *I wish we may. I'll consider of what you've said, and wish you well.*

S. *Farewell.* . . .

[Franklin next wrote as a layman to his brethren, urging that Hemphill's cause was part of the great cause of freedom of thought for all mankind.]

It is sufficiently known to all the thinking Part of Mankind, how difficult it is to alter Opinions long and universally receiv'd. The Prejudices of Education, Custom and Example, are generally very strong; it may therefore seem, in a manner, needless to publish any Thing contrary to such long imbib'd and generally receiv'd Opinions. It were, however, much to be wish'd, that Men would consider how glorious a Conquest they make, when they shake off all manner of Prejudice, and bring themselves to think *freely, fairly,* and *honestly*.

This is to think and act like Men; 'tis a Privilege common to Mankind; 'tis the only way to promote the Interests of Truth and Liberty in the World; and surely, none but Slaves and Lovers of Dominion and Darkness can be out of humour at it; nor would any Man, or any Set of Men, pretend to hinder others from a free impartial Enquiry into Matters of Religion especially, if they had not some sinister Designs in so doing.

My Brethren of the Laity, as it is to you that this Letter is address'd, and chiefly for your Sakes that I take the Liberty of Publishing it, it is hop'd you'll seriously consider the Contents of it. The Generality of the Clergy were always too fond of Power to quit their Pretensions to it, by any thing that was ever yet said by particular Persons; but my Brethren, how soon should we humble their Pride, did we all heartily and unanimously join in asserting our own natural Rights and Liberties in Opposition to their unrighteous Claims. Besides, we could make use of more prevailing Arguments than any that have been yet advanc'd, I mean such as oppose their temporal Interests. It is impossible they could long stand against the united Force of so powerful Antagonists. Truth manag'd by the Laity in Opposition to them and their temporal Interests, would do much. Their pretending to be the Directors of Men's Consciences, and Embassadors of the meek and lowly Jesus, ('twere greatly to be wish'd they study'd more to imitate so perfect a Model of Meekness and Humility, and pretended less to a Power that belongs not to 'em) and their assuming such like fine Titles, ought not to frighten us out of a good Cause, *The glorious Cause of Christian Liberty.* It is very probable, indeed, that according to their laudable Custom, they will make very free with the Characters of those that oppose their Schemes, and like sound, orthodox Divines, call them Hereticks, unsound in the Faith, and so on; but there is no Argument in such kind of Language, nor will it ever persuade. And we ought to value such ridiculous Epithets just as little as St. Paul did, Acts 24:14, since instead of a Reproach, they may be our greatest Glory and Honour. Such kind of Treatment was always look'd upon to be a strong Argument either of a bad Cause or a weak side. That it is our Duty to make a vigorous Opposition to them, is plain from these two Considerations: *First,* that when and wherever Men blindly submitted themselves to the Impositions of Priests, whether Popish, Presbyterian or Episcopal, &c. Ignorance and Error, Bigotry, Enthusiasm and Superstition, more or less, and in Proportion to such Submission, most certainly ensu'd, And *Secondly,* That all the Persecutions, Cruelties,

Mischiefs and Disturbances, that ever yet happen'd in the Church, took their rise from the usurp'd Power and Authority of her lawless Sons. Let us then to the utmost of our Power endeavour to preserve and maintain Truth, Common Sense, universal Charity, and brotherly Love, Peace and Tranquility, as recommended in the Gospel of Jesus, in this our infant and growing Nation, by steadily opposing those, whose Measures tend to nothing less than utterly to subvert and destroy all. Nothing, in all Probability, can prevent our being a very flourishing and happy People, but our suffering the Clergy to get upon our Backs, and ride us, as they do their Horses, where they please. . . .

[At the conclusion of his last effort in Hemphill's defense, disgusted with the vicious, persecuting spirit of the Presbyterian ministers who had succeeded in barring Hemphill from the pulpit, Franklin let loose a withering blast that reveals his deep animosity to those who said "Lord, Lord" but who, in Franklin's view, were hypocrites not the least interested in true Christianity and the welfare of mankind.]

. . . Thus, I think, I have examin'd the principal Things in this Vindication of the Rev. Commission; and upon the whole, it appears even from a plain Narration of Matter of Fact, that they (the leading Men among them at least) came to Philadelphia with Malice, Rancour and Prejudice in their Hearts, resolv'd at all Hazards to condemn the Man and his Doctrines; and their Aversion to both carry'd them those shameful Lengths which we have here shewn in their true Light. For if to justify a known Perjury, to lye openly and frequently in the Face of the World; if to condemn Doctrines agreeable to the main End and Design of the Gospel, and calculated for the common Welfare of Men; if to stamp an Appearance of Sanctity upon

Animosity, false Zeal, Injustice, Fraud, Oppression, by their own open Example as well as Precept; and to behave as bitter Adversaries instead of impartial Judges; if to do all this be truly *christian Candour, Charity and Truth,* then will I venture to say, these Rev. Gentlemen have given the most lively Instances of theirs. For all these Things have been so strongly charg'd and fairly prov'd upon 'em, that they must of Necessity confess their Guilt in Silence, or by endeavouring a Refutation of the plain Truth, plunge themselves deeper into the Dirt and Filth of Hypocrisy, Falsehood and Impiety, 'till at length they carry their quibbling Absurdities far enough to open the Eyes of the weakest and most unthinking Part of the Laity, from whom alone they can expect Support and Proselytes. . . .

FREEDOM OF THE PRESS

In his *Autobiography* Franklin tells of his long friendship with the great evangelist George Whitefield. During 1739 and 1740 thousands responded to Whitefield's preaching missions in Philadelphia, but at the same time he aroused the hostility of some local clergymen, especially those who objected to his emotionalism. Although Franklin admired Whitefield's oratory and the good effect it had, he objected to those intolerant of any criticism of the evangelist. Ebenezer Kinnersley, long a friend of Franklin's and later a collaborator in his electrical experiments, spoke against Whitefield. After the Baptist Church barred Kinnersley from its pulpit, he wrote a defense of his doctrines that Franklin printed. The statement that follows is Franklin's preface to that defense. The sermons by Reverend Archibald Cummings men-

---

Papers, II, 260–261; first printed in *The Pennsylvania Gazette,* July 24, 1740.

tioned by Franklin had been printed by his competitors in Philadelphia, Andrew and William Bradford.

It is a Principle among Printers, that when Truth has fair Play, it will always prevail over Falshood; therefore, though they have an undoubted Property in their own Press, yet they willingly allow, that any one is entitled to the Use of it, who thinks it necessary to offer his Sentiments on disputable Points to the Publick, and will be at the Expence of it. If what is thus publish'd be good, Mankind has the Benefit of it: If it be bad (I speak now in general without any design'd Application to any particular Piece whatever) the more 'tis made publick, the more its Weakness is expos'd, and the greater Disgrace falls upon the Author, whoever he be; who is at the same Time depriv'd of an Advantage he would otherwise without fail make use of, viz. of Complaining, *that Truth is suppress'd, and that he could say* MIGHTY MATTERS, *had he but the Opportunity of being heard.*

The Printers of this City have been unjustly reflected on, as if they were under some undue Influence, and guilty of great Partiality in favour of the Preaching lately admir'd among us, so as to refuse Printing any Thing in Opposition to it, how just or necessary soever. A Reflection entirely false and groundless, and without the least Colour of Fact to support it; which all will be convinc'd of when they see the following Piece from one Press, and the Rev. Mr. Cummings's Sermons against the Doctrines themselves, from the other.

Englishmen thought it an intolerable Hardship, when (tho' by an Act of their own Parliament) Thoughts, which should be free, were fetter'd and confin'd, and an Officer was erected over the Nation, call'd *a Licenser of the Press*, without whose Consent no Writing could be publish'd.

Care might indeed be taken in the Choice of this Officer, that he should be a Man of great Understanding, profound Learning, and extraordinary Piety; yet, as the greatest and best of Men may have *some* Errors, and have been often found averse to *some* Truths, it was justly esteem'd a National Grievance, that the People should have Nothing to read but the Opinions, or what was agreeable to the Opinions of ONE MAN. But should every petty Printer (who, if he can read his Hornbook, may be thought to have Learning enough to qualify him for his own Sphere) presume to erect himself into an Officer of this kind, and arbitrarily decide what ought and what ought not to be published, much more justly might the World complain. 'Tis true, where Invectives are contain'd in any Piece, there is no good-natur'd Printer but had much rather be employ'd in Work of another kind: However, tho' many personal Reflections be interwoven in the following Performance, yet as the Author *(who has subscrib'd his Name)* thought them necessary, to vindicate his own Conduct and Character, it is therefore hoped, on that Consideration, the Reader will excuse the Printer in publishing them.

THE CHARACTER OF ANDREW HAMILTON

Andrew Hamilton (1676–1741), long a power in Pennsylvania public life, often Speaker of its Assembly, and famous as the defender of John Peter Zenger, earned Franklin's personal friendship through many acts of kindness and sponsorship. When he died in 1741, Franklin regarded him very nearly as a model political leader and set down in his obituary some fundamental precepts that later guided Franklin's own career.

Papers, II, 327–328; first printed in *The Pennsylvania Gazette*, July 30, 1741.

... He lived not without Enemies: For, as he was himself open and honest, he took pains to unmask the Hypocrite, and boldly censured the Knave, without regard to Station and Profession. Such, therefore, may exult at his Death. He steadily maintained the Cause of Liberty; and the Laws made, during the time he was Speaker of the Assembly, which was many Years, will be a lasting Monument of his Affection to the People, and of his Concern for the welfare of this Province. He was no Friend to Power, as he had observed an ill use had been frequently made of it in the Colonies; and therefore was seldom upon good Terms with Governors. This Prejudice, however, did not always determine his Conduct towards them; for where he saw they meant well, he was for supporting them honourably, and was indefatigable in endeavouring to remove the Prejudices of others. He was long at the Top of his Profession here, and had he been as griping as he was knowing and active, he might have left a much greater Fortune to his Family than he has done: But he spent more Time in hearing and reconciling Differences in Private, to the Loss of his Fees, than he did in pleading Causes at the Bar. He was just, where he sat as a Judge; and tho' he was stern and severe in his Manner, he was compassionate in his Nature, and very slow to punish. He was the Poor Man's Friend, and was never known to with-hold his Purse or Service from the Indigent or Oppressed. He was a tender Husband and a fond Parent: But—these are Virtues which Fools and Knaves have sometimes in common with the Wise and the Honest. His free Manner of treating Religious Subjects, gave Offence to many, who, if a Man may judge by their Actions, were not themselves much in earnest. He feared God, loved Mercy, and did Justice: If he could not subscribe to the Creed of any particular Church, it was not for want of considering them All; for he had read much on Religious Subjects. He went through a tedious Sickness with uncommon Chearfulness, Constancy and Courage.

Nothing of affected Bravery or Ostentation appeared; But such a Composure and Tranquility of Mind, as results from the Reflection of a Life spent agreeable to the best of a Man's Judgment. . . .

ON LAWFUL PROCESS

Franklin shared the widespread colonial suspicion (especially strong in Quaker Pennsylvania) that lawyers and courts were worse than useless to humble citizens seeking justice. The following comment is but one of many printed in his newspaper and almanac from his pen and that of others berating the legal profession.

Honest Men often go to Law for their Right; when Wise Men would sit down with the Wrong, supposing the first Loss least. In some Countries the Course of the Courts is so tedious, and the Expence so high, that the Remedy, *Justice,* is worse than, *Injustice,* the Disease. In my Travels I once saw a Sign call'd *The Two Men at Law;* One of them was painted on one Side, in a melancholy Posture, all in Rags, with this Scroll, *I have lost my Cause.* The other was drawn capering for Joy, on the other Side, with these Words, *I have gain'd my Suit;* but he was stark naked.

THE EVILS OF TAVERNS

Among Franklin's other civic duties, he served on Philadelphia juries. There survives in his hand the following extract from

Papers, II, 339; first printed in *Poor Richard's Almanack,* 1742.
Papers, III, 10–11; document dated January 3, 1745.

a presentment of a grand jury on which he served condemning the excessive number of "Tipling Houses" in the city. Though it is not certain that Franklin drafted the presentment, its existence in his hand, and its style, suggest he was its author.

". . . The Grand Jury observe with great Concern the vast Number of Tipling Houses within this City, many of which they think are little better than Nurseries of Vice and Debauchery, and tend very much to encrease the Number of our Poor. They are like wise of Opinion, that the profane Language, horrid Oaths and Imprecations, grown of late so common in our Streets, so shocking to the Ears of the sober Inhabitants, and tending to destroy in the Minds of our Youth, all Sense of the Fear of God and the Religion of an Oath, owes its Increase in a great Measure to those disorderly Houses. The Jury therefore beg Leave to recommend it to the Court, to fall on some Method of limiting or diminishing the Number of Publick Houses, and preserving Good Order in such as shall be licenced for the future."

The Jury would only observe, that they had no Intention in the least to break in upon the Authority of the Magistrates; that they only complain'd of the great Number of Tipling Houses as a Grievance which they feel, and, far from prescribing to the Justices, they only requested them to fall upon some Methods among themselves of preventing it for the future: Which is no more than is practiced in like Cases by the Grand Juries of the City of London, as the Presentment they made of the great Increase of Gin Shops, to the Lord Mayor and Justices of that City, fully shows. For this Presentment the Jury were, as we are inform'd, *thank'd* by that honourable Court, and a Committee of the Bench appointed to enquire into the Grievance complain'd of, upon whose Report Measures were afterwards taken to remove it. The Grand Jury do therefore still think it their Duty to complain of the enormous Increase of Publick Houses in Philadelphia, especially since it now appears by the Constables Returns that there are upwards of One Hundred that have Licences, which, with the Retailers, make the Houses that sell strong Drink, by our Computation, near a tenth Part of the City; a Proportion that appears to us much too great, since by their Number they impoverish one another as well as the Neighbourhoods they live in, and, for want of better Customers, may, thro' Necessity, be under greater Temptations to entertain Apprentices, Servants, and even Negroes. The Jury therefore are glad to hear from the Bench, that the Magistrates are become sensible of this Evil, and purpose to apply a Remedy; for which they will deserve the Thanks of all good Citizens. . . .

SPEECH OF MISS POLLY BAKER

This famous hoax, probably composed by Franklin to amuse his friends, nevertheless shows his rational, pragmatic approach to matters of public policy and is a brilliant example of his ability to use wit and satire to focus attention on what he considered absurdities. There was, of course, no real Polly Baker and her "Speech" was a product of Franklin's fertile imagination, but the laws and attitudes satirized were far from fanciful.

The SPEECH of Miss POLLY BAKER, before a Court of Judicature, at Connecticut near Boston in New-England; where she was prosecuted the Fifth Time, for having a

---

Papers, III, 123–125; first printed in *The [London] General Advertiser*, April 15, 1747.

Bastard Child: Which influenced the Court to dispense with her Punishment, and induced one of her Judges to marry her the next Day

May it please the Honourable Bench to indulge me in a few Words: I am a poor unhappy Woman, who have no Money to fee Lawyers to plead for me, being hard put to it to get a tolerable Living. I shall not trouble your Honours with long Speeches; for I have not the Presumption to expect, that you may, by any Means, be prevailed on to deviate in your Sentence from the Law, in my Favour. All I humbly hope is, That your Honours would charitably move the Governor's Goodness on my Behalf, that my Fine may be remitted. This is the Fifth Time, Gentlemen, that I have been dragg'd before your Court on the same Account; twice I have paid heavy Fines, and twice have been brought to Publick Punishment, for want of Money to pay those Fines. This may have been agreeable to the Laws, and I don't dispute it; but since Laws are sometimes unreasonable in themselves, and therefore repealed, and others bear too hard on the Subject in particular Circumstances; and therefore there is left a Power somewhat to dispense with the Execution of them; I take the Liberty to say, That I think this Law, by which I am punished, is both unreasonable in itself, and particularly severe with regard to me, who have always lived an inoffensive Life in the neighbourhood where I was born, and defy my Enemies (if I have any) to say I ever wrong'd Man, Woman, or Child. Abstracted from the Law, I cannot conceive (may it please your Honours) what the Nature of my Offence is. I have brought Five fine Children into the World, at the Risque of my Life; I have maintain'd them well by my own Industry, without burthening the Township, and would have done it better, if it had not been for the heavy Charges and Fines I have paid. Can it be a Crime (in the Nature of Things I mean) to add to the Number of the

Business, Civic and Political Leader 41

King's Subjects, in a new Country that really wants People? I own it, I should think it a Praise-worthy, rather than a punishable Action. I have debauched no other Woman's Husband, nor enticed any Youth; these Things I never was charg'd with, nor has any one the least Cause of Complaint against me, unless, perhaps, the Minister, or Justice, because I have had Children without being married, by which they have missed a Wedding Fee. But, can ever this be a Fault of mine? I appeal to your Honours. You are pleased to allow I don't want Sense; but I must be stupified to the last Degree, not to prefer the Honourable State of Wedlock, to the Condition I have lived in. I always was, and still am willing to enter into it; and doubt not my behaving well in it, having all the Industry, Frugality, Fertility, and Skill in Economy, appertaining to a good Wife's Character. I defy any Person to say, I ever refused an Offer of that Sort: On the contrary, I readily consented to the only Proposal of Marriage that ever was made me, which was when I was a Virgin; but too easily confiding in the Person's Sincerity that made it, I unhappily lost my own Honour, by trusting to his; for he got me with Child, and then forsook me: That very Person you all know; he is now become a Magistrate of this Country; and I had Hopes he would have appeared this Day on the Bench, and have endeavoured to moderate the Court in my Favour; then I should have scorn'd to have mention'd it; but I must now complain of it, as unjust and unequal, That my Betrayer and Undoer, the first Cause of all my Faults and Miscarriages (if they must be deemed such) should be advanc'd to Honour and Power in the Government, that punishes my Misfortunes with Stripes and Infamy. I should be told, 'tis like, That were there no Act of Assembly in the Case, the Precepts of Religion are violated by my Transgressions. If mine, then, is a religious Offence, leave it to religious Punishments. You have already excluded me from the

Comforts of Your Church-Communion. Is not that sufficient? You believe I have offended Heaven, and must suffer eternal Fire: Will not that be sufficient? What Need is there, then, of your additional Fines and Whipping? I own, I do not think as you do; for, if I thought what you call a Sin, was really such, I could not presumptously commit it. But, how can it be believed, that Heaven is angry at my having Children, when to the little done by me towards it, God has been pleased to add his Divine Skill and admirable Workmanship in the Formation of their Bodies, and crown'd it, by furnishing them with rational and immortal Souls. Forgive me, Gentlemen, if I talk a little extravagantly on these Matters; I am no Divine, but if you, Gentlemen, must be making Laws, do not turn natural and useful Actions into Crimes, by your Prohibitions. But take into your wise Consideration, the great and growing Number of Batchelors in the Country, many of whom from the mean Fear of the Expences of a Family, have never sincerely and honourably courted a Woman in their Lives; and by their Manner of Living, leave unproduced (which is little better than Murder) Hundreds of their Posterity to the Thousandth Generation. Is not this a greater Offence against the Publick Good, than mine? Compel them, then, by Law, either to Marriage, or to pay double the Fine of Fornication every Year. What must poor young Women do, whom Custom have forbid to solicit the Men, and who cannot force themselves upon Husbands, when the Laws take no Care to provide them any; and yet severely punish them if they do their Duty without them; the Duty of the first and great Command of Nature, and of Nature's God, *Encrease and Multiply.* A Duty, from the steady Performance of which, nothing has been able to deter me; but for its Sake, I have hazarded the Loss of the Publick Esteem, and have frequently endured Publick Disgrace and Punishment; and therefore ought, in my

Business, Civic and Political Leader 43

humble Opinion, instead of a Whipping, to have a Statue erected to my Memory.

PLAIN TRUTH

In July 1747, during the War of the Austrian Succession (King George's War), French and Spanish privateers brought hostilities to the Delaware River and for the first time threatened Pennsylvania, founded on pacifist principles, with attack, plunder, and bloodshed. When the Assembly refused to arm the province, Franklin published *Plain Truth*, pleading for defense measures, chastising both political factions in the colony, and proposing a voluntary militia association which, since it did not require legislative action, by-passed the Assembly. The pamphlet had, Franklin wrote in his *Autobiography*, "a sudden and surprizing Effect." Its proposals were debated but in the end an association of over one thousand armed men, including Franklin, was formed in Philadelphia. The pamphlet heightened Franklin's popularity and made him thereafter a significant force in the politics of the colony.

. . . War, at this Time, rages over a great Part of the known World; our News-Papers are Weekly filled with fresh Accounts of the Destruction it every where occasions. Pennsylvania, indeed, situate in the Center of the Colonies, has hitherto enjoy'd profound Repose; and tho' our Nation is engag'd in a bloody War, with two great and powerful Kingdoms, yet, defended, in a great Degree, from the French on the one Hand by the Northern Provinces,

---

Papers, III, 188–204; published as a pamphlet, November 17, 1747, entitled *Plain Truth: or, Serious Considerations On the Present State of the City of Philadelphia, and Province of Pennsylvania. By a Tradesman of Philadelphia.*

and from the Spaniards on the other by the Southern, at no small Expence to each, our People have, till lately, slept securely in their Habitations.

There is no British Colony excepting this, but has made some Kind of Provision for its Defence; many of them have therefore never been attempted by an Enemy; and others that were attack'd, have generally defended themselves with Success. The Length and Difficulty of our Bay and River has been thought so effectual a Security to us, that hitherto no Means have been entered into that might discourage an Attempt upon us, or prevent its succeeding.

But whatever Security this might have been while both Country and City were poor, and the Advantage to be expected scarce worth the Hazard of an Attempt, it is now doubted whether we can any longer safely depend upon it. Our Wealth, of late Years much encreas'd, is one strong Temptation, our defenceless State another, to induce an Enemy to attack us; while the Acquaintance they have lately gained with our Bay and River, by Means of the Prisoners and Flags of Truce they have had among us; by Spies which they almost every where maintain, and perhaps from Traitors among ourselves; with the Facility of getting Pilots to conduct them; and the known Absence of Ships of War, during the greatest Part of the Year, from both Virginia and New-York, ever since the War began, render the Appearance of Success to the Enemy far more promising, and therefore highly encrease our Danger. . . .

. . . If this now flourishing City, and greatly improving Colony, is destroy'd and ruin'd, it will not be for want of Numbers of Inhabitants able to bear Arms in its Defence. 'Tis computed that we have at least (exclusive of the Quakers) 60,000 Fighting Men, acquainted with Fire-Arms, many of them Hunters and Marksmen, hardy and bold. All we want is Order, Discipline, and a few Cannon. At present we are like the separate Filaments of Flax before the Thread is form'd, without Strength because without Connection; but Union would make us strong and even formidable: Tho' the *Great* should neither help nor join us; tho' they should even oppose our Uniting, from some mean Views of their own, yet, if we resolve upon it, and it please God to inspire us with the necessary Prudence and Vigour, it *may* be effected. . . . Were this Union form'd, were we once united, thoroughly arm'd and disciplin'd, was every Thing in our Power done for our Security, as far as human Means and Foresight could provide, we might then, *with more Propriety,* humbly ask the Assistance of Heaven, and a Blessing on our lawful Endeavours. The very Fame of our Strength and Readiness would be a Means of Discouraging our Enemies; for 'tis a wise and true Saying, that *One Sword often keeps another in the Scabbard.* The Way to secure Peace is to be prepared for War. They that are on their Guard, and appear ready to receive their Adversaries, are in much less Danger of being attack'd, than the supine, secure and negligent. We have yet a Winter before us, which may afford a good and almost sufficient Opportunity for this, if we seize and improve it with a becoming Vigour. And if the Hints contained in this Paper are so happy as to meet with a suitable Disposition of Mind in his Countrymen and Fellow Citizens, the Writer of it will, in a few Days, lay before them a Form of an Association for the Purposes herein mentioned, together with a practicable Scheme for raising the Money necessary for the Defence of our Trade, City, and Country, without laying a Burthen on any Man.

May the GOD *of* Wisdom, Strength *and* Power, *the Lord of the Armies of Israel, inspire us with Prudence in this Time of* Danger; *take away from us all the Seeds of Contention and Division, and unite the Hearts and Counsels* of all of us, of whatever Sect or Nation, in one Bond of Peace, Brotherly Love, and generous Publick Spirit; May he give us Strength and Resolution to amend our Lives, and remove from among us every Thing that is displeasing to him; afford us his most gracious Protection, confound the Designs of our Enemies, and give Peace in all our Borders, is the sincere Prayer of

A Tradesman of Philadelphia.

PROPOSALS FOR A VOLUNTEER

AND REPUBLICAN MILITARY FORCE

Following the success of *Plain Truth* Franklin offered a plan for organizing men willing to bear arms into voluntary militia associations. The preamble to the plan, the first three articles, and Franklin's "Remarks" on them are reprinted here. Though the proposal that company officers be elected by the men in the ranks was novel in Great Britain and in the colonies from New York southward, it had long been the practice in Franklin's native New England. The tone of *Plain Truth*, appealing to the "middling Persons" against the leaders of the province, the extra-legal character of the proposed militia, and the democratic election of officers, all alarmed the constituted authorities in the colony. Proprietor Thomas Penn wrote of the plan and its proposer: "This Association is founded on a Contempt to Government, and cannot end in anything but Anarchy and Confusion. . . . tho very true in it self, that Obedience to Goverers is no more due that Protection to the People, yet it is not fit to be always in the heads

---

Papers, III, 205–209; first printed in *The Pennsylvania Gazette*, December 3, 1747.

of the Wild unthinking Multitude. . . . [Franklin] is a dangerous Man and I should be very Glad he inhabited any other Country, as I believe him of a very uneasy Spirit. However as he is a Sort of Tribune of the People, he must be treated with regard." [1]

We whose Names are hereunto subscribed, Inhabitants of the Province of Pennsylvania in America, taking into serious Consideration, that Great Britain, to which we are subject, is now engag'd in a War with two powerful Nations: That it is become too well known to our Enemies, that this Colony is in a naked, defenceless State, without Fortifications or Militia of any Sort, and is therefore exposed daily to Destruction from the Attacks of a very small Force: That we are at a great Distance from our Mother Country, and cannot, on any Emergency, receive Assistance from thence: That thro' the Multiplicity of other Affairs of greater Importance (as we presume) no particular Care hath hitherto been taken by the Government at Home of our Protection, an humble Petition to the Crown for that purpose, sign'd by a great Number of Hands, having yet had no visible Effect. That the Assemblies of this Province, by reason of their religious Principles, have not done, nor are likely to do any Thing for our Defence, notwithstanding repeated Applications to them for that Purpose: That being thus unprotected by the Government under which we live, against our foreign Enemies that may come to invade us, As we think it absolutely necessary, We Do hereby, for our mutual Defence and Security, and for the Security of our Wives, Children and Estates, and the Preservation of the Persons and Estates of others,

---

[1]Thomas Penn to Richard Peters, March 30 and June 9, 1748, Historical Society of Pennsylvania; quoted in *Papers*, III, 186 [Ed.].

our Neighbours and Fellow Subjects, form ourselves into an Association, and, imploring the Blessing of Heaven on our Undertaking, do agree *solemnly* with each other in Manner following; that is to say;

First, That we will each of us, before the first Day of January next, or as soon as possible, provide ourselves with a good Firelock, Cartouch Box, and at least twelve Charges of Powder and Ball, and as many of us as conveniently can, with a good Sword, Cutlass or Hanger, to be kept always in our respective Dwellings, in Readiness, and good Order.

Secondly, That we will before the said Day, form ourselves into Companies, from Fifty to One Hundred Men each, consisting of such as are situated most conveniently for meeting together.

Thirdly, That at the first Meetings of each Company, which shall be on the Day aforesaid, three Persons shall be chosen by Ballot out of, and by each Company, to be Captain, Lieutenant and Ensign of the same, whose Names shall be presented to the Governor for the Time being, or in his Absence to the President and Council of this Province, in order to obtain Commissions accordingly. Which Persons, so commissioned, shall be the Captains, Lieutenants and Ensigns, of each Company, respectively, for the ensuing Year. . . .

Remarks on the Preamble.

This contains the Reasons and the Necessity of our associating. Where a Government takes proper Measures to protect the People under its Care, such a Proceeding might have been thought both unnecessary and unjustifiable: But here it is quite the Reverse. For in our State (and perhaps if you search the World through, you will find it in ours only) the Government, that Part of it at least that holds the Purse, has always, from religious Considerations, refused to use the common Means for the Defence of the Country against an Enemy.

Remarks on Article I.

As *Use* is in our Case more to be regarded than *Uniformity*, and it would be difficult so suddenly to procure such a Number of Arms, exactly of the same Kind, the general Word *Firelock* is used (rather than *Musket*, which is the Name of a particular kind of Gun) most People having a Firelock of some kind or other already in their Hands. If the Cartouch Box should not contain the 12 Charges, the rest may be ready in the Pocket. It is said by some military Writers, that one fourth Part of the Weight of the Ball, is Powder sufficient for a Charge; an Over-quantity, that makes a Gun violently recoil, rendering the Shot less certain. They add, that the nicest Care ought to be taken in casting Bullets so much less than the Bore, that they may slip down with Ease, when rolled in Cartridges, even into a foul Gun, otherwise there is great Loss of Time and Fire in an Engagement, to the no small Advantage of the Enemy. Tho' Bayonets are not required, it would be well enough for some to provide them; for they may be as useful against a violent Onset from irregular Foot, as against Horse. Those who on Account of their Age or Infirmities ought to be excused from the common Exercises, yet will do well to keep Arms and Ammunition ready in their Houses, that when Occasion calls, they may either use them if they can, or lend them to those who happen to be unprovided. The Expence of providing these Arms is small, and may be saved in some other Article: and they will always fetch near the Money they cost.

Remarks on Article II.

This Article is intended to prevent People's sorting themselves into Companies, according to their Ranks in Life, their Quality or Station. 'Tis designed to mix the Great and Small together, for the sake of Union and Encouragement. Where Danger and Duty are equal to All, there should be no Distinction from Circumstances, but All be on the Level.

Remarks on Article III.

Where the Officers of a Militia are appointed by the Governor (as in some Colonies) it often happens, that Persons absolutely disagreeable to the People are impower'd to command them. This is attended with very ill Consequences, rendering the Meetings for military Exercise, instead of a Pleasure, a most grievous Burthen, and by Degrees discouraging them even to a total Disuse. But where those to be commanded chuse those that are to command, it is to be presumed the Choice will naturally fall on Men of the best Character for their military Skill; on such too, from whose Prudence and Good-nature there may be no Fear of Injustice or military Oppression: And as the Ballot prevents all Resentments, so the Choice for one Year only, will keep all Officers within the Bounds of Moderation and Decorum in the Exercise of their Power, and excite an Emulation in All to qualify themselves for being chosen in their Turn. The Rotation of military Offices may be objected to, as contrary to modern Practice; but the wonderful Success of the Old Romans proves it absolutely right. The Romans, without Doubt, affected Glory and Command as much as other People; but yet they disdained not to obey in their Armies the same Persons whom they had formerly commanded; and to serve as private Soldiers, where they had been formerly Generals. The Application to the Governor, &c. for Commissions, preserves the Prerogative, at the same time that these frequent Elections secure the Liberty of the People. And what can give more Spirit and martial Vigour to an Army of FREEMEN, than to be led by those of whom they have the best Opinion?

ADVICE TO A YOUNG TRADESMAN

Franklin's famous *personae*, thrifty Poor Richard and prudent Father Abraham (the guide to "The Way to Wealth"), though not primarily political in character, form an essential part both of Franklin's reputation as a public figure and of the attitude he took toward public questions. He was effective as a politician partly because he was world-famous as an apostle of thrift, and he believed earnestly in applying Poor Richard's maxims in affairs of state. Furthermore, he thought tradesmen with proper habits would make model citizens for the free societies of the New World. His earliest public statement on the precepts of frugality, other than the scattered adages in *Poor Richard's Almanack*, was in "Advice to a Young Tradesman." Although "Advice" is less famous than the longer "The Way to Wealth," it states fully Franklin's faith in thrift and prudence.

Remember that Time is Money. He that can earn Ten Shillings a Day by his Labour, and goes abroad, or sits idle one half of that Day, tho' he spends but Sixpence during his Diversion or Idleness, ought not to reckon That the only Expence; he has really spent or rather thrown away Five Shillings besides.

Papers, III, 306–308; first printed on July 21, 1748.

Remember that Credit is Money. If a Man lets his Money lie in my Hands after it is due, he gives me the Interest, or so much as I can make of it during that Time. This amounts to a considerable Sum where a Man has good and large Credit, and makes good Use of it.

Remember that Money is of a prolific generating Nature. Money can beget Money, and its Offspring can beget more, and so on. Five Shillings turn'd, is *Six:* Turn'd again, 'tis Seven and Three Pence; and so on 'til it becomes an Hundred Pound. The more there is of it, the more it produces every Turning, so that the Profits rise quicker and quicker. He that kills a breeding Sow, destroys all her Offspring to the thousandth Generation. He that murders a Crown, destroys all it might have produc'd, even Scores of Pounds.

Remember that Six Pounds a Year is but a Groat a Day. For this little Sum (which may be daily wasted either in Time or Expence unperciev'd) a Man of Credit may on his own Security have the constant Possession and Use of an Hundred Pounds. So much in Stock briskly turn'd by an industrious Man, produces great Advantage.

Remember this Saying, *That the good Paymaster is Lord of another Man's Purse.* He that is known to pay punctually and exactly to the Time he promises, may at any Time, and on any Occasion, raise all the Money his Friends can spare. This is sometimes of great Use: Therefore never keep borrow'd Money an Hour beyond the Time you promis'd, lest a Disappointment shuts up your Friends Purse forever.

The most trifling Actions that affect a Man's Credit, are to be regarded. The Sound of your Hammer at Five in the Morning or Nine at Night, heard by a Creditor, makes him easy Six Months longer. But if he sees you at a Billiard Table, or hears your Voice in a Tavern, when you should be at Work, he sends for his Money the next Day. Finer

Business, Civic and Political Leader 53

Cloaths than he or his Wife wears, or greater Expence in any particular than he affords himself, shocks his Pride, and he duns you to humble you. Creditors are a kind of People, that have the sharpest Eyes and Ears, as well as the best Memories of any in the World.

Good-natur'd Creditors (and such one would always chuse to deal with if one could) feel Pain when they are oblig'd to ask for Money. Spare 'em that Pain, and they will love you. When you receive a Sum of Money, divide it among 'em in 'Proportion to your Debts. Don't be asham'd of paying a small Sum because you owe a greater. Money, more or less, is always welcome; and your Creditor had rather be at the Trouble of receiving Ten Pounds voluntarily brought him, tho' at ten different Times or Payments, than be oblig'd to go ten Times to demand it before he can receive it in a Lump. It shews, besides, that you are mindful of what you owe; it makes you appear a careful as well as an honest Man; and that still encreases your Credit.

Beware of thinking all your own that you possess, and of living accordingly. 'Tis a Mistake that many People who have Credit fall into. To prevent this, keep an exact Account for some Time of both your Expences and your Incomes. If you take the Pains at first to mention Particulars, it will have this good Effect; you will discover how wonderfully small trifling Expences mount up to large Sums, and will discern what might have been, and may for the future be saved, without occasioning any great Inconvenience.

In short, the Way to Wealth, if you desire it, is as plain as the Way to Market. It depends chiefly on two Words, Industry and Frugality; i.e. Waste neither Time nor Money, but make the best Use of both. He that gets all he can honestly, and saves all he gets (necessary Expences excepted) will certainly become Rich, If that Being who governs the World, to whom all should look for a Blessing on their honest Endeavours, doth not in his wise Providence otherwise determine.

EDUCATION AND THE PUBLIC GOOD

Among Franklin's many promotions for civic improvement was the Academy and College of Philadelphia, which became the University of Pennsylvania. His proposals to emphasize English and other modern languages rather than the traditional ancient ones, and to offer training in subjects useful in commerce and agriculture, were novel, but his remarks on the purpose of the institution and its role in the public life of the colony were more conventional. Franklin's understanding of the importance of proper education in a self-governing society is an essential element of his political thought. His reasons for founding the Academy and for encouraging the study of morality and history are summarized in the following extracts from his *Proposals Relating to the Education of Youth in Pensilvania* and from a letter to a friend.

The good Education of Youth has been esteemed by wise Men in all Ages, as the surest Foundation of the Happiness both of private Families and of Commonwealths. Almost all Governments have therefore made it a principal Object of their Attention, to establish and endow with proper Revenues, such Seminaries of Learning, as might supply the succeeding Age with Men qualified to serve the Publick with Honour to themselves, and to their Country.

Many of the first Settlers of these Provinces, were Men who had received a good Education in Europe, and to

---

Papers, III, 399, 412–415; IV, 41; from a pamphlet first published in October 1749, and from a letter to Samuel Johnson, August 23, 1750.

their Wisdom and good Management we owe much of our present Prosperity. But their Hands were full, and they could not do all Things. The present Race are not thought to be generally of equal Ability: For though the American Youth are allow'd not to want Capacity; yet the best Capacities require Cultivation, it being truly with them, as with the best Ground, which unless well tilled and sowed with profitable Seed, produces only ranker Weeds. . . .

Morality, by descanting and making continual Observations on the Causes of the Rise or Fall of any Man's Character, Fortune, Power, &c. mention'd in History; the Advantages of Temperance, Order, Frugality, Industry, Perseverance, &c. &c. Indeed the general natural Tendency of Reading good History, must be, to fix in the Minds of Youth deep Impressions of the Beauty and Usefulness of Virtue of all Kinds, Publick Spirit, Fortitude, &c.

History will show the wonderful Effects of Oratory, in governing, turning and leading Great Bodies of Mankind, Armies, Cities, Nations. When the Minds of Youth are struck with Admiration at this, then is the Time to give them the Principles of that Art, which they will study with Taste and Application. Then they may be made acquainted with the best Models among the Antients, their Beauties being particularly pointed out to them. Modern Political Oratory being chiefly performed by the Pen and Press, its Advantages over the Antient in some Respects are to be shown; as that its Effects are more extensive, more lasting, &c.

History will also afford frequent Opportunities of showing the Necessity of a *Publick Religion,* from its Usefulness to the Publick; the Advantage of a Religious Character among private Persons; the Mischiefs of Superstition, &c. and the Excellency of the Christian Religion above all other ancient or modern.

History will also give Occasion to expatiate on the Advantage of Civil Orders and Constitutions, how Men and their Properties are protected by joining in Societies and establishing Government; their Industry encouraged and rewarded, Arts invented, and Life made more comfortable: The Advantages of *Liberty*, Mischiefs of *Licentiousness*, Benefits arising from good Laws and a due Execution of Justice, &c. Thus may the first Principles of sound *Politicks* be fix'd in the Minds of Youth.

On *Historical* Occasions, Questions of Right and Wrong Justice and Injustice, will naturally arise, and may be put to Youth, which they may debate in Conversation and in Writing. When they ardently desire Victory, for the Sake of the Praise attending it, they will begin to feel the Want, and be sensible of the Use of *Logic*, or the Art of Reasoning to *discover* Truth, and of Arguing to *defend* it, and *convince* Adversaries. This would be the Time to acquaint them with the Principles of that Art. Grotius, Puffendorff, and some other Writers of the same Kind, may be used on these Occasions to decide their Disputes. Publick Disputes warm the Imagination, whet the Industry, and strengthen the natural Abilities. . . .

. . . I think with you, that nothing is of more importance for the public weal, than to form and train up youth in wisdom and virtue. Wise and good men are, in my opinion, the *strength* of a state: much more so than riches or arms, which, under the management of Ignorance and Wickedness, often draw on destruction, instead of providing for the safety of a people. And though the culture bestowed on *many* should be successful only with a *few*, yet the influence of those few and the service in their power, may be very great. Even a single woman that was wise, by her wisdom saved a city.

I think also, that general virtue is more probably to be expected and obtained from the *education* of youth, than from the *exhortation* of adult persons; bad habits and vices of the mind, being, like diseases of the body, more easily prevented than cured.

I think moreover, that talents for the education of youth are the gift of God; and that he on whom they are bestowed, whenever a way is opened for the use of them, is as strongly *called* as if he heard a voice from heaven: nothing more surely pointing out *duty* in a public service, than *ability* and *opportunity* of performing it. . . .

HOSPITALS, CHARITY, AND THE PUBLIC GOOD

Franklin gave the same wholehearted and industrious support to the Pennsylvania Hospital (founded in 1751) he had lavished on the Library Company and on the Academy, and he had the same end in mind in each promotion: the organization of human good will into institutions for the improvement of the community in which he lived. This impulse was the foundation of his public philosophy and the source of his fame and effectiveness as a political leader. Portions of the petition he drafted for support of the hospital by the Pennsylvania Assembly, and the conclusion of his report on the benefits afforded by the Hospital are reprinted here.

TO THE

HONOURABLE HOUSE OF REPRESENTATIVES

OF THE PROVINCE OF PENNSYLVANIA

The PETITION of sundry Inhabitants of the said Province.

Papers, V, 285–286, 325–327; from a petition dated January 23, 1751, and from Franklin's *Account of the Pennsylvania Hospital*, May 1754.

Humbly sheweth,

That with the Numbers of People the Number of Lunaticks, or Persons distemper'd in Mind, and deprived of their rational Faculties, hath encreased in this Province.

That some of them going at large, are a Terror to their Neighbours, who are daily apprehensive of the Violences they may commit; and others are continually wasting their Substance, to the great Injury of themselves and Families, ill disposed Persons wickedly taking Advantage of their unhappy Condition, and drawing them into unreasonable Bargains, &c.

That few or none of them are so sensible of their Condition as to submit voluntarily to the Treatment their respective Cases require, and therefore continue in the same deplorable State during their Lives; whereas it has been found, by the Experience of many Years, that above two Thirds of the mad People received into Bethlehem Hospital, and there treated properly, have been perfectly cured.

Your Petitioners beg Leave farther to represent, that tho' the good Laws of this Province have made many compassionate and charitable Provisions for the Relief of the Poor, yet something farther seems wanting in Favour of such whose Poverty is made more miserable by the additional Weight of a grievous Disease, from which they might easily be relieved, if they were not situated at too great a Distance from regular Advice and Assistance, whereby many languish out their Lives, tortur'd perhaps with the Stone, devour'd by the Cancer, depriv'd of Sight by Cataracts, or gradually decaying by loathsome Distempers; who, if the Expence in the present Manner of nursing and attending them separately when they come to Town, were not so discouraging, might again, by the judicious Assistance of Physick and Surgery, be enabled to taste the Blessings of Health, and be made in a few Weeks useful Members of the Community, able to provide for themselves and Families.

The kind Care our Assemblies have heretofore taken for the Relief of Sick and distemper'd Strangers, by providing a Place for their Reception and Accommodation, leaves us no Room to doubt their shewing an equal tender Concern for the Inhabitants. And we hope they will be of Opinion with us, that a small Provincial Hospital, erected and put under proper Regulations, in the Care of Persons to be appointed by this House, or otherwise, as they shall think meet, with Power to receive and apply the charitable Benefactions of good People towards enlarging and supporting the same, and some other Provisions in a Law for the Purposes abovementioned, will be a good Work, acceptable to GOD, and to all the good People they represent. . . .

. . . It ought in Justice to be here observed, that the Practitioners have not only given their Advice and Attendance *gratis,* but have made their Visits with even greater Assiduity and Constancy than is sometimes used to their richer Patients; and that the Managers have attended their Monthly Boards, and the Committees the Visitations of two Days in every Week, with greater Readiness and Punctuality than has been usually known in any other publick Business, where Interest was not immediately concerned; owing, no Doubt, to that Satisfaction which naturally arises in humane Minds from a Consciousness of doing Good, and from the frequent pleasing Sight of Misery relieved, Distress removed, grievous Diseases healed, Health restored, and those who were admitted languishing, groaning, and almost despairing of Recovery, discharged sound and hearty, with chearful and thankful Countenances, gratefully acknowledging the Care that has been taken of them, praising GOD, and blessing their Benefactors, who by their bountiful Contributions founded so excellent an Institution. . . .

60 The Political Thought of Benjamin Franklin

CRIMINALS AND CITIZENSHIP

Authorities in Great Britain had long sought to empty jails in the mother country by transporting their inmates to the colonies. In 1731 colonial governors were instructed to prevent their assemblies from interfering with such transportation. News that a Pennsylvania law imposing duties on the imported convicts had been blocked in England caused Franklin to satirize the British rationalization that the criminals would help populate the colonies and become useful citizens there.

To the Printers of the Gazette:

By a Passage in one of your late Papers, I understand that the Government at home will not suffer our mistaken Assemblies to make any Law for preventing or discouraging the Importation of Convicts from Great Britain, for this kind Reason, *"That such Laws are against the Publick Utility, as they tend to prevent the* Improvement *and* well peopling of the Colonies."

Such a tender *parental* Concern in our *Mother Country* for the *Welfare* of her Children, calls aloud for the highest *Returns* of Gratitude and Duty. This every one must be sensible of: But 'tis said, that in our present Circumstances it is absolutely impossible for us to make *such* as are adequate to the Favour. I own it; but nevertheless let us do our Endeavour. 'Tis something to show a grateful Disposition.

In some of the uninhabited Parts of these Provinces, there are Numbers of these venomous Reptiles we call Rattle-Snakes; Felons-convict from the Beginning of the World: These, whenever we meet with them, we put to

---

Papers, IV, 131–133; first printed in *The Pennsylvania Gazette*, May 9, 1751.

Business, Civic and Political Leader 61

Death, by Virtue of an old Law, *Thou shalt bruise his Head.* But as this is a sanguinary Law, and may seem too cruel; and as however mischievous those Creatures are with us, they may possibly change their Natures, if they were to change the Climate; I would humbly propose, that this general Sentence of *Death* be changed for *Transportation.*

In the Spring of the Year, when they first creep out of their Holes, they are feeble, heavy, slow, and easily taken; and if a small Bounty were allow'd *per* Head, some Thousands might be collected annually, and *transported* to Britain. There I would propose to have them carefully distributed in St. James's Park, in the Spring-Gardens and other Places of Pleasure about London; in the Gardens of all the Nobility and Gentry throughout the Nation; but particularly in the Gardens of the *Prime Ministers,* the *Lords of Trade* and *Members of Parliament;* for to them we are *most particularly* obliged.

There is no human Scheme so perfect, but some Inconveniencies may be objected to it: Yet when the Conveniencies far exceed, the Scheme is judg'd rational, and fit to be executed. Thus Inconveniencies have been objected to that *good* and *wise* Act of Parliament, by virtue of which all the Newgates and Dungeons in Britain are emptied into the Colonies. It has been said, that these Thieves and Villains introduc'd among us, spoil the Morals of Youth in the Neighbourhoods that entertain them, and perpetrate many horrid Crimes: but let not *private Interests* obstruct *publick Utility.* Our *Mother* knows what is best for us. What is a little *Housebreaking, Shoplifting,* or *Highway Robbing;* what is a *Son* now and then *corrupted* and *hang'd,* a Daughter *debauch'd* and *pox'd,* a Wife *stabb'd,* a Husband's *Throat cut,* or a Child's *Brains beat out* with an Axe, compar'd with this "Improvement and well peopling of the Colonies!"

Thus it may perhaps be objected to my Scheme, that the *Rattle-Snake* is a mischievous Creature, and that his changing his Nature with the Clime is a mere Supposition, not yet confirm'd by sufficient Facts. What then? Is not Example more prevalent than Precept? And may not the honest rough British Gentry, by a Familiarity with these Reptiles, learn to *creep,* and to *insinuate,* and to *slaver,* and to *wriggle* into Place (and perhaps to *poison* such as stand in their Way) Qualities of no small Advantage to Courtiers! In comparison of which "*Improvement* and *Publick Utility,*" what is a *Child* now and then kill'd by their venomous Bite, — or even a favourite *Lap-Dog?*

I would only add, That this Exporting of Felons to the Colonies, may be consider'd as a Trade, as well as in the Light of a *Favour.* Now all Commerce implies *Returns:* Justice requires them: There can be no Trade without them. And *Rattle-Snakes* seem the most *suitable Returns* for the *Human Serpents* sent us by our *Mother* Country. In this, however, as in every other Branch of Trade, she will have the Advantage of us. She will reap *equal* Benefits without equal Risque of the Inconveniencies and Dangers. For the *Rattle-Snake* gives Warning before he attempts his Mischief; which the Convict does not. I am Yours, &c.

Americanus

OBSERVATIONS

CONCERNING THE INCREASE OF MANKIND

This famous essay on demography and what Franklin conceived was the glorious future of the British Empire is the foundation for all his later speculations and opinions, before and after

---

Papers, IV, 227–234; written in 1751 and first printed in 1755.

1776, on the growth and development of North America. He believed that the human fertility encouraged by the open lands and free society of the New World would make Pennsylvania and her neighbors a great and prosperous country regardless of which flag flew over them. Though there is no explicit thought of separation from the mother country in this essay, the destiny Franklin foresees for the colonies carries with it, unmistakably, the implication that forces were at work that would overpower any political efforts at unnatural restraint by Great Britain. The unfortunate strictures in the last two paragraphs on the German immigrants to Pennsylvania and on the "black and tawny" races were omitted, apparently at Franklin's direction, from editions of the essay printed in the 1760's.

1. Tables of the Proportion of Marriages to Births, of Deaths to Births, of Marriages to the Numbers of Inhabitants, &c. form'd on Observations made upon the Bills of Mortality, Christnings, &c. of populous Cities, will not suit Countries; nor will Tables form'd on Observations made on full settled old Countries, as Europe, suit new Countries, as America.

2. For People increase in Proportion to the Number of Marriages, and that is greater in Proportion to the Ease and Convenience of supporting a Family. When Families can be easily supported, more Persons marry, and earlier in Life.

3. In Cities, where all Trades, Occupations and Offices are full, many delay marrying, till they can see how to bear the Charges of a Family; which Charges are greater in Cities, as Luxury is more common: many live single during Life, and continue Servants to Families, Journeymen to Trades, &c. hence Cities do not by natural Generation supply themselves with Inhabitants; the Deaths are more than the Births.

4. In Countries full settled, the Case must be nearly

the same; all Lands being occupied and improved to the Heighth: those who cannot get Land, must Labour for others that have it; when Labourers are plenty, their Wages will be low; by low Wages a Family is supported with Difficulty; this Difficulty deters many from Marriage, who therefore long continue Servants and single. Only as the Cities take Supplies of People from the Country, and thereby make a little more Room in the Country; Marriage is a little more incourag'd there, and the Births exceed the Deaths.

5. Europe is generally full settled with Husbandmen, Manufacturers, &c. and therefore cannot now much increase in People: America is chiefly occupied by Indians, who subsist mostly by Hunting. But as the Hunter, of all Men, requires the greatest Quantity of Land from whence to draw his Subsistence, (the Husbandman subsisting on much less, the Gardner on still less, and the Manufacturer requiring least of all), The Europeans found America as fully settled as it well could be by Hunters; yet these having large Tracks, were easily prevail'd on to part with Portions of Territory to the new Comers, who did not much interfere with the Natives in Hunting, and furnish'd them with many Things they wanted.

6. Land being thus plenty in America, and so cheap as that a labouring Man, that understands Husbandry, can in a short Time save Money enough to purchase a Piece of new Land sufficient for a Plantation, whereon he may subsist a Family; such are not afraid to marry; for if they even look far enough forward to consider how their Children when grown up are to be provided for, they see that more Land is to be had at Rates equally easy, all Circumstances considered.

7. Hence Marriages in America are more general, and more generally early, than in Europe. And if it is reckoned there, that there is but one Marriage per Annum among

100 Persons, perhaps we may here reckon two; and if in Europe they have but 4 Births to a Marriage (many of their Marriages being late) we may here reckon 8, of which if one half grow up, and our Marriages are made, reckoning one with another at 20 Years of Age, our People must at least be doubled every 20 Years.

8. But notwithstanding this Increase, so vast is the Territory of North-America, that it will require many Ages to settle it fully; and till it is fully settled, Labour will never be cheap here, where no Man continues long a Labourer for others, but gets a Plantation of his own, no Man continues long a Journeyman to a Trade, but goes among those new Settlers, and sets up for himself, &c. Hence Labour is no cheaper now, in Pennsylvania, than it was 30 Years ago, tho' so many Thousand labouring People have been imported.

9. The Danger therefore of these Colonies interfering with their Mother Country in Trades that depend on Labour, Manufactures, &c. is too remote to require the Attention of Great-Britain.

10. But in Proportion to the Increase of the Colonies, a vast Demand is growing for British Manufactures, a glorious Market wholly in the Power of Britain, in which Foreigners cannot interfere, which will increase in a short Time even beyond her Power of supplying, tho' her whole Trade should be to her Colonies: Therefore Britain should not too much restrain Manufactures in her Colonies. A wise and good Mother will not do it. To distress, is to weaken, and weakening the Children, weakens the whole Family.

11. Besides if the Manufactures of Britain (by Reason of the American Demands) should rise too high in Price, Foreigners who can sell cheaper will drive her Merchants out of Foreign Markets; Foreign Manufactures will thereby be encouraged and increased, and consequently

foreign Nations, perhaps her Rivals in Power, grow more populous and more powerful; while her own Colonies, kept too low, are unable to assist her, or add to her Strength.

12. 'Tis an ill-grounded Opinion that by the Labour of Slaves, America may possibly vie in Cheapness of Manufactures with Britain. The Labour of Slaves can never be so cheap here as the Labour of working Men is in Britain. Any one may compute it. Interest of Money is in the Colonies from 6 to 10 per Cent. Slaves one with another cost £30 Sterling per Head. Reckon then the Interest of the first Purchase of a Slave, the Insurance or Risque on his Life, his Cloathing and Diet, Expences in his Sickness and Loss of Time, Loss by his Neglect of Business (Neglect is natural to the Man who is not to be benefited by his own Care or Diligence), Expence of a Driver to keep him at Work, and his Pilfering from Time to Time, almost every Slave being *by Nature* a Thief, and compare the whole Amount with the Wages of a Manufacturer of Iron or Wool in England, you will see that Labour is much cheaper there than it ever can be by Negroes here. Why then will Americans purchase Slaves? Because Slaves may be kept as long as a Man pleases, or has Occasion for their Labour; while hired Men are continually leaving their Master (often in the midst of his Business,) and setting up for themselves.

13. As the Increase of People depends on the Encouragement of Marriages, the following Things must diminish a Nation, viz. 1. The being conquered; for the Conquerors will engross as many Offices, and exact as much Tribute or Profit on the Labour of the conquered, as will maintain them in their new Establishment, and this diminishing the Subsistence of the Natives discourages their Marriages, and so gradually diminishes them, while the Foreigners increase. 2. Loss of Territory. Thus the Britons being

driven into Wales, and crowded together in a barren Country insufficient to support such great Numbers, diminished 'till the People bore a Proportion to the Produce, while the Saxons increas'd on their abandoned Lands; 'till the Island became full of English. And were the English now driven into Wales by some foreign Nation, there would in a few Years be no more Englishmen in Britain, than there are now People in Wales. 3. Loss of Trade. Manufactures exported, draw Subsistence from Foreign Countries for Numbers; who are thereby enabled to marry and raise Families. If the Nation be deprived of any Branch of Trade, and no new Employment is found for the People occupy'd in that Branch, it will also be soon deprived of so many People. 4. Loss of Food. Suppose a Nation has a Fishery, which not only employs great Numbers, but makes the Food and Subsistence of the People cheaper; If another Nation becomes Master of the Seas, and prevents the Fishery, the People will diminish in Proportion as the Loss of Employ, and Dearness of Provision, makes it more difficult to subsist a Family. 5. Bad Government and insecure Property. People not only leave such a Country, and settling Abroad incorporate with other Nations, lose their native Language, and become Foreigners; but the Industry of those that remain being discourag'd, the Quantity of Subsistence in the Country is lessen'd, and the Support of a Family becomes more difficult. So heavy Taxes tend to diminish a People. 6. The Introduction of Slaves. The Negroes brought into the English Sugar Islands, have greatly diminish'd the Whites there; the Poor are by this Means depriv'd of Employment, while a few Families acquire vast Estates; which they spend on Foreign Luxuries, and educating their Children in the Habit of those Luxuries; the same Income is needed for the Support of one that might have maintain'd 100. The Whites who have Slaves, not labouring, are enfeebled, and therefore not so generally prolific; the Slaves being work'd too hard, and ill fed, their Constitutions are broken, and the Deaths among them are more than the Births; so that a continual Supply is needed from Africa. The Northern Colonies having few Slaves increase in Whites. Slaves also pejorate the Families that use them; the white Children become proud, disgusted with Labour, and being educated in Idleness, are rendered unfit to get a Living by Industry.

14. Hence the Prince that acquires new Territory, if he finds it vacant, or removes the Natives to give his own People Room; the Legislator that makes effectual Laws for promoting of Trade, increasing Employment, improving Land by more or better Tillage; providing more Food by Fisheries; securing Property, &c. and the Man that invents new Trades, Arts or Manufactures, or new Improvements in Husbandry, may be properly called *Fathers* of their Nation, as they are the Cause of the Generation of Multitudes, by the Encouragement they afford to Marriage.

15. As to Privileges granted to the married, (such as the *Jus trium Liberorum* among the Romans), they may hasten the filling of a Country that has been thinned by War or Pestilence, or that has otherwise vacant Territory; but cannot increase a People beyond the Means provided for their Subsistence.

16. Foreign Luxuries and needless Manufactures imported and used in a Nation, do, by the same Reasoning, increase the People of the Nation that furnishes them, and diminish the People of the Nation that uses them. Laws therefore that prevent such Importations, and on the contrary promote the Exportation of Manufactures to be consumed in Foreign Countries, may be called (with Respect to the People that make them) *generative Laws*, as by increasing Subsistence they encourage Marriage. Such Laws likewise strengthen a Country, doubly, by increasing its own People and diminishing its Neighbours.

17. Some European Nations prudently refuse to consume the Manufactures of East-India. They should likewise forbid them to their Colonies; for the Gain to the Merchant, is not to be compar'd with the Loss by this Means of People to the Nation.

18. Home Luxury in the Great, increases the Nation's Manufacturers employ'd by it, who are many, and only tends to diminish the Families that indulge in it, who are few. The greater the common fashionable Expence of any Rank of People, the more cautious they are of Marriage. Therefore Luxury should never be suffer'd to become common.

19. The great Increase of Offspring in particular Families, is not always owing to greater Fecundity of Nature, but sometimes to Examples of Industry in the Heads, and industrious Education; by which the Children are enabled to provide better for themselves, and their marrying early, is encouraged from the Prospect of good Subsistence.

20. If there be a Sect therefore, in our Nation, that regard Frugality and Industry as religious Duties, and educate their Children therein, more than others commonly do; such Sect must consequently increase more by natural Generation, than any other Sect in Britain.

21. The Importation of Foreigners into a Country that has as many Inhabitants as the present Employments and Provisions for Subsistence will bear; will be in the End no Increase of People; unless the New Comers have more Industry and Frugality than the Natives, and then they will provide more Subsistence, and increase in the Country; but they will gradually eat the Natives out. Nor is it necessary to bring in Foreigners to fill up any occasional Vacancy in a Country; for such Vacancy (if the Laws are good, § 14, 16) will soon be filled by natural Generation. Who can now find the Vacancy made in Sweden, France or other Warlike Nations, by the Plague of Heroism 40 Years

ago; in France, by the Expulsion of the Protestants; in England, by the Settlement of her Colonies; or in Guinea, by 100 Years Exportation of Slaves, that has blacken'd half America? The thinness of Inhabitants in Spain is owing to National Pride and Idleness, and other Causes, rather than to the Expulsion of the Moors, or to the making of new Settlements.

22. There is in short, no Bound to the prolific Nature of Plants or Animals, but what is made by their crowding and interfering with each others Means of Subsistence. Was the Face of the Earth vacant of other Plants, it might be gradually sowed and overspread with one Kind only; as, for Instance, with Fennel; and were it empty of other Inhabitants, it might in a few Ages be replenish'd from one Nation only; as, for Instance, with Englishmen. Thus there are suppos'd to be now upwards of One Million English Souls in North-America, (tho' 'tis thought scarce 80,000 have been brought over Sea) and yet perhaps there is not one the fewer in Britain, but rather many more, on Account of the Employment the Colonies afford to Manufacturers at Home. This Million doubling, suppose but once in 25 Years, will in another Century be more than the People of England, and the greatest Number of Englishmen will be on this Side the Water. What an Accession of Power to the British Empire by Sea as well as Land! What Increase of Trade and Navigation! What Numbers of Ships and Seamen! We have been here but little more than 100 Years, and yet the Force of our Privateers in the late War, united, was greater, both in Men and Guns, than that of the whole British Navy in Queen Elizabeth's Time. How important an Affair then to Britain, is the present Treaty for settling the Bounds between her Colonies and the French, and how careful should she be to secure Room enough, since on the Room depends so much the Increase of her People?

23. In fine, A Nation well regulated is like a Polypus;

take away a Limb, its Place is soon supply'd; cut it in two, and each deficient Part shall speedily grow out of the Part remaining. Thus if you have Room and Subsistence enough, as you may by dividing, make ten Polypes out of one, you may of one make ten Nations, equally populous and powerful; or rather, increase a Nation ten fold in Numbers and Strength.

And since Detachments of English from Britain sent to America, will have their Places at Home so soon supply'd and increase so largely here; why should the Palatine Boors be suffered to swarm into our Settlements, and by herding together establish their Language and Manners to the Exclusion of ours? Why should Pennsylvania, founded by the English, become a Colony of *Aliens,* who will shortly be so numerous as to Germanize us instead of our Anglifying them, and will never adopt our Language or Customs, any more than they can acquire our Complexion.

24. Which leads me to add one Remark: That the Number of purely white People in the World is proportionably very small. All Africa is black or tawny. Asia chiefly tawny. America (exclusive of the new Comers) wholly so. And in Europe, the Spaniards, Italians, French, Russians and Swedes, are generally of what we call a swarthy Complexion; as are the Germans also, the Saxons only excepted, who with the English, make the principal Body of White People on the Face of the Earth. I could wish their Numbers were increased. And while we are, as I may call it, *Scouring* our Planet, by clearing America of Woods, and so making this Side of our Globe reflect a brighter Light to the Eyes of Inhabitants in Mars or Venus, why should we in the Sight of Superior Beings, darken its People? why increase the Sons of Africa, by Planting them in America, where we have so fair an Opportunity, by excluding all Blacks and Tawneys, of increasing the lovely White and Red? But perhaps I am partial to the Complexion of my Country, for such Kind of Partiality is natural to Mankind.

POVERTY AND THE EFFECTS OF GERMAN IMMIGRATION TO PENNSYLVANIA

Franklin sent his "Observations . . ." (see preceding document) to his friend the London merchant Peter Collinson who wrote him about it, eliciting these additional comments by Franklin.

I received your Favour of the 29th. August last and thank you for the kind and judicious remarks you have made on my little Piece. Whatever further occurs to you on the same subject, you will much oblige me in communicating it.

I have often observed with wonder, that Temper of the poor English Manufacturers and day Labourers which you mention, and acknowledge it to be pretty general. When any of them happen to come here, where Labour is much better paid than in England, their Industry seems to diminish in equal proportion. But it is not so with the German Labourers; They retain the habitual Industry and Frugality they bring with them, and now receiving higher Wages an accumulation arises that makes them all rich.

When I consider, that the English are the Offspring of Germans, that the Climate they live in is much of the same Temperature; when I can see nothing in Nature that should create this Difference, I am apt to suspect it must arise from Institution, and I have sometimes doubted, whether the Laws peculiar to England which compel the Rich to maintain the Poor, have not given the latter, a Dependance that very much lessens the care of providing against the wants of old Age.

Papers, IV, 479–486; from a letter to Peter Collinson, May 9, 1753.

I have heard it remarked that the Poor in Protestant Countries on the Continent of Europe, are generally more industrious than those of Popish Countries, may not the more numerous foundations in the latter for the relief of the poor have some effect towards rendering them less provident. To relieve the misfortunes of our fellow creatures is concurring with the Deity, 'tis Godlike, but if we provide encouragements for Laziness, and supports for Folly, may it not be found fighting against the order of God and Nature, which perhaps has appointed Want and Misery as the proper Punishments for, and Cautions against as well as necessary consequences of Idleness and Extravagancy.

Whenever we attempt to mend the scheme of Providence and to interfere in the Government of the World, we had need be very circumspect lest we do more harm than Good. In New England they once thought Black-birds useless and mischievous to their corn, they made Laws to destroy them, the consequence was, the Black-birds were diminished but a kind of Worms which devoured their Grass, and which the Black-birds had been used to feed on encreased prodigiously; Then finding their Loss in Grass much greater than their saving in corn they wished again for their Black-birds.

We had here some years since a Transylvanian Tartar, who had travelled much in the East, and came hither merely to see the West, intending to go home thro' the spanish West Indies, China &c. He asked me one day what I thought might be the Reason that so many and such numerous nations, as the Tartars in Europe and Asia, the Indians in America, and the Negroes in Africa, continued a wandring careless Life, and refused to live in Cities, and to cultivate the arts they saw practiced by the civilized part of Mankind. While I was considering what answer to make him; I'll tell you, says he in his broken English, God make man for Paradise, he make him for to live lazy; man make God angry, God turn him out of Paradise, and bid him work; man no love work; he want to go to Paradise again, he want to live lazy; so all mankind love lazy. Howe'er this may be it seems certain, that the hope of becoming at some time of Life free from the necessity of care and Labour, together with fear of penury, are the mainsprings of most peoples industry.

To those indeed who have been educated in elegant plenty, even the provision made for the poor may appear misery, but to those who have scarce ever been better provided for, such provision may seem quite good and sufficient, these latter have then nothing to fear worse than their present Conditions, and scarce hope for any thing better than a Parish maintainance; so that there is only the difficulty of getting that maintainance allowed while they are able to work, or a little shame they suppose attending it, that can induce them to work at all, and what they do will only be from hand to mouth.

The proneness of human Nature to a life of ease, of freedom from care and labour appears strongly in the little success that has hitherto attended every attempt to civilize our American Indians, in their present way of living, almost all their Wants are supplied by the spontaneous Productions of Nature, with the addition of very little labour, if hunting and fishing may indeed be called labour when Game is so plenty, they visit us frequently, and see the advantages that Arts, Sciences, and compact Society procure us, they are not deficient in natural understanding and yet they have never shewn any Inclination to change their manner of life for ours, or to learn any of our Arts; When an Indian Child has been brought up among us, taught our language and habituated to our Customs, yet if he goes to see his relations and make one Indian Ramble with them, there is no perswading him ever to return, and that this is not natural [to them] merely as Indians, but as men, is plain from this, that when white persons of either sex have been taken prisoners young by the Indians, and lived a while among them, tho' ransomed by their Friends, and treated with all imaginable tenderness to prevail with them to stay among the English, yet in a Short time they become disgusted with our manner of life, and the care and pains that are necessary to support it, and take the first good Opportunity of escaping again into the Woods, from whence there is no reclaiming them. One instance I remember to have heard, where the person was brought home to possess a good Estate; but finding some care necessary to keep it together, he relinquished it to a younger Brother, reserving to himself nothing but a gun and a match-Coat, with which he took his way again to the Wilderness.

Though they have few but natural wants and those easily supplied. But with us are infinite Artificial wants, no less craving than those of Nature, and much more difficult to satisfy; so that I am apt to imagine that close Societies subsisting by Labour and Arts, arose first not from choice, but from necessity: When numbers being driven by war from their hunting grounds and prevented by seas or by other nations were crowded together into some narrow Territories, which without labour would not afford them Food. However as matters [now] stand with us, care and industry seem absolutely necessary to our well being; they should therefore have every Encouragement we can invent, and not one Motive to diligence be subtracted, and the support of the Poor should not be by maintaining them in Idleness, But by employing them in some kind of labour suited to their Abilities of body &c. as I am informed of late begins to be the practice in many parts of England, where work houses are erected for that purpose. If these were general I should think the Poor would be more careful and work voluntarily and lay up something for themselves against a rainy day, rather than run the risque of being obliged to work at the pleasure of others for a bare subsistence and that too under confinement. The little value Indians set on what we prize so highly under the name of Learning appears from a pleasant passage that happened some years since at a Treaty between one of our Colonies and the Six Nations; when every thing had been settled to the Satisfaction of both sides, and nothing remained but a mutual exchange of civilities, the English Commissioners told the Indians, they had in their Country a College for the instruction of Youth who were there taught various languages, Arts, and Sciences; that there was a particular foundation in favour of the Indians to defray the expense of the Education of any of their sons who should desire to take the Benefit of it. And now if the Indians would accept of the Offer, the English would take half a dozen of their brightest lads and bring them up in the Best manner; The Indians after consulting on the proposal replied that it was remembered some of their Youths had formerly been educated in that College, but it had been observed that for a long time after they returned to their Friends, they were absolutely good for nothing being neither acquainted with the true methods of killing deer, catching Beaver or surprizing an enemy. The Proposition however, they looked on as a mark of the kindness and good will of the English to the Indian Nations which merited a grateful return; and therefore if the English Gentlemen would send a dozen or two of their Children to Onondago the great Council would take care of their Education, bring them up in really what was the best manner and make men of them.

I am perfectly of your mind, the measures of great Temper are necessary with the Germans: and am not without Apprehensions, that thro' their indiscretion or Ours, or both, great disorders and inconveniences may one day arise among us; Those who come hither are generally of the most ignorant Stupid Sort of their own Nation, and as Ignorance is often attended with Credulity when Knavery would mislead it, and with Suspicion when Honesty would set it right; and as few of the English understand the German Language, and so cannot address them either from the Press or Pulpit, 'tis almost impossible to remove any prejudices they once entertain. Their own Clergy have very little influence over the people; who seem to take an uncommon pleasure in abusing and discharging the Minister on every trivial occasion. Not being used to Liberty, they know not how to make a modest use of it; and as Kolben says of the young Hottentots, that they are not esteemed men till they have shewn their manhood by beating their mothers, so these seem to think themselves not free, till they can feel their liberty in abusing and insulting their Teachers. Thus they are under no restraint of Ecclesiastical Government; They behave, however, submissively enough at present to the Civil Government which I wish they may continue to do: For I remember when they modestly declined intermeddling in our Elections, but now they come in droves, and carry all before them, except in one or two Counties; Few of their children in the Country learn English; they import many Books from Germany; and of the six printing houses in the Province, two are entirely German, two half German half English, and but two entirely English; They have one German News-paper, and one half German. Advertisments intended to be general are now printed in Dutch and English; the Signs in our Streets have inscriptions in both languages, and in some places only German: They begin of late to make all their Bonds and other legal Writings in their own Language, which (though I think it ought not to be) are allowed good in our Courts, where the German

Business so encreases that there is continual need of Interpreters; and I suppose in a few years they will be also necessary in the Assembly, to tell one half of our Legislators what the other half say; In short unless the stream of their importation could be turned from this to other Colonies, as you very judiciously propose, they will soon so out number us, that all the advantages we have will not [in My Opinion] be able to preserve our language, and even our Government will become precarious. The French who watch all advantages, are now [themselves] making a German settlement back of us in the Ilinoes Country, and by means of those Germans they may in time come to an understanding with ours, and indeed in the last war our Germans shewed a general disposition that seems to bode us no good; for when the English who were not Quakers, alarmed by the danger arising from the defenceless state of our Country entered unanimously into an Association within this Government and the lower Countries [Counties] raised armed and Disciplined [near] 10,000 men, the Germans except a very few in proportion to their numbers refused to engage in it, giving out one among another, and even in print, that if they were quiet the French should they take the Country would not molest them; at the same time abusing the Philadelphians for fitting out Privateers against the Enemy; and representing the trouble hazard and Expence of defending the Province, as a greater inconvenience than any that might be expected from a change of Government. Yet I am not for refusing entirely to admit them into our Colonies: all that seems to be necessary is, to distribute them more equally, mix them with the English, establish English Schools where they are now too thick settled, and take some care to prevent the practice lately fallen into by some of the Ship Owners, of sweeping the German Goals to make up the number of their Passengers. I say I am not against the Admission of

Germans in general, for they have their Virtues, their industry and frugality is exemplary; They are excellent husbandmen and contribute greatly to the improvement of a Country.

I pray God long to preserve to Great Britain the English Laws, Manners, Liberties and Religion notwithstanding the complaints so frequent in Your public papers, of the prevailing corruption and degeneracy of your People; I know you have a great deal of Virtue still subsisting among you, and I hope the Constitution is not so near a dissolution, as some seem to apprehend; I do not think you are generally become such Slaves to your Vices, as to draw down that *Justice* Milton speaks of when he says that

>   ——sometimes Nations will descend so low
>   From reason, which is virtue, that no Wrong,[1]
>   But Justice, and some fatal curse annex'd
>   Deprives them of their *outward* liberty,
>   Their *inward* lost.   Parad: lost.

In history we find that Piety, Public Spirit and military Prowess have their Flows, as well as their ebbs, in every nation, and that the Tide is never so low but it may rise again; But should this dreaded fatal change happen in my time, how should I even in the midst of the Affliction rejoice, if we have been able to preserve those invaluable treasures, and can invite the good among you to come and partake of them! O let not Britain seek to oppress us, but like an affectionate parent endeavour to secure freedom to her children; they may be able one day to assist her in defending her own—Whereas a Mortification begun in the Foot may spread upwards to the destruction of the nobler parts of the Body. . . .

---

[1] In the original, *Paradise Lost*, XII: 98, Milton had written "From vertue, which is reason . . ." [Ed.].

THE SOCIAL VALUE
OF A RELIGION OF GOOD WORKS

Franklin received frequent admonition from orthodox Christians warning him that his espousal of good works and his own good deeds would not earn him eternal salvation, and urging him thus to pay more attention to faith and doctrine. In a reply to one such entreaty Franklin explained his own humility and his understanding of the kind of Christianity that would be useful to human society in this world.

. . . For my own Part, when I am employed in serving others, I do not look upon my self as conferring Favours, but as paying Debts. In my Travels and since my Settlement I have received much Kindness from Men, to whom I shall never have any Opportunity of making the least direct Return. And numberless Mercies from God, who is infinitely above being benefited by our Services. These Kindnesses from Men I can therefore only return on their Fellow-Men; and I can only show my Gratitude for those Mercies from God, by a Readiness to help his other Children and my Brethren. For I do not think that Thanks, and Compliments, tho' repeated Weekly, can discharge our real Obligations to each other, and much less those to our Creater.

You will see in this my Nation of Good Works, that I am far from expecting (as you suppose) that I shall merit Heaven by them. By Heaven we understand, a State of Happiness, infinite in Degree, and eternal in Duration: I can do nothing to deserve such Reward: He that for giving a Draught of Water to a thirsty Person should expect to be

---

Papers, IV, 504-506; from a letter to Joseph Huey, June 6, 1753.

paid with a good Plantation, would be modest in his Demands, compar'd with those who think they deserve Heaven for the little Good they do on Earth. Even the mix'd imperfect Pleasures we enjoy in this World are rather from God's Goodness than our Merit; how much more such Happiness of Heaven. For my own part, I have not the Vanity to think I deserve it, the Folly to expect it, nor the Ambition to desire it; but content myself in submitting to the Will and Disposal of that God who made me, who has hitherto preserv'd and bless'd me, and in whose fatherly Goodness I may well confide, that he will never make me miserable, and that even the Afflictions I may at any time suffer shall tend to my Benefit.

The Faith you mention has doubtless its use in the World; I do not desire to see it diminished, nor would I endeavour to lessen it in any Man. But I wish it were more productive of Good Works than I have generally seen it: I mean real good Works, Works of Kindness, Charity, Mercy, and Publick Spirit; not Holiday-keeping, Sermon-Reading or Hearing, performing Church Ceremonies, or making long Prayers, fill'd with Flatteries and Compliments, despis'd even by wise Men, and much less capable of pleasing the Deity. The Worship of God is a Duty, the hearing and reading of Sermons may be useful; but if Men rest in Hearing and Praying, as too many do, it is as if a Tree should value itself on being water'd and putting forth Leaves, tho' it never produc'd any Fruit.

Your great Master tho't much less of these outward Appearances and Professions than many of his modern Disciples. He prefer'd the Doers of the Word to the meer Hearers; the Son that seemingly refus'd to obey his Father and yet perform'd his Commands, to him that profess'd his Readiness but neglected the Works; the heretical but charitable Samaritan, to the uncharitable tho' orthodox Priest and sanctified Levite: and those who gave Food to the hungry, Drink to the Thirsty, Raiment to the Naked, Entertainment to the Stranger, and Relief to the Sick, &c. tho' they never heard of his Name, he declares shall in the last Day be accepted, when those who cry Lord, Lord; who value themselves on their Faith tho' great enough to perform Miracles but have neglected good Works shall be rejected. He profess'd that he came not to call the Righteous but Sinners to Repentance; which imply'd his modest Opinion that there were some in his Time so good that they need not hear even him for Improvement; but now a days we have scarce a little Parson, that does not think it the Duty of every Man within his Reach to sit under his petty Ministrations, and that whoever omits them offends God. I wish to such more Humility, and to you Health and Happiness, being Your Friend and Servant B FRANKLIN

THE EVILS OF THE INDIAN TRADE

As a conflict with the French in the Ohio Valley seemed more and more inevitable, leaders of the English colonies moved to secure the friendship of as many Indians as possible, depending primarily on their bond with the Iroquois, or Six Nations. Pennsylvania held a treaty with Iroquois chiefs and their dependent tribes, the Delawares, Shawnee, Miami, and Wyandots, at Carlisle in the fall of 1753. At the conclusion of the treaty, at which Franklin was a commissioner, he and his colleagues submitted an addendum to the report of the proceedings placing the blame for the deteriorating Indian relations where it belonged.

. . . In Justice to these Indians, and the Promises we made them, we cannot close our Report, without taking

---

Papers, V, 107; first printed at the conclusion of the *Treaty* . . . *at Carlisle*, November 1, 1753.

Notice, That the Quantities of strong Liquors sold to these Indians in the Places of their Residence, and during their Hunting Seasons, from all Parts of the Counties over Sasquehannah, have encreased of late to an inconceivable Degree, so as to keep these poor Indians continually under the Force of Liquor, that they are hereby become dissolute, enfeebled and indolent when sober, and untractable and mischievous in their Liquor, always quarrelling, and often murdering one another: That the Traders are under no Bonds, nor give any Security for their Observance of the Laws, and their good Behavior; and by their own Intemperance, unfair Dealings, and Irregularities, will, it is to be feared, entirely estrange the Affections of the Indians from the English; deprive them of their natural Strength and Activity, and oblige them either to abandon their Country, or submit to any Terms, be they ever so unreasonable, from the French. These Truths, may it please the Governor, are of so interesting a Nature, that we shall stand excused in recommending in the most earnest Manner, the deplorable State of these Indians, and the heavy Discouragements under which our Commerce with them at present labours, to the Governor's most serious Consideration, that some good and speedy Remedies may be provided, before it be too late.

THE ALBANY PLAN OF UNION

In June 1754, delegates from New Hampshire, Massachusetts Bay, Connecticut, Rhode Island, New York, Pennsylvania, and Maryland met at Albany, New York, to treat with the Iroquois and to lay plans to resist more effectively French encroachments on the British colonies in North America. Franklin, a delegate from Pennsylvania, took the lead in seeking a closer union of the

---

Papers, V, 387–392; approved by the Albany Congress, July 10, 1754.

84 *The Political Thought of Benjamin Franklin*

colonies, and his proposals were the basis for the Plan of Union approved by the delegates. As to the fate of the Plan, Franklin later reported: "The Crown disapprov'd it, as having plac'd too much weight in the democratic Part of the Constitution [the Grand Council]; and every Assembly as having allow'd too much to Prerogative [the President General]. So it was rejected." It nevertheless was an important step in the moves toward union which culminated in the Federal Constitution of 1787, and shows Franklin's persistent belief in the value of human accord.

Plan of a Proposed Union of the Several Colonies of Masachusets-bay, New Hampshire, Coneticut, Rhode Island, New York, New Jerseys, Pensilvania, Maryland, Virginia, North Carolina, and South Carolina, For their Mutual Defence and Security, and for Extending the British Settlements in North America.

That humble Application be made for an Act of the Parliament of Great Britain, by Virtue of which, one General Government may be formed in America, including all the said Colonies, within and under which Government, each Colony may retain its present Constitution, except in the Particulars wherein a Change may be directed by the said Act, as hereafter follows.

That the said General Government be administred by a President General, To be appointed and Supported by the Crown, and a Grand Council to be Chosen by the Representatives of the People of the Several Colonies, met in their respective Assemblies.

That within Months after the passing of such Act, The House of Representatives in the Several Assemblies, that Happen to be Sitting within that time or that shall be Specially for that purpose Convened, may and Shall Choose Members for the Grand Council in the following Proportions, that is to say.

Masachusets-Bay	7.
New Hampshire	2.
Conecticut	5.
Rhode-Island	2.
New-York	4.
New-Jerseys	3.
Pensilvania	6.
Maryland	4.
Virginia	7.
North-Carolina	4.
South-Carolina	4.
	48.

Who shall meet for the first time at the City of Philadelphia, in Pensilvania, being called by the President General as soon as conveniently may be, after his Appointment.

That there shall be a New Election of Members for the Grand Council every three years; And on the Death or Resignation of any Member his Place shall be Supplyed by a New Choice at the next Sitting of the Assembly of the Colony he represented.

That after the first three years, when the Proportion of Money arising out of each Colony to the General Treasury can be known, The Number of Members to be Chosen, for each Colony shall from time to time in all ensuing Elections be regulated by that proportion (yet so as that the Number to be Chosen by any one Province be not more than Seven nor less than Two).

That the Grand Council shall meet once in every Year, and oftner if Occasion require, at such Time and place as they shall adjourn to at the last preceeding meeting, or as they shall be called to meet at by the President General, on any Emergency, he having first obtained in Writing the

Consent of seven of the Members to such call, and sent due and timely Notice to the whole.

That the Grand Council have Power to Chuse their Speaker, and shall neither be Dissolved, prorogued nor Continue Sitting longer than Six Weeks at one Time without their own Consent, or the Special Command of the Crown.

That the Members of the Grand Council shall be Allowed for their Service ten shillings Sterling per Diem, during their Sessions or Journey to and from the Place of Meeting; Twenty miles to be reckoned a days Journey.

That the Assent of the President General be requisite, to all Acts of the Grand Council, and that it be His Office, and Duty to cause them to be carried into Execution.

That the President General with the Advice of the Grand Council, hold or Direct all Indian Treaties in which the General Interest or Welfare of the Colony's may be Concerned; And make Peace or Declare War with the Indian Nations. That they make such Laws as they Judge Necessary for regulating all Indian Trade. That they make all Purchases from Indians for the Crown, of Lands not within the Bounds of Particular Colonies, or that shall not be within their Bounds when some of them are reduced to more Convenient Dimensions. That they make New Settlements on such Purchases, by Granting Lands in the Kings Name, reserving a Quit Rent to the Crown, for the use of the General Treasury. That they make Laws for regulating and Governing such new Settlements, till the Crown shall think fit to form them into Particular Governments.

That they raise and pay Soldiers, and build Forts for the Defence of any of the Colonies, and equip Vessels of Force to Guard the Coasts and Protect the Trade on the Ocean, Lakes, or Great Rivers; But they shall not Impress

Men in any Colonies, without the Consent of its Legislature. That for these purposes they have Power to make Laws And lay and Levy such General Duties, Imposts, or Taxes, as to them shall appear most equal and Just, Considering the Ability and other Circumstances of the Inhabitants in the Several Colonies, and such as may be Collected with the least Inconvenience to the People, rather discouraging Luxury, than Loading Industry with unnecessary Burthens. That they may Appoint a General Treasurer and a Particular Treasurer in each Government, when Necessary, And from Time to Time may Order the Sums in the Treasuries of each Government, into the General Treasury, or draw on them for Special payments as they find most Convenient; Yet no money to Issue, but by joint Orders of the President General and Grand Council Except where Sums have been Appropriated to particular Purposes, And the President General is previously impowered By an Act to draw for such Sums.

That the General Accounts shall be yearly Settled and Reported to the Several Assembly's.

That a Quorum of the Grand Council impower'd to Act with the President General, do consist of Twenty-five Members, among whom there shall be one, or more from a Majority of the Colonies. That the Laws made by them for the Purposes aforesaid, shall not be repugnant but as near as may be agreeable to the Laws of England, and Shall be transmitted to the King in Council for Approbation, as Soon as may be after their Passing and if not disapproved within Three years after Presentation to remain in Force.

That in case of the Death of the President General The Speaker of the Grand Council for the Time Being shall Succeed, and be Vested with the Same Powers, and Authority, to Continue until the King's Pleasure be known.

That all Military Commission Officers Whether for Land

or Sea Service, to Act under this General Constitution, shall be Nominated by the President General But the Approbation of the Grand Council, is to be Obtained before they receive their Commissions, And all Civil Officers are to be Nominated, by the Grand Council, and to receive the President General's Approbation, before they Officiate; But in Case of Vacancy by Death or removal of any Officer Civil or Military under this Constitution, The Governor of the Province, in which such Vacancy happens, may Appoint till the Pleasure of the President General and Grand Council can be known. That the Particular Military as well as Civil Establishments in each Colony remain in their present State, this General Constitution Notwithstanding. And that on Sudden Emergencies any Colony may Defend itself, and lay the Accounts of Expence thence Arisen, before the President General and Grand Council, who may allow and order payment of the same As far as they Judge such Accounts Just and reasonable.

REASONS AND MOTIVES

FOR THE ALBANY PLAN OF UNION

After the delegates had adopted the Albany Plan of Union, at the request of Thomas Pownall, Franklin set down the "Reasons and Motives" behind it as part of the argument to be presented to the Board of Trade, which would largely decide the Plan's fate in Great Britain. The general defense of the Plan, and arguments in favor of some of its more important parts, are reprinted here. See the preceding document for the clauses in the Albany Plan of Union to which the reasons refer.

Papers, V, 399-416; drafted by Franklin in July 1754.

I. REASONS AND MOTIVES ON WHICH THE PLAN OF UNION WAS FORMED.

The Commissioners from a number of the northern colonies being met at Albany, and considering the difficulties that have always attended the most necessary general measures for the common defence, or for the annoyance of the enemy, when they were to be carried through the several particular assemblies of all the colonies; some assemblies being before at variance with their governors or councils, and the several branches of the government not on terms of doing business with each other; others taking the opportunity, when their concurrence is wanted, to push for favourite laws, powers, or points that they think could not at other times be obtained, and so *creating* disputes and quarrels; one assembly waiting to see what another will do, being afraid of doing more than its share, or desirous of doing less; or refusing to do any thing, because its country is not at present so much exposed as others, or because another will reap more immediate advantage; from one or other of which causes, the assemblies of six (out of seven) colonies applied to, had granted no assistance to Virginia, when lately invaded by the French, though purposely convened, and the importance of the occasion earnestly urged upon them: Considering moreover, that one principal encouragement to the French, in invading and insulting the British American dominions, was their knowledge of our disunited state, and of our weakness arising from such want of union; and that from hence different colonies were, at different times, extremely harassed, and put to great expence both of blood and treasure, who would have remained in peace, if the enemy had had cause to fear the drawing on themselves the resentment and power of the whole; the said Commissioners, considering also the present incroachments of the French, and the mischievous consequences that may be expected from them, if not opposed with our force, came to an unanimous resolution, *That an union of the colonies is absolutely necessary for their preservation.*

The *manner* of forming and establishing this union was the next point. When it was considered that the colonies were seldom all in equal danger at the same time, or equally near the danger, or equally sensible of it; that some of them had particular interests to manage, with which an union might interfere; and that they were extremely jealous of each other; it was thought impracticable to obtain a joint agreement of all the colonies to an union, in which the expence and burthen of defending any of them should be divided among them all; and if ever acts of assembly in all the colonies could be obtained for that purpose, yet as any colony, on the least dissatisfaction, might repeal its own act and thereby withdraw itself from the union, it would not be a stable one, or such as could be depended on: for if only one colony should, on any disgust withdraw itself, others might think it unjust and unequal that they, by continuing in the union, should be at the expence of defending a colony which refused to bear its proportionable part, and would therefore one after another, withdraw, till the whole crumbled into its original parts. Therefore the commissioners came to another previous resolution, viz. *That it was necessary the union should be established by act of parliament.*

They then proceeded to sketch out a *plan of union,* which they did in a plain and concise manner, just sufficient to shew their sentiments of the kind of union that would best suit the circumstances of the colonies, be most agreeable to the people, and most effectually promote his Majesty's service and the general interest of the British empire. This was respectfully sent to the assemblies of the several colonies for their consideration, and to receive such alterations and improvements as they should think fit and necessary; after which it was proposed to be transmitted to England to be perfected, and the establishment of it there humbly solicited.

This was as much as the commissioners could do.

II. REASONS AGAINST PARTIAL UNIONS.

It was proposed by some of the Commissioners to form the colonies into two or three distinct unions; but for these reasons that proposal was dropped even by those that made it; [viz.]

1. In all cases where the strength of the whole was necessary to be used against the enemy, there would be the same difficulty in degree, to bring the several unions to unite together, as now the several colonies; and consequently the same delays on our part and advantage to the enemy.

2. Each union would separately be weaker than when joined by the whole, obliged to exert more force, be more oppressed by the expence, and the enemy less deterred from attacking it.

3. Where particular colonies have *selfish views*, as New York with regard to Indian trade and lands; or are *less exposed*, being covered by others, as New Jersey, Rhode Island, Connecticut, Maryland; or have *particular whims and prejudices* against warlike measures in general, as Pensylvania, where the Quakers predominate; such colonies would have more weight in a partial union, and be better able to oppose and obstruct the measures necessary for the general good, than where they are swallowed up in the general union.

4. The Indian trade would be better regulated by the union of the whole than by partial unions. And as Canada

is chiefly supported by that trade, if it could be drawn into the hands of the English, (as it might be if the Indians were supplied on moderate terms, and by honest traders appointed by and acting for the public) that alone would contribute greatly to the weakening of our enemies.

5. The establishing of new colonies westward on the Ohio and the lakes, (a matter of considerable importance to the increase of British trade and power, to the breaking that of the French, and to the protection and security of our present colonies,) would best be carried on by a joint union.

6. It was also thought, that by the frequent meetings-together of commissioners or representatives from all the colonies, the circumstances of the whole would be better known, and the good of the whole better provided for; and that the colonies would by this connection learn to consider themselves, not as so many independent states, but as members of the same body; and thence be more ready to afford assistance and support to each other, and to make diversions in favour even of the most distant, and to join cordially in any expedition for the benefit of all against the common enemy. . . .

. . . It was thought that it would be best the President General should be supported as well as appointed by the crown; that so all disputes between him and the Grand Council concerning his salary might be prevented; as such disputes have been frequently of mischievous consequence in particular colonies, especially in time of public danger. The quit-rents of crown-lands in America, might in a short time be sufficient for this purpose. The choice of members for the grand council is placed in the house of representatives of each government, in order to give the people a share in this new general government, as the crown has its share by the appointment of the President General.

But it being proposed by the gentlemen of the council of New York, and some other counsellors among the commissioners, to alter the plan in this particular, and to give the governors and council of the several provinces a share in the choice of the grand council, or at least a power of approving and confirming or of disallowing the choice made by the house of representatives, it was said:

"That the government or constitution proposed to be formed by the plan, consists of two branches; a President General appointed by the crown, and a council chosen by the people, or by the people's representatives, which is the same thing.

"That by a subsequent article, the council chosen by the people can effect nothing without the consent of the President General appointed by the crown; the crown possesses therefore full one half of the power of this constitution.

"That in the British constitution, the crown is supposed to possess but one third, the Lords having their share.

"That this constitution seemed rather more favourable for the crown.

"That it is essential to English liberty, [that] the subject should not be taxed but by his own consent or the consent of his elected representatives.

"That taxes to be laid and levied by this proposed constitution will be proposed and agreed to by the representatives of the people, if the plan in this particular be preserved:

"But if the proposed alteration should take place, it seemed as if matters may be so managed as that the crown shall finally have the appointment not only of the President General, but of a majority of the grand council; for, seven out of eleven governors and councils are appointed by the crown:

"And so the people in all the colonies would in effect be taxed by their governors.

"It was therefore apprehended that such alterations of the plan would give great dissatisfaction, and that the colonies could not be easy under such a power in governors, and such an infringement of what they take to be English liberty.

"Besides, the giving a share in the choice of the grand council would not be equal with respect to all the colonies, as their constitutions differ. In some, both governor and council are appointed by the crown. In others, they are both appointed by the proprietors. In some, the people have a share in the choice of the council; in others, both government and council are wholly chosen by the people. But the house of representatives is every where chosen by the people; and therefore placing the right of choosing the grand council in the representatives, is equal with respect to all.

"That the grand council is intended to represent all the several houses of representatives of the colonies, as a house of representatives doth the several towns or counties of a colony. Could all the people of a colony be consulted and unite in public measures, a house of representatives would be needless: and could all the assemblies conveniently consult and unite in general measures, the grand council would be unnecessary.

"That a house of commons or the house of representatives, and the grand council, are thus alike in their nature and intention. And as it would seem improper that the King or house of Lords should have a power of disallowing or appointing members of the house of commons; so likewise that a governor and council appointed by the crown should have a power of disallowing or appointing members of the grand council, (who, in this constitution, are to be the representatives of the people.)

"If the governors and councils therefore were to have a share in the choice of any that are to conduct this general government, it should seem more proper that they chose the President General. But this being an office of great trust and importance to the nation, it was thought better to be filled by the immediate appointment of the crown.

"The power proposed to be given by the plan to the grand council is only a concentration of the powers of the several assemblies in certain points for the general welfare; as the power of the President General is of the powers of the several governors in the same points.

"And as the choice therefore of the grand council by the representatives of the people, neither gives the people any new powers, nor diminishes the power of the crown, it was thought and hoped the crown would not disapprove of it."

Upon the whole, the commissioners were of opinion, that the choice was most properly placed in the representatives of the people. . . .

[To justify letting the Grand Council determine its own adjournments:]

. . . Governors have sometimes wantonly exercised the power of proroguing or continuing the sessions of assemblies, merely to harass the members and compel a compliance; and sometimes dissolve them on slight disgusts. This it was feared might be done by the President General, if not provided against: and the inconvenience and hardship would be greater in the general government than in particular colonies, in proportion to the distance the members must be from home, during sittings, and the long journies some of them must necessarily take. . . .

. . . The assent of the President General to all acts of the grand council was made necessary, in order to give the crown its due share of influence in this government, and connect it with that of Great Britain. The President General, besides one half of the legislative power, hath in his hands the whole executive power. . . .

. . . The laws which the President General and grand

council are impowered to make, *are such only* as shall be necessary for the government of the settlements; the raising, regulating and paying soldiers for the general service; the regulating of Indian trade; and laying and collecting the general duties and taxes. (They should also have a power to restrain the exportation of provisions to the enemy from any of the colonies, on particular occasions, in time of war.) But it is not intended that they may interfere with the constitution and government of the particular colonies; who are to be left to their own laws, and to lay, levy, and apply their own taxes as before. . . .

[To justify the requirement that the President General and the Grand council share in the appointment of military and civil officers:]

. . . It was thought it might be very prejudicial to the service, to have officers appointed unknown to the people, or unacceptable; the generality of Americans serving willingly under officers they know; and not caring to engage in the service under strangers, or such as are often appointed by governors through favour or interest. The service here meant, is not the stated settled service in standing troops; but any sudden and short service, either for defence of our own colonies, or invading the enemies country; (such as, the expedition to Cape Breton in the last war; in which many substantial farmers and tradesmen engaged as common soldiers under officers of their own country, for whom they had an esteem and affection; who would not have engaged in a standing army, or under officers from England.) It was therefore thought best to give the council the power of approving the officers, which the people will look upon as a great security of their being good men. And without some such provision as this, it was thought the expence of engaging men in the service on any emergency would be much greater, and the number who could be induced to engage much less; and that therefore it would be most for the King's service and general benefit of the nation, that the prerogative should relax a little in this particular throughout all the colonies in America; as it had already done much more in the charters of some particular colonies, viz. Connecticut and Rhode Island.

The civil officers will be chiefly treasurers and collectors of taxes; and the suitable persons are most likely to be known by the council. . . .

LETTERS

TO WILLIAM SHIRLEY ON THE PLACE

OF THE COLONIES IN THE BRITISH EMPIRE

A few months after the Albany Congress and during a visit by Franklin to Boston, Governor William Shirley of Massachusetts showed him a plan of union which gave the colonial assemblies much less power that that proposed at Albany. In reply, Franklin wrote three letters which became famous as an early statement of colonial resistance to "taxation without representation." The last two letters were often reprinted on both sides of the Atlantic following their first publication in the *London Chronicle,* February 8, 1766.

. . . I apprehend, that excluding the *People* of the Colonies from all share in the choice of the Grand Council, will give extreme dissatisfaction, as well as the taxing them by Act of Parliament, where they have no Representative. It is

---

Papers, V, 443-451; from letters written December 3, 4, and 22, 1754.

very possible, that this general Government might be as well and faithfully administer'd without the people, as with them; but where heavy burthens are to be laid on them, it has been found useful to make it, as much as possible, their own act; for they bear better when they have, or think they have some share in the direction; and when any public measures are generally grievous or even distasteful to the people, the wheels of Government must move more heavily.

. . . In Matters of General Concern to the People, and especially where Burthens are to be laid upon them, it is of Use to consider as well what they will *be apt* to think and say, as what they *ought* to think: I shall, therefore, as your Excellency requires it of me, briefly mention what of either Kind occurs at present, on this Occasion.

First, they will say, and perhaps with Justice, that the Body of the People in the Colonies are as loyal, and as firmly attach'd to the present Constitution and reigning Family, as any Subjects in the King's Dominions; that there is no Reason to doubt the Readiness and Willingness of their Representatives to grant, from Time to Time, such Supplies, for the Defence of the Country, as shall be judg'd necessary, so far as their Abilities will allow: That the People in the Colonies, who are to feel the immediate Mischiefs of Invasion and Conquest by an Enemy, in the Loss of their Estates, Lives and Liberties, are likely to be better Judges of the Quantity of Forces necessary to be raised and maintain'd, Forts to be built and supported, and of their own Abilities to bear the Expence, than the Parliament of England at so great a Distance. That Governors often come to the Colonies meerly to make Fortunes, with which they intend to return to Britain, are not always Men of the best Abilities and Integrity, have no Estates here, nor any natural Connections with us, that should make them heartily concern'd for our Welfare; and might possibly be sometimes fond of raising and keeping up more Forces than necessary, from the Profits accruing to themselves, and to make Provision for their Friends and Dependents. That the Councellors in most of the Colonies, being appointed by the Crown, on the Recommendation of Governors, are often of small Estates, frequently dependant on the Governors for Offices, and therefore too much under Influence. That there is therefore great Reason to be jealous of a Power in such Governors and Councils, to raise such Sums as they shall judge necessary, by Draft on the Lords of the Treasury, to be afterwards laid on the Colonies by Act of Parliament, and paid by the People here; since they might abuse it, by projecting useless Expeditions, harrassing the People, and taking them from their Labour to execute such Projects, and meerly to create Offices and Employments, gratify their Dependants and divide Profits. That the Parliament of England is at a great Distance, subject to be misinform'd by such Governors and Councils, whose united Interests might probably secure them against the Effect of any Complaints from hence. That it is suppos'd an undoubted Right of Englishmen not to be taxed but by their own Consent given thro' their Representatives. That the Colonies have no Representatives in Parliament. That to propose taxing them by Parliament, and refusing them the Liberty of chusing a Representative Council, to meet in the Colonies, and consider and judge of the Necessity of any General Tax and the Quantum, shews a Suspicion of their Loyalty to the Crown, or Regard for their Country, or of their Common Sense and Understanding, which they have not deserv'd. That compelling the Colonies to pay Money without their Consent would be rather like raising Contributions in an Enemy's Country, than taxing of Englishmen for their own publick Benefit. That it would be treating them as a conquer'd People, and not as true British Subjects. That a Tax laid by the Representatives of the Colonies might easily be lessened as the Occasions should lessen, but being once laid by Parliament, under the Influence of the Representations made by Governors, would probably be kept up and continued, for the Benefit of Governors, to the grievous Burthen and Discouragement of the Colonies, and preventing their Growth and Increase. That a Power in Governors to march the Inhabitants from one End of the British and French Colonies to the other, being a Country of at least 1500 Miles square, without the Approbation or Consent of their Representatives first obtain'd to such Expeditions, might be grievous and ruinous to the People, and would put them on a Footing with the Subjects of France in Canada, that now groan under such Oppression from their Governor, who for two Years past has harrass'd them with long and destructive Marches to the Ohio. That if the Colonies in a Body may be well governed by Governors and Councils appointed by the Crown, without Representatives, particular Colonies may as well or better be so governed; a Tax may be laid on them all by Act of Parliament, for Support of Government, and their Assemblies be dismiss'd as a useless Part of their Constitution. That the Powers propos'd, by the Albany Plan of Union to be vested in a Grand Council representative of the People, even with Regard to Military Matters, are not so great as those the Colonies of Rhode-Island and Connecticut are intrusted with, and have never abused; for by this Plan the President-General is appointed by the Crown, and controls all by his Negative; but in those Governments the People chuse the Governor, and yet allow him no Negative. That the British Colonies, bordering on the French, are properly Frontiers of the British Empire; and that the Frontiers of an Empire are properly defended at the joint Expence of the Body of People in such Empire. It would now be thought hard, by Act of

Parliament, to oblige the Cinque Ports or Sea Coasts of Britain to maintain the whole Navy, because they are more immediately defended by it, not allowing them, at the same Time, a Vote in chusing Members of Parliament: And if the Frontiers in America must bear the Expence of their own Defence, it seems hard to allow them no Share in Voting the Money, judging of the Necessity and Sum, or advising the Measures. That besides the Taxes necessary for the Defence of the Frontiers, the Colonies pay yearly great Sums to the Mother Country unnotic'd: For Taxes, paid in Britain by the Land holder or Artificer, must enter into and increase the Price of the Produce of Land, and of Manufactures made of it; and great Part of this is paid by Consumers in the Colonies, who thereby pay a considerable Part of the British Taxes. We are restrain'd in our Trade with Foreign Nations, and where we could be supplied with any Manufactures cheaper from them, but must buy the same dearer from Britain, the Difference of Price is a clear Tax to Britain. We are oblig'd to carry great Part of our Produce directly to Britain, and where the Duties there laid upon it lessens its Price to the Planter, or it sells for less than it would in Foreign Markets, the Difference is a Tax paid to Britain. Some Manufactures we could make, but are forbid, and must take them of British Merchants; the whole Price of these is a Tax paid to Britain. By our greatly increasing the *Consumption* and *Demand* of British Manufactures, their Price is considerably rais'd of late Years; the Advance is clear Profit to Britain, and enables its People better to pay great Taxes; and much of it being paid by us is clear Tax to Britain. In short, as we are not suffer'd to regulate our Trade, and restrain the Importation and Consumption of British Superfluities, (as Britain can the Consumption of Foreign Superfluities) our whole Wealth centers finally among the Merchants and Inhabitants of Britain, and if we make them richer, and enable them better to pay their Taxes, it is nearly the same as being taxed ourselves, and equally beneficial to the Crown. These Kind of Secondary Taxes, however, we do not complain of, tho' we have no Share in the Laying or Disposing of them; but to pay immediate heavy Taxes, in the Laying Appropriation or Disposition of which, we have no Part, and which perhaps we may know to be as unnecessary as grievous, must seem hard Measure to Englishmen, who cannot conceive, that by hazarding their Lives and Fortunes in subduing and settling new Countries, extending the Dominion and encreasing the Commerce of their Mother Nation, they have forfeited the native Rights of Britons, which they think ought rather to have been given them, as due to such Merit, if they had been before in a State of Slavery.

These, and such Kind of Things as these, I apprehend will be thought and said by the People, if the propos'd Alteration of the Albany Plan should take Place. Then, the Administration of the Board of Governors and Council so appointed, not having any Representative Body of the People to approve and unite in its Measures, and conciliate the Minds of the People to them, will probably become suspected and odious. Animosities and dangerous Feuds will arise between the Governors and Governed, and every Thing go into confusion. Perhaps I am too apprehensive in this Matter, but having freely given my Opinion and Reasons, your Excellency can better judge whether there be any Weight in them. . . .

Since the conversation your Excellency was pleased to honour me with, on the subject of uniting the Colonies more intimately with Great Britain, by allowing them Representatives in Parliament, I have something further considered that matter, and am of opinion, that such an Union would be very acceptable to the Colonies, provided they had a reasonable number of Representatives allowed them; and that all the old Acts of Parliament restraining the trade or cramping the manufactures of the Colonies, be at the same time repealed, and the British Subjects on this side the water put, in those respects, on the same footing with those in Great Britain, 'till the new Parliament, representing the whole, shall think it for the interest of the whole to re-enact some or all of them: It is not that I imagine so many Representatives will be allowed the Colonies, as to have any great weight by their numbers; but I think there might be sufficient to occasion those laws to be better and more impartially considered, and perhaps to overcome the private interest of a petty corporation, or of any particular set of artificers or traders in England, who heretofore seem, in some instances, to have been more regarded than all the Colonies, or than was consistent with the general interest, or best national good. I think too, that the government of the Colonies by a Parliament, in which they are fairly represented, would be vastly more agreeable to the people, than the method lately attempted to be introduced by Royal Instructions, as well as more agreeable to the nature of an English Constitution, and to English Liberty; and that such laws as now seem to bear hard on the Colonies, would (when judged by such a Parliament for the best interest of the whole) be more chearfully submitted to, and more easily executed.

I should hope too, that by such an union, the people of Great Britain and the people of the Colonies would learn to consider themselves, not as belonging to different Communities with different Interests, but to one Community with one Interest, which I imagine would contribute to strengthen the whole, and greatly lessen the danger of future separations.

It is, I suppose, agreed to be the general interest of any state, that it's people be numerous and rich; men enow to fight in its defence, and enow to pay sufficient taxes to defray the charge; for these circumstances tend to the security of the state, and its protection from foreign power: But it seems not of so much importance whether the fighting be done by John or Thomas, or the tax paid by William or Charles: The iron manufacture employs and enriches British Subjects, but is it of any importance to the state, whether the manufacturers live at Birmingham or Sheffield, or both, since they are still within its bounds, and their wealth and persons at its command? Could the Goodwin Sands be laid dry by banks, and land equal to a large country thereby gain'd to England, and presently filled with English Inhabitants, would it be right to deprive such Inhabitants of the common privileges enjoyed by other Englishmen, the right of vending their produce in the same ports, or of making their own shoes, because a merchant, or a shoemaker, living on the old land, might fancy it more for his advantage to trade or make shoes for them? Would this be right, even if the land were gained at the expence of the state? And would it not seem less right, if the charge and labour of gaining the additional territory to Britain had been borne by the settlers themselves? And would not the hardship appear yet greater, if the people of the new country should be allowed no Representatives in the Parliament enacting such impositions? Now I look on the Colonies as so many Counties gained to Great Britain, and more advantageous to it than if they had been gained out of the sea around its coasts, and joined to its land: For being in different climates, they afford greater variety of produce, and materials for more manufactures; and being separated by the ocean, they increase much more its shipping and seamen; and since they are all included in the British Empire, which has only extended itself by their means; and the strength and wealth of the parts is the strength and wealth of the whole; what imports it to the general state, whether a merchant, a smith, or a hatter, grow rich in *Old* or *New* England? And if, through increase of people, two smiths are wanted for one employed before, why may not the *new* smith be allowed to live and thrive in the *new Country,* as well as the *old* one in the *Old?* In fine, why should the countenance of a state be *partially* afforded to its people, unless it be most in favour of those, who have most merit? and if there be any difference, those, who have most contributed to enlarge Britain's empire and commerce, encrease her strength, her wealth, and the numbers of her people, at the risque of their own lives and private fortunes in new and strange countries, methinks ought rather to expect some preference. . . .

PLAN FOR ESTABLISHING ENGLISH

COLONIES IN THE OHIO VALLEY

Consistent with the propositions laid down in the "Observations Concerning the Increase of Mankind" (see above), Franklin believed that the only sure foundation for English power in North America was the spread of English settlements across the continent; against such, Indians, French arms, or Jesuit missionaries would be unable to prevail. To this end he planned to settle two colonies in the Ohio Valley.

The great country back of the Apalachian mountains, on both sides the Ohio, and between that river and the lakes; is now well known both to the English and French, to be

---

Papers, V, 457–462; from a proposal drafted sometime in the last months of 1754.

one of the finest in North America, for the extreme richness and fertility of the land; the healthy temperature of the air, and mildness of the climate; the plenty of hunting, fishing, and fowling; the facility of trade with the Indians; and the vast convenience of inland navigation or water-carriage by the lakes and great rivers, many hundred of leagues around.

From these natural advantages it must undoubtedly (perhaps in less than another century) become a populous and powerful dominion; and a great accession of power, either to England or France.

The French are now making open encroachments on these territories, in defiance of our known rights; and, if we longer delay to settle that country, and suffer them to possess it, these *inconveniences and mischiefs* will probably follow:

1. Our people, being confined to the country between the sea and the mountains, cannot much more increase in number; people increasing in proportion to their room and means of subsistence. (See the Observations on the Increase of Mankind, &c. p. 1.)

2. The French will increase much more, by that acquired room and plenty of subsistence, and become a great people behind us.

3. Many of our debtors, and loose English people, our German servants, and slaves, will probably desert to them; and increase their numbers and strength, to the lessening and weakening of ours.

4. They will cut us off from all commerce and alliance with the western Indians, to the great prejudice of Britain, by preventing the sale and consumption of its manufactures.

5. They will both in time of peace and war (as they have always done against New England) set the Indians on to harass our frontiers, kill and scalp our people, and drive in

the advanced settlers; and so, in preventing our obtaining more subsistence by cultivating of new lands, they discourage our marriages, and keep our people from increasing; thus (if the expression may be allowed) killing thousands of our children before they are born.

If two strong colonies of English were settled between the Ohio and lake Erie, in the places hereafter to be mentioned, these *advantages* might be expected:

1. They would be a great security to the frontiers of our other colonies; by preventing the incursions of the French and French Indians of Canada, on the back parts of Pensylvania, Maryland, Virginia, and the Carolinas; and the frontiers of such new colonies would be much more easily defended, than those of the colonies last mentioned now can be, as will appear hereafter.

2. The dreaded junction of the French settlements in Canada, with those of Louisiana would be prevented.

3. In case of a war, it would be easy, from those new colonies, to annoy Louisiana by going down the Ohio and Mississippi; and the southern part of Canada by sailing over the lakes; and thereby confine the French within narrower limits.

4. We should secure the friendship and trade of the Miamis or Twigtwees, (a numerous people, consisting of many tribes, inhabiting the country between the west end of lake Erie, and the south end of lake Hurons, and the Ohio;) who are at present dissatisfied with the French, and fond of the English, and would gladly encourage and protect an infant English settlement in or near their country, as some of their chiefs have declared to the writer of this memoir. Further, by means of the lakes, the Ohio, and the Mississippi, our trade might be extended through a vast country, among many numerous and distant nations, greatly to the benefit of Britain.

5. The settlement of all the intermediate lands, between

the present frontiers of our colonies on one side, and the lakes and Mississippi on the other; would be facilitated and speedily executed, to the great increase of Englishmen, English trade, and English power. . . .

The difficulty of settling the first English colonies in America, at so great a distance from England; must have been vastly greater than the settling these proposed new colonies: for it would be the interest and advantage of all the present colonies to support these new ones; as they would cover their frontiers, and prevent the growth of the French power behind or near their present settlements; and the new country is nearly at equal distance from all the old colonies; and could easily be assisted from all of them.

And as there are already in the old colonies, many thousands of families that are ready to swarm, wanting more land; the richness and natural advantage of the Ohio country would draw most of them thither, were there but a tolerable prospect of a safe settlement. So that the new colonies would soon be full of people; and from the advantage of their situation, become much more terrible to the French settlements, than those are now to us. The gaining of the back Indian trade from the French, by the navigation of the lakes, &c. would of itself greatly weaken our enemies: it being now their principal support, it seems highly probable that in time they must be subjected to the British crown, or driven out of the country.

Such settlements may better be made now, than fifty years hence, because it is easier to settle ourselves, and thereby prevent the French settling there, as they seem now to intend, than to remove them when strongly settled.

If these settlements are postponed, then more forts and stronger, and more numerous and expensive garrisons must be established, to secure the country, prevent their settling, and secure our present frontiers; the charge of which, may probably exceed the charge of the proposed settlements, and the advantage nothing near so great. . . .

HUMILITY AND THE SEARCH FOR TRUTH

Franklin's scientific habit of mind (as well as his fame as a scientist) taught him lessons applicable in public affairs, as this reply to a request for an explanation of a curious electrical phenomenon shows.

. . . You require the reason; I do not know it. Perhaps you may discover it, and then you will be so good as to communicate it to me. I find a frank acknowledgment of one's ignorance is not only the easiest way to get rid of a difficulty, but the likeliest way to obtain information, and therefore I practice it: I think it an honest policy. Those who affect to be thought to know every thing, and so undertake to explain every thing, often remain long ignorant of many things that others could and would instruct them in, if they appeared less conceited. . . .

A PARABLE AGAINST PERSECUTION

Nothing pleased Franklin more than to combine wit and precept. One of his most famous and successful sallies of this kind was the "Parable against Persecution," an apocryphal "Fifty-first Chapter of Genesis," wherein he imitated biblical language to tell a story in the life of Abraham teaching the duty of religious toleration. Franklin delighted to amuse and instruct his friends

---

Papers, V, 526; from a letter to John Lining, March 19, 1755.
Papers, VI, 122–124; probably written in July 1755 or shortly before.

by appearing to turn to a Bible and read a chapter as he recited his own "Parable," thus confounding "Scriptuarians" and giving one of his favorite lessons a force it could not have in more sober dress.

1. And it came to pass after these Things, that Abraham sat in the Door of his Tent, about the going down of the Sun.

2. And behold a Man, bowed with Age, came from the Way of Wilderness, leaning on a Staff.

3. And Abraham arose and met him, and said unto him, Turn in, I pray thee, and wash thy Feet, and tarry all Night, and thou shalt arise early on the Morrow, and go on thy Way.

4. And the Man said, Nay, for I will abide under this Tree.

5. But Abraham pressed him greatly; so he turned, and they went into the Tent; and Abraham baked unleavened Bread, and they did eat.

6. And when Abraham saw that the Man blessed not God, he said unto him, Wherefore dost thou not worship the most high God, Creator of Heaven and Earth?

7. And the Man answered and said, I do not worship the God thou speakest of; neither do I call upon his Name; for I have made to myself a God, which abideth alway in mine House, and provideth me with all Things.

8. And Abraham's Zeal was kindled against the Man; and he arose, and fell upon him, and drove him forth with Blows into the Wilderness.

9. And at Midnight God called unto Abraham, saying, Abraham, where is the Stranger?

10. And Abraham answered and said, Lord, he would not worship thee, neither would he call upon thy Name; therefore have I driven him out from before my Face into the Wilderness.

11. And God said, Have I born with him these hundred ninety and eight Years, and nourished him, and cloathed him, notwithstanding his Rebellion against me, and couldst not thou, that art thyself a Sinner, bear with him one Night?

12. And Abraham said, Let not the Anger of my Lord wax hot against his Servant. Lo, I have sinned; forgive me, I pray Thee:

13. And Abraham arose and went forth into the Wilderness, and sought diligently for the Man, and found him, and returned with him to his Tent; and when he had entreated him kindly, he sent him away on the Morrow with Gifts.

14. And God spake again unto Abraham, saying, For this thy Sin shall thy Seed be afflicted four Hundred Years in a strange Land:

15. But for thy Repentance will I deliver them; and they shall come forth with Power, and with Gladness of Heart, and with much Substance.

THE RIGHTS OF A COLONIAL ASSEMBLY

In August 1755, in the fear and confusion that followed Braddock's defeat, the Pennsylvania Assembly sought to use the pressure of war to tax for the first time the estates of the Proprietors in Pennsylvania. The expenses of war undertaken to protect that property along with other estates in the province, the Assembly reasoned, should be borne by a tax on *all* property. Governor Robert Hunter Morris, bound by instructions from the Proprietors not to approve any tax on their estates and himself a stout defender of executive prerogative, fought a war of words with the

---

Papers, VI, 135–138, 161–163, 194–196, 209–210, 241–242, and 263–266; in Pennsylvania Assembly documents dated August 8, 19, September 29, November 11, and 25, 1755.

Assembly during which the legislators not only set down their case in this particular dispute, but also stated the rights they claimed as an assembly of freeborn Englishmen. Governor Morris explained Franklin's part in the struggle to his superiors in London: he "is at the head of these extraordinary measures taken by the Assembly, writes their Messages and directs their motions." (To Thomas Robinson, August 28, 1755; quoted in *Papers*, VI, 130 n.).

On August 2, 1755, the Assembly passed a £50,000 tax measure which did not exempt the proprietary estates, whereupon Morris rejected the bill and opened a debate on the theory of colonial government by making four objections in principle to the measure. Here is the reply of the Assembly, in the words of its penman Franklin.

. . . To the first we shall only say, That we do not propose to tax the Proprietary as Governor, but as a Fellow Subject, a Landholder and Possessor of an Estate in Pennsylvania; an Estate that will be more benefited by a proper Application of the Tax, than any other Estate in the Province. The Proprietary, may it please the Governor, does *not* govern us. The Province supports a Lieutenant to do that Duty for him, by a large Revenue arising from Licences, and other Fees and Perquisites. But if the Proprietary actually governed us, and had a Support allowed him on that Account, we should not therefore think it less reasonable to tax him as a Landholder, for the Security of that Land. The Representatives of the People have also some Support as a Part of the Government, by the Wages they are allowed for their Service in Assembly; would the Governor think this a good Reason, that as Owners of Estates they should be exempt from Taxes? Can the Proprietary, as Governor, have, from the Nature of his Office, more of this pretended Right of Exemption from Taxes than the King himself? Are not the Tenants of the King's Lands (who by every Land Tax Act of Parliament are to pay the Poundage) impowered to deduct the same out of their Rent? And are not the Receivers of his Majesty's Rents obliged, under severe Penalties, to allow of such Deduction? But this is not the first Instance by many, in which Proprietors and Governors of petty Colonies have assumed to themselves greater Powers, Privileges, Immunities, and Prerogatives, than were ever claimed by their Royal Master on the Imperial Throne of all his extensive Dominions.

On the second it may be sufficient to observe, that the positive Law of this Province, hinted at by the Governor as exempting the Proprietaries Estates from Taxes, is no other than the Law for raising County Rates and Levies, which are in the same Act appropriated to Purposes for which the Proprietaries could not reasonably be charged; such as the Payment of Assemblymens Wages, and of the Rewards for killing of Wolves, Crows, Foxes, with other Matters more immediately for the Peoples Benefit; it is not, as the Governor would insinuate, a general constitutional Law of the Province, made to enforce a natural Right, but is confined to County Affairs, and has no Relation to Provincial Taxes, especially to such as are intended for the Benefit and Advantage of the Proprietary Estate more than of any other Estate in the Province; which will be evident to the Governor, on his perusing it with the smallest Degree of Attention. 'Tis true it is, as the Governor calls it, a *positive Law,* so far as it extends; but to apply it to the present Case, seems inconsistent with both Equity and Reason. We have likewise a *positive Law,* that the Peoples Representatives shall dispose of the Peoples Money, and this seems to us consistent generally with Reason and natural Right; but does the Governor think that, because it is a positive Law, it ought to be extended to all Cases in Government? If so, we humbly conceive he would have proposed some other Amendments to the Bill, and different from those he has thought fit to send us: For we, considering the Intention of the Grant, have allowed him a Share in the Disposition of the Fifty Thousand Pounds; and he proposes, by his last Amendment, to have a Share likewise in the Disposition of the Overplus, if any.

On the third Reason, we would only beg Leave to ask, Whether, supposing the Proprietary Estate to be taxed, it would be equitable that he should have a Negative in the Choice of the Assessors; since that would give him Half the Choice, tho' he were to pay perhaps not a Hundredth Part of the Tax? In our Estimation, and we think we are not mistaken, he may have Friends, Officers and other Dependents enow in every County, to vote as much in his Behalf, or more, than his Share of the Tax can possibly amount to. But if the Proprietary shrinks at the Injustice of being taxed, where he has no Choice in the Assessors, with what Face of Justice can he desire and insist on having Half the Power of disposing of the Money levied, to which he would contribute not a single Farthing? By the Words the Governor chuses to express the Power of the Assessors, viz. "Taxing the Proprietaries Estate *at Discretion*," one would think their Power unlimited, and the Proprietary left at their Mercy; but in the Valuation of Estates, they are confined by the Bill within certain moderate Bounds, are enjoined, and sworn or solemnly affirmed "to assess themselves, and all others, equally and impartially, and to spare no Person for Favour or Affection, nor grieve any for Hatred or Ill-will;" which we think gives the Proprietary as good Security for Equity and Justice as any Subject in the King's Dominions.

As to the Governor's fourth Reason, deduced from the Usage in this and the other Proprietary Governments, we think Usage and Custom, against Reason and Justice, ought to have but little Weight. But though it may have been the Usage in this Government, and perhaps in others, to exempt the Proprietary Estate from Taxes in Cases where their Estates could not by the Application of such Taxes be any way benefited, that Usage can, as we conceive, have no Relation to the present Case, which, as we have shewn, is of a widely different Nature. Nor, if the Governor's Rule from Usage could be allowed, viz. *That the Lands or Estates of Proprietaries, exercising Government by themselves or their Lieutenants, ought to be exempt from Taxes,* would it operate in Favour of the Estates of Proprietaries who not only do not exercise Government by themselves, but would restrain their Lieutenants in the Exercise of the just Powers they are vested with by the Royal Charter.

On the Whole, we beg the Governor would again calmly and seriously consider our Bill, to which End we once more send it up to him. We know that without his Assent the Money cannot be raised, nor the good Ends so earnestly desired and expected from it be obtained, and we fear his Resolution to refuse it. But we entreat him to reflect with what Reluctance a People born and bred in Freedom, and accustomed to equitable Laws, must undergo the Weight of this uncommon Tax, and even expose their Persons for the Defence of *his* Estate, who by Virtue of his Power only, and without even a Colour of Right, should refuse to bear the least Share of the Burthen, though to receive so great a Benefit! With what Spirit can they exert themselves in his Cause, who will not pay the smallest Part of their grievous Expences? How odious must it be to a sensible manly People, to find *him* who ought to be their Father and Protector, taking Advantage of Publick Calamity and Distress, and their Tenderness for their bleeding Country, to force down their Throats Laws of Imposition, abhorrent to common Justice and common Reason! Why will the Governor make himself the hateful

Instrument of reducing a free People to the abject State of Vassalage; of depriving us of those Liberties, which have given Reputation to our Country throughout the World, and drawn Inhabitants from the remotest Parts of Europe to enjoy them? Liberties not only granted us of Favour, but of Right; Liberties which in Effect we have bought and paid for, since we have not only performed the Conditions on which they were granted, but have actually given higher Prices for our Lands on their Account; so that the Proprietary Family have been doubly paid for them, in the Value of the Lands, and in the Increase of Rents with Increase of People: Let not our Affections be torn in this Manner from a Family we have long loved and honoured! Let that novel Doctrine, hatched by their mistaken Friends, that Privileges granted to promote the Settlement of a Country, are to be abridged when the Settlement is obtained, iniquitous as it is, be detested as it deserves, and banished from all our publick Councils; and let the Harmony, so essential to the Welfare of both Governors and Governed, be once again restored; since it can never be more necessary to our Affairs than in their present melancholy Situation. We hope the Governor will excuse some Appearance of Warmth, in a Cause of all others in the World the most interesting, and believe us to be, with all possible Respect and Duty to the Proprietary Family and to himself, his and their sincere Friends and Well-wishers.

[On August 12 Morris replied at length to this message, and on the 19th the Assembly responded, charging the Governor with efforts to enslave the province and returning his personal invective.]

The Governor thinks himself injuriously treated by our Request, "that he would not make himself the hateful Instrument of reducing a free People to the abject State of

Vassalage," and asks, "What Grounds have you, Gentlemen, for this heavy Charge? What Laws of Imposition abhorrent to common Justice and common Reason have I attempted to force down your Throats?" &c. A Law to tax the People of Pennsylvania to defend the Proprietary Estate, and to exempt the Proprietary Estate from bearing any Part of the Tax, is, may it please the Governor, a Law *abhorrent to common Justice, common Reason,* and *common Sense.* This is a Law of Imposition that the Governor would force down our Throats, by taking Advantage of the Distress of our Country, the Defence of which he will not suffer us to provide for, unless we will comply with it. Our Souls rise against it. We cannot swallow it. What other Instance would the Governor desire us to give of his endeavouring to reduce us to a State of Vassalage? He calls upon us for an Instance. We give him the very Law in Question, as the strongest of Instances. Vassals must *follow* their Lords to the Wars in Defence of their Lands; our Lord Proprietary, though a Subject like ourselves, would *send* us out to fight *for* him, while he keeps himself a thousand Leagues remote from Danger! Vassals fight at their Lords Expence, but our Lord would have us defend his Estate at our own Expence! This is not merely Vassalage, it is worse than any Vassalage we have heard of; it is something we have no adequate Name for; it is even more slavish than Slavery itself. And if the Governor can accomplish it, he *will be* deemed the hateful Instrument (how much soever he is disgusted with the Epithet) as long as History can preserve the Memory of his Administration. Does the Governor think to exculpate himself, by calling upon us to prove him guilty of Crimes we have never charged him with? *Whose Liberty have I taken away? Whose Property have I invaded?* If he can force us into this Law, the Liberty and Property, not only of one Man, but of all the Men in the Province, will be invaded and taken away; and this to aggrandize our *intended Lord,* encrease and secure his Estate at our Cost, and give him the glorious Privilege that no British Nobleman enjoys, of having his Lands free from Taxes, and defended gratis. But what is the Loss of even Liberty and Property, compared with the Loss of our good Name and Fame, which the Governor has, by every Artifice, endeavoured to deprive us of, and to ruin us in the Estimation of all Mankind. Accusations secretly despersed in the neighbouring Provinces and our Mother Country; nameless Libels put into the Hands of every Member of Parliament, Lords and Commons! But these were modest Attacks compared with his publick Messages, filled with the most severe and heavy Charges against us, without the least Foundation; such as those in his Message of the Sixteenth of May last; some of which, tho' then fully refuted, he now ventures to renew, by exclaiming in these Terms, "Had you any Regard for your bleeding Country, would you have been *deaf* to all the affectionate Warnings and Calls of his Majesty? and would you have *refused* the proper, necessary and timely Assistance to an Army sent to protect these Colonies?" For is it not well known that we have essayed every Method, consistent with our Rights and Liberties, to comply with the Calls of the Crown, which have frequently been defeated either by Proprietary Instructions or the Perverseness of our Governor? Did we not supply that Army plentifully with all they ask'd of us, and even more than all? in Testimony of which, have we not Letters from the late General, and other principal Officers, acknowledging our Care, and thanking us cordially for our Services? These Things are well known here: But there is no Charge that the Governor cannot allow himself to throw out against us, so it may have the least Chance of gaining some small Credit some where, though of the shortest Continuance.

In fine, we are sincerely grieved at the present unhappy

Business, Civic and Political Leader 119

State of our Affairs; but must endeavour patiently to wait for that Relief which Providence may, in due Time, think fit to favour us with, having, if this Bill is still refused, little farther Hopes of any Good from our present Governor.

[With the tax bill still unpassed as its session ended on September 29, the Assembly responded to Morris' message of the 24th (an especially abusive and inflammatory one) with a further definition of the rights they claimed as Englishmen, and a renewed personal assault on Morris.]

. . . The Governor denies, that our Claim of the Privilege "of having our Bills granting Supplies passed as they are tendered without Amendments, is warranted by the Words of the Charter;" though it gives us "all the Powers and Privileges of an Assembly, according to the Rights of the Free-born Subjects of England, and as is usual in any of the King's Plantations in America." If the Freeborn Subjects of England *do not* exercise this Right by their Representatives in Parliament, and it *is not* usual in *any* of the King's Plantations in America; then we are in the wrong to claim it, and the Governor is right in denying it. But Facts are for us; and these, in this Case, the Governor does not deny. Our Predecessors may in some few Instances have waved that Right, but they have never given it up, nor will, as we hope, those that shall succeed us. We trust they will rather be more cautious of suffering such dangerous Precedents, when they see how fond Governors are of seizing the Advantage for diminishing our Privileges. . . .

. . . The Governor is pleased to say, That "the common Security of the People requires that they should not be taxed but by the Voice of the whole Legislature;" and that "we might as well set up a Democracy at once, as claim an exclusive Right to the Disposition of Publick Money." To this we beg Leave to answer, that though we are not so absurd as to "design a Democracy," of which the Governor is pleased to accuse us; yet in this Particular, all our late Attempts to raise Money "for the common Security of the People," being obstructed and defeated by the Governor's having a Voice in that Matter, would rather induce us to think, that his having such a Voice, *is not* best for their Security; and such a Conduct in a Governor, appears to us the most likely Thing in the World to make People incline to a Democracy, who would otherwise never have dreamt of it.

But the Governor is pleased to tell us, that "our Claim of a natural exclusive Right to the Disposition of Publick Money, because it is the Peoples, is *against Reason, the Nature of an English Government,* and the *Usage of this Province.*" He has, however, never produced *that Reason* to us; and we still think, that as every Man has, so every Body of Men have a natural Right to the Disposition of their own Money, by themselves or their Representatives; and that the Proprietary's Claim of a Voice in the Disposition of Money to which he will contribute no Part, is a Claim contrary to Reason. The Wisdom of the Crown has thought fit to allow different Constitutions to different Colonies, suitable to their different Circumstances, and as they have been long settled and established, we apprehend that if the Governor could have Power to unsettle them all, and make in every one such Changes as would be necessary to reduce them to a Conformity with *his Idea* of an "English Government," the Reformation would be productive of more Inconvenience than Advantage. The general "Usage of this Province" in the Disposition of Publick Money, was ever what it now is; and as the Province has flourished with it, and no Inconvenience has attended it, we hope it will still continue. Particular Laws may, in a very few Instances, have given the Disposition of particular Sums to the Governor, or to Commissioners, for particular Services; but a few such Instances do not make *an Usage,* and the Governor must in that Point have been greatly misinformed. . . .

. . . The Governor concludes with telling us, that "if our Minutes be examined for Fifteen Years past, in them will be found more frivolous Controversies, unparalleled Abuses of Governors, and more Undutifulness to the Crown, than in all the rest of his Majesty's Colonies put together." The Minutes are printed, and in many Hands, who may judge on examining them whether any Abuses of Governors and Undutifulness to the Crown are to be found in them. *Controversies,* indeed, there are too many; but as our Assemblies are yearly changing, while our Proprietaries, during that Term, have remained the same, and have probably given their Governors the same Instructions, we must leave others to guess from what Root it is most likely that those Controversies should continually spring. As to *frivolous* Controversies, we never had so many of them as since our present Governor's Administration, and all raised by himself; and we may venture to say, that during that one Year, scarce yet expired, there have been more "unparallelled Abuses" of this People, and their Representatives in Assembly, than in all the Years put together, since the Settlement of the Province.

We are now to take our Leave of the Governor; and indeed, since he hopes no Good from us, nor we from him, 'tis Time we should be parted. If our Constituents disapprove our Conduct, a few Days will give them an Opportunity of changing us by a new Election; and could the Governor be as soon and as easily changed, Pennsylvania would, we apprehend, deserve much less the Character he gives it, of *an unfortunate Country.*

[In November, after Pennsylvania had for the first time experienced Indian warfare on its frontier, the Assembly passed a £60,000 tax bill which Morris refused to approve.

In its message of November 11, the Assembly turned its fire on the proprietary instructions which Morris used as an excuse for rejecting the tax measure, and sharpened its argument that it and it alone, as the body representing the people, could of right control measures in their defense.]

Our Assemblies have of late had so many Supply Bills, and of such different Kinds, rejected on various Pretences; Some for not complying with obsolete occasional Instructions (tho' other Acts exactly of the same Tenor had been past since those Instructions, and received the Royal Assent;) Some for being inconsistent with the supposed *Spirit of an Act of Parliament,* when the Act itself did not any way affect us, being made expresly for other Colonies; Some for being, as the Governor was pleased to say, "*of an extraordinary Nature,*" without informing us wherein that extraordinary Nature consisted; and others for disagreeing with new discovered Meanings, and forced Constructions of a Clause in the Proprietary Commission; that we are now really at a Loss to divine what Bill can possibly pass. The Proprietary Instructions are Secrets to us; and we may spend much Time, and much of the Publick Money, in preparing and framing Bills for Supply, which, after all, must, from those Instructions, prove abortive. If we are thus to be driven from Bill to Bill, without one solid Reason afforded us; and can raise no Money for the King's Service, and Relief or Security of our Country, till we fortunately hit on the only Bill the Governor is allowed to pass, or till we consent to make such as the Governor or Proprietaries direct us to make, we see little Use of Assemblies in this Particular; and think we might as well leave it to the Governor or Proprietaries to make for us what Supply Laws they please, and save ourselves and the Country the Expence and Trouble. All Debates and all Reasonings are vain, where Proprietary Instructions, just or unjust, right or wrong, must inviolably be observed. We have only to find out, if we can, what they are, and then submit

Business, Civic and Political Leader 123

and obey. But surely the Proprietaries Conduct, whether as Fathers of their Country, or Subjects to their King, must appear extraordinary, when it is considered that they have not only formally refused to bear any Part of our yearly heavy Expenses in cultivating and maintaining Friendship with the Indians, tho' they reap such immense Advantages by that Friendship; but they now, by their Lieutenant, refuse to contribute any Part towards resisting an Invasion of the King's Colony, committed to their Care; or to submit their Claim of Exemption to the Decision of their Sovereign.

In fine, we have the most sensible Concern for the poor distressed Inhabitants of the Frontiers. We have taken every Step in our Power, consistent with the just Rights of the Freemen of Pennsylvania, for their Relief, and we have Reason to believe, that in the Midst of their Distresses they themselves do not wish us to go farther. Those who would give up essential Liberty, to purchase a little temporary Safety, deserve neither Liberty nor Safety. Such as were inclined to defend themselves, but unable to purchase Arms and Ammunition, have, as we are informed, been supplied with both, as far as Arms could be procured, out of Monies given by the last Assembly for the King's Use; and the large Supply of Money offered by this Bill, might enable the Governor to do every Thing else that should be judged necessary for their farther Security, if he shall think fit to accept it. Whether he could, as he supposes, "if his Hands had been properly strengthened, have put the Province into such a Posture of Defence, as might have prevented the present Mischiefs," seems to us uncertain; since late Experience in our neighbouring Colony of Virginia (which had every Advantage for that Purpose that could be desired) shows clearly, that it is next to impossible to guard effectually an extended Frontier, settled by scattered single Families at two or three Miles Distance, so as to secure them from the insiduous Attacks of small Parties of skulking Murderers: But thus much is certain, that by refusing our Bills from Time to Time, by which great Sums were seasonably offered, he has rejected all the Strength that Money could afford him; and if his Hands are still weak or unable, he ought only to blame himself, or those who have tied them. . . .

[A final Assembly message of November 25 was not delivered because immediately after its presentation word arrived that the Proprietors had made a gift of £5000 for the defense of the province which the Assembly accepted in lieu of taxes, and then passed a tax bill, acceptable to Governor Morris, exempting the proprietary estates. The Message nevertheless summarized the Assembly case and represents the final position and mood of Franklin's strenuous, bitter campaign for Assembly privileges in the fall of 1755.]

The Governor is pleased to tell us, "The Constitution of this Province is founded on certain Royal and Proprietary Charters." It is true, and one of those Charters expresly says, "That the Assemblies of this Province shall have Power to chuse a Speaker, and other their Officers; and shall be judges of the Qualifications and Elections of their own Members; sit upon their own Adjournments; appoint Committees; prepare Bills, in order to pass into Laws; impeach Criminals, and redress Grievances; and shall have ALL OTHER Powers and Privileges of an Assembly, according to the Rights of the Freeborn Subjects of England, and as is usual in ANY of the King's Plantations in America." These very Words are also to be found in a Law of the Province, enacted in the Fourth of Queen ANNE, and to this Day in Force. That the "Freeborn Subjects of England" have a Right to grant Money by their Representatives in Parliament, in Bills that shall suffer no Amendment, the Governor does not deny; nor that it is usual in any of the King's Plantations in America: If therefore the Freeborn Subjects of England have this Right, we have it by our Charter, and our Laws. And if we had it not by our Charter and Laws, we should nevertheless have it; for the Freeborn Subjects of England do not lose their essential Rights by removing into the King's Plantations, extending the British Dominions at the Hazard of their Lives and Fortunes, and encreasing the Power, Wealth and Commerce of their Mother Country; they have, on the contrary, particular Privileges justly granted and added to their native Rights, for their Encouragement in so useful and meritorious an Undertaking. . . .

. . . In one Thing, indeed, it is our Misfortune, that our Constitution differs from that of England. The King has a natural Connection with His Subjects. The Crown descends to His Posterity; and the more his People prosper and flourish, the greater is the Power, Wealth, Strength and Security of his Family and Descendants. But Plantation Governors are frequently transient Persons, of broken Fortunes, greedy of Money, without any Regard to the People, or natural Concern for their Interests, often their Enemies, and endeavouring not only to oppress but defame them, and render them obnoxious to their Sovereign, and odious to their Fellow Subjects. Our present Governor not only denies us the Privileges of an English Constitution, but would, as far as in his Power, introduce a French one, by reducing our Assemblies to the Insignificance of their Parliaments, incapable of making Laws, but by Direction, or of qualifying their own Gifts and Grants, and only allowed to register his Edicts. He would even introduce a worse; he requires us to defend our Country, but will not permit us to raise the Means, unless we will give up some of those Liberties that make the Country worth defending; this is demanding *Brick without Straw*, and is so far *similar* to the Egyptian Constitution. He has got us indeed into *similar* Circumstances with the poor Egyptians, and takes the same Advantage of our Distress; for as they were to perish by Famine, so he tells us we must by the Sword, unless we will become Servants to our Pharaoh, and make him an *absolute Lord,* as he is pleased to stile himself *absolute Proprietary.* . . .

. . . What those "many other Ways of granting Money" are, "to which the Governor has no Objection," we must own ourselves totally ignorant; as well as what the other Bill may be "that he shall think consistent with his Duty to pass." He thinks it inconsistent with his Duty to pass any Bill contrary to his Instructions from the Proprietary, and those (like the Instructions of the President and Council of the North, mentioned by Lord Coke, IVth Inst. P. 246) are to us impenetrable Secrets. That great Lawyer's Remark on Governing by such Instructions, is truly just, viz. *Misera est Servitus, ubi Jus est vagum aut incognitum.* Wretched is the Slavery, where Law is either uncertain or unknown. It is vain for us therefore to look out for other Ways of raising Money, or to form other Bills: Here we must rest till His Majesty shall graciously please to relieve us; since with the Governor we can no otherwise hope to end our unhappy Disputes, than by submitting to one Part or the other of the miserable Alternative he mentions, either not to have "a Privilege worth disputing about, or be deprived of a Country to dispute it in."

A MILITIA ACT PROTECTING

CONSCIENTIOUS OBJECTORS

When war with France and Indian attacks on the frontier in 1755 made the pacifist Quakers who had dominated Pennsylvania politics for seventy years face the need for self-defense, they

---

Papers, VI, 269-273, 296-306; from a Militia Act passed by the Pennsylvania Assembly, November 25, 1755, and "A Dialogue between X, Y, and Z," first published in *The Pennsylvania Gazette,* December 18, 1755.

found Franklin a useful ally. He sought to protect pacifists from having to bear arms and to relieve Quakers in the Assembly from having to support measures onerous to their brethren, but he sought also to permit those who wanted to bear arms to do so under the laws of the province. He therefore drafted the militia bill portions of which are reprinted here, the first such measure ever adopted in Pennsylvania, and wrote "A Dialogue between X, Y, and Z" (extracts follow) explaining the usefulness of the act and urging people to execute it with integrity, good will, and patriotism. Franklin thought his "Dialogue" had a "great Effect" in helping to organize militia companies under the new Act, but in fact opposition from the anti-Quaker party led by Governor Morris vitiated it; they termed it a "solemn Farce," and a "villainous absurd law" designed to enhance Franklin's personal power. The provision for election of company officers by the rank-and-file, the absence of strict military discipline, and the exemption of pacifists from any obligation at all were fatal flaws in their view. In spite of this political obstruction and the Act's prompt disallowance by the Privy Council, it was a significant step for a colony previously pacifist. It also showed Franklin's conciliatory talents and his sometimes too-easy optimism that measures depending on the good will and voluntary efforts of the people would be practical under trying wartime conditions and amid the most bitter political disputes.

An act for the better Ordering and Regulating such as are willing and desirous to be united for Military Purposes within this Province.

Whereas this Province was first settled by (and a Majority of the Assemblies have ever since been) of the People called Quakers, who, though they do not, as the World is now circumstanced, condemn the Use of Arms in others, yet are principled against bearing Arms themselves; and to make any Law to compel them thereto against their Consciences, would not only be to violate a Fundamental in our Constitution, and be a direct Breach of our Charter of Privileges, but would also in Effect be to commence Persecution against all that Part of the Inhabitants of the Province: And for them by any Law to compel others to bear Arms, and exempt themselves, would be inconsistent and partial. Yet forasmuch as by the general Toleration and Equity of our Laws, great Numbers of People of other religious Denominations are come among us, who are under no such Restraint, some of whom have been disciplined in the Art of War, and conscientiously think it their Duty to fight in Defence of their Country, their Wives, their Families and Estates, and such have an equal Right to Liberty of Conscience with others. And whereas a great Number of Petitions from the several Counties of this Province have been presented to this House, setting forth, That the Petitioners are very willing to defend themselves and their Country, and desirous of being formed into regular Bodies for that Purpose, instructed and disciplined under proper Officers, with suitable and legal Authority; representing withal, that unless Measures of this Kind are taken, so as to unite them together, subject them to due Command, and thereby give them Confidence in each other, they cannot assemble to oppose the Enemy, without the utmost Danger of exposing themselves to Confusion and Destruction. And whereas the voluntary Assembling of great Bodies of armed Men, from different Parts of the Province, on any occasional Alarm, whether true or false, as of late hath happened, without Call or Authority from the Government, and without due Order and Direction among themselves, may be attended with Danger to our neighbouring Indian Friends and Allies, as well as to the internal Peace of the Province. And whereas the Governor hath frequently recommended it to the Assembly, that in preparing and passing a Law for such Purposes, they should have a due Regard to scrupulous and tender Consciences, which cannot be done where compulsive Means are used to force Men into Military Service; therefore as we represent all the People of the Province, and are composed of Members of different religious Persuasions, we do not think it reasonable that any should, through a Want of legal Powers, be in the least restrained from doing what they judge it their Duty to do for their own Security and the Publick Good; we, in Compliance with the said Petitions and Recommendations, do offer it to the Governor to be enacted, and be it enacted . . .That from and after the Publication of this Act, it shall and may be lawful for the Freemen of this Province to form themselves into Companies, as heretofore they have used in Time of War without Law, and for each Company, by Majority of Votes, in the Way of Ballot, to chuse its own Officers, to wit, a Captain, Lieutenant and Ensign, and present them to the Governor or Commander in Chief for the Time being for his Approbation; which Officers so chosen, if approved and commissioned by him, shall be the Captain, Lieutenant and Ensign of each Company respectively, according to their Commissions, and the said Companies being divided into Regiments by the Governor or Commander in Chief, it shall and may be lawful for the Officers so chosen and commissioned for the several Companies of each Regiment to meet together, and, by Majority of Votes, in the Way of Ballot, to chuse a Colonel, Lieutenant-Colonel and Major, for the Regiment, and present them to the Governor or Commander in Chief for his Approbation; which Officers so chosen, if approved and commissioned by him, shall be the Colonel, Lieutenant-Colonel and Major of the Regiment, according to their Commissions, during the Continuance of this Act. Provided always, That if the Governor or Commander in Chief shall not think fit to grant his Commission to any Officer so first chosen and presented, it shall and may be lawful for the Electors of such Officer to chuse two other Persons in his Stead, and present them to the Governor or Commander in Chief, one of whom, at his Pleasure, shall receive his Commission, and be the Officer as aforesaid. . . .

A DIALOGUE between X, Y, and Z, concerning the present State of Affairs in Pennsylvania.

. . . Z. I have heard this objected, That it were better the Governor should appoint the Officers; for the Choice being in the People, a Man very unworthy to be an Officer, may happen to be popular enough to get himself chosen by the undiscerning Mob.

X. 'Tis possible. And if all Officers appointed by Governors were always Men of Merit, and fully qualified for their Posts, it would be wrong ever to hazard a popular Election. It is reasonable, I allow, that the Commander in Chief should not have Officers absolutely forced upon him, in whom, from his Knowledge of their Incapacity, he can place no Confidence. And, on the other Hand, it seems likely that the People will engage more readily in the Service, and face Danger with more Intrepidity, when they are commanded by a Man they know and esteem, and on whose Prudence and Courage, as well as Good will and Integrity, they can have Reliance, than they would under a Man they either did not know, or did not like. For supposing Governors ever so judicious and upright in the Distribution of Offices, they cannot know every Body, in every Part of the Province, and are liable to be imposed on by partial Recommendations; but the People generally know their Neighbours. And to me, the Act in question seems to have hit a proper Medium, between the two Modes of appointing: The People chuse, and if the Governor approves, he grants the Commission; if not, they are to chuse a second, and even a third Time. Out of three Choices, 'tis probable one may be right; and where an Officer is approved both by Superior and Inferiors, there is the greater Prospect of those Advantages that attend a good Agreement in the Service. This Mode of Choice is moreover agreeable to the Liberty and Genius of our Constitution. 'Tis similar to the Manner in which by our Laws Sheriffs and Coroners are chosen and approved. And yet it has more Regard to the Prerogative than the Mode of Choice in some Colonies, where the military Officers are either chosen absolutely by the Companies themselves, or by the House of Representatives, without any Negative on that Choice, or any Approbation necessary from the Governor.

Y. But is that agreeable to the English Constitution?

X. Considered in this Light, I think it is; British Subjects, by removing into America, cultivating a Wilderness, extending the Dominion, and increasing the Wealth, Commerce and Power of their Mother Country, at the Hazard of their Lives and Fortunes, ought not, and in Fact do not thereby lose their native Rights. There is a Power in the Crown to grant a Continuance of those Rights to such Subjects, in any Part of the World, and to their Posterity born in such new Country; and for the farther Encouragement and Reward of such Merit, to grant *additional* Liberties and Privileges, not used in England, but suited to the different Circumstances of different Colonies. If then the Grants of those additional Liberties and Privileges may be regularly made under an English Constitution, they may be enjoyed agreeable to that Constitution. . . .

Z. Though the Quakers and others conscientiously scrupulous of bearing Arms, are exempted, as you say, by Charter; they might, being a Majority in the Assembly, have made the Law compulsory on others. At present, 'tis so loose, that no body is obliged by it, who does not voluntarily engage.

X. They might indeed have made the Law compulsory

on all others. But it seems they thought it more equitable and generous to leave to all as much Liberty as they enjoy themselves, and not lay even a seeming Hardship on others, which they themselves declined to bear. They have however granted all we asked of them. Our Petitions set forth, that "we were freely willing and ready to defend ourselves and Country, and all we wanted was legal Authority, Order and Discipline." These are now afforded by the Law, if we think fit to make use of them. And indeed I do not see the Advantage of compelling People of any Sect into martial Service merely for the Sake of raising Numbers. I have been myself in some Service of Danger, and I always thought Cowards rather *weakened,* than *strengthened,* the Party. Fear is contagious, and a Pannick once begun spreads like Wildfire, and infects the stoutest Heart. All Men are not by Nature brave: And a few who are so, will do more effectual Service by themselves, than when accompanied by, and mixed with, a Multitude of Poltroons, who only create Confusion, and give Advantage to the Enemy. . . .

Z. But if this Act should be carried into Execution, prove a good One, and answer the End; what shall we have to say against the Quakers at the next Election?

X. O my Friends, let us on this Occasion cast from us all these little Party Views, and consider ourselves as Englishmen and Pennsylvanians. Let us think only of the Service of our King, the Honour and Safety of our Country, and Vengeance on its Murdering Enemies. If Good be done, what imports it by whom 'tis done? The Glory of serving and saving others, is superior to the Advantage of being served or secured. Let us resolutely and generously unite in our Country's Cause (in which to die is the sweetest of all Deaths) and may the God of Armies bless our honest Endeavours.

A REBUKE TO COWARDS AND IDLERS

Franklin spent nearly two months (1755-1756) on the Pennsylvania frontier in considerable personal danger organizing defenses against Indian attacks. He generally sympathized with the suffering inhabitants, but as this letter shows, he had little use for shirkers nor did he approve the Moravian settlement at Bethlehem, under Spangenberg's leadership, becoming a haven for those unwilling to defend or feed themselves.

As the Forts are built, and the Ranging Companies in Motion beyond the Mountains, to cover the Inner Parts of the Country, I think the People may now very safely stay at their Places. The Government is at a great Expence to afford them this Defence; If they have no regard to it, but run away in so shameful and cowardly a Manner every time an Indian or two appears in any Part of the Province, and abandon their Plantations, I believe the Government will not think it worth while to keep up those Guards merely to secure empty Houses and uncultivated Fields, but will demolish the Forts, withdraw the Companies from your Frontier, and send them to other Parts to defend a better and more manly People. Of this be pleased to acquaint them; and farther that the Commissioners desire no Allowance may be made of Provisions on Account of the Government to any Refugees at your Place after this time; for some of them, as long as they can live in Idleness with you, and be fed, will think little of returning to their Places, or of the Duty of caring and labouring for their own Livelihood. . . .

Papers, VI, 414; from a letter to Augustus Spangenberg, March 1, 1756.

FRANKLIN'S POLITICAL PRINCIPLES, 1756

The dispute over Franklin's Militia Act (see above) soon led to a debate in the newspapers between the proprietary party and the so-called Quaker party led by Franklin. A spokesman for the Quaker party set down its case in a newspaper article that is the best statement of the principles motivating Franklin during the crucial years when he first became fully engaged in politics. Though he seems not to have prepared the draft submitted to the newspaper, he probably did help formulate its argument, and he undoubtedly approved it as a full summary of the cause he supported.

. . . The People of this Province are generally of the middling sort, and at present pretty much upon a Level. They are chiefly industrious Farmers, Artificers, or Men in Trade; they enjoy and are fond of Freedom, *and the meanest among them* thinks he has a Right to Civility from the greatest. They see with Concern in a neighbouring Province [Maryland], the vast Sums levied from the groaning People, and paid in exorbitant Fees to numerous great Officers, appointed by the Proprietor, who in return treat the poor Planter with Haughtiness, and the Artificer with Contempt; while both must stand Cap-in-hand when they speak to the Lordlings, and *your Honour* begins or ends every Sentence. Our People therefore dread the Growth of Proprietary Power, and are for holding fast those Privileges that tend to balance it or keep it down.

At present, the Representatives of the People having the Right of disposing of the People's Money, granting Salaries, and paying Accounts; the sole Appointment to some

---

The Pennsylvania Journal, supplement, March 25, 1756; essay signed "Pensylvanus."

Business, Civic and Political Leader 135

Offices of Profit, and a Share in the Appointment to others; and not subject to Prorogations or Dissolutions at a Governor's Pleasure, they are of Course a respectable Part of the Government. And as they are to be chosen annually, the common People whose Votes are so frequently necessary in Elections, are generally better treated by their Superiors on that Account. Besides as Assembly-men may so soon be chang'd and mix'd again among the People, it is scarce worth the Proprietaries while to bribe them with an Office, nor worth theirs to accept of it, to oppress their Constituents with unnessary heavy Taxes, or other burthensome Laws, since a Post may fail while the Burthens continue, and they come in to bear their Share of them. Hence the People are commonly attach'd to the Assembly, and jealous of its Priviledges and Independency, as knowing that their own Freedom and Happiness, and the Publick Welfare, depend on the Support of those Privileges, and that Independency. . . .

[After explaining the devices the proprietary party favored to limit the power of the Assembly, "Pensylvanus" outlined the principles that party set forth to justify the limitations.]

. . . They say they have studied Politicks in learned Authors, and are convinc'd that our Constitution is defective in those Particulars; that the People have too much Power, the Governor too little; hence the *lower Sort* are not respectful enough to the *better Sort;* hence the Laws are lax, and the Execution of them more so. That in every well fram'd Government, there ought to be Checks on the Disposition of Publick Money, to prevent Misapplications; that the Governor's Negative would be a proper Check on the Assembly's Grants. That our Offices are too few; for if we had more, we might encourage more Men of *Sense* and

Ability to come from *other* Places and fill them; and if the Fees were higher, it would be better worth a *Gentleman's* while to accept of them. That the appointing Militia Officers is an inherent Right in the Governor; and that the People are not fit to be trusted with any Share in it, being ignorant of the necessary Qualifications of an Officer, and easily byass'd to a wrong Choice: At least, if they are, from Favour, allow'd to chuse, it ought not to be by *private* Ballot but by *open* Election; for so those in Power may have an Opportunity of knowing who does and who does not vote as he should do, and by that Means influence a better Election. That a Legislative Council is absolutely necessary for the better and more weighty Consideration of proposed Laws, and is moreover agreeable to the British Constitution, as similar to the House of Lords. That no popular Assembly ought to meet, or sit, or continue, but at the Governor's Pleasure, least they should carry on Designs against the Government, or promote Rebellion. Nor have the Appointment of any Officers least it increase their Influence, and strengthen their Hands. That the Proprietor is a very good Man, has a sincere Love to the Country, is a true Friend to the Constitution, and if he aims at a few Alterations in it, tis for its Improvement only, and for the Sake of Order, internal Peace and better Government. These are the Principles by which *the most thinking Persons* of that Side justify their Conduct. . . . —Now let me tell you what the other Side says.

They say, Sir, that all the Powers in Possession of the Assembly are necessary to the Publick Wellfare. That the flourishing of this Province beyond its Neighbours, is a Proof of the Goodness of its Constitution, under which we long lived happily, and in which no Flaw was ever found 'till these Tinkers attempted to mend it. That Assemblies more rarely misuse their Power than Governors, their

Interest and that of the Publick being one and the same. That our Publick Business is as well transacted with *few Offices* and *small Fees*, as in other Governments with more and larger. That an Increase of Offices and of Fees to be paid by the People, is an Increase of Burthen, to no Purpose; an Impoverishment of the Inhabitants, and weakening of the State. That the People ought to chuse their own Militia Officers, to be commission'd by the Governor, for they know their Neighbours Loyalty, Courage, and Abilities, better than the Governor can know them; and, if they have not this Privilege, they are in a worse Condition than common Soldiers in the King's Troops, who may chuse under what Captain they will inlist. That if the Proprietor's Influence over the Assembly is so increas'd, as that they are render'd dependent and subservient to his Pleasure, it may as well be left to him to make the Laws, Assemblies thenceforth will be Cyphers; they will be worse than Cyphers, they will become the Instruments of Oppression. That if no Officer can be appointed, or Money appropriated, without the Proprietor's Consent or his Deputy's, we cannot so much as chuse an Agent to represent our Grievances at Home [England] on any Occasion, or pay him for his Services. That a Check in the Governor's Hands on the Disposition of public Money, may prevent right Applications as well as Misapplications, and in Fact more frequently does so in other Colonies. That tho' a Council of Advice may be useful, a Legislative Council is by long Experience found unnecesary; and they cannot be similar to a British House of Lords, while they are removeable at the Proprietor's Pleasure. That there is no Danger of Assemblies sitting to hatch Rebellion: they are all loyal, and take the legal Qualifications. That Elections by private Ballot, are fairest, and best show the free Inclination and Judgment of the People; and that if Persons in Power, and those who are called *Gentlemen,* will take care to increase in Virtue as they do in Wealth, they can never fail of sufficient Respect from the People. . . .

POPULAR SUPPORT

AND RESISTING THE PROPRIETORS

While fighting the Proprietors of Pennsylvania Franklin wrote his friend Peter Collinson of his reasons for resistance and at the same time displayed some vanity over his own popularity; Franklin had been touched and perhaps made a little conceited by the acclaim he received for his military and political efforts.

. . . The Proprietors, you write me word, are greatly incensed at some Parts of my late Conduct. I am not much concern'd at that, because if I have offended them *by acting right,* I can, whenever I please, remove their Displeasure, *by acting wrong.* Tho' at present I have not the least Inclination to be in their good Graces on those Terms. I have some natural Dislike to Persons who so far *Love Money,* as to be *unjust* for its sake: I despise their *Meanness,* (as it appears to me) in several late Instances, most cordially, and am thankful that I never had any Connection with them, or Occasion to ask or receive a Favour at their hands. For now I am persuaded that I do not oppose their Views from Pique, Disappointment, or personal Resentment, but, as I think, from a Regard to the Publick Good. I may be mistaken in what is that Publick Good; but at least I mean well. And whenever they appear to me to have the Publick Good in View, I think I would as readily

---

Papers, VII, 14–15; from a letter to Peter Collinson, November 5, 1756.

serve them as if they were my best Friends. I am sometimes asham'd for them, when I see them differing with their People for Trifles, and instead of being ador'd, as they might be, like Demi Gods, become the Objects of universal Hatred and Contempt. How must they have managed, when, with all the Power their Charter, the Laws and their Wealth give them, a private Person (forgive your Friend a little Vanity, as it's only between ourselves) can do more Good in their Country than they, because he has the Affections and Confidence of their People, and of course some Command of the Peoples Purses. You are ready now to tell me, that Popular Favour is a most uncertain Thing. You are right. I blush at having valued myself so much upon it. I have done. . . .

PART TWO

Spokesman for America in England

1757-1775

CONVERSATION WITH A NOBLE LORD

ON LEGISLATION FOR THE COLONIES

Within a month of Franklin's arrival in London he was taken to visit Lord Granville, President of the Privy Council, where after some talk of affairs in America, Granville addressed Franklin on what was to become the root cause of American Independence.

'You Americans have wrong Ideas of the Nature of your Constitution; you contend that the King's Instructions to his Governors are not Laws, and think yourselves at Liberty to disregard them at your own Discretion. But those Instructions are not like the Pocket Instructions given to a Minister going abroad, for regulating his Conduct in some trifling Point of Ceremony. They are first drawn up by Judges learned in the Laws; they are then considered, debated and perhaps amended in Council, after which they are signed by the King. They are then so far as relates to you, the *Law of the Land;* for the King is the Legisla-

The Autobiography of Benjamin Franklin, Leonard W. Labaree and others, eds. (New Haven: Yale University Press, 1964), pp. 261–262; Franklin's account of a conversation with John Carteret, first Earl Granville, in August 1757.

tor of the Colonies.' I told his Lordship this was new Doctrine to me. I had always understood from our Charters, that our Laws were to be made by our Assemblies, to be presented indeed to the King for his Royal Assent, but that being once given the King could not repeal or alter them. And as the Assemblies could not make permanent Laws without his Assent, so neither could he make a Law for them without theirs. He assur'd me I was totally mistaken. I did not think so however. And his Lordship's Conversation having a little alarm'd me as to what might be the Sentiments of the Court concerning us, I wrote it down as soon as I return'd to my Lodgings.

THE SOCIAL VALUE OF RELIGION

Shortly after reaching London, Franklin received from an unidentified deist a manuscript for a book which ridiculed other religious tenets while upholding those of the author. Franklin expressed his own strong feelings on the usefulness of religion, especially religious training for children, and also gave pragmatic support to voluntary suppression of certain kinds of publications.

I have read your Manuscrit with some Attention. By the Arguments it contains against the Doctrine of a particular Providence, tho' you allow a general Providence, you strike at the Foundation of all Religion: For without the Belief of a Providence that takes Cognizance of, guards and guides and may favour particular Persons, there is no Motive to Worship a Deity, to fear its Displeasure, or to pray for its Protection. I will not enter into any Discussion of your Principles, tho' you seem to desire it; At present I

Papers, VII, 294–295; from a letter to an unidentified person, December 13, 1757.

shall only give you my Opinion that tho' your Reasonings are subtle, and may prevail with some Readers, you will not succeed so as to change the general Sentiments of Mankind on that Subject, and the Consequence of printing this Piece will be a great deal of Odium drawn upon your self, Mischief to you and no Benefit to others. He that spits against the Wind, spits in his own Face. But were you to succeed, do you imagine any Good would be done by it? You yourself may find it easy to live a virtuous Life without the Assistance afforded by Religion; you having a clear Perception of the Advantages of Virtue and the Disadvantages of Vice, and possessing a Strength of Resolution sufficient to enable you to resist common Temptations. But think how great a Proportion of Mankind consists of weak and ignorant Men and Women, and of inexperienc'd and inconsiderate Youth of both Sexes, who have need of the Motives of Religion to restrain them from Vice, to support their Virtue, and retain them in the Practice of it till it becomes *habitual,* which is the great Point for its Security; And perhaps you are indebted to her originally that is to your Religious Education, for the Habits of Virtue upon which you now justly value yourself. You might easily display your excellent Talents of reasoning on a less hazardous Subject, and thereby obtain Rank with our most distinguish'd Authors. For among us, it is not necessary, as among the Hottentots that a Youth to be receiv'd into the Company of Men, should prove his Manhood by beating his Mother.[1] I would advise you therefore not to attempt unchaining the Tyger, but to burn this Piece before it is seen by any other Person, whereby you will save yourself a great deal of Mortification from the Enemies it may raise

---

[1] Franklin at first intended to insert here but then crossed out: "If you had a Constitution of Body capable of resisting all the Inclemencies of the Air, and that received no Damage by sleeping under the Hedges, would you therefore burn all our Houses?" [Ed.]

against you, and perhaps a good deal of Regret and Repentance. If Men are so wicked as we now see them *with Religion* what would they be if *without it?* I intend this Letter itself as a *Proof* of my Friendship and therefore add no *Professions* of it, but subscribe simply Yours

B.F.

THE VICES OF BRITISH GOVERNMENT
AND THE VIRTUES OF WILLIAM PITT

Franklin arrived in England at a low point in her war with France: an English fleet had been humiliated, her armies were defeated in North America and in Europe, and corruption raged unabated at home. Only the wisdom, energy, and integrity of William Pitt seemed capable of rescuing the nation from defeat. Franklin wrote of his reaction to both the calamitous situation and the prospective deliverer.

. . . A great Force is now going to America, where, it is said, very vigorous Measures are to be pursu'd this ensuing Campaign. If it should prove such another as the last, the Nation would be quite dispirited. It knows and feels itself so universally corrupt and rotten from Head to Foot, that it has little Confidence in any publick Men or publick Measures; and the Want of that Confidence turns, thro' Disunion, all their Strength into Weakness. Mr. Pitt's Abilities, and hitherto steady and disinterested Conduct, indeed seems at present their principal Foundation of Hope. They have reason therefore to pray for some Success this Year to strengthen his Hands and his Interests, as

---

Papers, VII, 375–376; from a letter to Joseph Galloway, February 17, 1758.

well as for his Life or Health; for if he should fall through, it is thought by many that his Place could scarcely be supplied, and that everything would go into Confusion. His universal Character of Integrity is what gave him his present Power, rather than the Favour of the King which he had not, or Party Interest which was little more than popular Esteem and Opinion. Men of Abilities were in the Ministry before, but one of that kind seem'd to be wanting for a Center of Union, who was, or at least was generally believ'd to be, an honest Man. Measures proposed by a Man of Abilities without Honesty, are always suspected, and he becomes weak thro' the Diffidence of those that should concur with and help him; but the Man of moderate Talents who is believ'd to mean well, and to act uprightly for the common Good, has everyone's ready Assistance, and thereby is able to do more than the other of superior Parts: But when Ability and Integrity meet in the same Person, his Power of doing Good must be greater, as he can himself plan right Measures, will receive all necessary Advice, can distinguish what is good, and can have all the necessary Assistance in the Execution. It is thought, however, by some, that Mr. Pitt fail'd of the last Particular at Rochfort; for that Envy, and an Apprehension lest Success in that Attempt might establish his Power, influenc'd the Inaction now so much complain'd of. But as he seems more confirm'd in his Station, it is hop'd the Commanders for the ensuing Year, will be more solicitous of recommending themselves to his Favour. They cannot indeed wish for a finer Opportunity of recommending themselves to the publick Favour, and gaining infinite Applause; for a long Series of ill Success has created such an Appetite for good News, that a small Victory obtain'd would be magnify'd to a great one, and the Man who procures us a Bonfire and a Holiday, would be almost ador'd as a Hero. . . .

FRIENDS AND FOES

OF AMERICA IN ENGLAND

After eighteen months in England, Franklin understood very well that the protection of colonial rights depended on the struggle to extend freedom in Great Britain, and the support of the friends of liberty there. In assessing ways to present colonial appeals in England, and in speculating on the likely disposition of a case pending before the Privy Council, Franklin gave Isaac Norris, the Speaker of the Pennsylvania Assembly and long a political ally of Franklin, a candid account of British government in the generation before the American Revolution.

The case referred to in the last paragraph of this document is that of the Reverend William Smith, imprisoned by the Pennsylvania Assembly for contempt because of his role in disseminating a scurrilous attack on the Assembly written by William Moore. The Assembly denied Smith the right to appeal for a writ of habeas corpus and otherwise acted high-handedly in retaining him, claiming in justification all the privileges and prerogatives of the House of Commons in Great Britain. Sensing that Ministers in London would disapprove this claim, the Proprietors of Pennsylvania and their lawyer, Ferdinand J. Paris, supported Smith's petition to the Privy Council for redress. As agent for the Assembly Franklin opposed the appeal and in the process learned a good deal about the cross-currents of British politics. His concluding conjecture proved correct; the Privy Council upheld Smith and rejected the wide claim of privileges by the Pennsylvania Assembly, but did not restrain its authority generally.

. . . The Prevailing Opinion, as far as I am able to collect it, among the Ministers and great Men here, is, that

---

Papers, VIII, 291-297; from a letter to Isaac Norris, March 10, 1759.

the Colonies have too many and too great Privileges; and that it is not only the Interest of the Crown but of the Nation to reduce them. An absolute Subjection to Orders sent from hence in the Shape of Instructions, is the Point to be carried if possible. Lord G[ranville] who you know is President of the [Privy] Council told me frankly in a Conversation he honoured me with on that Head, . . .
[Here Franklin repeated his account of the conversation, reprinted above, "Conversation with a Noble Lord . . ."]
. . . Lord Hardwike, is next at the Council Board; than whom no one is supposed to be for carrying the Prerogative higher in all Respects even on this Side the Water; all his Actions they say, on all Occasions, have shown this; and he makes little less Scruple than the President in declaring his Opinions of this kind. These two govern at that Board, so that one may easily conjecture what Reception a Petition concerning Privileges from the Colonies may meet with from those who are known to think that even the People of England have too many. As to the Board of Trade, you know who presides and governs all there [Lord Halifax], and if his sentiments were no other ways to be known, the fruitless Experiment he has tryed at the Nation's Cost, of a military Government for a Colony, sufficiently shows what he thinks would be best for us. The Speaker of the House, indeed, is looked on as a stanch Friend to Liberty; and so is the Secretary Mr. Pitt; the Attorney General [Charles Pratt, later Lord Camden] is likewise *inclined* to that Side in all Questions, though the Nature of his Office requires him to be something of a Prerogative Man; but the *Sollicitor* General who is Lord H[ardwick]'s *Son* is wholly and strongly tinctured with high Notions of the Prerogative, imbited from his Father, and may be said to be dyed in grain.

From this Sketch of Leading Characters, you will judge, that if the Proprietor does not agree with us, our best Chance in an Application is directly to Parliament; and yet that at this Time is something hazardous, for though there are many Members in both Houses who are Friends to Liberty and of noble Spirits, yet a good deal of Prejudice still prevails against the Colonies, the Courtiers think us not sufficiently obedient; the illicit Trade from Holland, etc. greatly offends the Trading and Manufactoring Interest; and the Landed Interest begin to be jealous of us as a Corn Country, that may interfere with them in the Markets to which they export that Commodity: I wish indeed that the illicit Trade could be wholly prevented, for it is not to be justified. As to other Things, I am meditating a Pamphlet that I hope may help to introduce less partial, more generous, and sounder Politicks.

Smith is here, and by the Help of Paris worries the Attorney and Sollicitor General for a Report on his Case, who did not intend to make any. The Attorney is greatly perplexed, angry with the Council for referring the Affair to them, and with Smith for urging a Report; He has opened his Mind to a Friend of mine on this Head; says, "the Council he knows are for Clipping the Wings of Assemblies in their Claims of all the Privileges of a House of Commons; the House of Commons are thought to claim too many, some very unfit and unreasonable, and not for the common Good; but the Council have let the Colonies go on so long in this Way that it will now be difficult to restrain them; and the Council would now make the Attorney and Sollicitor the first Instruments of so odious a Measure; that they (the Council) should have carried it into Parliament, but they are afraid the Parliament would establish more Liberty in the Colonies than is proper or necessary, and therefore do not care the Parliament should meddle at all with the Government of the Colonies; they rather chuse to carry every Thing there by the *Weight of Prerogative,* which by Degrees may bring Things to a proper Situation. Most Attorney Generals (he said) would immediately do what they knew would be pleasing to the Council; but he could not: He must however make some kind of Report." This is the Substance of his Discourse to my Friend, who communicated it to me with Leave to mention it to you and the Committee, as it contains some Hints that are of Importance, but it is to go no farther. It is some Comfort that the Council are doubtful of the Parliament. The West India Interest in the House, in any general Attack on the Colonies would doubtless be of use to us, and perhaps that may be a little apprehended, and it may be thought not proper to disoblige those Members as they make a considerable Body: But at the same Time it is known here that if the Ministry make a Point of carrying *any thing* in Parliament, they can carry it. On the whole, it is conjectured the Attorney and Sollicitor General's Report, will be of a special kind; some Censure perhaps passed on Modes and Expressions in your Proceeding; but the general Authority of an Assembly not impeached. This, however, is only Conjecture. . . .

THE FUTURE OF THE BRITISH EMPIRE

IN NORTH AMERICA

As British forces conquered Canada during the French and Indian War, a dispute arose over the wisdom of retaining possession. Franklin began a propaganda campaign favoring retention in London newspapers in the fall of 1759, and stated the heart of his argument in a letter to the Scottish philosopher Lord Kames.

. . . No one can more sincerely rejoice than I do, on the reduction of Canada; and this is not merely as I am a colo-

---

Writings, IV, 4; from a letter to Lord Kames, January 3, 1760.

nist, but as I am a Briton. I have long been of opinion, that the *foundations of the future grandeur and stability of the British empire lie in America;* and though, like other foundations, they are low and little seen, they are, nevertheless, broad and strong enough to support the greatest political structure human wisdom ever yet erected. I am therefore by no means for restoring Canada. If we keep it, all the country from the St. Lawrence to the Mississippi will in another century be filled with British people. Britain itself will become vastly more populous, by the immense increase of its commerce; the Atlantic sea will be covered with your trading ships; and your naval power, thence continually increasing, will extend your influence round the whole globe, and awe the world! If the French remain in Canada, they will continually harass our colonies by the Indians, and impede if not prevent their growth; your progress to greatness will at best be slow, and give room for many accidents that may for ever prevent it. But I refrain, for I see you begin to think my notions extravagant, and look upon them as the ravings of a mad prophet. . . .

THE INTEREST OF GREAT BRITAIN CONSIDERED WITH REGARD TO HER COLONIES AND THE ACQUISITION OF CANADA AND GUADALOUPE

Franklin developed his full argument for retaining Canada in the peace settlement with France in this pamphlet, widely reprinted in England and in America and credited with some influence in persuading British negotiators of the Treaty of Paris

---

Writings, IV, 32–82; from a pamphlet first published in April 1760.

Spokesman for America in England 151

in 1763 to acquire the vast French possessions on the North American continent. The basic argument was an old one to Franklin (see above, "Observations Concerning the Increase of Mankind . . ." 1751); in this pamphlet he simply applied it to the contention then raging over Canada. He wrote specifically in response to some anonymous "Remarks" urging that the rich and highly developed sugar island of Guadaloupe in the West Indies would be more valuable to Britain than the unsettled wilderness of Canada. The argument Franklin quotes to refute is from these "Remarks." He wrote, furthermore, as a Briton rather than as a colonialist to give his pamphlet more power as a plea to the self-interest of the influential people in London whom he hoped to persuade. "The Interest of Great Britain Considered . . . ," usually called "The Canada Pamphlet," was one of Franklin's most skilful propaganda ventures and shows his characteristic ability to combine special pleading with general precepts, and appeals to self-interest with those to humane considerations.

. . . While the war continues, its final event is quite uncertain. The Victorious of this year may be the vanquish'd of the next. It may therefore be too early to say, what advantages we ought absolutely to insist on, and make the *sine quibus non* of a peace. If the necessity of our affairs should oblige us to accept of terms less advantageous than our present successes seem to promise us, an intelligent people as ours is, must see that necessity, and will acquiesce. But as a peace, when it is made, may be made hastily; and as the unhappy continuance of the war affords us time to consider, among several advantages gain'd or to be gain'd, which of them may be most for our interest to retain, if some and not all may possibly be retained; I do not blame the public disquisition of these points, as premature or useless. Light often arises from a collision of opinions, as fire from flint and steel; and if we can obtain the benefit of the *light*, without danger from the *heat* sometimes produc'd by controversy, why should we discourage it? . . .

. . . *Canada*, in the hands of *Britain*, will endanger the kingdom of *France* as little as any other cession; and from its situation and circumstances cannot be hurtful to any other state. Rather, if peace be an advantage, this cession may be such to all *Europe*. The present war teaches us, that disputes arising in *America* may be an occasion of embroiling nations who have no concerns there. If the *French* remain in *Canada* and *Louisiana*, fix the boundaries as you will between us and them, we must border on each other for more than 1500 miles. The people that inhabit the frontiers are generally the refuse of both nations, often of the worst morals and the least discretion, remote from the eye, the prudence, and the restraint of government. Injuries are therefore frequently, in some part or other of so long a frontier, committed on both sides, resentment provoked, the colonies are first engaged, and then the mother countries. And two great nations can scarce be at war in *Europe*, but some other prince or state thinks it a convenient opportunity to revive some ancient claim, seize some advantage, obtain some territory, or enlarge some power at the expence of a neighbour. The flames of war once kindled, often spread far and wide, and the mischief is infinite. Happy it prov'd to both nations, that the *Dutch* were prevailed on finally to cede the *New Netherlands* (now the province of *New York*) to us at the peace of 1674; a peace that has ever since continued between us, but must have been frequently disturbed, if they had retained the possession of that country, bordering several hundred miles on our colonies of *Pensilvania* westward, *Connecticut* and the *Massachusetts* eastward. Nor is it to be wondered at that people of different language, religion, and manners, should in those remote parts engage in frequent quarrels, when we find, that even the people of our own colonies have frequently been so exasperated against each other in their disputes about boundaries, as to proceed to open violence and bloodshed. . . .

. . . Our *North American* colonies are to be considered as the frontier of the *British* empire on that side. The frontier of any dominion being attack'd, it becomes not merely *"the cause"* of the people immediately affected, (the inhabitants of that frontier) but properly *"the cause"* of the whole body. Where the frontier people owe and pay obedience, there they have a right to look for protection. No political proposition is better established than this. It is therefore invidious to represent the "blood and treasure" spent in this war, as spent in "the cause of the colonies" only, and that they are "absurd and ungrateful" if they think we have done nothing unless we "make conquests for them," and reduce *Canada* to gratify their "vain ambition," &c. It will not be a conquest for them, nor gratify any vain ambition of theirs. It will be a conquest for the whole; and all our people will, in the increase of trade, and the ease of taxes, find the advantage of it.

Should we be obliged at any time to make a war for the protection of our commerce, and to secure the exportation of our manufactures, would it be fair to represent such a war merely as blood and treasure spent in the cause of the weavers of *Yorkshire, Norwich,* or the *West,* the cutlers of *Sheffield,* or the button-makers of *Birmingham?* I hope it will appear before I end these sheets, that if ever there was a *national war,* this is truly such a one: a war in which the interest of the *whole* nation is directly and fundamentally concerned. Those who would be thought deeply skilled in human nature, affect to discover self-interested views everywhere at the bottom of the fairest, the most generous conduct. Suspicions and charges of this kind, meet with ready reception and belief in the minds even of the multitude; and therefore less acuteness and address than the *remarker* is possessed of, would be sufficient to persuade the nation generally, that all the zeal and spirit manifested and exerted by the colonies in this war, was only in "their own cause," to "make conquest for themselves," to engage us to make more for them, to gratify their own "vain ambition." . . .

. . . In fact, the occasion for *English* goods *North America*, and the inclination to have and use them, is, and must be for ages to come, much greater than the ability of the people to pay for them; they must therefore, as they now do, deny themselves many things they would otherwise chuse to have, or increase their industry to obtain them; and thus, if they should at any time manufacture some coarse article, which on account of its bulk or some other circumstance, cannot so well be brought to them from *Britain*, it only enables them the better to pay for finer goods that otherwise they could not indulge themselves in: So that the exports thither are not diminished by such manufacture, but rather increased. The single article of manufacture in these colonies, mentioned by the *remarker*, is *hats* make in *New England*. It is true there have been, ever since the first settlement of that country, a few hatters there, drawn thither probably at first by the facility of getting beaver, while the woods were but little clear'd, and there was plenty of those animals. The case is greatly alter'd now. The beaver skins are not now to be had in *New England*, but from very remote places and at great prices. The trade is accordingly declining there, so that, far from being able to make hats in any quantity for exportation, they cannot supply their home demand; and it is well known that some thousand dozens are sent thither yearly from *London, Bristol*, and *Liverpool*, and sold cheaper than the inhabitants can make them of equal goodness.

In fact, the colonies are so little suited for establishing of manufactures, that they are continually losing the few branches they accidentally gain. The working brasiers, cutlers, and pewterers, as well as hatters, who have happened to go over from time to time and settle in the colonies, gradually drop the working part of their business, and import their respective goods from England, whence they can have them cheaper and better than they can make them. They continue their shops indeed, in the same way of dealing; but become *sellers* of brasiery, cutlery, pewter, hats, &c. brought from England, instead of being *makers* of those goods.

Thus much as to the apprehension of our colonies becoming *useless* to us. I shall next consider the other supposition, that their growth may render them *dangerous*. Of this, I own, I have not the least conception, when I consider that we have already fourteen separate governments on the maritime coast of the continent, and if we extend our settlements shall probably have as many more behind them on the inland side. Those we now have, are not only under different governors, but have different forms of government, different laws, different interests, and some of them different religious persuasions, and different manners.

Their jealousy of each other is so great, that however necessary an union of the colonies has long been, for their common defence and security against their enemies, and how sensible soever each colony has been of that necessity, yet they have never been able to effect such an union among themselves, nor even to agree in requesting the mother country to establish it for them. Nothing but the immediate command of the crown has been able to produce even the imperfect union, but lately seen there, of the forces of some colonies. If they could not agree to unite for their defence against the *French* and *Indians*, who were perpetually harassing their settlements, burning their villages, and murdering their people; can it reasonably be supposed there is any danger of their uniting against their own nation, which protects and encourages them, with which they have so many connections and ties of blood, interest and affection, and which 'tis well known they all love much more than they love one another?

In short, there are so many causes that must operate to prevent it, that I will venture to say, an union amongst them for such a purpose is not merely improbable, it is impossible; and if the union of the whole is impossible, the attempt of a part must be madness: as those colonies, that did not join the rebellion, would join the mother country in suppressing it. When I say such an union is impossible, I mean without the most grievous tyranny and oppression. People who have property in a country which they may lose, and privileges which they may endanger, are generally dispos'd to be quiet; and even to bear much, rather than hazard all. While the government is mild and just, while important civil and religious rights are secure, such subjects will be dutiful and obedient. The waves do not rise but when the winds blow. . . .

The *Romans* well understood that policy which teaches the security arising to the chief government from separate states among the governed, when they restored the liberties of the states of *Greece* (oppressed but united under *Macedon*) by an edict that every state should live under its own laws. They did not even name a governor. *Independence of each other, and separate interests,* tho' among a people united by common manners, language, and I may say religion, inferior neither in wisdom, bravery, nor their love of liberty, to the *Romans* themselves, was all the security the sovereigns wished for their sovereignty.

It is true, they did not call themselves sovereigns; they set no value on the title; they were contented with possessing the thing; and possess it they did, even without a standing army. What can be a stronger proof of the security of their possession? And yet by a policy similar to this throughout, was the *Roman* world subdued and held: a world composed of above a hundred languages and sets of manners, different from those of their masters. Yet this dominion was unshakeable, till the loss of liberty and corruption of manners in the sovereign state overturned it. . . .

. . . The objection I have often heard, that if we had *Canada*, we could not people it, without draining *Britain* of its inhabitants, is founded on ignorance of the nature of population in new countries. When we first began to colonize in *America*, it was necessary to send people, and to send seed-corn; but it is not now necessary that we should furnish, for a new colony, either the one or the other. The annual increment alone of our present colonies, without diminishing their numbers, or requiring a man from hence, is sufficient in ten years to fill *Canada* with double the number of *English*, that it now has of *French* inhabitants. Those who are protestants among the *French* will probably chuse to remain under the *English* government; many will chuse to remove, if they can be allowed to sell their lands, improvements, and effects: the rest in that thin-settled country will in less than half a century, from the crowds of *English* settling round and among them, be blended and incorporated with our people both in language and manners.

In *Guadalupe* the case is somewhat different; and though I am far from thinking we have sugar-land enough, I cannot think *Guadalupe* is so desirable an increase of it, as other objects the enemy would probably be infinitely more ready to part with. A country *fully inhabited* by any nation is no proper possession for another of different language, manners and religion. It is hardly ever tenable at less expence than it is worth. . . .

I have before said I do not deny the utility of the conquest, or even of our future possession of *Guadalupe*, if not bought too dear. The trade of the *West Indies* is one of our most valuable trades. Our possessions there deserve our greatest care and attention. So do those of *North America*. I shall not enter into the invidious task of comparing their due estimation. It would be a very long and a very disagreeable one, to run through every thing material on this head. It is enough to our present point, if I have shown, that the value of *North America* is capable of an immense increase, by an acquisition and measures, that must necessarily have an effect the direct contrary of what we have been industriously taught to fear; and that *Guadalupe* is, in point of advantage, but a very small addition to our *West India* possessions, rendered many ways less valuable to us, than it is to the *French*, who will probably set more value upon it than upon a country that is much more valuable to us than to them. . . .

THE BARBARISM

AND INJUSTICE OF "WHITE SAVAGES"

When Franklin returned to Pennsylvania for two years, 1762–1764, he again found himself deeply involved in the bitter partisan politics and heated emotions of Indian warfare he had left five years before. Pontiac's uprising of Indians in the Ohio

---

Writings, IV, 297–312; from the pamphlet A *Narrative of the Late Massacres, in Lancaster County, of a Number of Indians, Friends of this Province, by Persons Unknown. With Some Remarks on the Same;* first printed in Philadelphia, January 1764.

Spokesman for America in England 159

Valley spread eastward into the Susquehanna Valley, and aroused frontiersmen there to bloody reprisals on peaceful Indians settled near Lancaster; twenty of them were murdered in December 1763. In an effort to calm tempers and prevent further bloodshed, Franklin wrote and published this pamphlet protesting the injustice of the murders and pleading for the human rights of peaceful Indians. After an account of the murders, Franklin turned his wrath on those who excused them.

. . . There are some, (I am ashamed to hear it,) who would extenuate the enormous Wickedness of these Actions, by saying, "The Inhabitants of the Frontiers are exasperated with the Murder of their Relations, by the Enemy *Indians*, in the present War." It is possible; — but though this might justify their going out into the Woods, to seek for those Enemies, and avenge upon them those Murders, it can never justify their turning into the Heart of the Country, to murder their Friends.

If an *Indian* injures me, does it follow that I may revenge that Injury on all *Indians?* It is well known, that *Indians* are of different Tribes, Nations and Languages, as well as the White People. In *Europe*, if the *French*, who are White People, should injure the *Dutch*, are they to revenge it on the *English*, because they too are White People? The only Crime of these poor Wretches seems to have been, that they had a reddish-brown Skin, and black Hair; and some People of that Sort, it seems, had murdered some of our Relations. If it be right to kill Men for such a Reason, then, should any Man, with a freckled Face and red Hair, kill a Wife or Child of mine, it would be right for me to revenge it, by killing all the freckled red-haired Men, Women and Children, I could afterwards anywhere meet with.

But it seems these People think they have a better Justification; nothing less than the *Word of God*. With the Scriptures in their Hands and Mouths, they can set at nought that express Command, *Thou shalt do no Murder;* and justify their Wickedness by the Command given *Joshua* to destroy the Heathen. Horrid Perversion of Scripture and of Religion! To father the worst of Crimes on the God of Peace and Love! Even the *Jews*, to whom that particular Commission was directed, spared the *Gibeonites*, on Account of their Faith once given. The Faith of this Government has been frequently given to those *Indians;* but that did not avail them with People who despise Government.

We pretend to be *Christians*, and, from the superior Light we enjoy, ought to exceed *Heathens*, *Turks*, *Saracens*, *Moors*, *Negroes* and *Indians*, in the Knowledge and Practice of what is right. I will endeavour to show, by a few Examples from Books and History, the Sense those People have had of such Actions. . . .

[Franklin then cited a series of instances in which the Indians had shown much more humanity and mercy than the blood-thirsty frontiersmen. He concluded with a plea for compassion.]

These poor People have been always our Friends. Their Fathers received ours, when Strangers here, with Kindness and Hospitality. Behold the Return we have made them! When we grew more numerous and powerful, they put themselves under our *Protection*. See, in the mangled Corpses of the last Remains of the Tribe, how effectually we have afforded it to them!

Unhappy People! to have lived in such Times, and by such Neighbours! We have seen, that they would have been safer among the ancient *Heathens*, with whom the Rites of Hospitality were *sacred*. They would have been considered as *Guests* of the Publick, and the Religion of the Country would have operated in their Favour. But our Frontier People call themselves *Christians!* They would have been safer, if they had submitted to the *Turks;* for ever since *Mahomet's* Reproof to *Khaled,* even the cruel *Turks* never kill Prisoners in cold Blood. These were not even Prisoners. But what is the Example of *Turks* to Scripture *Christians?* They would have been safer, though they had been taken in actual War against the *Saracens,* if they had once drank Water with them. These were not taken in War against us, and have drank with us, and we with them, for Fourscore Years. But shall we compare *Saracens* to *Christians?*

They would have been safer among the *Moors* in *Spain,* though they had been Murderers of Sons; if Faith had once been pledged to them, and a Promise of Protection given. But these have had the Faith of the *English* given to them many Times by the Government, and, in Reliance on that Faith, they lived among us, and gave us the Opportunity of murdering them. However, what was honourable in *Moors,* may not be a Rule to us; for we are *Christians!* They would have been safer it seems among *Popish Spaniards,* even if Enemies, and delivered into their Hands by a Tempest. These were not Enemies; they were born among us, and yet we have killed them all. But shall we imitate *idolatrous Papists,* we that are *enlightened Protestants?* They would have even been safer among the *Negroes* of *Africa,* where at least one manly Soul would have been found, with Sense, Spirit and Humanity enough, to stand in their Defence. But shall *Whitemen* and *Christians* act like a *Pagan Negroe?* In short it appears, that they would have been safe in any Part of the known World, except in the Neighbourhood of the Christian white Savages of *Peckstang* and *Donegall!*

ROYAL GOVERNMENT BETTER THAN PROPRIETARY RULE

Though during his five years in England Franklin established, with the support of Lord Mansfield and other British Ministers, the right of the Pennsylvania Assembly to tax the proprietary estates, the quarrels with the Proprietor-appointed governor continued. After eighteen months at home Franklin wrote a tract arguing that the only way to end the disputes was to eliminate the Proprietors' voice in the government by placing the colony under the rule of the Crown, as was already the case with most of the other colonies. Shortly after publication of *Cool Thoughts* . . . , Franklin as Speaker of the Assembly signed a petition to the King for royal government in Pennsylvania.

. . . I do not purpose entering into the Merits of the Disputes between the Proprietaries and the People. I only observe it as a Fact known to us all, that such Disputes there are, and that they have long subsisted, greatly to the Prejudice of the Province, clogging and embarrassing all the Wheels of Government, and exceedingly obstructing the publick Defence, and the Measures wisely concerted by our Gracious Sovereign, for the common Security of the Colonies. I may add it as another Fact, that *we are all heartily tired of these Disputes.* . . .

. . . *Pennsylvania* had scarce been settled Twenty Years, when these Disputes began between the first Proprietor and the original Settlers; they continued, with some Intermissions, during his whole Life; his Widow

---

Writings, IV, 226–241; from the pamphlet *Cool Thoughts on the Present Situation of Our Public Affairs,* printed in Philadelphia and dated April 12, 1764.

took them up, and continued them after his Death. Her Sons resum'd them very early, and they still subsist. Mischievous and distressing as they have been found to both Proprietors and People, it does not appear that there is any Prospect of their being extinguish'd, till either the Proprietary Purse is unable to support them, or the Spirit of the People so broken, that they shall be willing to submit to any Thing, rather than continue them. The first is not very likely to happen, as that immense Estate goes on increasing.

Considering all Circumstances, I am at length inclin'd to think, that the Cause of these miserable Contentions is not to be sought for merely in the Depravity and Selfishness of human Minds. For tho' it is not unlikely that in these, as well as in other Disputes, there are *Faults on both Sides,* every glowing Coal being apt to inflame its Opposite; yet I see no Reason to suppose that all Proprietary Rulers are worse Men than other Rulers, nor that all People in Proprietary Governments are worse People than those in other Governments. I suspect therefore, that the Cause is radical, interwoven in the Constitution, and so become of the very Nature, of Proprietary Governments; and will therefore produce its Effects, as long as such Governments continue. And, as some Physicians say, every Animal Body brings into the World among its original Stamina the Seeds of that Disease that shall finally produce its Dissolution; so the Political Body of a Proprietary Government, contains those convulsive Principles that will at length destroy it.

I may not be Philosopher enough to develop those Principles, nor would this Letter afford me Room, if I had Abilities, for such a Discussion. The *Fact* seems sufficient for our Purpose, and the *Fact* is notorious, that such Contentions have been in all Proprietary Governments, and have brought, or are now bringing, them all to a Conclusion. I will only mention one Particular common to them all. Proprietaries must have a Multitude of private Accounts and Dealings with almost all the People of their Provinces, either for Purchase money or Quit-rents. Dealings often occasion Differences, and Differences produce mutual Opinions of Injustice. If Proprietaries do not insist on small Rights, they must on the Whole lose large Sums; and if they do insist on small Rights, they seem to descend, their Dignity suffers in the Opinion of the People, and with it the Respect necessary to keep up the Authority of Government. The People, who think themselves injured in Point of Property, are discontented with the Government, and grow turbulent; and the Proprietaries using their Powers of Government to procure for themselves what they think Justice in their Points of Property, renders those Powers odious. I suspect this has had no small Share in producing the Confusions incident to those Governments. They appear, however, to be, *of all others,* the most unhappy.

At present we are in a wretched Situation. The Government that ought to keep all in Order, is itself weak, and has scarce Authority enough to keep the common Peace. Mobs assemble and kill (we scarce dare say *murder*) Numbers of innocent People in cold Blood, who were under the Protection of the Government. Proclamations are issued to bring the Rioters to Justice. Those Proclamations are treated with the utmost Indignity and Contempt. Not a Magistrate dares wag a Finger towards discovering or apprehending the *Delinquents,* (we must not call them *Murderers.*) They assemble again, and with Arms in their Hands approach the Capital. The Government truckles, condescends to cajole them, and drops all Prosecution of their Crimes; whilst honest Citizens, threatened in their Lives and Fortunes, flie the Province, as having no Confidence in the Publick Protection. We are daily threatened with more of these Tumults; and the Government, which in its Distress call'd aloud on the sober Inhabitants to come with Arms to its Assistance, now sees those who afforded that Assistance daily libell'd, abus'd, and menac'd by its Partizans for so doing; whence it has little Reason to expect such Assistance on another Occasion: —

In this Situation, what is to be done? By what Means is that Harmony between the two Branches of Government to be obtain'd, without which the internal Peace of the Province cannot be well secured? One Project is, to turn all *Quakers* out of the Assembly; or, by obtaining more Members for the Back Counties, to get a Majority in, who are not *Quakers*. This, perhaps, is not very difficult to do; and more Members for those Counties may, on other Accounts, be proper; but I much question if it would answer this End, as I see among the Members, that those who are not *Quakers*, and even those from the Back Counties, are as hearty and unanimous in opposing what they think Proprietary Injustice, as the *Quakers* themselves, if not more so. Religion has happily nothing to do with our present Differences, tho' great Pains is taken to lug it into the Squabble. And even were the *Quakers* extirpated, I doubt whether the Proprietaries, while they pursue the same Measures, would be a Whit more at their Ease.

Another Project is, to chuse none for Assembly-men but such as are Friends to the Proprietaries. The Number of Members is not so great, but that I believe this Scheme may be practicable, if you look for Representatives among Proprietary Officers and Dependants. Undoubtedly it would produce great Harmony between Governor and Assembly: But how would both of them agree with the People? Their Principles and Conduct must greatly change, if they would be elected a second Year. But that might be needless. Six Parts in Seven agreeing with the Governor, could make the House perpetual. This, however, would not probably establish Peace in the Province.

The Quarrel the People now have with the Proprietaries, would then be with both the Proprietaries and Assembly. There seems to remain, then, but one Remedy for our Evils, a Remedy approved by Experience, and which has been tried with Success by other Provinces; I mean that of an immediate *Royal Government,* without the Intervention of Proprietary Powers, which, like unnecessary Springs and Movements in a Machine are so apt to produce Disorder. . . .

. . . In fine, it does not appear to me, that this *Change of Government* can possibly hurt us; and I see many Advantages that may flow from it. The Expression, *Change of Government,* seems, indeed, to be too extensive; and is apt to give the Idea of a general and total Change of our Laws and Constitution. It is rather and only a *Change of Governor,* that is, instead of self-interested Proprietaries, a gracious King! His Majesty who has no Views but for the Good of the People, will thenceforth appoint the Governor, who, unshackled by Proprietary Instructions, will be at Liberty to join with the Assembly in enacting wholesome Laws. At present, when the King requires Supplies of his faithful Subjects, and they are willing and desirous to grant them, the Proprietaries intervene and say, *unless our private Interests in certain Particulars are served,* nothing shall be done. This insolent Tribunitial VETO has long encumbered all our Publick Affairs, and been productive of many Mischiefs. By the Measure proposed, not even the Proprietaries can justly complain of any Injury. The being oblig'd to fulfill a fair Contract is no Injury. The Crown will be under no Difficulty in compleating the old Contract made with their Father, as there needs no Application to Parliament for the necessary Sum, since half the Quit-Rents of the Lower Counties belongs to the King, and the many Years Arrears in the Proprietaries' Hands, who are the Collectors, must vastly exceed what they have a Right to demand, or any Reason to expect.

On the whole, I cannot but think, the more the Proposal is considered, of *an humble Petition to the* King *to take this Province under his Majesty's immediate Protection and Government,* the more unanimously we shall go into it. We are chiefly People of *three Countries: British* Spirits can no longer bear the Treatment they have received, nor will they put on the Chains prepared for them by a Fellow Subject. And the *Irish* and *Germans* have felt too severely the Oppressions of *hard-hearted Landlords and arbitrary Princes,* to wish to see, in the Proprietaries of *Pennsylvania,* both the one and the other united.

THE FOOLISHNESS

OF BRITISH COMMERCIAL RESTRICTIONS

Nothing more offended Franklin's sense of the benefit to all of a free exchange of goods than the trade restrictions secured from Parliament by special interests. The restraints, Franklin hinted, posed a threat to the prosperity and ultimately to the very existence of the British Empire.

. . . We are in your Hands as Clay in the Hands of the Potter; and so in one more Particular than is generally consider'd: for as the Potter cannot waste or spoil his Clay without injuring himself, so I think there is scarce anything you can do that may be hurtful to us, but what will be as much or more so to you. This must be our chief Security; for Interest with you we have but little. The West Indians vastly outweigh us of the Northern Colonies. What we get above a Subsistence we lay out with you for your Manufactures.

Writings, IV, 243-245; from a letter to Peter Collinson, April 30, 1764.

Therefore what you get from us in Taxes you must lose in Trade. The Cat can yield but her skin. And as you must have the whole Hide, if you first cut Thongs out of it, 'tis at your own Expence. The same in regard to our Trade with the foreign West India Islands. If you restrain it in any Degree, you restrain in the same Proportion our Power of making Remittances to you & of course our Demand for your Goods; for you will not clothe us out of Charity, tho' to receive 100 per cent for it in Heaven. In time perhaps Mankind may be wise enough to let Trade take its own Course, find its own Channels, and regulate its own Proportions, etc. At present, most of the Edicts of Princes, Placaerts, Laws & Ordinances of Kingdoms & States for that purpose, prove political Blunders. The Advantages they produce not being *general* for the Commonwealth; but *particular,* to private Persons or Bodies in the State who procur'd them, and *at the Expence of the rest of the People.* Does no body see, that if you confine us in America to your own Sugar Islands for that Commodity, it must raise the Price of it upon you in England? Just so much as the Price advances, so much is every Englishman tax'd to the West Indians.

Apropos, Now we are on the Subject of Trade and Manufactures, let me tell you a Piece of News, that though it might displease a very respectable Body among you, the Button-makers, will be agreable to yourself as a Virtuoso; It is, that we have discover'd a Beach in a Bay several Miles round, the Pebbles of which are all in the Form of Buttons, whence it is called *Button-mold Bay;* where thousands of Tons may be had for fetching; and as the Sea washes down the slaty Cliff, more are continually manufacturing out of the Fragments by the Surge. I send you a Specimen of Coat, Wastecoat & Sleeve Buttons; just as Nature has turn'd them. But I think I must not mention the Place, lest some Englishman get a Patent for this *Button-*

mine, as one did for the *Coalmine* at Louisburgh, and by neither suffering others to work it, nor working it himself, deprive us of the Advantage God & Nature seem to have intended us. As we have now got Buttons, 'tis something towards our Cloathing; and who knows but in time we may find out where to get Cloth?—for as to our being always supply'd by you, 'tis folly to expect it. Only consider *the rate of our Increase*, and tell me if you can increase your Wooll in that Proportion, and where, in your little Island you can feed the Sheep. Nature has put Bounds to your Abilities, tho' none to your Desires. Britain would, if she could, manufacture & trade for all the World; England for all Britain;—London for all England;—and every Londoner for all London. So selfish is the human Mind! But 'tis well there is One above that rules these Matters with a more equal Hand. He that is pleas'd to feed the Ravens, will undoubtedly take care to prevent a Monopoly of the Carrion. . . .

ON PASSAGE OF THE STAMP ACT

Though the first of these letters has often been cited as evidence that Franklin too readily acquiesed in the Stamp Act, in fact he himself had it printed, together with Thomson's reply underscoring the Act's oppressive aspects and the violent opposition it might arouse, in a London newspaper as part of a campaign for its repeal. Its last two sentences appear not to have been in the original sent to Thomson, but apparently were added

---

Writings, IV, 390, 391–392, and Crane, *Franklin's Letters to the Press* (Chapel Hill, N. C.:, The University of North Carolina Press, 1950), p. 36; from letters to Charles Thomson, July 11, 1765, and to John Hughes, August 9, 1765. The paragraph from the letter to Thomson, with the two additional sentences, appeared in the *London Chronicle*, November 16, 1765.

by Franklin when he gave it to the newspaper as part of his persistent effort to convince English merchants that America did not *need* her trade with Britain. The second letter, to the man for whom Franklin secured the stamp agent's office in Philadelphia, shows more candidly what Franklin thought America's response to the Stamp Act should be.

. . . Depend upon it, my good neighbour, I took every step in my power to prevent the passing of the Stamp Act. Nobody could be more concerned in interest than myself to oppose it sincerely and heartily. But the Tide was too strong against us. The nation was provoked by American Claims of Independence, and all Parties joined in resolving by this act to settle the point. We might as well have hindered the sun's setting. That we could not do. But since 'tis down, my Friend, and it may be long before it rises again, let us make as good a night of it as we can. We may still light candles. Frugality and Industry will go a great way toward indemnifying us. Idleness and Pride tax with a heavier hand than Kings and Parliaments; if we can get rid of the former, we may easily bear the latter. Our country produces, or is capable of producing, all the *necessaries* of life, the wasting *superfluities* come from hence. Let us have but the wisdom to be content awhile with our own, and this country will soon feel, that its loss in point of commerce, is infinitely more than its gain in taxes.

. . . The Account you give me of the Indiscretion of some People with you, concerning the Government here, I do not wonder at. 'Tis of a Piece with the rest of their Conduct. But the Rashness of the Assembly in Virginia is amazing! I hope however that ours will keep within the Bounds of Prudence and Moderation; for that is the only way to lighten or get clear of our Burthens.

As to the Stamp Act, tho' we purpose doing our Endeavour to get it repeal'd, in which I am sure you would concur with us, yet the Success is uncertain: — If it continues, your undertaking to execute it may make you unpopular for a Time, but your acting with Coolness and Steadiness, and with every Circumstance in your Power of Favour to the People, will by degrees reconcile them. In the mean time, a firm Loyalty to the Crown & faithful Adherence to the Government of this Nation, which it is the Safety as well as Honour of the Colonies to be connected with, will always be the wisest Course for you and I to take, whatever may be the Madness of the Populace or their blind Leaders, who can only bring themselves and Country into Trouble and draw on greater Burthens by Acts of rebellious Tendency — . . . .

REPEAL OF THE STAMP ACT

During December 1765 and January 1766, after news of the riots in America over the Stamp Act reached England and while its repeal was under consideration in Parliament, Franklin conducted a vigorous campaign in London newspapers urging repeal and defending America from aspersions cast by supporters of the Act. On December 28, 1765, Franklin wrote this letter in response to a letter signed "Vindex Patriae" attacking American manners, character, and concepts of government.

I would fain know what good purpose can be answered, by the frequent invectives published in your and other papers against the Americans. Do these small writers hope to provoke the nation by their oratory, to embrue its hands

Crane, *Franklin's Letters to the Press*, pp. 42–59; *Writings*, IV, 393–395; from letters printed in the London *Gazetteer* and the *Public Advertiser*, December 28, 1765 – January 29, 1766.

in the blood of its, perhaps mistaken children? And if this should be done, do they imagine it could be of any advantage to this country? Do they expect to convince the Americans, and reduce them to submission, by their flimsey arguments of *virtual representation,* and *of Englishmen by fiction of law only,* mixed with insolence, contempt, and abuse? Can it be supposed that such treatment will make them rest satisfied with the unlimited claim set up, of a power to tax them *ad libitum,* without their consent; while they are to work only for us, and our profit; restrained in their foreign trade by our laws, however profitable it might be to them; forbidden to manufacture their own produce, and obliged to purchase the work of our artificers at our own prices? Is this the state we wish to keep them in? And can it be thought such writings (which are unfortunately reprinted in all *their* papers) will induce them to bear it with greater patience, and during a longer period of time?

The gentle terms of *republican race, mixed rabble of Scotch, Irish and foreign vagabonds, descendants of convicts, ungrateful rebels* &c. are some of the sweet flowers of English rhetorick, with which our colonists have of late been regaled. Surely, if we are so much their superiors, we should shew the superiority of our breeding by our better manners! Our slaves they may be thought: But every master of slaves ought to know, that though all the slave possesses is the property of the master, his *good-will* is his own, he bestows it where he pleases; and it is of *some importance* to the master's *profit,* if he can obtain that *good-will* at the cheap rate of a few kind words, with fair and gentle usage.

These people, however, are not, never were, nor ever will be our slaves. The first settlers of New England particularly, were English gentlemen of fortune, who, being Puritans, left this country with their families and followers, in times of persecution, for the sake of enjoying, though in a wilderness, the blessings of civil and religious liberty; of which they retain to this day, as high a sense as any Briton whatsoever; and possess as much virtue, humanity, civility, and let me add, *loyalty to their Prince*, as is to be found among the like number of people in any part of the world; and the other colonies merit and maintain the same character. They should then be treated with *decency* and with *candour*.

Your correspondent Vindex Patriae, who is indeed more of a reasoner than a railer, has nevertheless thought fit to assert, that "their refusing submission to the stamp act, proceeds *only* from their *ambition* of becoming *independent*; and that it is plain the colonies have no other aim but a *total enfranchisement* from obedience to our Parliament." These are strong charges; but the proofs of such ambitious and rebellious views no where appear in his paper. He has, however, condescended to give us his proofs of another point, viz. "That the colonies have no tenderness for their mother country;" (and of course I suppose, the mother country is to have none for them.) "The sugar, teas, and other commodities, says he, which they daily buy from St. Eustatia and Monte Christi, in particular, are too *convincing proofs*, that they have *no tenderness* for their mother country." May one ask this profound writer; are sugar and teas the produce of the mother country? does not she herself buy her teas from strangers? were the North Americans to buy all the sugars they consume, even of our own Islands, would not that raise the price of such sugars upon us here in England? is not then their buying them of Foreigners, if it proves any thing, a Proof rather of their tenderness for the mother country? But the grocerly argument of tea and sugar, is not inferior to the lawyerly argument with which he demonstrates that, "by a *fiction* between us and the colonists,

Connecticut is in England, and therefore represented in the British parliament." I am afraid the common Americans will be as much at a loss as I am, to understand what he means by his *estoppers*, and his *averments*, and therefore not in the least convinced by his demonstration. They will only find out upon the whole, that he is not their friend; and perhaps conclude from that and his learning in the law, that he is one of their *virtual representatives* by *fiction* in P——t.

I hope, however, to see prudent measures taken by our rulers, such as may heal and not widen our breaches. The Americans, I am sure, for I know them, have not the least desire of independence; they submit, in general, to all the laws we make for them; they desire only a continuance of what they think a *right*, the privilege of manifesting their loyalty by granting their own money, when the occasions of their prince shall call for it. This right they say they have always enjoyed and exercised, and never misused; and they think it wrong that any body of men whatever, should claim a power of giving what is not their own, and make to themselves a merit with the sovereign and their own constituents, by granting away the property of others who have no representatives in that body, and therefore make no part of the *common consent in parliament,* by which alone, according to *magna charta* and the *petition of right,* taxes can be legally laid upon the subject. These are their notions. They may be errors; 'tis a part of our common constitution perhaps not hitherto sufficiently considered. 'Tis fit for the discussion of wise and learned men, who will, I doubt not, settle it wisely and benevolently. Cowardice and cruelty are indeed almost inseparable companions, and none are more ready to propose sending out fleets and armies, and to expose friends and foes to one common carnage, than such pusillanimous men as would tremble at a sword drawn in their presence tho' with the most peaceable Intention. But Britons, as a people, are equally brave and generous; prodigal of their blood and treasure where there are just calls for its expence; and by no means niggards of those rights, liberties and privileges, that make the subjects of Britain the envy and admiration of the universe.

[Responding again to "Vindex Patriae" on January 15, 1766, Franklin defended the American diet, observance of the Sabbath, and all the non-English Britons disdained by the imperious "Vindex."]

JOHN BULL shews in nothing more his great veneration for good eating, and how much he is always thinking of his belly, than in his making it the constant topic of his contempt for other nations, that *they do not eat so well as himself*. The *roast beef of Old England* he is always exulting in, as if no other country had beef to roast; — reproaching, on every occasion, the *Welsh* with their leeks and toasted cheese, the *Irish* with their potatoes, and the *Scotch* with their oatmeal. And now that we are a little out of favour with him, he has begun, by his attorney VINDEX PATRIAE, to examine our eating and drinking, in order, I apprehend, to fix some horrible scandal of the same kind upon us poor *Americans*.

I did but say a word or two in favour of *Indian corn*, which he had treated as "disagreable and indigestible," and this vindictive gentleman grows angry. "Let him tell the world, IF HE DARES (says he) that the Americans prefer it to a place at their own tables." Ah, Sir, I see the dilemma you have prepared for me. If I should not *dare* to say, that we do prefer it to a place at our tables, then you demonstrate, that we must come to England for tea, or go without our breakfasts: and if I do *dare* to say it, you fix upon me and my countrymen for ever, the indelible disgrace of being *Indian corn-eaters*.

I am afraid, Mr. Printer, that you will think this too trifling a dispute to deserve a place in your paper: but, pray, good sir, consider, as you are yourself an Englishman, that we Americans, who are allowed even by Mr. VINDEX to have some English blood in our veins, may think it a very serious thing to have the honour of our eating impeached in any particular whatsoever.

"Why doth he not deny the fact (says VINDEX) that it is assigned to the slaves for their food? To proclaim the *wholesomeness* of this corn, without assigning a reason why white men give it to their slaves, when they can get other food, is only satirizing the good sense of their brethren in America." In truth I cannot deny the fact, though it should reflect ever so much on the *good sense* of my countrymen. I own we do give food made of Indian corn to our slaves, as well as eat it ourselves; not, as you suppose, because it is *"indigestible* and *unwholesome";* but because it keeps them healthy, strong and hearty, and fit to go through all the labour we require of them. Our slaves, Sir, cost us money, and we buy them to make money by their labour. If they are sick, they are not only unprofitable, but expensive. Where then was your *English good sense,* when you imagined we gave our slaves our Indian corn, because we knew it to be *unwholesome?*

In short, this is only another of Mr. VINDEX's paradoxes, in which he is a great dealer. The first endeavoured to persuade us, that we were represented in the British Parliament *virtually,* and by *fiction:* — Then that we were *really* represented there, because the Manor of East Greenwich in Kent is represented there, and all the Americans live in East Greenwich. And now he undertakes to prove to us, that taxes are the most profitable things in the world to those that pay them; for that Scotland is grown rich since the Union, by paying English taxes. I wish he would accommodate himself a little better to our dull capacities. We Americans have a great many heavy taxes of our own, to support our several governments, and pay off the enormous debt contracted by the war; we never conceived ourselves the richer for paying taxes, and are willing to leave all new ones to those that like them. At least, if we must with Scotland, participate in your taxes, let us likewise, with Scotland, participate in the Union, and in all the privileges and advantages of commerce that accompanied it.

VINDEX, however, will never consent to this. He has made us partakers in all the odium with which he thinks fit to load Scotland:—"They resemble the Scots in sentiments, (says he) their religion is Scottish; their customs and *laws* are Scottish; like the Scotch they Judaically observe what *they call* the Sabbath, persecute old women for witches, are intolerant to other sects, &c." But we must not, like the Scots, be admitted into Parliament; for that, he thinks, would increase "the Scotch interest in England, which is equally hostile to the cause of liberty, and the cause of our church."

Pray, Sir, who informed you that our "*laws* are Scottish?" The same, I suppose, that told you our Indian corn is unwholesome. Indeed, Sir, your information is very imperfect. The common law of England is, I assure you, the common law of the colonies: and if the civil law is what you mean by the Scottish law, we have none of it but which is forced upon us by England, in its courts of Admiralty, depriving us of that inestimable part of the common law, trials by juries. And do you look upon keeping the *Sabbath,* as part of the Scottish law? "The Americans, like the Scots, (you say) observe what *they call* the Sabbath." Pray, Sir, you who are so zealous for your church (in abusing other Christians) what *do you call* it? and where the harm of their *observing* it? If you look into your prayer-book, or over your altars, you will find these words written, *Remember to keep holy the* SABBATH *Day.* This law, tho' it may be observed in Scotland, and has been *countenanced* by some of your statutes, is, Sir, originally one of *God's Commandments:* a body of laws still in force in America, tho' they may have become *obsolete* in *some other* countries.

Give me leave, Master JOHN BULL, to remind you, that you are *related to all mankind;* and therefore it less becomes you than any body, to affront and abuse other nations. But you have mixed with your many virtues, a pride, a haughtiness, and an insolent contempt for all but yourself, that, I am afraid, will, if not abated, procure you one day or other a handsome drubbing. Besides your rudeness to foreigners, you are far from being civil even to your own family. The Welch you have always despised for submitting to your government: But why despise your own English, who conquered and settled Ireland for you; who conquered and settled America for you? Yet these you now think you may treat as you please, because, forsooth, they are a *conquered* people. Why despise the Scotch, who fight and die for you all over the world? Remember, you courted Scotland for one hundred years, and would fain have had your *wicked will* of her. She virtuously resisted all your importunities, but at length kindly consented to become your lawful wife. You then solemnly promised to *love, cherish,* and *honour* her, as long as you both should live; and yet you have ever since treated her with the utmost contumely, which you now begin to extend to your common children. But, pray, when your enemies are uniting in a *Family Compact* against you, can it be discreet in you to kick up in your own house a *Family Quarrel?* And at the very time you are inviting foreigners to settle on your lands, and when you have more to settle than ever you had before, is it prudent to suffer your lawyer, VINDEX, to abuse those who have settled there already, because they cannot yet speak "Plain English?"—It is my opinion, Master BULL, that the Scotch and Irish, as well as the colonists, are capable of speaking much *plainer English* than they have ever yet spoke, but which I hope they will never be provoked to speak.

To be brief, Mr. VINDEX, I pass over your other accusations of the Americans, and of the Scotch, that we "Persecute old women for witches, and are intolerant to other sects," observing only, that we were wise enough to leave off both those foolish tricks, long before Old England made the act of toleration, or repealed the statute against witchcraft; so that even *you yourself* may safely travel through all Scotland and the Colonies, without the least danger of being persecuted as a churchman, or taken (up) for a conjurer. And yet I own myself so far of an intolerant spirit, that though I thank you for the box-in-the-ear you have given TOM HINT, as being, what you justly call him, "a futile calumniator," I cannot but wish he would give you another—for the same reason.

One word more, however, about the *Indian corn*, which I began and must end with, even though I should hazard your remarking that it is certainly "indigestible," as it plainly appears to *stick in my stomach*. "Let him tell the world. IF HE DARES, (you say) that the Americans prefer it to a place at their tables."—And, pray, if I should DARE, —what then?—why then—"You would enter upon a discussion of its salubrity and pleasant taste."—Really? —Would you venture to write on the salubrity and *pleasant taste* of Indian corn, when you never in your life have tasted a *single grain* of if?—But why should that hinder you writing on it? Have you not written even on *politics?*

[In a final essay Franklin rejected more of "Vindex Patriae's" slurs on America, and introduced a theme which was to prove crucial to his conclusion, nine years later, that America had to be independent: to remain connected with

England would mean only to be poisoned by her corruption and depravity.]

In your paper of Friday last, VINDEX PATRIAE justifies his involving all the people of the colonies in the guilt of the late riots, because they were not prevented. He seems not to have considered that riots are sudden things which often are not foreseen, and therefore cannot be prevented. Scarce a year passes, in which England, and even London, how well soever governed, do not afford ample instances of this, which are therefore never, by reasonable people, imputed to the "whole community."

His repeated arguments about "East Greenwich" and "*America in England*," and the "total illegality of the power of assemblies to raise money," I pass over, as I do not find that any body is convinced by them, but himself, and I believe no one elsewhere will be. I would only remark another instance of his unacquaintance with facts. He denies, that the people of New England are restrained (as I heard they were) in "working their own beaver into hats, their wool into cloth, or their iron into steel:"—Let him but consult the statutes under the several heads, and he will see how much those operations are fettered in America, and perhaps be sensible of his mistake.

His justification of the abuses with which he has treated the Americans, is curious. "I agree, says he, that reflections on the morals of the Americans ought to be shunned, *except when the Americans make it necessary to display their true character*. Had it never been proposed to subject us to America, by introducing Members from thence into our legislature, I had never touched that point; but when a proposal of this sort is made, it is necessary that their *true characters* should be looked into and published," &c. Now after affirming, from my certain knowledge of, and long acquaintance with both countries, that the "Morals of the

Americans" in general, considered in the whole *as a people*, are much purer, much less corrupt, than the general morals of the *English*, a difference naturally to be expected, and always to be expected, between *young* countries and *old* ones; the remark of SWIFT being equally applicable to states as to single persons, when he said, he would venture great odds in a wager, that the *greatest* knave in England was the *oldest*. I say, after affirming this of the Americans, and observing, that whatever might *"make it necessary* to display their *true character,* nothing could make it necessary to give them a *false one";* I would ask this gentleman, where is the foundation he mentions for supposing "The Americans made it necessary" to give them any character at all? Have *they* ever "proposed to introduce Members from thence into the legislature here?" Has there ever been the least petition, memorial, or request to that purpose sent hither from America? Does he imagine the people there have the least inclination towards it?—If he does, he never was more mistaken. There never was any danger to the public, which he had less reason to apprehend. For in the first place, the Americans not only *never have,* asked such a privilege, but, he may depend on it, *they never will;* for they have not the least conception that it could be of any use to them. They are contented with their own little legislatures, if they may be permitted to enjoy the privileges belonging to them. They read the political papers and pamphlets of this country; they see that the parties, into which the great are continually divided, are for ever mutually accusing each other with the grossest *venality* and *corruption*. At so great a distance, they can be but little acquainted with the particular merit of personal characters, and therefore, to be impartial, they believe both sides. They could propose to themselves no advantage, if they did not send their best and honestest men; and those they are not willing to expose to the danger of being corrupted, or themselves to the *legal* mischiefs that might be the consequence of such corruption. In the next place, though I think it *highly* to the *interest* of *this country* to consolidate its dominions, by *inviting*, and even (if it has a power) *compelling* the Americans as well as the Irish to submit to an union, send representatives hither, and make one common P——t of the whole; yet I am persuaded that *will never be done*, as every ministry has already difficulty enough to satisfy those, who think they have a right to divide, or to recommend the division of all posts, profits and emoluments; and those who think they have such right, will never agree to increase their own number, by which the chance in favour of each would be diminished. Agreable to the shrewd remark of one of Sir *Robert Walpole's* friends, that of late he found their party increasing, which he did not like. How so, says Sir *Robert*. Why, z——ds, Sir, says he, don't we lie *two in a bed* already?

AN EXAMINATION

BEFORE THE HOUSE OF COMMONS

Franklin's appearance before the House of Commons to answer questions about taxation in America established his standing as *the* American representative in Great Britain. His direct, moderate, well-informed answers impressed Englishmen, and his stout defense of American rights made him a champion to his fellow colonials. The frequent reprinting of the transcript of the interrogation on both sides of the Atlantic made it a major

---

Writings, IV, 412–448; Franklin appeared in the House of Commons on February 12–13, 1766; the transcript was first printed in North America in September 1766, and in England in 1767.

contribution to the constitutional controversy leading to the American Revolution.

Q. What is your name, and place of abode?
A. Franklin, of Philadelphia.
Q. Do the Americans pay any considerable taxes among themselves?
A. Certainly many, and very heavy taxes.
Q. What are the present taxes in Pennsylvania, laid by the laws of the colony?
A. There are taxes on all estates real and personal, a poll tax, a tax on all offices, professions, trades and businesses, according to their profits; an excise on all wine, rum, and other spirits; and a duty of Ten Pounds per head on all Negroes imported, with some other duties.
Q. For what purposes are those taxes laid?
A. For the support of the civil and military establishments of the country, and to discharge the heavy debt contracted in the last war.
Q. How long are those taxes to continue?
A. Those for discharging the debt are to continue till 1772, and longer, if the debt should not be then all discharged. The others must always continue.
Q. Was it not expected that the debt would have been sooner discharged?
A. It was, when the peace was made with France and Spain — But, a fresh war breaking out with the Indians, a fresh load of debt was incurred; and the taxes, of course, continued longer by a new law.
Q. Are not all the people very able to pay those taxes?
A. No. The frontier counties, all along the continent, having been frequently ravaged by the enemy and greatly impoverished, are able to pay very little tax. And therefore,

in consideration of their distresses, our late tax laws do expressly favour those counties, excusing the sufferers; and I suppose the same is done in other governments. . . .

Q. What may be the amount of one year's imports into Pennsylvania from Britain?

A. I have been informed that our merchants compute the imports from Britain to be above 500,000 Pounds.

Q. What may be the amount of the produce of your province exported to Britain?

A. It must be small, as we produce little that is wanted in Britain. I suppose it cannot exceed 40,000 Pounds.

Q. How then do you pay the balance?

A. The balance is paid by our produce carried to the West-Indies, and sold in our own islands, or to the French, Spaniards, Danes, and Dutch; by the same carried to other colonies in North-America, as to New-England, Nova-Scotia, Newfoundland, Carolina, and Georgia; by the same, carried to different parts of Europe, as Spain, Portugal, and Italy. In all which places we receive either money, bills of Exchange, or commodities that suit for remittance to Britain; which, together with all the profits on the industry of our merchants and mariners, arising in those circuitous voyages, and the freights made by their ships, center finally in Britain to discharge the balance, and pay for British manufactures continually used in the province, or sold to foreigners by our traders. . . .

Q. Do you think it right that America should be protected by this country and pay no part of the expence?

A. That is not the case. The Colonies raised, cloathed and payed, during the last war, near 25000 men, and spent many millions.

Q. Were you not reimbursed by parliament?

A. We were only reimbursed what, in your opinion, we had advanced beyond our proportion, or beyond what might reasonably be expected from us; and it was a very small part of what we spent. Pennsylvania, in particular, disbursed about 500,000 Pounds, and the reimbursements, in the whole, did not exceed 60,000 Pounds. . . .

Q. Do not you think the people of America would submit to pay the stamp duty, if it was moderated?

A. No, never, unless compelled by force of arms. . . .

Q. What was the temper of America towards Great Britain before the year 1763?

A. The best in the world. They submitted willingly to the government of the Crown, and paid, in all their courts, obedience to acts of parliament. Numerous as the people are in the several provinces, they cost you nothing in forts, citadels, garrisons, or armies, to keep them in subjection. They were governed by this country at the expence only of a little pen, ink and paper. They were led by a thread. They had not only a respect, but an affection for Great-Britain; for its laws, its customs and manners, and even a fondness for its fashions, that greatly increased the commerce. Natives of Britain were always treated with particular regard; to be an Old-England man was, of itself, a character of some respect, and gave a kind of rank among us.

Q. And what is their temper now?

A. O, very much altered.

Q. Did you ever hear the authority of parliament to make laws for America questioned till lately?

A. The authority of parliament was allowed to be valid in all laws, except such as should lay internal taxes. It was never disputed in laying duties to regulate commerce. . . .

Q. In what light did the people of America use to consider the parliament of Great-Britain?

A. They considered the parliament as the great bulwark and security of their liberties and privileges, and always spoke of it with the utmost respect and veneration. Arbitrary ministers, they thought, might possibly, at times, attempt to oppress them; but they relied on it, that the parliament, on application, would always give redress. They remembered, with gratitude, a strong instance of this, when a bill was brought into parliament, with a clause, to make royal instructions laws in the colonies, which the House of Commons would not pass, and it was thrown out.

Q. And have they not still the same respect for parliament?

A. No, it is greatly lessened.

Q. To what causes is that owing?

A. To a concurrence of causes; the restraints lately laid on their trade, by which the bringing of foreign gold and silver into the Colonies was prevented; the prohibition of making paper money among themselves; and then demanding a new and heavy tax by stamps; taking away, at the same time, trials by juries, and refusing to receive and hear their humble petitions. . . .

Q. Have not you heard of the resolutions of this House, and of the House of Lords, asserting the right of parliament relating to America, including a power to tax the people there?

A. Yes, I have heard of such resolutions.

Q. What will be the opinion of the Americans on those resolutions?

A. They will think them unconstitutional and unjust.

Q. Was it an opinion in America before 1763, that the parliament had no right to lay taxes and duties there?

A. I never heard any objection to the right of laying duties to regulate commerce; but a right to lay internal taxes was never supposed to be in parliament, as we are not represented there.

Q. On what do you found your opinion, that the people in America made any such distinction?

A. I know that whenever the subject has occurred in

conversation where I have been present, it has appeared to be the opinion of every one, that we could not be taxed by a parliament where we were not represented. But the payment of duties laid by an act of parliament, as regulations of commerce, was never disputed. . . .

Q. But in case a governor, acting by instruction, should call on an assembly to raise the necessary supplies, and the assembly should refuse to do it, do you not think it would then be for the good of the people of the colony, as well as necessary to government, that the parliament should tax them?

A. I do not think it would be necessary. If an assembly could possibly be so absurd, as to refuse raising the supplies requisite for the maintenance of government among them, they could not long remain in such a situation; the disorders and confusion occasioned by it must soon bring them to reason.

Q. If it should not, ought not the right to be in Great Britain of applying a remedy?

A. A right, only to be used in such a case, I should have no objection to; supposing it to be used merely for the good of the people of the Colony.

Q. But who is to judge of that, Britain or the Colony?

A. Those that feel can best judge.

Q. You say the Colonies have always submitted to external taxes, and object to the right of parliament only in laying internal taxes; now can you shew, that there is any kind of difference between the two taxes to the Colony on which they may be laid?

A. I think the difference is very great. An external tax is a duty laid on commodities imported; that duty is added to the first cost and other charges on the commodity, and, when it is offered to sale, makes a part of the price. If the people do not like it at that price, they refuse it; they are not obliged to pay it. But an internal tax is forced from the people without their consent, if not laid by their own representatives. The stamp act says, we shall have no commerce, make no exchange of property with each other, neither purchase, nor grant, nor recover debts; we shall neither marry nor make our wills, unless we pay such and such sums; and thus it is intended to extort our money from us, or ruin us by the consequences of refusing to pay it. . . .

Q. Can any thing less than a military force carry the stamp act into execution?

A. I do not see how a military force can be applied to that purpose.

Q. Why may it not?

A. Suppose a military force sent into America, they will find nobody in arms; what are they then to do? They cannot force a man to take stamps who chuses to do without them. They will not find a rebellion; they may indeed make one.

Q. If the act is not repealed, what do you think will be the consequences?

A. A total loss of the respect and affection the people of America bear to this country, and of all the commerce that depends on that respect and affection.

Q. How can the commerce be affected?

A. You will find, that if the act is not repealed, they will take very little of your manufactures in a short time.

Q. Is it in their power to do without them?

A. I think they may very well do without them.

Q. Is it their interest not to take them?

A. The goods they take from Britain are either necessaries, mere conveniences, or superfluities. The first, as cloth, &c. with a little industry they can make at home; the second they can do without, till they are able to provide them among themselves; and the last, which are much the greatest part, they will strike off immediately. They are mere articles of fashion, purchased and consumed because the fashion in a respected country; but will now be detested and rejected. The people have already struck off, by general agreement, the use of all goods fashionable in mournings, and many thousand pounds worth are sent back as unsaleable.

Q. Is it their interest to make cloth at home?

A. I think they may at present get it cheaper from Britain, I mean of the same fineness and workmanship; but, when one considers other circumstances, the restraints on their trade, and the difficulty of making remittances, it is their interest to make every thing.

Q. Suppose an act of internal regulations connected with a tax; how would they receive it?

A. I think it would be objected to.

Q. Then no regulation with a tax would be submitted to?

A. Their opinion is, that, when aids to the Crown are wanted, they are to be asked of the several assemblies, according to the old established usage; who will, as they always have done, grant them freely. And that their money ought not to be given away, without their consent, by persons at a distance, unacquainted with their circumstances and abilities. The granting aids to the Crown is the only means they have of recommending themselves to their sovereign; and they think it extremely hard and unjust, that a body of men, in which they have no representatives, should make a merit to itself of giving and granting what is not its own, but theirs; and deprive them of a right they esteem of the utmost value and importance, as it is the security of all their other rights. . . .

Q. But suppose Great-Britain should be engaged in a war in Europe, would North-America contribute to the support of it?

A. I do think they would as far as their circumstances

would permit. They consider themselves as a part of the British empire, and as having one common interest with it; they may be looked on here as foreigners, but they do not consider themselves as such. They are zealous for the honour and prosperity of this nation; and, while they are well used, will always be ready to support it, as far as their little power goes. . . .

Q. Do you think the assemblies have a right to levy money on the subject there, to grant to the Crown?

A. I certainly think so; they have always done it.

Q. Are they acquainted with the declaration of rights? And do they know, that, by that statute, money is not to be raised on the subject but by consent of parliament?

A. They are very well acquainted with it.

Q. How then can they think they have a right to levy money for the Crown, or for any other than local purposes?

A. They understand that clause to relate to subjects only within the realm; that no money can be levied on them for the Crown, but by consent of parliament. The Colonies are not supposed to be within the realm; they have assemblies of their own, which are their parliaments, and they are, in that respect, in the same situation with Ireland. When money is to be raised for the Crown upon the subject in Ireland, or in the Colonies, the consent is given in the Parliament of Ireland, or in the assemblies of the Colonies. They think the parliament of Great-Britain cannot properly give that consent, till it has representatives from America; for the petition of right expressly says, it is to be by common consent in parliament; and the people of America have no representatives in parliament, to make a part of that common consent. . . .

Q. If the stamp act should be repealed, would it induce the assemblies of America to acknowledge the rights of parliament to tax them, and would they erase their resolutions?

A. No, never.

Q. Are there no means of obliging them to erase those resolutions?

A. None that I know of; they will never do it, unless compelled by force of arms.

Q. Is there a power on earth that can force them to erase them?

A. No power, how great soever, can force men to change their opinions. . . .

Q. What used to be the pride of the Americans?

A. To indulge in the fashions and manufactures of Great Britain.

Q. What is now their pride?

A. To wear their old cloaths over again, till they can make new ones.

THE AMERICAN INTEREST IN PARLIAMENT

Though Franklin gave strong expression to American rights in opposing the Stamp Act, he nevertheless continued to believe American interests could be defended within the frame of British government by encouraging the factions in England well-disposed toward the colonies.

Our Friends here are in Pain, lest the Condescension of Parliament, in repealing the Stamp-Act, will encourage the Americans to farther Excesses; and our Enemies, who have predicted it, hope to see their Prophecies fulfilled, that they may disgrace the present Ministry; but I hope we shall behave prudently, and disappoint them, which will

---

Crane, *Franklin's Letters to the Press*, p. 76; from a letter to Joseph Galloway, April 12, 1766.

establish the Ministry, and *thereby effectually secure* the American Interest in Parliament. Indeed I wish this Ministry well, for their own Sakes, as well as ours, as they appear to me to be really very honest worthy Men, with the best Intentions; by no means deficient in Abilities, very attentive to Business, and of course daily improving in their Acquaintance with it. . . .

ON A COMMON PARLIAMENT FOR THE BRITISH EMPIRE

No question interested Franklin more, nor was more important to a final settlement of the dispute between mother country and colonies, than that of how the parts could maintain control over local questions and yet submit to the authority of the whole. Franklin explained his opinion shortly after repeal of the Stamp Act.

. . . My private opinion concerning a union in Parliament between the two countries is, that it would be best for the whole. But I think it will never be done. For though I believe, that, if we had no more representatives than Scotland has, we should be sufficiently strong in the House to prevent, as they do for Scotland, any thing ever passing to our disadvantage; yet we are not able at present to furnish and maintain such a number, and, when we are more able, we shall be less willing than we are now. The Parliament here do at present think too highly of themselves to admit representatives from us, if we should ask it; and, when they will be desirous of granting it, we shall

---

Writings, IV, 456; from a letter to Cadwallader Evans, May 9, 1766.

think too highly of ourselves to accept of it. It would certainly contribute to the strength of the whole, if Ireland and all the dominions were united and consolidated under one common council for general purposes, each retaining its particular council or parliament for its domestic concerns. But this should have been more early provided for. In the infancy of our foreign establishments it was neglected, or was not thought of. And now the affair is nearly in the situation of Friar Bacon's project of making a brazen wall round England for its eternal security. His servant, Friar Bungey, slept while the brazen head, which was to dictate how it might be done, said *Time is,* and *Time was.* He only waked to hear it say, *Time is past.* An explosion followed, that tumbled their house about the conjuror's ears. . . .

THE USES OF PAPER CURRENCY

A report by the Board of Trade, February 9, 1764, gave six reasons for restraining the issue of paper currency in America, most of them directed at emissions to which it objected in particular colonies. Franklin defended colonial monetary practices generally and set down the necessary qualities of a circulating medium that would be adequate for an expanding trade. The Board's reasons to which Franklin responded are set in italics.

. . . That Paper Money carries the Gold and Silver out of the Province, and so ruins the Country, as Experience has shewn in every Colony where it has been practised in any great Degree. This seems to be a mere speculative

---

Writings, V, 2–9; from "Remarks" printed in the *Pennsylvania Chronicle,* June 1, 1767, but probably drafted in March 1767.

Opinion, not founded on Fact in any of the Colonies. The Truth is, that the Balance of their Trade with Britain being generally against them, the Gold and Silver is drawn out to pay that Balance; and then the Necessity of some Medium of Trade has induced the making of Paper Money, which could not be carried away. Thus, if carrying out all the Gold and Silver ruins a Country, every Colony was ruined before it made Paper Money. But, far from being ruined by it, the Colonies, that have made Use of Paper Money, have been and are all in a thriving Condition. Their Debt indeed to *Britain* has increased, because their Numbers, and of course their Trade, has increased; for all Trade having always a Proportion of Debt outstanding, which is paid in its Turn, while fresh Debt is contracted, that Proportion of Debt naturally increases as the Trade increases; but the Improvement and Increase of Estates in the Colonies has been in a greater Proportion than their Debt. . . .

. . . That every Medium of Trade should have an intrinsic Value, which Paper Money has not: Gold and Silver are therefore the fittest for this Medium, as they are an Equivalent, which Paper never can be. However fit a particular Thing may be for a particular Purpose, wherever that Thing is not to be had, or not to be had in sufficient Plenty, it becomes necessary to use something else, the fittest that can be got, in lieu of it. Gold and Silver are not the Produce of *North-America,* which has no Mines; and that which is brought thither, cannot be kept there in sufficient Quantity for a Currency. *Britain,* an independent great State, when its Inhabitants grow too fond of the expensive Luxuries of foreign Countries, that draw away its Money, can, and frequently does, make Laws to discourage or prohibit such Importations; and, by that Means, can retain its Cash.

The Colonies are dependent Governments, and their People, having naturally great Respect for the sovereign

Country, and being thence immoderately fond of its Modes, Manufactures, and Superfluities, cannot be restrained, in purchasing them, by any Province Law; because such Law, if made there, would immediately be repealed here as prejudicial to the Trade and Interest of *Britain*. It seems hard therefore to draw all their real Money from them, and then refuse them the poor Privilege of using Paper instead of it. Bank Bills and Bankers' Notes are daily used here as a Medium of Trade, and in large Dealings perhaps the greater Part is transacted by their Means; and yet they have no intrinsic Value, but rest on the Credit of those that issue them, as Paper Bills in the Colonies do on the Credit of the respective Governments there: Their being payable in Cash upon Sight by the Drawers, is indeed a Circumstance that cannot attend the Colony Bills for the Reason just above mentioned, their Cash being drawn from them by the *British* Trade; but the legal Tender being substituted in its Place, is rather a greater Advantage to the Possessor, since he need not be at the Trouble of going to a particular Bank or Banker to demand his Money, finding wherever he has Occasion to lay out Money in the Province, a Person that is obliged to take the Bills. So that even out of the Province, the Knowledge that every Man within that Province is obliged to take its Money, gives the Bills a Credit among its Neighbours nearly equal to what they have at home. And were it not for the Laws here, [in England] that restrain or prohibit, as much as possible, all losing Trades, the Cash of this Country would soon be exported; every Merchant, who had Occasion to remit it, would run to the Bank with all its Bills, that came into his Hands, and take out his Part of its Treasure for that Purpose, so that in a short Time it would be no more able to pay Bills in Money upon Sight, than it is now in the Power of a Colony Treasury so to do. If Government afterwards should have Occasion for the

Credit of the Bank, it must of Necessity make its Bills a legal Tender, funding them however on Taxes by which they may in Time be paid off, as has been the general Practice in the Colonies.

At this very Time even the Silver Money in *England* is obliged to the legal Tender for Part of its Value, that Part which is the Difference between its real Weight and its Denomination. Great Part of the Shillings and Sixpences now current, are by wearing become 5, 10, 20, and some of the Sixpences even 50 *per Cent.* too light. For this Difference between the *real* and *nominal*, you have no *intrinsic* Value, you have not so much as Paper, you have nothing. It is the legal Tender only, that makes Three-Pennyworth of Silver pass for Sixpence. Gold and Silver have undoubtedly some Properties, that give them a Fitness above Paper, as a Medium of Exchange; particularly their universal Estimation, especially in Cases where a Country has Occasion to carry its Money abroad, either as a Stock to trade with, or to purchase Allies and foreign Succours; otherwise that very universal Estimation is an Inconvenience which Paper Money is free from, since it tends to deprive a Country of even the Quantity of Currency that should be retained as a necessary Instrument of its internal Commerce; and obliges it to be continually on its Guard, in making and executing at a great Expence, the Laws that are to prevent the Trade which exports it.

Paper Money, well funded, has another great Advantage over Gold and Silver, its Lightness of Carriage, and the little Room that is occupied by a great Sum, whereby it is capable of being more easily, and more safely, because more privately conveyed from Place to Place. Gold and Silver are not *intrinsically* of equal Value with Iron, a Metal in itself capable of many more beneficial Uses to Mankind. Their Value rests chiefly in the Estimation they happen to be in among the Generality of Nations, and the

Credit given to the Opinion that that Estimation will continue: Otherwise a Pound of Gold would not be a real Equivalent for even a Bushel of Wheat. Any other well-founded Credit is as much an Equivalent as Gold and Silver, and in some Cases more so, or it would not be preferred by commercial People in different Countries. . . .

THE NATURE OF THE BRITISH EMPIRE

A year after repeal of the Stamp Act and following further British plans to require a full submission of the colonies to parliamentary authority, the Scottish philosopher Lord Kames wrote Franklin of his plan for a closer union of the parts of the British Empire. In response Franklin outlined his own theory of the Empire.

. . . It becomes a matter of great importance that clear ideas should be formed on solid principles, both in Britain and America, of the true political relation between them, and the mutual duties belonging to that relation. Till this is done, they will be often jarring. I know none whose knowledge, sagacity and impartiality qualify him so thoroughly for such a service, as yours do you. I wish therefore you would consider it. You may thereby be the happy instrument of great good to the nation, and of preventing much mischief and bloodshed. I am fully persuaded with you, that a *Consolidating Union,* by a fair and equal representation of all the parts of this empire in Parliament, is the only firm basis on which its political grandeur and prosperity can be founded. Ireland once wished it, but

---

Writings, V, 17-22; from a letter to Lord Kames, April 11, 1767.

now rejects it. The time has been, when the colonies might have been pleased with it: they are now *indifferent* about it; and if it is much longer delayed, they too will *refuse* it. But the pride of this people cannot bear the thought of it, and therefore it will be delayed. Every man in England seems to consider himself as a piece of a sovereign over America; seems to jostle himself into the throne with the King, and talks of *our subjects in the Colonies.* The Parliament cannot well and wisely make laws suited to the Colonies, without being properly and truly informed of their circumstances, abilities, temper, &c. This it cannot be, without representatives from thence: and yet it is fond of this power, and averse to the only means of acquiring the necessary knowledge for exercising it; which is desiring to be *omnipotent,* without being *omniscient.*

I have mentioned that the contest is likely to be revived. It is on this occasion. In the same session with the stamp act, an act was passed to regulate the quartering of soldiers in America; when the bill was first brought in, it contained a clause, empowering the officers to quarter their soldiers in private houses: this we warmly opposed, and got it omitted. The bill passed, however, with a clause, that empty houses, barns, &c., should be hired for them, and that the respective provinces where they were should pay the expence and furnish firing, bedding, drink, and some other articles to the soldiers *gratis.* There is no way for any province to do this, but by the Assembly's making a law to raise the money. The Pennsylvanian Assembly has made such a law: the New York Assembly has refused to do it: and now all the talk here is of sending a force to compel them.

The reasons given by the Assembly to the Governor, for the refusal, are, that they understand the act to mean the furnishing such things to **soldiers,** only while on their march through the country, **and not** to great bodies of soldiers, to be fixt as at present, in the province; the burthen in the latter case being greater than the inhabitants can bear: That it would put it in the power of the Captain-General to oppress the province at pleasure, &c. But there is supposed to be another reason at bottom, which they intimate, though they do not plainly express it; to wit, that it is of the nature of an *internal tax* laid on them by Parliament, which has no right so to do. Their refusal is here called *Rebellion*, and punishment is thought of.

Now waving that point of right, and supposing the Legislatures in America subordinate to the Legislature of Great Britain, one might conceive, I think, a power in the superior Legislature to forbid the inferior Legislatures making particular laws; but to enjoin it to make a particular law contrary to its own judgment, seems improper; an Assembly or Parliament not being an *executive* officer of Government, whose duty it is, in law-making, to obey orders, but a *deliberative* body, who are to consider what comes before them, its propriety, practicability, or possibility, and to determine accordingly: The very nature of a Parliament seems to be destroyed, by supposing it may be bound, and compelled by a law of a superior Parliament, to make a law contrary to its own judgment.

Indeed, the act of Parliament in question has not, as in other acts, when a duty is enjoined, directed a penalty on neglect or refusal, and a mode of recovering that penalty. It seems, therefore, to the people in America as a mere requisition, which they are at liberty to comply with or not, as it may suit or not suit the different circumstances of different provinces. Pennsylvania has therefore voluntarily complied. New York, as I said before, has refused. The Ministry that made the act, and all their adherents, call for vengeance. The present Ministry are perplext, and the measures they will finally take on the occasion, are yet unknown. But sure I am, that, if *Force* is used, great mischief will ensue; the affections of the people of America to this country will be alienated; your commerce will be diminished; and a total separation of interests be the final consequence.

It is a common, but mistaken notion here, that the Colonies were planted at the expence of Parliament, and that therefore the Parliament has a right to tax them, &c. The truth is, they were planted at the expence of private adventurers, who went over there to settle, with leave of the King, given by charter. On receiving this leave, and those charters, the adventurers voluntarily engaged to remain the King's subjects, though in a foreign country; a country which had not been conquered by either King or Parliament, but was possessed by a free people.

When our planters arrived, they purchased the lands of the natives, without putting King or Parliament to any expence. Parliament had no hand in their settlement, was never so much as consulted about their constitution, and took no kind of notice of them, till many years after they were established. I expect only the two modern Colonies, or rather attempts to make Colonies, (for they succeed but poorly, and as yet hardly deserve the name of Colonies), I mean Georgia and Nova Scotia, which have hitherto been little better than Parliamentary jobs. Thus all the colonies acknowledge the King as their sovereign; his Governors there represent his person: Laws are made by their Assemblies or little Parliaments, with the Governor's assent, subject still to the King's pleasure to confirm or annul them: Suits arising in the Colonies, and differences between Colony and Colony, are determined by the King in Council. In this view, they seem so many separate little states, subject to the same Prince. The *sovereignty of the* King is therefore easily understood. But nothing is more common here than to talk of the *sovereignty* of PARLIAMENT, and the *sovereignty of* THIS NATION over the Colonies; a kind of sovereignty, the idea of which is not so clear, nor does it clearly appear on what foundation it is established. On the other hand, it seems necessary for the common good of the empire, that a power be lodged somewhere, to regulate its general commerce: this can be placed nowhere so properly as in the Parliament of Great Britain; and therefore, though that power has in some instances been executed with great partiality to Britain, and prejudice to the Colonies, they have nevertheless always submitted to it. Custom-houses are established in all of them, by virtue of laws made here, and the duties constantly paid, except by a few smugglers, such as are here and in all countries; but internal taxes laid on them by Parliament, are still and ever will be objected to, for the reasons that you will see in the mentioned Examination.

Upon the whole, I have lived so great a part of my life in Britain, and have formed so many friendships in it, that I love it, and sincerely wish it prosperity; and therefore wish to see that Union, on which alone I think it can be secured and established. As to America, the advantages of such a union to her are not so apparent. She may suffer at present under the arbitrary power of this country; she may suffer for a while in a separation from it; but these are temporary evils that she will outgrow. Scotland and Ireland are differently circumstanced. Confined by the sea, they can scarcely increase in numbers, wealth and strength, so as to overbalance England. But America, an immense territory, favoured by Nature with all advantages of climate, soil, great navigable rivers, and lakes, &c. must become a great country, populous and mighty; and will, in a less time than is generally conceived, be able to shake off any shackles that may be imposed on her, and perhaps place them on the imposers. In the mean time, every act of oppression will sour their tempers, lessen greatly, if not annihilate the profits of your commerce with them, and hasten their final revolt; for the seeds of liberty are universally found there, and nothing can eradicate them. And yet, there remains among that people, so much respect, veneration and affection for Britain, that, if cultivated prudently, with kind usage, and tenderness for their privileges, they might be easily governed still for ages, without force, or any considerable expence. But I do not see here a sufficient quantity of the wisdom, that is necessary to produce such a conduct, and I lament the want of it. . . .

AMERICA AND BRITISH POLITICS

In 1767 the impact of an approaching election on the debate in Parliament over ways to govern America spurred Franklin to explain how American interests were affected, for better and for worse, by the strains and stresses of British politics.

. . . There has lately been an attempt to make a kind of coalition of parties in a new ministry, but it fell through, and the present set is like to continue for some time longer, which I am rather pleased with, as some of those who were proposed to be introduced are professed adversaries to America, which is now made one of the distinctions of party here; those who have in the two last sessions shown a disposition to favour us, being called by way of reproach, Americans; while the others, adherents to Grenville and Bedford, value themselves on being true to the interests of Britain, and zealous for maintaining its dignity and sovereignty over the colonies.

This distinction will, it is apprehended, be carried much higher in the next session, for the political purpose of

---

Writings, V, 41–42; from a letter to Joseph Galloway, August 8, 1767.

influencing the ensuing election. It is already given out that the compliance of New York, in providing for the quarters, without taking notice of its being done in obedience to the act of Parliament, is evasive and unsatisfactory. That it is high time to put the right and power of this country to tax the colonies out of dispute, by an act of taxation, effectually carried into execution, and that all the colonies should be obliged explicitly to acknowledge that right. Every step is taken to render the taxing America a popular measure here, by continually insisting on the topics of our wealth and flourishing circumstances, while this country is loaded with debt, great part of it incurred on our account, the distress of the poor here by the multitude and weight of taxes, &c. &c.; and though the traders and manufacturers may possibly be kept in our interest, the idea of an American tax is very pleasing to the landed men, who therefore readily receive and propagate these sentiments wherever they have influence.

If such a bill should be brought in, it is hard to say what would be the event of it, or what would be the effects. Those who oppose it, though they should be strong enough to throw it out, would be stigmatized as Americans, betrayers of Old England, &c., and perhaps, our friends by this means being excluded, a majority of our adversaries may get in, and then the act infallibly passes the following session. To avoid the danger of such exclusion, perhaps little opposition will be given, and then it passes immediately. I know not what to advise on this occasion, but that we should all do our endeavours on both sides of the water to lessen the present unpopularity of the American cause, conciliate the affections of people here towards us, increase by possible means the number of our friends, and be careful not to weaken their hands and strengthen those of our enemies, by rash proceedings on our side, the mischiefs of which are inconceivable. . . .

ON SMUGGLING

To embarrass Englishmen who declaimed excessively against American resistance to laws of Parliament, Franklin wrote an essay on British evasions of the law and at the same time set down some thoughts on the obligations of citizens.

There are many people that would be thought, and even think themselves, *honest Men,* who fail nevertheless in particular points of honesty, deviating from that Character sometimes by the prevalence of mode or custom, and sometimes thro' mere inattention; so that their honesty is *partial* only, and not *general* or universal. Thus one who would scorn to overreach you in a bargain, shall make no scruple of tricking you a little now and then at Cards. Another that plays with the utmost fairness, shall with great freedom cheat you in the sale of a horse. But there is no kind of dishonesty into which otherwise good people more easily and frequently fall, than that of defrauding Government of its revenues, by Smuggling when they have an opportunity, or encouraging Smugglers by buying their goods.

I fell into these reflections the other day on hearing two gentlemen of reputation discoursing about a small estate which one of them was inclined to sell and the other to buy; when the Seller, in recommending the Place, remark'd, that the Situation was very advantageous on this Account, that being on the Sea-Coast, in a Smuggling Country, one had frequent Opportunities of buying many of the expensive Articles used in a Family (such as Tea, Coffee, Chocolate, Brandy, Wines, Cambrics, Brussels Laces, French Silks, and all kinds of India Goods,) 20, 30,

---

Writings, V, 60–65; first printed in *The London Chronicle,* November 24, 1767.

and in some articles 50 per cent cheaper than they could be had in the more interior Parts, where they must be bo't of Traders that paid Duty. The other *honest* Gentleman allow'd this to be an Advantage, but insisted, that the Seller, in the advanc'd Price he demanded on that Account, rated the Advantage much above its Value. And neither of them seem'd to think Dealing with Smugglers a Practice, that an *honest* Man (provided he got his Goods cheaper) had the least Reason to be asham'd of.

At a Time when the Load of our Publick Debt, and the heavy Expence of maintaining our Fleets and Armies to be ready for our Defence on Occasion, make it necessary, not only to continue old Taxes, but often to look out for new Ones, perhaps it may not be unuseful to state this Matter in a Light, that few seem to have consider'd it in.

The People of Great Britain, under the happy Constitution of this Country, have a Privilege few other Countries enjoy, that of chusing the third Branch of the Legislature, which Branch has alone the Power of regulating their Taxes. Then when the Government finds it necessary for the common Benefit, Advantage, and Safety of the Nation, for the Security of our Liberties, Property, Religion, and every thing that is dear to us, that certain Sums shall be yearly raised by Taxes, Duties, &c., and paid into the publick Treasury, thence to be dispens'd by Government for those purposes; ought not every *honest Man* freely and willingly to pay his just Proportion of this necessary Expence? Can he possibly preserve a Right to that Character, if, by any Fraud, Stratagem, or Contrivance, he avoids that Payment in whole or in Part?

What should we think of a Companion, who, having sup'd with his Friends at a Tavern, and partaken equally of the Joys of the Evening with the rest of us, would nevertheless contrive by some Artifice to shift his share of the reckoning upon others, in order to go off scot free? If a man who practised this would when detected, be deemed and called a scoundrel, what ought he to be call'd, who can enjoy all the inestimable Benefits of Publick Society, and yet by Smuggling or dealing with Smugglers contrive to evade paying his just share of the Expence, as settled by his own Representatives in Parliament, and wrongfully throw it upon his honester, and perhaps, much poorer Neighbours? He will, perhaps, be ready to tell me, that he does not wrong his Neighbours, he scorns the imputation: He only cheats the King a little, who is very able to bear it. This, however, is a mistake; the Publick Treasure is the Treasure of the Nation, to be applied for national purposes. And when a Duty is laid for a particular Publick and necessary Purpose, if, through Smuggling, that Duty falls short of raising the sum required, and other Duties must therefore be laid to make up the Deficiency; all the additional Sum laid by the new Duties and paid by other people, tho' it should amount to no more than a Half-penny or a Farthing per Head, is so much actually picked out of the Pockets of those other People by the Smugglers and their Abettors and Encouragers; Are they then any better or other than Pickpockets? And what mean, low, rascally Pickpockets must those be, that can pick Pockets for Half-pence and for Farthings?

I would not, however, be supposed to allow, in what I have just said, that cheating the King is a less offence against honesty, than cheating the public. The King and the public, in this case, are different names for the same thing; but, if we consider the King distinctly, it will not lessen the crime; it is no justification of a robbery, that the person robbed was rich and able to bear it. The King has as much right to justice as the meanest of his subjects; and, as he is truly the common *father* of his people, those that rob him fall under the Scripture woe, pronounced against the son *that robbeth his father, and saith it is no sin.*

Mean as this Practice is, do we not daily see people of Character and Fortune engaged in it for trifling Advantages to themselves? Is any Lady asham'd to request of a Gentleman of her Acquaintance, that when he returns from abroad, he would Smuggle her home a piece of Silk, or Lace, from France or Flanders? Is any Gentleman asham'd to undertake, and execute the commission? No. They will talk of it freely even before their Friends whose pockets they are thus contriving to pick by this piece of Knavery.

Among other Branches of the Revenue, that of the Post-Office is by a late Law appropriated to the Discharge of our Publick Debt, and defray the Expences of the State. None but Members of Parliament, and a few Publick Officers have now a right to avoid, by a Frank, the payment of Postage. Whenever any Letter not written by them or on their Business, if frank'd by any of them, tis a Fraud upon the Revenue; a Fraud which they must now take the Pains to conceal by writing the whole Superscription themselves. And yet such is our Insensibility to justice in this Particular, that nothing is more common than to see, even in reputable Company, a *very honest* Gentleman or Lady declare his or her Intention to cheat the Nation of Three pence by a Frank, and without Blushing apply to one of the very Legislators themselves, with a modest Request, that he would please to become an Accomplice in the Crime, and assist in the Perpetration of it.

There are those who by these Practices take a great deal in a Year out of the Publick Purse, and put the Money into their own private Pockets. If, passing thro' a Room where Publick Treasure is deposited, a Man takes the Opportunity of clandestinely pocketing and carrying off a Guinea, is he not truly and properly a Thief? And if another evades paying into the Treasury a Guinea that he ought to pay in, and Applys it to his own use, when he knows it belongs to the Publick as much as that which has been paid in, what

Difference is there in the Nature of the Crime, or the Baseness of committing it?

Some Laws make the Receiving of stolen Goods equally penal with Stealing, and upon this Principle, that if there were no Receivers, there would be few Thieves. Our Proverb says truly that *the Receiver is as bad as the Thief.*

By the same Reasoning, as there would be few Smugglers, if there were none who knowingly encourage them by buying their Goods, we may say, that the Encouragers of Smuggling are as bad as the Smugglers; and that, as Smugglers are Thieves, both equally deserve the Punishment of Thievery.

In this view of wronging the Revenue, what must we think of great Officers in the N——y, who eat their Country's Bread, if such should run Goods by Boatfulls *vi et armis,* in open Day, with Threats of immediate Death to an Officer of the Customs who desired Leave to do his Duty in searching the Boat if he did not instantly withdraw. What must we think of Sen——rs who can evade paying for their Wheels or their Plate, in Defiance of Law and Justice, and yet declaim against Corruption, as if their own Hearts and Hands were pure and unsullied? The Americans offend us grievously, when, contrary to our Laws, they smuggle Goods into their own Country; and yet they had no hand in making those Laws. I do not however pretend from thence to justify them. But I think the Offence much greater in those, who either directly or indirectly have been concern'd in making the very Laws they break. And when I hear them exclaim'g against the Americans, and for every little infringement on the acts of trade, or obstruction given by a petty mob to an officer of our customs in that country, calling for vengeance against the whole people as REBELS and TRAITORS, I cannot help thinking there are still those in the world who can *see a mote in their brother's eye, while they do not discern a beam in their own;* and that the old saying is as true now as ever it was, *One man may better steal a horse, than another look over the hedge.*

B. F.

CAUSES OF

THE AMERICAN DISCONTENTS BEFORE 1768

Following passage of the Townshend Acts (July 1767) and receipt of news of resistance to them in America, Franklin addressed the English public as one acquainted with the attitudes of Americans toward the measures then being pursued by the Ministry. He sought, he said, not to justify the Americans, but merely to let Englishmen better consult their own self-interest by giving them an accurate picture of some unanticipated results of a policy that threatened bonds across the Atlantic important to those who lived on each side.

As the cause of the present ill-humour in America, and of the resolutions taken there to purchase less of our manufactures, does not seem to be generally understood, it may afford some satisfaction to your Readers, if you give them the following short historical state of facts.

From the time that the Colonies were first considered as capable of granting aids to the Crown, down to the end of the last war, it is said, that the constant mode of obtaining those aids was by *Requisition* made from the Crown through its Governors to the several Assemblies, in circular letters from the Secretary of State in his Majesty's

---

Writings, V, 78–89; first published in *The London Chronicle,* January 7, 1768.

name, setting forth the occasion, requiring them to take the matter into consideration; and expressing a reliance on their prudence, duty and affection to his Majesty's Government, that they would grant such sums, or raise such numbers of men, as were suitable to their respective circumstances.

The Colonies, being accustomed to this method, have from time to time granted money to the Crown, or raised troops for its service, in proportion to their abilities; and during all the last war beyond their abilities, so that considerable sums were returned them yearly by Parliament, as they had exceeded their proportion.

Had this happy method of Requisition been continued, (a method that left the King's subjects in those remote countries the pleasure of showing their zeal and loyalty, and of imagining that they recommended themselves to their Sovereign by the liberality of their voluntary grants) there is no doubt but all the money that could reasonably be expected to be raised from them in any manner, might have been obtained, without the least heart-burning, offence, or breach of the harmony, of affections and interests, that so long subsisted between the two countries.

It has been thought wisdom in a Government exercising sovereignty over different kinds of people, to have some regard to prevailing and established opinions among the people to be governed, wherever such opinions might, in their effects obstruct or promote public measures. If they tend to obstruct public service, they are to be changed, if possible, before we attempt to act against them; and they can only be changed by reason and persuasion. But if public business can be carried on without thwarting those opinions, if they can be, on the contrary, made subservient to it, they are not unnecessarily to be thwarted, how absurd so ever such popular opinions may be in their nature.

This had been the wisdom of our Government with

respect to raising money in the Colonies. It was well known, that the Colonists universally were of opinion, that no money could be levied from English subjects, but by their own consent given by themselves or their chosen Representatives: That therefore, whatever money was to be raised from the people in the Colonies, must first be granted by their Assemblies, as the money raised in Britain is first to be granted by the House of Commons: That this right of granting their own money, was essential to English liberty: And that if any man, or body of men, in which they had no Representative of their choosing, could tax them at pleasure, they could not be said to have any property, any thing they could call their own. But as these opinions did not hinder their granting money voluntarily and amply whenever the Crown by its servants came into their Assemblies (as it does into its Parliaments of Britain or Ireland) and demanded aids; therefore that method was chosen rather than the hateful one of arbitrary taxes. . . .

[After reciting American reasons for opposing some particular measures, Franklin turned to their grounds for resisting alien rulers.]

. . . They say then as to Governors, that they are not like Princes whose posterity have an inheritance in the government of a nation, and therefore an interest in its prosperity; they are generally strangers to the Provinces they are sent to govern, have no estate, natural connexion, or relation there, to give them an affection for the country; that they come only to make money as fast as they can; are sometimes men of vicious characters and broken fortunes, sent by a Minister merely to get them out of the way; that as they intend staying in the country no longer than their government continues, and purpose to leave no family behind them, they are apt to be regardless of the good will of the people, and care not what is said or thought of them after they are gone.

Their situation at the same time gives them many opportunities of being vexatious, and they are often so, notwithstanding their dependance on the Assemblies for all that part of their support that does not arise from fees established by law; but would probably be much more so, if they were to be supported by money drawn from the people without their consent or good will, which is the professed design of this new act. That if by means of these forced duties Government is to be supported in America, without the intervention of the Assemblies, their Assemblies will soon be looked upon as useless, and a Governor will not call them, as having nothing to hope from their meeting, and perhaps something to fear from their inquiries into and remonstrances against this Mal-administration. That thus the people will be deprived of their most essential rights. That it being, as at present, a Governor's interest to cultivate the good will by promoting the welfare of the people he governs, can be attended with no prejudice to the Mother Country, since all the laws he may be prevailed on to give his assent to are subject to revision here, and, if reported against by the Board of Trade, are immediately repealed by the Crown; nor dare he pass any law contrary to his instructions, as he holds his office during the pleasure of the Crown, and his Securities are liable for the penalties of their bonds if he contravenes those instructions. This is what they say as to *Governors.*

As to *Judges,* they alledge, that being appointed from hence, and holding their commissions *not* during *good behaviour,* as in Britain, but during *pleasure,* all the weight of interest or influence would be thrown into one of the scales, (which ought to be held even) if the salaries are also to be paid out of duties raised upon the people without their consent, and independent of their Assemblies' approbation or disapprobation of the Judge's behaviour. That it is true, Judges should be free from all influence; and therefore whenever Government here will grant commissions to able and honest Judges during good behaviour, the Assemblies will settle permanent and ample salaries on them during their commissions: But at present they have no other means of getting rid of an ignorant or an unjust Judge (and some of scandalous characters have, they say, been sometimes sent them) but by starving him out.

I do not suppose these reasonings of theirs will appear here to have much weight. I do not produce them with an expectation of convincing your readers. I relate them merely in pursuance of the task I have imposed on myself, to be an impartial historian of American facts and opinions. . . .

[Franklin then summarized American resentment at the mercantile policies which subordinated colonial interests to those of the mother country, and moved on to other grievances.]

Added to these, the Americans remembered the Act authorizing the most cruel insult that perhaps was ever offered by one people to another, that of *emptying our goals* into their settlements: Scotland too having within these two years obtained the privilege it had not before, of sending its rogues and villains also to the plantations. I say, reflecting on these things, they said one to another (their newspapers are full of such discourses) these people are not content with making a monopoly of us, forbidding us to trade with any other country of Europe, and compelling us to buy every thing of them, though in many articles we could furnish ourselves 10, 20, and even to 50 per cent cheaper elsewhere; but now they have as good as declared they have a right to tax us *ad libitum* internally and externally, and that our constitutions and liberties shall all be taken away, if we do not submit to that claim.

They are not content with the high prices at which they sell us their goods, but have now begun to enhance those prices by new duties; and, by the expensive apparatus of a new set of officers, appear to intend an augmentation and multiplication of those burthens that shall still be more grievous to us. Our people have been foolishly fond of their superfluous modes and manufactures, to the impoverishing our country, carrying off all our cash, and loading us with debt: they will not suffer us to restrain the luxury of our inhabitants, as they do that of their own, by laws; they can make laws to discourage or prohibit the importation of French superfluities; but though those of England are as ruinous to us as the French ones are to them, if we make a law of that kind, they immediately repeal it.

Thus they get all our money from us by trade, and every profit we can anywhere make by our fisheries, our produce, or our commerce, centres finally with them; but this does not signify. It is time then to take care of ourselves by the best means in our power. Let us unite in solemn resolutions and engagements with and to each other, that we will give these new officers as little trouble as possible, by not consuming the British manufactures on which they are to levy the duties. Let us agree to consume no more of their expensive gewgaws. Let us live frugally, and let us industriously manufacture what we can for ourselves: Thus we shall be able honourably to discharge the debts we already owe them, and after that we may be able to keep some money in our country, not only for the uses of our internal commerce, but for the service of our gracious Sovereign, whenever he shall have occasion for it, and think proper to require it of us in the old *constitutional* manner. For, notwithstanding the reproaches thrown out against us in their public papers and pamphlets, notwithstanding we have been reviled in their senate as *Rebels* and *Traitors*, we are truly a loyal people. Scotland has had its rebellions, and England its plots against the present Royal Family; but America is untainted with those crimes; there is in it scarce a man, there is not a single native of our country, who is not firmly attached to his King by principle and by affection.

But a new kind of loyalty seems to be required of us, a loyalty to Parliament; a loyalty that is to extend, it is said, to a surrender of all our properties, whenever a House of Commons, (in which there is not a single member of our choosing) shall think fit to grant them away without our consent; and to a patient suffering the loss of our privileges as Englishmen, if we cannot submit to make such surrender. We were separated too far from Britain by the Ocean, but we were united to it by respect and love, so that we could at any time freely have spent our lives and little fortunes in its cause: But this unhappy new system of politics tends to dissolve those bands of union, and to sever us for ever.

These are the wild ravings of the at present half distracted Americans. To be sure, no reasonable man in England can approve of such sentiments, and, as I said before, I do not pretend to support or justify them: But I sincerely wish, for the sake of the manufactures and commerce of Great-Britain, and for the sake of the strength which a firm union with our growing colonies would give us, that these people had never been thus needlessly driven out of their senses.

216   *The Political Thought of Benjamin Franklin*

THE BRITISH CONSTITUTION

In response to some public letters asserting the absolute sovereignty of Parliament in all parts of the Empire, Franklin begged "leave to give a short sketch of the British constitution."

. . . The British state or empire consists of several islands and other distant countries, asunder in different parts of the globe, *but all united in allegiance to one Prince*, and to the *common law* (Scotland excepted) as it existed in the old provinces or mother country, before the colonies or new provinces were formed. The prince, with a select parliament, or assembly, make the legislative power of and for each province within itself. Where vicinity made it convenient, several islands and provinces were at sundry times consolidated, and represented by one parliament, as the Isle of Wight, Cornwall, Wales, Cheshire, Durham, and Scotland; by which means all Great Britain and its contiguous isles, are unitedly represented in one assembly in parliament. It has not as yet been thought proper to unite Ireland to the old provinces, though lying very near; nor any of the provinces of America, which lie at a great distance. But notwithstanding this state of separate assemblies, the allegiance of the distant provinces to the crown will remain for ever unshaken, while they enjoy the rights of Englishmen; that is, with the consent of their sovereign, the right of legislation each for themselves; for this puts them on an exact level, in this respect, with their fellow subjects in the old provinces, and better than this they could not be by any change in their power. But if the old provinces should often exercise the right of making laws

---

Crane, *Franklin's Letters to the Press*, pp. 110–112; from an essay first published in *Gentleman's Magazine*, January 1768.

for the new, they would probably grow as restless as the Corsicans, when they perceived they were no longer fellow subjects, but the subjects of subjects.

To illustrate this matter by a comparison; Should it happen, through the revolutions of time, that some future king should make choice of Ireland for his seat of government, and that the parliament of that kingdom, with his majesty's concurrence, should assume the right of taxing the people of England, would the people of England quietly acquiesce, or implicitly pay obedience to laws made by virtue of an assumed right? And yet, as there is no law in being to prevent his majesty from making any part of his dominions the seat of his government, the case is by no means foreign to the present question.

The laws made here to tax the Americans affect them as a distinct body, in which the law makers are in no manner whatever, comprehended; whereas the laws made to tax Great-Britain, affect alike every member who gives his concurrence to such law. And hence arises the essential difference between *real* and *virtual* representations, so much agitated. . . .

CORRUPTION

IN PARLIAMENTARY ELECTIONS

Franklin's horrified reaction to the wholesale fraud practiced in parliamentary elections was probably more important than any other single factor in transforming him from a loyal subject proud of the British constitution into an American anxious to be free from England's contaminating influence. His description of one election is significant.

Writings, V, 99–100, 112; from letters to Joseph Galloway, February 17 and March 13, 1768.

... The Parliament have of late been acting an egregious farce, calling before them the mayor and aldermen of Oxford, for proposing a sum to be paid by their old members on being rechosen at the next election; and sundry printers and brokers, for advertising and dealing in boroughs, &c. The Oxford people were sent to Newgate, and discharged, after some days, on humble petition, and receiving the Speaker's reprimand upon their knees. The House could scarcely keep countenances, knowing as they all do, that the practice is general. People say, they mean nothing more than to *beat down the price* by a little discouragement of borough jobbing, now that their own elections are all coming on. The price indeed is grown exorbitant, no less than *four thousand pounds* for a member.

Mr. Beckford has brought in a bill for preventing bribery and corruption in elections, wherein was a clause to oblige every member to swear, on their admission into the House, that he had not directly or indirectly given any bribe to any elector, &c.; but this was so universally exclaimed against, as answering no end but perjuring the members, that he has been obliged to withdraw that clause. It was indeed a cruel contrivance of his, worse than the gunpowder plot; for that was only to blow the Parliament up to heaven, this to sink them all down to——. Mr. Thurlow opposed his bill by a long speech. Beckford, in reply, gave a dry hit to the House, that is repeated everywhere. "The honourable gentleman," says he, "in his learned discourse, gave us first one definition of corruption, then he gave us another definition of corruption, and I think he was about to give us a third. Pray does that gentleman imagine *there is any member of this House that does not* KNOW what corruption is?" which occasioned only a roar of laughter, for they are so hardened in the practice, that they are very little ashamed of it. This between ourselves. ...

Spokesman for America in England 219

. . . All the members are now in their counties and boroughs among their drunken electors; much confusion and disorder in many places, and such profusion of money as never was known before on any similar occasion. The first instance of bribery to be chosen a member, taken notice of on the journals, is no longer ago than Queen Elizabeth's time, when the being sent to Parliament was looked upon as a troublesome service, and therefore not sought after. It is said that such a one, "being a simple man, and conceiving it might be of some advantage to him, had given *four pounds* to the mayor and corporation, that they might choose him to serve them in Parliament."

The price is monstrously risen since that time, for it is now no less than *four thousand pounds!* It is thought, that near two millions will be spent this election; but those, who understand figures and act by computation, say the crown has *two millions a year in places and pensions to dispose of,* and it is well worth while to engage in such a seven years' lottery, though all that have tickets should not get prizes.

ON THE LABOURING POOR

In the midst of Franklin's almost rebellious political tracts he extolled diligence and hard work in a way which must have pleased the ruling circles.

I have met with much invective in the papers, for these two years past, against the hard-heartedness of the rich, and much complaint of the great oppressions suffered in

---

Writings, V, 122-127; first published in *Gentleman's Magazine,* April 1768.

this country by the labouring poor. Will you admit a word or two on the other side of the question? I do not propose to be an advocate for oppression or oppressors. But when I see that the poor are, by such writings, exasperated against the rich, and excited to insurrections, by which much mischief is done, and some forfeit their lives, I could wish the true state of things were better understood, the poor not made by these busy writers more uneasy and unhappy than their situation subjects them to be, and the nation not brought into disrepute among foreigners, by public groundless accusations of ourselves, as if the rich in England had no compassion for the poor, and Englishmen wanted common humanity.

In justice, then to this country, give me leave to remark, that the condition of the poor here is, by far, the best in Europe, for that, except in England and her American colonies, there is not in any country of the known world, not even in Scotland or Ireland, a provision by law to enforce a support of the poor. Everywhere else necessity reduces to beggary. This law was not made by the poor. The legislators were men of fortune. By that act they voluntarily subjected their own estates, and the estates of all others, to the payment of a tax for the maintenance of the poor, incumbering those estates with a kind of rent-charge for that purpose, whereby the poor are vested with an inheritance, as it were, in all the estates of the rich. I wish they were benefited by this generous provision in any degree equal to the good intention, with which it was made, and is continued: But I fear the giving mankind a dependance on any thing for support, in age or sickness, besides industry and frugality during youth and health, tends to flatter our natural indolence, to encourage idleness and prodigality, and thereby to promote and increase poverty, the very evil it was intended to cure; thus multiplying beggars instead of diminishing them.

Besides this tax, which the rich in England have subjected themselves to, in behalf of the poor, amounting in some places to five or six shillings in the pound, of the annual income, they have, by donations and subscriptions, erected numerous schools in various parts of the kingdom, for educating gratis the children of the poor in reading and writing, and in many of those schools the children are also fed and cloathed. They have erected hospitals at an immense expence for the reception and cure of the sick, the lame, the wounded, and the insane poor, for lying-in women, and deserted children. They are also continually contributing towards making up losses occasioned by fire, by storms, or by floods, and to relieve the poor in severe seasons of frost, in times of scarcity, &c., in which benevolent and charitable contributions no nation exceeds us. Surely, there is some gratitude due for so many instances of goodness.

Add to this all the laws made to discourage foreign manufactures, by laying heavy duties on them, or totally prohibiting them, whereby the rich are obliged to pay much higher prices for what they wear and consume, than if the trade was open: These are so many laws for the support of our labouring poor, made by the rich, and continued at their expence; all the difference of price, between our own and foreign commodities, being so much given by our rich to our poor; who would indeed be enabled by it to get by degrees above poverty, if they did not, as too generally they do, consider every encrease of wages, only as something that enables them to drink more and work less; so that their distress in sickness, age, or times of scarcity, continues to be the same as if such laws had never been made in their favour.

Much malignant censure have some writers bestowed upon the rich for their luxury and expensive living, while the poor are starving, &c.; not considering that what the rich expend, the labouring poor receive in payment for their labour. It may seem a paradox if I should assert, that our labouring poor do in every year receive *the whole revenue of the nation;* I mean not only the public revenue, but also the revenue or clear income of all private estates, or a sum equivalent to the whole.

In support of this position I reason thus. The rich do not work for one another. Their habitations, furniture, cloathing, carriages, food, ornaments, and every thing in short, that they or their families use and consume, is the work or produce of the labouring poor, who are, and must be continually, paid for their labour in producing the same. In these payments the revenues of private estates are expended, for most people live up to their incomes. In cloathing or provision for troops, in arms, ammunition, ships, tents, carriages, &c. &c., (every particular the produce of labour,) much of the public revenue is expended. The pay of officers, civil and military, and of the private soldiers and sailors, requires the rest; and they spend that also in paying for what is produced by the labouring poor.

I allow that some estates may increase by the owners spending less than their income; but then I conceive that other estates do at the same time diminish by the owners spending more than their income, so that when the enriched want to buy more land, they easily find lands in the hands of the impoverished, whose necessities oblige them to sell; and thus this difference is equalled. I allow also, that part of the expence of the rich is in foreign produce or manufactures, for producing which the labouring poor of other nations must be paid; but then I say, we must first pay our own labouring poor for an equal quantity of our manufactures or produce, to exchange for those foreign productions, or we must pay for them in money, which money, not being the natural produce of our country, must first be purchased from abroad, by sending out its value in the produce or manufactures of this country, for which manufactures our labouring poor are to be paid. And indeed, if we did not export more than we import, we could have no money at all. I allow farther, that there are middle men, who make a profit, and even get estates, by purchasing the labour of the poor, and selling it at advanced prices to the rich; but then they cannot enjoy that profit, or the incomes of estates, but by spending them in employing and paying our labouring poor, in some shape or other, for the products of industry. Even beggars, pensioners, hospitals, and all that are supported by charity, spend their incomes in the same manner. So that finally, as I said at first, *our labouring poor receive annually the whole of the clear revenues of the nation,* and from us they can have no more.

If it be said that their wages are too low, and that they ought to be better paid for their labour, I heartily wish any means could be fallen upon to do it, consistent with their interest and happiness; but, as the cheapness of other things is owing to the plenty of those things, so the cheapness of labour is in most cases owing to the multitude of labourers, and to their under-working one another in order to obtain employment. How is this to be remedied? A law might be made to raise their wages; but, if our manufactures are too dear, they will not vend abroad, and all that part of employment will fail, unless by fighting and conquering we compel other nations to buy our goods, whether they will or no, which some have been mad enough at times to propose.

Among ourselves, unless we give our working people less employment, how can we, for what they do, pay them higher than we do? Out of what fund is the additional price of labour to be paid, when all our present incomes are, as it were, mortgaged to them? Should they get higher wages, would that make them less poor, if, in consequence, they worked fewer days of the week proportionably? I have said, a law might be made to raise their wages; but I doubt much whether it could be executed to any purpose, unless another law, now indeed almost obsolete, could at the same time be revived and enforced; a law, I mean, that many have often heard and repeated, but few have ever duly considered. SIX *days shalt thou labour.* This is as positive a part of the commandment, as that which says, *The* SEVENTH *day thou shalt rest.* But we remember well to observe the indulgent part, and never think of the other. *Saint Monday* is generally as duly kept by our working people as *Sunday;* the only difference is, that, instead of employing their time cheaply at church, they are wasting it expensively at the alehouse.

RIOTS IN LONDON

OVER "WILKES AND LIBERTY"

Though American Whigs generally applauded the campaign of the English radical John Wilkes to gain a seat in Parliament, and saw the cause of American liberty as entwined with Wilkes's efforts on behalf of English liberty, Franklin's observation in London of the riots precipitated by Wilkes's followers led him to some strictures on popular tumults.

. . . Even this capitol, the residence of the King, is now a daily scene of lawless riot and confusion. Mobs patrolling the streets at noonday, some knocking all down that will not roar for Wilkes and liberty; courts of justice afraid

---

Writings, V, 133, 134–135; from letters to John Ross and to Joseph Galloway, May 14, 1768.

to give judgment against him; coal-heavers and porters pulling down the houses of coal merchants, that refuse to give them more wages; sawyers destroying sawmills; sailors unrigging all the outward bound ships, and suffering none to sail till merchants agree to raise their pay; watermen destroying private boats and threatening bridges; soldiers firing among the mobs and killing men, women, and children, which seems only to have produced a universal sullenness, that looks like a great black cloud coming on, ready to burst in a general tempest.

What the event will be God only knows. But some punishment seems preparing for a people, who are ungratefully abusing the best constitution, and the best King, any nation was ever blessed with, intent on nothing but luxury, licentiousness, power, places, pensions, and plunder; while the ministry, divided in their counsels, with little regard for each other, worried by perpetual oppositions, in continual apprehension of changes, intent on securing popularity in case they should lose favour, have for some years past had little time or inclination to attend to our small affairs, whose remoteness makes them appear still smaller. . . .

. . . While I am writing, a great mob of coal porters fills the street, carrying a wretch of their business upon poles to be ducked, and otherwise punished at their pleasure for working at the old wages. All respect to law and government seems to be lost among the common people, who are moreover continually inflamed by seditious scribblers, to trample on authority and every thing that used to keep them in order.

The Parliament is now sitting, but will not continue long together, nor undertake any material business. The court of King's Bench postponed giving sentence against Wilkes on his outlawry till the next term, intimidated as some say by his popularity, and willing to get rid of the affair for a time, till it should be seen what the Parliament would conclude as to his membership. The Commons at least some of them, resent that conduct, which has thrown a burthen on them it might have eased them of, by pillorying or punishing him in some infamous manner, that would have given better ground for expelling him from the House. His friends complain of it as a delay of justice, say the court knew the outlawry to be defective, and that they must finally pronounce it void, but would punish him by long confinement. Great mobs of his adherents have assembled before the prison, the guards have fired on them; it is said five or six are killed, and sixteen or seventeen wounded; and some circumstances have attended this military execution, such as its being done by the Scotch regiment, the pursuing a lad, and killing him at his father's house, &c. &c., that exasperate people exceedingly, and more mischief seems brewing. Several of the soldiers are imprisoned. If they are not hanged, it is feared there will be more and greater mobs; and, if they are, that no soldier will assist in suppressing any mob hereafter. The prospect either way is gloomy. It is said the English soldiers cannot be confided in, to act against these mobs, being suspected as rather inclined to favour and join them. . . .

POSITIONS TO BE EXAMINED,

CONCERNING NATIONAL WEALTH

In July 1768, a few months after a trip to France where he had enjoyed the company of French intellectuals and scientists, Franklin wrote Du Pont de Nemours that he "received from it a

---

Writings, V, 200–202; from a manuscript dated April 4, 1769.

great deal of instruction." The doctrines of the physiocrats, emphasizing the supreme importance of agriculture, came propitiously to Franklin's attention. They helped him understand theoretically the shortcomings of England's manufacturing and commercial system at a time when he had strong political reasons for resenting it. He worked out some physiocratic ideas in a commentary on national wealth.

1. All food or subsistence for mankind arises from the earth or waters.

2. Necessaries of life, that are not food, and all other conveniences, have their values estimated by the proportion of food consumed while we are employed in procuring them.

3. A small people, with a large territory, may subsist on the productions of nature, with no other labour than that of gathering the vegetables and catching the animals.

4. A large people, with a small territory, finds these insufficient, and, to subsist, must labour the earth, to make it produce greater quantities of vegetable food, suitable for the nourishment of men, and of the animals they intend to eat.

5. From this labour arises a *great increase* of vegetable and animal food, and of materials for clothing, as flax, wool, silk, &c. The superfluity of these is wealth. With this wealth we pay for the labour employed in building our houses, cities, &c., which are therefore only subsistence thus metamorphosed.

6. *Manufactures* are only *another shape* into which so much provisions and subsistence are turned, as were equal in value to the manufactures produced. This appears from hence, that the manufacturer does not, in fact, obtain from the employer, for his labour, *more* than a mere subsistence, including raiment, fuel, and shelter; all which de-

rive their value from the provisions consumed in procuring them.

7. The produce of the earth, thus converted into manufactures, may be more easily carried to distant markets than before such conversion.

8. *Fair commerce is*, where equal values are exchanged for equal, the expense of transport included. Thus, if it costs A in England as much labour and charge to raise a bushel of wheat, as it costs B in France to produce four gallons of wine, then are four gallons of wine the fair exchange for a bushel of wheat, A and B meeting at half distance with their commodities to make the exchange. The advantage of this fair commerce is, that each party increases the number of his enjoyments, having, instead of wheat alone, or wine alone, the use of both wheat and wine.

9. Where the labour and expense of producing both commodities are known to both parties, bargains will generally be fair and equal. Where they are known to one party only, bargains will often be unequal, knowledge taking its advantage of ignorance.

10. Thus, he that carries one thousand bushels of wheat abroad to sell, may not probably obtain so great a profit thereon, as if he had first turned the wheat into manufactures, by subsisting therewith the workmen while producing those manufactures; since there are many expediting and facilitating methods of working, not generally known; and strangers to the manufactures, though they know pretty well the expense of raising wheat, are unacquainted with those short methods of working, and, thence being apt to suppose more labour employed in the manufactures than there really is, are more easily imposed on in their value, and induced to allow more for them than they are honestly worth.

11. Thus the advantage of having manufactures in a

country does not consist, as is commonly supposed, in their highly advancing the value of rough materials, of which they are formed; since, though six pennyworth of flax may be worth twenty shillings, when worked into lace, yet the very cause of its being worth twenty shillings, is, that, besides the flax, it has cost nineteen shillings and sixpence in subsistence to the manufacturer. But the advantage of manufactures is, that under their shape provisions may be more easily carried to a foreign market; and, by their means, our traders may more easily cheat strangers. Few, where it is not made, are judges of the value of lace. The importer may demand forty, and perhaps get thirty, shillings for that which cost him but twenty.

12. Finally, there seem to be but three ways for a nation to acquire wealth. The first is by *war,* as the Romans did, in plundering their conquered neighbours. This is *robbery.* The second by *commerce,* which is generally *cheating.* The third by *agriculture,* the only *honest way,* wherein man receives a real increase of the seed thrown into the ground, in a kind of continual miracle, wrought by the hand of God in his favour, as a reward for his innocent life and his virtuous industry.

A STRATEGY

FOR RESISTING BRITISH OPPRESSION

Though Franklin did not receive formal appointment as agent for Massachusetts until 1770, through correspondence with friends there he had long been party to the most exacerbated conflict between a colony and the mother country. As Boston took the lead in nonimportation measures against British goods and

---

Writings, V, 203–205; from a letter to Samuel Cooper, April 27, 1769.

endured the presence of British troops, Franklin championed the cause in London and wrote words of advice to his friends in Massachusetts.

. . . I hope my Country folks will remain as fix'd in their Resolutions of Industry and Frugality till these Acts are repeal'd. And, if I could be sure of that, I should almost wish them never to be repealed; being persuaded, that we shall reap more solid and extensive Advantages from the steady Practice of those two great Virtues, than we can possibly suffer Damage from all the Duties the Parliament of this kingdom can levy on us. They flatter themselves you cannot long subsist without their Manufactures. They believe you have not Virtue enough to persist in such Agreements, — they imagine the Colonies will differ among themselves, deceive and desert one another, and quietly one after the other submit to the Yoke, and return to the Use of British Fineries. They think, that, tho' the Men may be contented with homespun stuffs, the Women will never get the better of their Vanity and Fondness for English Modes and Gewgaws. The ministerial People all talk in this Strain, and many even of the Merchants. I have ventured to assert, that they will all find themselves mistaken; and I rely so much on the Spirit of my Country, as to be confident I shall not be found a false Prophet, tho' at present not believed.

I hope nothing that has happened, or may happen, will diminish in the least our Loyalty to our Sovereign, or Affection for this Nation in general. I can scarcely conceive a King of better Dispositions, of more exemplary Virtues, or more truly desirous of promoting the Welfare of all his Subjects. The Experience we have had of the Family in the two preceding mild Reigns, and the good Temper of our young Princes, so far as can yet be discovered, promise us a Continuance of this Felicity. The Body of this People, too, is of a noble and generous Nature, loving and honouring the Spirit of Liberty, and hating arbitrary Power of all sorts. We have many, very many, friends among them.

But as to the Parliament! tho' I might excuse that which made the Acts, as being surpriz'd & misled into the Measure; I know not how to excuse this, which, under the fullest Conviction of its being a wrong one, resolves to continue it. It is decent, indeed, in your publick Papers to speak as you do of the *"Wisdom and the Justice of Parliament;"* but now that the Subject is more thoroughly understood, if this new Parliament had been really *wise*, it would not have refused even to *receive* a Petition against the Acts; and, if it had been *just*, it would have repealed them, and refunded the Money. Perhaps it may be *wiser* and *juster* another Year, but that is not to be depended on.

If under all the Insults and Oppressions you are now exposed to, you can prudently, as you have lately done, continue quiet, avoiding Tumults, but still resolutely keeping up your Claim and asserting your Rights, you will finally establish them, and this military Cloud that now blusters over you will pass away, and do no more Harm than a Summer Thunder Shower. But the Advantages of your Perseverance in Industry and Frugality will be great and permanent. Your Debts will be paid, your Farms will be better improv'd, and yield a greater Produce; your real Wealth will increase in a Plenty of every useful home Production, and all the true Enjoyments of Life, even tho' no foreign Trade should be allow'd you; and this handicraft, shop-keeping State, will, for its own sake, learn to behave more civilly to its Customers. . . .

FABLES ON THE MOTHER COUNTRY AND HER COLONIES

Franklin was never content with mere learned argument and syllogisms in his campaigns in the press. In 1770 he wrote and had printed three fables teaching the foolishness of punitive measures against the colonies.

FABLE I.

A Herd of Cows had long afforded Plenty of Milk, Butter and Cheese to an avaritious Farmer, who grudged them the Grass they subsisted on, and at length mowed it to make Money of the Hay, leaving them to *shift for Food* as they could, and yet still expected to *milk them* as before; but the Cows, offended with his Unreasonableness, resolved for the future *to suckle one another*.

FABLE II.

An Eagle, King of Birds, sailing on his Wings aloft over a Farmer's Yard, saw a Cat there basking in the Sun, *mistook it for a Rabbit*, stoop'd, seized it, and carried it up into the Air, *intending to prey on it*. The Cat turning, set her Claws into the Eagle's Breast; who, finding his Mistake, opened his Talons, and would have let her drop; but Puss, unwilling to fall so far, held faster; and the Eagle, to get rid of the Inconvenience, found it necessary to *set her down where he took her up*.

Crane, *Franklin's Letters to the Press,* pp. 166–167; first printed in the *Public Advertiser,* January 2, 1770.

Spokesman for America in England 233

FABLE III.

A Lion's Whelp was put on board a Guinea Ship bound to America as a Present to a Friend in that Country: It was tame and harmless as a Kitten, and therefore not confined, but suffered to walk about the Ship at Pleasure. A stately, full-grown English Mastiff, belonging to the Captain, despising the Weakness of the young Lion, frequently took it's *Food* by Force, and often turned it out of its Lodging Box, when he had a Mind to repose therein himself. The young Lion nevertheless grew daily in Size and Strength, and the Voyage being long, he became at last a more equal Match for the Mastiff; who continuing his Insults, received a stunning Blow from the Lion's Paw that fetched his Skin over his Ears, and deterred him from any future Contest with such growing Strength; regretting that he had not rather secured it's Friendship than provoked it's Enmity.

THE RIGHT TO VOTE

Franklin's major effort to persuade Parliament to repeal all the Townshend Duties, including that on tea, was a series of eleven essays entitled "The Colonist's Advocate," in which he reviewed at length the by-now familiar arguments denying parliamentary power to tax the colonies because of their rights under the English constitution. He also argued, as he had many times, the imprudence and impracticality of such taxation. In one essay he hinted at the justice of a wider suffrage than had yet been allowed on either side of the Atlantic.

Crane, *Franklin's Letters to the Press*, pp. 173–174; from an essay first printed in the *Public Advertiser*, January 11, 1770.

Suppose some long-headed Minister should invent a Tax to be imposed *only* on those Subjects, residing in Britain, who have no Vote in any Election for Members of Parliament. Suppose the British Government to publish a formal Declaration, That they have a Right to give and grant away the Property of many Millions of their Fellow-Subjects, without, or against their Consent, and for the declared Purpose of saving their own, what Idea would this Proceeding give Foreigners of the hitherto justly boasted Equity of the British Government? But does it make any Difference, as to Equity, whether the Individuals taxed without, or against their own Consent, be Subjects residing on the Eastern, or on the Western Side of the Atlantick? If it does, the Advantage is plainly on the Side of the Tax here supposed; for the Members of the British Parliament, or at least the Majority of them (and the Majority decides) cannot be supposed competent Judges of the Ability of the Colonists to bear Taxes; whereas, they are Judges of the Ability of their Fellow-Subjects resident in Britain.

Again, suppose the Form of Representation was the same in England, as it is in some Parts of America, viz. That every Parish should send so many Deputies to the Assembly of Lawmakers. Suppose each County to exclude one Parish from the Privilege of Representation, and yet to lay Taxes on the unrepresented Parishes, as if they were represented. Suppose the Legislature to declare, that the County of Middlesex has a Right to tax the Parish of Islington, and at the same Time a Right to refuse to admit Deputies from that Parish to the County-Meeting, in which the Contingent for each Parish was settled, could it be reasonably expected that the Inhabitants of the Parish of Islington should contentedly submit to such gross Partiality? Yet this gross Partiality would be more reasonable than the British Parliament's assuming a Right to tax the unrepresented Colonists, because the Representatives of the other Parishes of Middlesex (and so of the rest) must, at least, be supposed competent Judges of the Abilities of the Inhabitants of Islington. . . .

AN EVIL PARLIAMENT AND A GOOD KING

Franklin sought often to stiffen resistance to parliamentary oppression by asking Americans, as Englishmen had done traditionally, to enlist the King in their cause.

. . . That the Colonies originally were constituted distinct States, and intended to be continued such, is clear to me from a thorough Consideration of their original Charters, and the whole Conduct of the Crown and Nation towards them until the Restoration. Since that Period, the Parliament here has usurp'd an Authority of making Laws for them, which before it had not. We have for some time submitted to that Usurpation, partly through Ignorance and Inattention, and partly from our Weakness and Inability to contend: I hope, when our Rights are better understood here, we shall, by prudent and proper Conduct, be able to obtain from the Equity of this Nation a Restoration of them. And in the mean time, I could wish, that such Expressions as *the Supreme Authority of Parliament; the Subordinacy of our Assemblies to the Parliament,* and the like, (which in Reality mean nothing, if our Assemblies, with the King, have a true Legislative Authority); I say, I could wish that such Expressions were no more seen in our publick Pieces. They are too strong for Compliment, and tend to confirm a Claim of Subjects in one Part of the

---

Writings, V, 260–261; from a letter to Samuel Cooper, June 8, 1770.

King's Dominions to be Sovereigns over their Fellow Subjects in another Part of his Dominions, when in truth they have no such Right, and their Claim is founded only in Usurpation, the several States having equal Rights and Liberties, and being only connected, as England and Scotland were before the Union, by having one common Sovereign, the King.

This kind of Doctrine the Lords and Commons here would deem little less than Treason against what they think their Share of the Sovereignty over the Colonies. To me those Bodies seem to have been long encroaching on the Rights of their and our Sovereign, assuming too much of his Authority, and betraying his Interests. By our Constitution he is, with his plantation Parliaments, the sole Legislator of his American Subjects, and in that Capacity is, and ought to be, free to exercise his own Judgment, unrestrained and unlimited by his Parliament here. And our Parliaments have right to grant him Aids without the Consent of this Parliament, a Circumstance, which, by the way, begins to give it some Jealousy. Let us, therefore, hold fast our Loyalty to our King, who has the best Disposition towards us, and has a Family Interest in our Prosperity; as that steady Loyalty is the most probable means of securing us from the arbitrary Power of a corrupt Parliament, that does not like us, and conceives itself to have an Interest in keeping us down and fleecing us.

If they should urge the *inconvenience* of an empire's being divided into so many separate States, and from thence conclude, that we are not so divided, I would answer, that an Inconvenience proves nothing but itself. England and Scotland were once separate States, under the same King. The Inconvenience found in their being separate States did not prove, that the Parliament of England had a right to govern Scotland. A formal Union was thought necessary, and England was a hundred Years soliciting it, before she could bring it about. If Great Britain now think such a Union necessary with us, let her propose her Terms, and we may consider them. Were the general Sentiments of this Nation to be consulted in the Case, I should hope the Terms, whether practicable or not, would at least be equitable; for I think, that, except among those with whom the spirit of Toryism prevails, the popular Inclination here is, to wish us well, and that we may preserve our Liberties. . . .

ON OFFICE-HOLDING

Franklin's defense of American rights led to efforts to deprive him of his office as deputy postmaster general for North America. When rumors of these attempts reached Boston, Franklin's sister, Jane Mecom, wrote him, worried about the loss and embarrassment he might suffer. He replied, somewhat self-righteously, but he nevertheless set down a high standard of independence and integrity for office-holders.

. . . I have heard of some great Man, whose Rule it was, with regard to Offices, *never to ask for them, and never to refuse them;* to which I have always added, in my own Practice, *never to resign them.* As I told my Friends, I rose to that Office through a long Course of Service in the inferior Degrees of it. Before my Time, through bad Management, it never produced the Salary annex'd to it; and, when I received it, no Salary was to be allowed, if the Office did not produce it. During the first four Years it was so far from defraying itself, that it became nine hundred and fifty Pounds Sterling in Debt to me and my Colleague.

Writings, V, 289-291; from a letter to Jane Mecom, December 30, 1770.

I had been chiefly instrumental in bringing it to its present flourishing State, and therefore thought I had some kind of Right to it. I had hitherto executed the Duties of it faithfully, and to the perfect Satisfaction of my Superiors, which I thought was all that should be expected of me on that Account. As to the Letters complained of, it was true I did write them, and they were written in compliance with another Duty, that to my Country; a Duty quite distinct from that of PostMaster.

My Conduct in this respect was exactly similar to that I held on a similar Occasion but a few Years ago, when the then Ministry were ready to hug me for the Assistance I afforded them of repealing a former revenue Act. My Sentiments were still the same, that no such Acts should be made here for America; or, if made, should as soon as possible be repealed; and I thought it should not be expected of me to change my political Opinions every time his Majesty thought fit to change his Ministers. This was my Language on the occasion; and I have lately heard, that, though I was thought much to blame, it being understood that every man who holds an office should act with the ministry, whether agreeable or not to his own judgment, yet, in consideration of the goodness of my private character (as they were pleased to compliment me), the office was not to be taken from me.

Possibly they may still change their minds, and remove me; but no apprehension of that sort will, I trust, make the least alteration in my political conduct. My rule, in which I have always found satisfaction, is, never to turn aside in public affairs through views of private interest; but to go straight forward in doing what appears to me right at the time, leaving the consequences with Providence. What in my younger days enabled me more easily to walk upright, was, that I had a trade, and that I knew I could live upon little; and thence (never having had views of making a fortune) I was free from avarice, and contented with the plentiful supplies my business afforded me. And now it is still more easy for me to preserve my freedom and integrity, when I consider that I am almost at the end of my journey, and therefore need less to complete the expense of it; and that what I now possess, through the blessing of God, may, with tolerable economy, be sufficient for me (great misfortunes excepted), though I should add nothing more to it by any office or employment whatsoever. . . .

THE SEEDS OF A "TOTAL DISUNION"

BETWEEN GREAT BRITAIN AND AMERICA

In efforts in England to make colonial officials independent of colonial assemblies, and especially in moves to deprive Massachusetts of the power to thwart her royal governor, Franklin saw the most dangerous and unwelcome signs.

. . . I think one may clearly see, in the system of customs to be exacted in America by act of Parliament, the seeds sown of a total disunion of the two countries, though, as yet, that event may be at a considerable distance. The course and natural progress seems to be, first, the appointment of needy men as officers, for others do not care to leave England; then, their necessities make them rapacious, their office makes them proud and insolent, their insolence and rapacity make them odious, and, being conscious that they are hated, they become malicious; their malice urges them to a continual abuse of the inhab-

---

Writings, V, 317–319; from a letter to the Committee of Correspondence in Massachusetts, May 15, 1771.

itants in their letters to administration, representing them as disaffected and rebellious, and (to encourage the use of severity) as weak, divided, timid, and cowardly. Government believes all; thinks it necessary to support and countenance its officers; their quarrelling with the people is deemed a mark and consequence of their fidelity; they are therefore more highly rewarded, and this makes their conduct still more insolent and provoking.

The resentment of the people will, at times and on particular incidents, burst into outrages and violence upon such officers, and this naturally draws down severity and acts of further oppression from hence. The more the people are dissatisfied, the more rigor will be thought necessary; severe punishments will be inflicted to terrify; rights and privileges will be abolished; greater force will then be required to secure execution and submission; the expense will become enormous; it will then be thought proper, by fresh exactions, to make the people defray it; thence, the British nation and government will become odious, the subjection to it will be deemed no longer tolerable; war ensues, and the bloody struggle will end in absolute slavery to America, or ruin to Britain by the loss of her colonies; the latter most probable, from America's growing strength and magnitude.

But, as the whole empire must, in either case, be greatly weakened, I cannot but wish to see much patience and the utmost discretion in our general conduct, that the fatal period may be postponed, and that, whenever this catastrophe shall happen, it may appear to all mankind, that the fault has not been ours. And, since the collection of these duties has already cost Britain infinitely more, in the loss of commerce, than they amount to, and that loss is likely to continue and increase by the encouragement given to our manufactures through resentment; and since the best pretence for establishing and enforcing the duties is the regulation of trade for the general advantage, it seems to me, that it would be much better for Britain to give them up, on condition of the colonies undertaking to enforce and collect such, as are thought fit to be continued, by laws of their own, and officers of their own appointment, for the public uses of their respective governments. This would alone destroy those seeds of disunion, and both countries might thence much longer continue to grow great together, more secure by their united strength, and more formidable to their common enemies. But the power of appointing friends and dependents to profitable offices is too pleasing to most administrations, to be easily parted with or lessened; and therefore such a proposition if it were made, is not very likely to meet with attention.

I do not pretend to the gift of prophecy. History shows, that, by these steps, great empires have crumbled heretofore; and the late transactions we have so much cause to complain of show, that we are in the same train, and that, without a greater share of prudence and wisdom, than we have seen both sides to be possessed of, we shall probably come to the same conclusion. . . .

A REALISTIC APPRAISAL

OF THE BRITISH EMPIRE

In the period of improved relations between Britain and America that followed repeal of all the duties except that on tea, Franklin wrote privately and candidly to the chairman of the Massachusetts Committee of Correspondence of the steps that would maintain American rights and yet not diminish British honor and prestige in a way gratifying to her (and to America's) enemies.

Writings, V, 323-327; from a letter to Thomas Cushing, June 10, 1771.

... All Views or Expectations of drawing any considerable Revenue to this Country from the Colonies are, I believe, generally given over, and it seems probable that nothing of that kind will ever again be attempted. But as Foreign Courts appear to have taken great Pleasure in the Prospect of our Disunion, it seems now to be thought necessary for supporting the National Weight and the Influence of our Court abroad, that there should be an Appearance as if all was pacified in America; and, as I said before, I think the general Wish is that it may be really so. But then there is an Apprehension lest a too sudden yielding to all our Claims should be deem'd the Effect of Weakness, render the British Court contemptible in the Eyes of Foreigners; make us more presumptuous, and promote more extravagant Demands such as could never be granted, and thence still greater Danger of a fatal Rupture. I am thus particular, that you may judge whether it will not be prudent in us to indulge the Mother Country in this Concern for her own Honour, so far as may be consistent with the Preservation of our essential Rights, especially as that Honour may in some Cases be of Importance to the General Welfare. And in this View, whether it will not be better gradually to wear off the assum'd Authority of Parliament over America, which we have in too many Instances given countenance to, with our indiscrete Acknowledgment of it in Publick Acts, than by a general open Denial and Resistance to it, bring on prematurely a Contest to which, if we are not found equal, that Authority will by the Event be more strongly establish'd; and if we should prove superior, yet by the Division, the general strength of the British Nation must be greatly diminished. I do not venture to advise in this Case, because I see in this seemingly prudent Course some Danger of a diminishing Attention to our Rights, instead of a persevering Endeavor to recover and establish them; but I rely a good deal on the growing Knowledge of them among the Americans, and the daily increasing Strength and Importance of that Country to this, which must give such Weight in time to our just Claims as no selfish Spirit in this Part of the Empire will be able to resist. In the meantime, while we are declining the usurped Authority of Parliament, I wish to see a steady dutiful Attachment to the King and his Family maintained among us; and that however we may be induced for Peace-sake, or from a Sense of our present Inability, to submit at present in some Instances to the Exercise of that unjust Authority, we shall continue from time to time to assert our Rights in occasional solemn Resolves and other publick Acts, never yielding them up, and avoiding even the slightest Expressions that seem confirmatory of the Claim that has been set up against them. My Opinion has long been that Parliament had originally no Right to bind us by any kind of Law whatever without our Consent. We have indeed in a manner consented to some of them, at least tacitly. But for the future methinks we should be cautious how we add to those Instances, and never adopt or acknowledge an Act of Parliament but by a formal Law of our own. . . .

I do not at present see the least likelihood of preventing the Grant of Salaries or Pensions from hence to the King's Officers in America, by any Application in Behalf of the People there. It is look'd on as a strange thing here to object to the King's paying his own servants sent among us to do his Business; and they say we would seem to have much more Reason of Complaint if it were requir'd of us to pay them. And the more we urge the Impropriety of their not depending on us for their Support, the more Suspicion it breeds that we are desirous of influencing them to betray the Interests of their Master or of this Nation. Indeed if the money is rais'd from among us against our Wills, the Injustice becomes more evident than where it arises from

hence. I do not think, however, that the Effect of these Salaries is likely to be so considerable, either in favour of Government here, or in our Prejudice, as may be generally apprehended. The Love of Money is not a Thing of certain Measure, so as that it may be easily filled and satisfied. Avarice is infinite; and where there is not good Economy, no Salary, however large, will prevent Necessity. . . .

THE FARMERS OF GREAT BRITAIN
AND NEW ENGLAND COMPARED

Franklin's thorough knowledge of the conditions of life in the New World and his pride in his own remarkable rise to fame and fortune there made him especially sensitive to the wretched circumstances under which the common people of other lands lived—and, more significantly, to the pathological role played by the government and social structure of those lands in sustaining the wretchedness.

. . . I have lately made a Tour thro' Ireland and Scotland. In those Countries a small Part of the Society are Landlords, great Noblemen, and Gentlemen, extreamly opulent, living in the highest Affluence and Magnificence: The Bulk of the People Tenants, extreamly poor, living in the most sordid Wretchedness, in dirty Hovels of Mud and Straw, and cloathed only in Rags.

I thought often of the Happiness of New England, where every Man is a Freeholder, has a Vote in publick Affairs, lives in a tidy, warm House, has plenty of good Food and Fewel, with whole cloaths from Head to Foot, the Manufacture perhaps of his own Family. Long may

---

Writings, V, 362–363; from a letter to Joshua Babcock, January 13, 1772.

they continue in this Situation! But if they should ever envy the Trade of these Countries, I can put them in a Way to obtain a Share of it. Let them with three fourths of the People of Ireland live the Year round on Potatoes and Buttermilk, without Shirts, then may their Merchants export Beef, Butter, and Linnen. Let them, with the Generality of the Common People of Scotland, go Barefoot, then may they make large Exports in Shoes and Stockings: And if they will be content to wear Rags, like the Spinners and Weavers of England, they may make Cloths and Stuffs for all Parts of the World.

Farther, if my Countrymen should ever wish for the honour of having among them a gentry enormously wealthy, let them sell their Farms & pay rack'd Rents; the Scale of the Landlords will rise as that of the Tenants is depress'd, who will soon become poor, tattered, dirty, and abject in Spirit. Had I never been in the American Colonies, but was to form my Judgment of Civil Society by what I have lately seen, I should never advise a Nation of Savages to admit of Civilization: For I assure you, that, in the Possession & Enjoyment of the various Comforts of Life, compar'd to these People every Indian is a Gentleman: And the Effect of this kind of Civil Society seems only to be, depressing the Multitudes below the Savage State that a few may be rais'd above it. . . .

TOLERATION IN

OLD ENGLAND AND NEW ENGLAND

As the dispute between Great Britain and her colonies wore on and enlarged, the alarm of American dissenters (non-Anglican Protestants) at the persistent effort to plant an Anglican episco-

---

Writings, V, 399–405; first printed in the *London Packet*, June 3, 1772.

pate in the colonies increased. Though they objected on doctrinal grounds and feared the religious oppression bishops might undertake, American dissenters sought mainly to prevent the characteristic Toryism of the Anglican bishops from spreading in the colonies. Thus, in defending dissenters in Great Britain and in refuting the charge that dissenters in America were less tolerant than Anglicans in England, Franklin knew very well that he fought for the Whig cause in the colonies.

I understand from the public papers, that in the debates on the bill for relieving the Dissenters in the point of subscription to the church articles, sundry reflections were thrown out against that people, importing, "that they themselves are of a persecuting, intolerant spirit; for that, when they had the superiority, they persecuted the church, and still persecute it in America, where they compel its members to pay taxes for maintaining the Presbyterian or Independent worship, and, at the same time, refuse them a toleration in the full exercise of their religion by the administrations of a bishop."

If we look back into history for the character of the present sects in Christianity we shall find few that have not in their turns been persecutors, and complainers of persecution. The primitive Christians thought persecution extremely wrong in the Pagans, but practised it on one another. The first Protestants of the church of England blamed persecution in the Romish church, but practised it against the Puritans. These found it wrong in the bishops, but fell into the same practise themselves, both here and in New England. To account for this we should remember, that the doctrine of *toleration* was not then known, or had not prevailed in the world. Persecution was, therefore, not so much the fault of the sect as of the times. It was not in those days deemed wrong *in itself*. The general opinion was only, that those *who are in error* ought not to persecute *the truth;* but the *possessors of truth* were in the right to persecute *error* in order to destroy it. Thus every sect, believing itself possessed of *all truth,* and that every tenet differing from theirs was *error,* conceived, that, when the power was in their hands, persecution was a duty required of them by that God, whom they supposed to be offended with heresy. By degrees more moderate *and more modest* sentiments have taken place in the Christian world; and among Protestants, particularly, all disclaim persecution, none vindicate it, and but few practise it. We should then cease to reproach each other with what was done by our ancestors, but judge of the present character of sects or churches by their *present conduct* only.

Now, to determine on the justice of this charge against the present Dissenters, particularly those in America, let us consider the following facts. They went from England to establish a new country for themselves, *at their own expense,* where they might enjoy the free exercise of religion in their own way. When they had purchased the territory of the natives, they granted the lands out in townships, requiring for it neither purchase-money nor quit-rent, but this condition only to be complied with, that the freeholders should for ever support a gospel minister, (meaning probably one of the governing sects,) and a free-school, within the township. Thus what is commonly called Presbyterianism became the *established religion* of that country. All went on well in this way while the same religious opinions were general, the support of minister and school being raised by a proportionate tax on the lands. But, in process of time some becoming Quakers, some Baptists, and, of late years, some returning to the church of England (through the laudable endeavours, and a *proper application* of their funds, by the Society for Propagating the Gospel), objections were made to the payment

248   *The Political Thought of Benjamin Franklin*

of a tax appropriated to the support of a church they disapproved and had forsaken.

The civil magistrates, however, continued for a time to collect and apply the tax according to the original laws, which remained in force; and they did it more freely, as thinking it just and equitable, that the holders of lands should pay what was contracted to be paid when they were granted, as the only consideration for the grant, and what had been considered by all subsequent purchasers as a perpetual incumbrance on the estate, bought therefore at a proportionably cheaper rate; a payment which it was thought no honest man ought to avoid, under the pretence of his having changed his religious persuasion. And this, I suppose, is one of the best grounds of demanding tithes of Dissenters now in England. But the practice being clamoured against by the Episcopalians as persecution, the legislature of the province of Massachusetts Bay, near thirty years since, passed an act for their relief, requiring indeed the tax to be paid as usual, but directing that the several sums levied from members of the Church of England, should be paid over to the minister of that church, with whom such members usually attended divine worship, which minister had power given him to receive, and on occasion *to recover the same by law.*

It seems that the legislature considered the *end* of the tax was to secure and improve the morals of the people, and promote their happiness, by supporting among them the public worship of God, and the preaching of the Gospel; that where particular people fancied a particular mode, that mode might probably, therefore, be of most use to those people; and that, if the good was done, it was not so material in what mode or by whom it was done. The consideration that their brethren, the Dissenters in England, were still compelled to pay tithes to the clergy of the church, had not weight enough with the legislature to prevent this moderate act, which still continues in full force; and I hope no uncharitable conduct of the church towards the Dissenters will ever provoke them to repeal it.

With regard to a *bishop*, I know not upon what grounds the Dissenters, either here or in America, are charged with refusing the benefit of such an officer to the church in that country. *Here* they seem to have naturally no concern in the affair. *There* they have no power to prevent it, if government should think fit to send one. They would probably *dislike*, indeed, to see an order of men established among them, from whose persecutions their fathers fled into that wilderness, and whose future domination they may possibly fear, *not knowing that their natures are changed*. But the non-appointment of bishops for America seems to arise from another quarter. The same wisdom of government, probably, that prevents the sitting of convocations, and forbids by *noli-prosequis* the persecution of Dissenters for non-subscription, avoids establishing bishops where the minds of the people are not yet prepared to receive them cordially, lest the public peace should be endangered.

And now let us see how this *persecution account* stands between the parties.

In New England, where the legislative bodies are almost to a man dissenters from the church of England,

1. There is no test to prevent churchmen from holding offices.

2. The sons of churchmen have the full benefit of the universities.

3. The taxes for support of public worship, when paid by churchmen, are given to the Episcopal minister.

In Old England,

1. Dissenters are excluded from all offices of profit and honour.

2. The benefits of education in the universities are appropriated to the sons of churchmen.

3. The clergy of the Dissenters receive none of the

tithes paid by their people, who must be at the additional charge of maintaining their own separate worship.

But it is said, the Dissenters of America *oppose* the introduction of a bishop.

In fact, it is not alone the Dissenters there that give opposition (if *not encouraging* must be termed *opposing*), but the laity in general dislike the project, and some even of the clergy. The inhabitants of Virginia are almost all Episcopalians. The church is fully established there, and the Council and General Assembly are perhaps to a man its members; yet, when lately, at a meeting of the clergy, a resolution was taken to apply for a bishop, against which several however protested, the Assembly of the province at their next meeting expressed their disapprobation of the thing in the strongest manner, by unanimously ordering the thanks of the House to the protesters; for many of the American laity of the church think it some advantage, whether their own young men come to England for ordination and improve themselves at the same time with the learned here, or the congregations are supplied by Englishmen, who have had the benefit of education in English universities, and are ordained before they come abroad. They do not, therefore, see the necessity of a bishop merely for ordination, and confirmation is deemed among them a ceremony of no very great importance, since few seek it in England, where bishops are in plenty. These sentiments prevail with many churchmen there, not to promote a design which they think must sooner or later saddle them with great expenses to support it. As to the Dissenters, their minds might probably be more conciliated to the measure, if the bishops here should, in their wisdom and goodness, think fit to set their sacred character in a more friendly light, by dropping their opposition to the Dissenters' application for relief in subscription, and declaring their willingness that Dissenters should be capable of offices, enjoy the benefit of education in the universities, and the privilege of appropriating their tithes to the support of their own clergy. In all these points of toleration they appear far behind the present Dissenters of New England, and it may seem to some a step below the dignity of bishops to follow the example of such inferiors. I do not however despair of their doing it some time or other, since nothing of the kind is too hard for *true Christian humility.* I am, Sir, yours, &c.

A NEW ENGLAND MAN

ADVICE TO THE COLONIES:

UNION, MODERATION, AND FIRMNESS

In June 1773, George III rejected a Massachusetts petition for redress of grievances. Though disappointed at the rejection, Franklin wrote sympathetically of the King's dilemma caused by his dependence on Parliament (or so Franklin supposed), and then considered "How are we to obtain Redress?" After noting how English Ministers spoke more kindly of the colonies when their aid seemed necessary as war threatened, Franklin assessed relations within the Empire.

. . . But as the Strength of an Empire depends not only on the *Union* of its Parts, but on their *Readiness* for united Exertion of their common Force: And as the Discussion of Rights may seem unseasonable in the Commencement of actual War; and the Delay it might occasion be prejudicial to the common Welfare. As likewise the Refusal of one or a few Colonies would not be so much regarded, if the others

---

Writings, VI, 76–79; from a letter to Thomas Cushing, July 7, 1773.

granted liberally, which perhaps by various Artifices and Motives they might be prevailed on to do; and as this want of Concert would defeat the Expectation of general Redress, that otherwise might be justly formed; perhaps it would be best and fairest for the Colonies, in a general Congress now in Peace to be assembled, or by means of the Correspondence lately proposed, after a full and solemn Assertion and Declaration of their Rights, to engage firmly with each other, that they will never grant Aids to the Crown in any General War, till those Rights are recogniz'd by the King and both Houses of Parliament; communicating at the same time to the Crown this their Resolution. Such a Step I imagine will bring the Dispute to a Crisis; and whether our Demands are immediately comply'd with, or compulsory Measures thought of to make us rescind them, our Ends will finally be obtain'd; for even the Odium accompanying such compulsory Attempts will contribute to unite and strengthen us, and in the mean time all the World will allow, that our Proceeding has been honourable.

No one doubts the Advantage of a strict Union between the Mother Country and the Colonies, if it may be obtain'd and preserv'd on equitable Terms. In every fair Connection, each Party should find its own Interest. Britain will find hers in our joining with her in every War she makes, to the greater Annoyance and Terror of her Enemies; in our Employment of her Manufactures, and Enriching of her Merchants by our Commerce; and her Government will feel some additional Strengthening of its Hands by the Disposition of our profitable Posts and Places. On our side, we have to expect the Protection she can afford us, and the Advantage of a common Umpire in our Disputes, thereby preventing Wars we might otherwise have with each other; so that we can without Interruption go on with our Improvements, and increase our Numbers. We ask no more of her, and she should not think of forcing more from us.

By the Exercise of prudent Moderation on her part, mix'd with a little Kindness; and by a decent Behaviour on ours, excusing where we can excuse from a Consideration of Circumstances, and bearing a little with the Infirmities of her Government, as we would with those of an aged Parent, tho' firmly asserting our Privileges, and declaring that we mean at a proper time to vindicate them, this advantageous Union may still be long continued. We wish it, and we may endeavour it; but God will order it as to his Wisdom shall seem most suitable. The Friends of Liberty here, wish we may long preserve it on our side the Water, that they may find it there if adverse Events should destroy it here. They are therefore anxious and afraid, lest we should hazard it by premature Attempts in its favour. They think we may risque much by violent Measures, and that the Risque is unnecessary, since a little Time must infallibly bring us all we demand or desire, and bring it us in Peace and Safety. I do not presume to advise. There are many wiser men among you, and I hope you will be directed by a still superior Wisdom.

With regard to the Sentiments of People in general here, concerning America, I must say that we have among them many Friends and Wellwishers. The Dissenters are all for us, and many of the Merchants and Manufacturers. There seems to be, even among the Country Gentlemen, a general Sense of our growing Importance, a Disapprobation of the harsh Measures with which we have been treated, and a Wish that some Means may be found of perfect Reconciliation. A few Members of Parliament in Both Houses, and perhaps some in high Office, have in a Degree the same Ideas; but none of these seem willing as yet to be active in our favour, lest Adversaries should take Advantage, and charge it upon them as a Betraying the Interests

254 *The Political Thought of Benjamin Franklin*

of this Nation. In this State of things, no Endeavour of mine, or our other Friends here, "to obtain a Repeal of the Acts so oppressive to the Colonists, or the Orders of the Crown so destructive of the Charter Rights of our Province in particular," can expect a sudden Success. By Degrees, and a judicious Improvement of Events, we may work a Change in Minds and Measures; but otherwise such great Alterations are hardly to be look'd for. . . .

RULES BY WHICH A GREAT EMPIRE MAY BE REDUCED TO A SMALL ONE

AND

AN EDICT BY THE KING OF PRUSSIA

Following passage of the act giving the East India Company a virtual monopoly on tea sales in America (without rescinding the detested Townshend duty collected in America), and as evidence accumulated that Great Britain meant to persist in a harsh policy toward the colonies, Franklin wrote two attacks on that policy which are among the most skilful and effective satires ever written in English. He preferred the first ("Rules . . .") "for the quantity and variety of the matter contained, and a kind of spirited ending of each paragraph." Others, though, liked the "Edict . . ." better, partly because when they read it they "were, as the phrase is, *taken in,* till they had got half through it, and imagined it a real edict." Its greatest effect came, Franklin wrote in describing the reaction of one of his friends, when he "soon began to smoke it, and looking at my face said *I'll be hanged if*

Writings, VI, 127–137, 118–124; first printed in the *Public Advertiser,* September 11 and 22, 1773.

this is not some of your American jokes upon us." Delighted, Franklin wrote his sister: "Of late . . . I have been saucy, and in two Papers . . . I have held up a Looking-Glass in which some Ministers may see their ugly Faces, and the Nation its Injustice. The Papers have been much taken Notice of, many are pleas'd with them, and a few very angry."

RULES BY WHICH A GREAT EMPIRE

MAY BE REDUCED TO A SMALL ONE

PRESENTED TO A LATE MINISTER, WHEN HE

ENTERED UPON HIS ADMINISTRATION

An ancient Sage boasted, that, tho' he could not fiddle, he knew how to make a *great city* of a *little one*. The science that I, a modern simpleton, am about to communicate, is the very reverse.

I address myself to all ministers who have the management of extensive dominions, which from their very greatness are become troublesome to govern, because the multiplicity of their affairs leaves no time for *fiddling*.

I. In the first place, gentlemen, you are to consider, that a great empire, like a great cake, is most easily diminished at the edges. Turn your attention, therefore, first to your *remotest* provinces; that, as you get rid of them, the next may follow in order.

II. That the possibility of this separation may always exist, take special care the provinces are never incorporated with the mother country; that they do not enjoy the same common rights, the same privileges in commerce; and that they are governed by *severer* laws, all of *your enacting*, without allowing them any share in the choice of the legislators. By carefully making and preserving such distinctions, you will (to keep to my simile of the cake) act like a wise gingerbread-baker, who, to facilitate a division, cuts his dough half through in those places where, when baked, he would have it *broken to pieces.*

III. Those remote provinces have perhaps been acquired, purchased, or conquered, at the *sole expence* of the settlers, or their ancestors, without the aid of the mother country. If this should happen to increase her *strength,* by their growing numbers, ready to join in her wars; her *commerce,* by their growing demand for her manufactures; or her *naval power,* by greater employment for her ships and seamen, they may probably suppose some merit in this, and that it entitles them to some favour; you are therefore to *forget it all, or resent it,* as if they had done you injury. If they happen to be zealous whigs, friends of liberty, nurtured in revolution principles, *remember all that* to their prejudice, and resolve to punish it; for such principles, after a revolution is thoroughly established, are of *no more use;* they are even *odious* and *abominable.*

IV. However peaceably your colonies have submitted to your government, shewn their affection to your interests, and patiently borne their grievances; you are to *suppose* them always inclined to revolt, and treat them accordingly. Quarter troops among them, who by their insolence may *provoke* the rising of mobs, and by their bullets and bayonets *suppress* them. By this means, like the husband who uses his wife ill *from suspicion,* you may in time convert your *suspicions* into *realities.*

V. Remote provinces must have *Governors* and *Judges,* to represent the Royal Person, and execute everywhere the delegated parts of his office and authority. You ministers know, that much of the strength of government depends on the *opinion* of the people; and much of that opinion on the *choice of rulers* placed immediately over them. If you send them wise and good men for governors, who study the interest of the colonists, and advance their prosperity, they will think their King wise and good, and that he wishes the welfare of his subjects. If you send them learned and upright men for Judges, they will think him a lover of justice. This may attach your provinces more to his government. You are therefore to be careful whom you recommend for those offices. If you can find prodigals, who have ruined their fortunes, broken gamesters or stockjobbers, these may do well as *governors;* for they will probably be rapacious, and provoke the people by their extortions. Wrangling proctors and pettifogging lawyers, too, are not amiss; for they will be for ever disputing and quarrelling with their little parliaments. If withal they should be ignorant, wrongheaded, and insolent, so much the better. Attornies' clerks and Newgate solicitors will do for *Chief Justices,* especially if they hold their places *during your pleasure;* and all will contribute to impress those ideas of your government, that are proper for a people *you would wish to renounce it.*

VI. To confirm these impressions, and strike them deeper, whenever the injured come to the capital with complaints of mal-administration, oppression, or injustice, punish such suitors with long delay, enormous expence, and a final judgment in favour of the oppressor. This will have an admirable effect every way. The trouble of future complaints will be prevented, and Governors and Judges will be encouraged to farther acts of oppression and injustice; and thence the people may become more disaffected, and at length desperate.

VII. When such Governors have crammed their coffers, and made themselves so odious to the people that they can no longer remain among them, with safety to their persons, *recall and reward* them with pensions. You may make them *baronets* too, if that respectable order should not think fit to resent it. All will contribute to encourage new governors in the same practice, and make the supreme government, *detestable.*

VIII. If, when you are engaged in war, your colonies should vie in liberal aids of men and money against the common enemy, upon your simple requisition, and give far beyond their abilities, reflect that a penny taken from them by your power is more honourable to you, than a pound presented by their benevolence; despise therefore their voluntary grants, and resolve to harass them with novel taxes. They will probably complain to your parliaments, that they are taxed by a body in which they have no representative, and that this is contrary to common right. They will petition for redress. Let the Parliaments flout their claims, reject their petitions, refuse even to suffer the reading of them, and treat the petitioners with the utmost contempt. Nothing can have a better effect in producing the alienation proposed; for though many can forgive injuries, *none ever forgave contempt.*

IX. In laying these taxes, never regard the heavy burthens those remote people already undergo, in defending their own frontiers, supporting their own provincial governments, making new roads, building bridges, churches, and other public edifices, which in old countries have been done to your hands by your ancestors, but which occasion constant calls and demands on the purses of a new people. Forget the *restraints* you lay on their trade for *your own* benefit, and the advantage a *monopoly* of this trade gives your exacting merchants. Think nothing of the wealth those merchants and your manufacturers acquire by the colony commerce; their encreased ability thereby to pay taxes at home; their accumulating, in the price of their commodities, most of those taxes, and so levying them from their consuming customers; all this, and the employment and support of thousands of your poor by the colonists, you are *intirely to forget.* But remember to make your arbitrary tax more grievous to your provinces, by public declarations importing that your power of taxing them has *no limits;* so that when you take from them without their consent one shilling in the pound, you have a clear right to the other nineteen. This will probably weaken every idea of *security in their property,* and convince them, that under such a government they *have nothing they can call their own;* which can scarce fail of producing the *happiest consequences!*

X. Possibly, indeed, some of them might still comfort themselves, and say, "Though we have no property, we have yet *something* left that is valuable; we have constitutional *liberty,* both of person and of conscience. This King, these Lords, and these Commons, who it seems are too remote from us to know us, and feel for us, cannot take from us our *Habeas Corpus* right, or our right of trial *by a jury of our neighbours;* they cannot deprive us of the exercise of our religion, alter our ecclesiastical constitution, and compel us to be Papists, if they please, or Mahometans." To annihilate this comfort, begin by laws to perplex their commerce with infinite regulations, impossible to be remembered and observed; ordain seizures of their property for every failure; take away the trial of such property by Jury, and give it to arbitrary Judges of your own appointing, and of the lowest characters in the country, whose salaries and emoluments are to arise out of the duties or condemnations, and whose appointments are *during pleasure.* Then let there be a formal declaration of both Houses, that opposition to your edicts is *treason,* and that any person suspected of treason in the provinces may, according to some obsolete law, be seized and sent to the metropolis of the empire for trial; and pass an act, that those there charged with certain other offences, shall be sent away in chains from their friends and country to be tried in the same manner for felony. Then erect a new

Court of Inquisition among them, accompanied by an armed force, with instructions to transport all such suspected persons; to be ruined by the expence, if they bring over evidences to prove their innocence, or be found guilty and hanged, if they cannot afford it. And, lest the people should think you cannot possibly go any farther, pass another solemn declaratory act, "that King, Lords, Commons had, hath, and of right ought to have, full power and authority to make statutes of sufficient force and validity to bind the unrepresented provinces IN ALL CASES WHATSOEVER." This will include *spiritual* with temporal, and, taken together, must operate wonderfully to your purpose; by convincing them, that they are at present under a power something like that spoken of in the scriptures, which can not only *kill their bodies,* but *damn their souls* to all eternity, by compelling them, if it pleases, *to worship the Devil.*

XI. To make your taxes more odious, and more likely to procure resistance, send from the capital a board of officers to superintend the collection, composed of the most *indiscreet, ill-bred,* and *insolent* you can find. Let these have large salaries out of the extorted revenue, and live in open, grating luxury upon the sweat and blood of the industrious; whom they are to worry continually with groundless and expensive prosecutions before the abovementioned arbitrary revenue Judges; *all at the cost of the party prosecuted,* tho' acquitted, because *the King is to pay no costs.* Let these men, *by your order,* be exempted from all the common taxes and burthens of the province, though they and their property are protected by its laws. If any revenue officers are *suspected* of the least tenderness for the people, discard them. If others are justly complained of, protect and reward them. If any of the under officers behave so as to provoke the people to drub them, promote those to better offices: this will encourage others to procure for themselves such profitable drubbings, by multiplying and enlarging such provocations, and *all will work towards the end you aim at.*

XII. Another way to make your tax odious, is to misapply the produce of it. If it was originally appropriated for the *defence* of the provinces, the better support of government, and the administration of justice, where it may be *necessary,* then apply none of it to that *defence,* but bestow it where it is *not necessary,* in augmented salaries or pensions to every governor, who has distinguished himself by his enmity to the people, and by calumniating them to their sovereign. This will make them pay it more unwillingly, and be more apt to quarrel with those that collect it and those that imposed it, who will quarrel again with them, and all shall contribute to your *main purpose,* of making them *weary of your government.*

XIII. If the people of any province have been accustomed to support their own Governors and Judges to satisfaction, you are to apprehend that such Governors and Judges may be thereby influenced to treat the people kindly, and to do them justice. This is another reason for applying part of that revenue in larger salaries to such Governors and Judges, given, as their commissions are, *during your pleasure* only; forbidding them to take any salaries from their provinces; that thus the people may no longer hope any kindness from their Governors, or (in Crown cases) any justice from their Judges. And, as the money thus misapplied in one province is extorted from all, probably *all will resent the misapplication.*

XIV. If the parliaments of your provinces should dare to claim rights, or complain of your administration, order them to be harrassed with *repeated dissolutions.* If the same men are continually returned by new elections, adjourn their meetings to some country village, where they cannot be accommodated, and there keep them *during pleasure;* for this, you know, is your Prerogative; and an excellent one it is, as you may manage it to promote discontents among the people, diminish their respect, and *increase their disaffection.*

XV. Convert the brave, honest officers of your *navy* into pimping tide-waiters and colony officers of the *customs.* Let those, who in time of war fought gallantly in defence of the commerce of their countrymen, in peace be taught to prey upon it. Let them learn to be corrupted by great and real smugglers; but (to shew their diligence) scour with armed boats every bay, harbour, river, creek, cove, or nook throughout the coast of your colonies; stop and detain every coaster, every wood-boat, every fisherman, tumble their cargoes and even their ballast inside out and upside down; and, if a penn'orth of pins is found un-entered, let the whole be seized and confiscated. Thus shall the trade of your colonists suffer more from their friends in time of peace, than it did from their enemies in war. Then let these boats crews land upon every farm in their way, rob the orchards, steal the pigs and the poultry, and insult the inhabitants. If the injured and exasperated farmers, unable to procure other justice, should attack the aggressors, drub them, and burn their boats; you are to call this *high treason and rebellion,* order fleets and armies into their country, and threaten to carry all the offenders three thousand miles to be hanged, drawn, and quartered. *O! this will work admirably!*

XVI. If you are told of discontents in your colonies, never believe that they are general, or that you have given occasion for them; therefore do not think of applying any remedy, or of changing any offensive measure. Redress no grievance, lest they should be encouraged to demand the redress of some other grievance. Grant no request that is just and reasonable, lest they should make another that is unreasonable. Take all your informations of the state of the colonies from your Governors and officers in enmity with them. Encourage and reward these *leasing-makers;* secrete their lying accusations, lest they should be confuted; but act upon them as the clearest evidence; and believe nothing you hear from the friends of the people: suppose all *their* complaints to be invented and promoted by a few factious demagogues, whom if you could catch and hang, all would be quiet. Catch and hang a few of them accordingly; and the *blood of the Martyrs* shall *work miracles* in favour of your purpose.

XVII. If you see *rival nations* rejoicing at the prospect of your disunion with your provinces, and endeavouring to promote it; if they translate, publish, and applaud all the complaints of your discontented colonists, at the same time privately stimulating you to severer measures, let not that *alarm* or offend you. Why should it, since you all mean *the same thing?*

XVIII. If any colony should at their own charge erect a fortress to secure their port against the fleets of a foreign enemy, get your Governor to betray that fortress into your hands. Never think of paying what it cost the country, for that would look, at least, like some regard for justice; but turn it into a citadel to awe the inhabitants and curb their commerce. If they should have lodged in such fortress the very arms they bought and used to aid you in your conquests, seize them all; it will provoke like *ingratitude* added to *robbery.* One admirable effect of these operations will be, to discourage every other colony from erecting such defences, and so your enemies may more easily invade them; to the great disgrace of your government, and of course *the furtherance of your project.*

XIX. Send armies into their country under pretence of protecting the inhabitants; but, instead of garrisoning the forts on their frontiers with those troops, to prevent incursions, demolish those forts, and order the troops into the heart of the country, that the savages may be encouraged to attack the frontiers, and that the troops may be protected by the inhabitants. This will seem to proceed from your ill will or your ignorance, and contribute farther to produce and strengthen an opinion among them, *that you are no longer fit to govern them.*

XX. Lastly, invest the General of your army in the provinces, with great and unconstitutional powers, and free him from the controul of even your own Civil Governors. Let him have troops enow under his command, with all the fortresses in his possession; and who knows but (like some provincial Generals in the Roman empire, and encouraged by the universal discontent you have produced) he may take it into his head to set up for himself? If he should, and you have carefully practised these few *excellent rules* of mine, take my word for it, all the provinces will immediately join him; and you will that day (if you have not done it sooner) get rid of the trouble of governing them, and all the *plagues* attending their *commerce* and connection from henceforth and for ever.

Q. E. D.

AN EDICT BY THE KING OF PRUSSIA
Dantzic, Sept. 5, [1773.]

We have long wondered here at the supineness of the English nation, under the Prussian impositions upon its trade entering our port. We did not, till lately, know the claims, ancient and modern, that hang over that nation; and therefore could not suspect that it might submit to those impositions from a sense of duty or from principles of equity. The following Edict, just made publick, may, if serious, throw some light upon this matter.

"FREDERICK, by the grace of God, King of Prussia, &c. &c. &c., to all present and to come, (*à tous présens et à venir,*) Health. The peace now enjoyed throughout our dominions, having afforded us leisure to apply ourselves to the regulation of commerce, the improvement of our finances, and at the same time the easing our domestic subjects in their taxes: For these causes, and other good considerations us thereunto moving, we hereby make known, that, after having deliberated these affairs in our council, present our dear brothers, and other great officers of the state, members of the same, we, of our certain knowledge, full power, and authority royal, have made and issued this present Edict, viz.

"Whereas it is well known to all the world, that the first German settlements made in the Island of Britain, were by colonies of people, subject to our renowned ducal ancestors, and drawn from their dominions, under the conduct of Hengist, Horsa, Hella, Uff, Cerdicus, Ida, and others; and that the said colonies have flourished under the protection of our august house for ages past; have never been emancipated therefrom; and yet have hitherto yielded little profit to the same: And whereas we ourself have in the last war fought for and defended the said colonies, against the power of France, and thereby enabled them to make conquests from the said power in America, for which we have not yet received adequate compensation: And whereas it is just and expedient that a revenue should be raised from the said colonies in Britain, towards our indemnification; and that those who are decendants of our ancient subjects, and thence still owe us due obedience, should contribute to the replenishing of our royal coffers as they must have done, had their ancestors remained in the territories now to us appertaining: We do therefore hereby ordain and command, that, from and after the date of these presents, there shall be levied and paid to our officers of the *customs*, on all goods, wares, and merchandizes, and on all grain and other produce of the earth, exported from the said Island of Britain, and on all goods of whatever kind imported into the same, a duty of four and a half per cent *ad valorem*, for the use of us and our successors. And that the said duty may more effectually be collected, we do hereby ordain, that all ships or vessels bound from Great Britain to any other part of the world, or from any other part of the world to Great Britain, shall in their respective voyages touch at our port of Koningsberg, there to be unladen, searched, and charged with the said duties.

"And whereas there hath been from time to time discovered in the said island of Great Britain, by our colonists there, many mines or beds of iron-stone; and sundry subjects, of our ancient dominion, skilful in converting the said stone into metal, have in time past transported themselves thither, carrying with them and communicating that art; and the inhabitants of the said island, presuming that they had a natural right to make the best use they could of the natural productions of their country for their own benefit, have not only built furnaces for smelting the said stone into iron, but have erected plating-forges, slitting-mills, and steel-furnaces, for the more convenient manufacturing of the same; thereby endangering a diminution of the said manufacture in our ancient dominion;—we do therefore hereby farther ordain, that, from and after the date hereof, no mill or other engine for slitting or rolling of iron, or any plating-forge to work with a tilt-hammer, or any furnace for making steel, shall be erected or continued in the said island of Great Britain: And the Lord Lieutenant of every county in the said island is hereby commanded, on information of any such erection within his county, to order and by force to cause the same to be abated and destroyed; as he shall answer the neglect thereof to us at his peril. But we are nevertheless graciously pleased to permit the inhabitants of the said island to transport their iron into Prussia, there to be manufactured, and to them returned; they paying our Prussian subjects for the workmanship, with all the costs of commission, freight, and risk, coming and returning; any thing herein contained to the contrary notwithstanding.

"We do not, however, think fit to extend this our indulgence to the article of wool; but, meaning to encourage, not only the manufacturing of woollen cloth, but also the raising of wool, in our ancient dominions, and to prevent both, as much as may be, in our said island, we do hereby absolutely forbid the transportation of wool from thence, even to the mother country, Prussia; and that those islanders may be farther and more effectually restrained in making any advantage of their own wool in the way of manufacture, we command that none shall be carried out of one county into another; nor shall any worsted, bay, or woollen yarn, cloth, says, bays, kerseys, serges, frizes, druggets, cloth-serges, shalloons, or any other drapery stuffs, or woollen manufactures whatsoever, made up or mixed with wool in any of the said counties, be carried into any other county, or be waterborne even across the smallest river or creek, on penalty of forfeiture of the same, together with the boats, carriages, horses, &c., that shall be employed in removing them. Nevertheless, our loving subjects there are hereby permitted (if they think proper) to use all their wool as manure for the improvement of their lands.

"And whereas the art and mystery of making hats hath arrived at great perfection in Prussia, and the making of hats by our remoter subjects ought to be as much as possible restrained: And forasmuch as the islanders before mentioned, being in possession of wool, beaver and other furs, have presumptuously conceived they had a right to make some advantage thereof, by manufacturing the same into hats, to the prejudice of our domestic manufacture: We do therefore hereby strictly command and ordain, that no hats or felts whatsoever, dyed or undyed, finished or unfinished, shall be loaded or put into or upon any vessel, cart, carriage, or horse, to be transported or conveyed out of one county in the said island into another county, or to any other place whatsoever, by any person or persons whatsoever; on pain of forfeiting the same, with a penalty of five hundred pounds sterling for every offence. Nor shall any hat-maker, in any of the said counties, employ more than two apprentices, on penalty of five pounds sterling per month; we intending hereby, that such hat-makers, being so restrained, both in the production and sale of their commodity, may find no advantage in continuing their business. But, lest the said islanders should suffer inconveniency by the want of hats, we are farther graciously pleased to permit them to send their beaver furs to Prussia; and we also permit hats made thereof to be exported from Prussia to Britain; the people thus favoured to pay all costs and charges of manufacturing, interest, commission to our merchants, insurance and freight going and returning, as in the case of iron.

"And, lastly, being willing farther to favour our said colonies in Britain, we do hereby also ordain and command, that all the *thieves,* highway and street robbers, house-breakers, forgerers, murderers, s — d — tes, and villains of every denomination, who have forfeited their lives to the law in Prussia; but whom we, in our great clemency, do not think fit here to hang, shall be emptied out of our gaols into the said island of Great Britain, for the better peopling of that country.

"We flatter ourselves, that these our royal regulations

and commands will be thought just and reasonable by our much-favoured colonists in England; the said regulations being copied from their statutes of 10 and 11 William III. c. 10, 5 Geo. II. c. 22, 23, Geo. II. c. 29, 4 Geo. I. c. 11, and from other equitable laws made by their parliaments; or from instructions given by their Princes; or from resolutions of both Houses, entered into for the good government of their *own colonies in Ireland and America.*

"And all persons in the said island are hereby cautioned not to oppose in any wise the execution of this our Edict, or any part thereof, such opposition being high treason; of which all who are suspected shall be transported in fetters from Britain to Prussia, there to be tried and executed according to the Prussian law.

"Such is our pleasure.

"Given at Potsdam, this twenty-fifth day of the month of August, one thousand seven hundred and seventy-three, and in the thirty-third year of our reign.

"By the King, in his Council.
"RECHTMAESSIG, *Sec.*"

Some take this Edict to be merely one of the King's *Jeux d'Esprit:* others suppose it serious, and that he means a quarrel with England; but all here think the assertion it concludes with, "that these regulations are copied from acts of the English parliament respecting their colonies," a very injurious one; it being impossible to believe, that a people distinguished for their love of liberty, a nation so wise, so liberal in its sentiments, so just and equitable towards its neighbours, should, from mean and injudicious views of petty immediate profit, treat its own children in a manner so arbitrary and tyrannical!

THE NATURAL RIGHT OF EMIGRATION

A proposed act of Parliament to limit emigration from the British Isles to the colonies caused Franklin to sketch again his vision of a dynamic, freedom-extending British Empire, and to include freedom of movement in pursuit of opportunity among the rights of man. He thought what his father had done in 1683 and what he himself had done in 1723 was a priceless human privilege. He opposed the proposed restraint on four counts.

. . . 1ST. AS TO THE NECESSITY OF IT.

If any country has more people than can be comfortably subsisted in it, some of those who are incommoded may be induced to emigrate. As long as the new situation shall be *far* preferable to the old, the emigration may possibly continue. But when many of those, who at home interfered with others of the same rank (in the competition for farms, shops, business, offices, and other means of subsistence), are gradually withdrawn, the inconvenience of that competition ceases; the number remaining no longer half starve each other; they find they can now subsist comfortably, and though perhaps not quite so well as those who have left them, yet the inbred attachment to a native country is sufficient to overbalance a moderate difference; and thus the emigration ceases naturally. The waters of the ocean may move in currents from one quarter of the globe to another, as they happen in some places to be accumulated, and in others diminished; but no law, beyond the law of gravity, is necessary to prevent their abandoning any coast entirely. Thus the different degrees of happiness of different countries and situations find, or rather make,

---

Writings, VI, 294–299; drafted for publication in the *Public Advertiser* in November 1773, but probably never printed.

their level by the flowing of people from one to another; and where that level is once found, the removals cease. Add to this, that even a real deficiency of people in any country, occasioned by a wasting war or pestilence, is speedily supplied by earlier and more prolific marriages, encouraged by the greater facility of obtaining the means of subsistence. So that a country half depopulated would soon be repeopled, till the means of subsistence were equalled by the population. All increase beyond that point must perish, or flow off into more favourable situations. Such overflowings there have been of mankind in all ages, or we should not now have had so many nations. But to apprehend absolute depopulation from that cause, and call for a law to prevent it, is calling for a law to stop the Thames, lest its waters, by what leave it daily at Gravesend, should be quite exhausted. Such a law, therefore, I do not conceive to be NECESSARY.

2DLY. AS TO THE PRACTICABILITY.

When I consider the attempts of this kind that have been made, first in the time of Archbishop Laud, by orders of Council, to stop the Puritans, who were flying from his persecutions into New England, and next by Louis the Fourteenth, to retain in his kingdom the persecuted Huguenots; and how ineffectual all the power of our crown, with which the Archbishop armed himself, and all the more absolute power of that great French monarch, were, to obtain the end for which they were exerted; and when I consider, too, the extent of coast to be guarded, and the multitude of cruisers necessary effectually to make a prison of the Island for this confinement of free Englishmen, who naturally love liberty, and would probably by the very restraint be more stimulated to break through it; I cannot but think such a law IMPRACTICABLE. The offices would not be applied to for licenses, the ports would not be used for embarkation. And yet the people disposed to leave us would, as the Puritans did, get away by shipfuls.

3DLY. AS TO THE POLICY OF THE LAW.

Since I have shown there is no danger of depopulating Britain, but that the place of those that depart will soon be filled up equal to the means of obtaining a livelihood, let us see whether there are not some general *advantages* to be expected from the present emigration. The new settlers in America, finding plenty of subsistence, and land easily acquired whereon to seat their children, seldom postpone marriage through fear of poverty. Their natural increase is therefore in proportion far beyond what it would have been, if they had remained here. New farms are daily everywhere forming in those immense forests; new towns and villages rising; hence a growing demand for our merchandise, to the greater employment of our manufacturers, and the enriching of our merchants. By this natural increase of people, the strength of the empire is increased; men are multiplied, out of whom new armies may be formed on occasion, or the old recruited. The long-extended seacoast, too, of that vast country, the great maritime commerce of its ports with each other, its many navigable rivers and lakes, and its plentiful fisheries, breed multitudes of seamen, besides those created and supported by its voyages to Europe; a thriving nursery this, for the manning of our fleets in time of war, and maintaining our importance among foreign nations by that navy, which is also our best security against invasions from our enemies. An extension of empire by conquest of inhabited countries is not so easily obtained, it is not so easily secured; it alarms more the neighbouring states; it is more subject to revolts, and more apt to occasion new wars.

The increase of dominion by colonies proceeding from yourselves, and by the natural growth of your own people, cannot be complained of by your neighbours as an injury; none have a right to be offended with it. Your new possessions are therefore more secure, they are more cheaply gained, they are attached to your nation by natural alliance and affection; and thus they afford an additional strength more certainly to be depended on, than any that can be acquired by a conquering power, though at an immense expense of blood and treasure. These, methinks, are national advantages, that more than equiponderate with the inconveniences suffered by a few Scotch or Irish landlords, who perhaps may find it necessary to abate a little of their present luxury, or of those advanced rents they now so unfeelingly demand. From these considerations, I think I may conclude, that the restraining law proposed would, if practicable, be IMPOLITIC.

4THLY. AS TO THE JUSTICE OF IT.

I apprehend that every Briton, who is made unhappy at home, has a right to remove from any part of his King's dominions into those of any other prince, where he can be happier. If this should be denied me, at least it will be allowed, that he has a right to remove into any other part of the same dominions. For by this right so many Scotchmen remove into England, easing their own country of its supernumeraries, and benefiting ours by their industry. And this is the case with those who go to America. Will not these Scottish lairds be satisfied unless a law passes to pin down all tenants to the estate they are born on, (*adscripti glebæ,*) to be bought and sold with it? God has given to the beasts of the forest, and to the birds of the air, a right, when their subsistence fails in one country, to migrate to another, where they can get a more comfortable living; and shall man be denied a privilege enjoyed by brutes, merely to gratify a few avaricious landlords? Must misery be made *permanent,* and suffered by *many* for the emolument of *one;* while the increase of human beings is prevented, and thousands of their offsprings stifled, as it were, in the birth, that this petty Pharaoh may enjoy an *excess* of opulence? God commands to increase and replenish the earth; the proposed law would forbid increasing, and confine Britons to their present number, keeping half that number too in wretchedness. The common people of Britain and of Ireland contributed by the taxes they paid, and by the blood they lost, to the success of that war, which brought into our hands the vast unpeopled territories of North America; a country favored by Heaven with all the advantages of climate and soil. Germans are now pouring into it, to take possession of it, and fill it with their posterity; and shall Britons and Irelanders, who have a much better right to it, be forbidden a share of it, and, instead of enjoying there the plenty and happiness that might reward their industry, be compelled to remain here in poverty and misery? Considerations such as these persuade me, that the proposed law would be both UNJUST and INHUMAN.

If then it is *unnecessary, impracticable, impolitic,* and *unjust,* I hope our Parliament will never receive the bill, but leave landlords to their own remedy, an abatement of rents, and frugality of living; and leave the liberties of Britons and Irishmen at least as extensive as it found them. I am, Sir, yours, &c.

A FRIEND TO THE POOR.

Spokesman for America in England 275

DEFENSE

OF FRANKLIN'S CAREER AS AGENT

AND THE LOSS OF HIS OFFICES:

THE HUTCHINSON LETTERS

Late in 1772 Franklin received in confidence some letters Governor Thomas Hutchinson of Massachusetts had written in 1768-1769 to a third party urging the British Ministry to take firm, repressive measures in the colonies. Incensed, Franklin sent the letters, again in confidence, to his friends in Boston, to show them that they had enemies there as well as in London. Sensing that publication of the letters would arouse the public against Hutchinson as the radical leaders sought always to do, they were printed in Boston newspapers. When news of this publication reached London it caused a duel between the persons involved in giving the letters to Franklin in the first place. Caught in his own limited violation of a trust by the more flagrant violation of his Boston friends, to prevent a renewal of the duel Franklin acknowledged publicly that he, not the person challenged, had transmitted the letters to America. The Ministry saw its chance at last to humiliate the troublesome agent; he was caught red-handed, they alleged, betraying a friend in order to promote his seditious plans in America. On January 29, 1774, ostensibly at the hearing of a petition from the Massachusetts Assembly for removal of Governor Hutchinson, Franklin stood for more than an hour at the Cockpit before the Privy Council while Solicitor General Alexander Wedderburn delivered a bitter, brutal assault on his reputation and on his conduct as an

---

Writings, VI, 258-262, 189-191; from a tract written in 1774, and a letter to Thomas Cushing, February 15, 1774.

agent. The next day he was dismissed as deputy postmaster general, and he never again appeared officially in London as agent for any of the colonies.

Sometime later in 1774 he wrote a long defense "Relative to the Affair of Hutchinson's Letters" intended for publication but never given to the press. In it he commented on abuse of public figures and stated the principles upon which he had based his agency.

Having been from my Youth more or less engag'd in publick Affairs, it has often happened to me in the Course of my Life to be censured sharply for the Part I took in them. Such Censures I have generally passed over in Silence, conceiving, when they were just, that I ought rather to amend than defend; and when they were undeserved, that a little Time would justify me. Splashes of Dirt thrown upon my Character, I suffered while fresh to remain: I did not chuse to spread by endeavouring to remove them, but rely'd on the vulgar Adage *that they would all rub off when they were dry.* Much Experience has confirm'd my Opinion of the Propriety of this Conduct; for notwithstanding the frequent, and sometimes the virulent Attacks which the Jostlings of Party Interests have drawn upon me, I have had the Felicity of bringing down to a good old Age as fair a Reputation (may I be permitted to say it?) as most publick Men that I have known, and have never had reason to repent my neglecting to defend it. . . .

. . . It has long appeared to me, that the only true British Politicks were those which aim'd at the Good of the *Whole British Empire,* not that which sought the Advantage of *one Part* in the Disadvantage of the others; therefore all Measures of procuring Gain to the Mother Country arising from Loss to her Colonies, and all of Gain to the

Colonies arising from or occasioning Loss to Britain, especially where the Gain was small and the Loss great, every Abridgment of the Power of the Mother Country, where that Power was not prejudicial to the Liberties of the Colonists, and every Diminution of the Privileges of the Colonists, where they were not prejudicial to the Welfare of the Mo. Country, I, in my own Mind, condemned as improper, partial, unjust, and mischievous; tending to create Dissensions, and weaken that Union, on which the Strength, Solidity, and Duration of the Empire greatly depended; and I opposed, as far as my little Powers went, all Proceedings, either here or in America, that in my Opinion had such Tendency. Hence it has often happened to me, that while I have been thought here too much of an American, I have in America been deem'd too much of an Englishman. . . .

[On February 15, 1774, Franklin wrote Thomas Cushing of his reaction to Wedderburn's abuse.]

. . . It may be supposed, that I am very angry on this occasion, and therefore I did purpose to add no reflections of mine on the treatment the Assembly and their agent have received, lest they should be thought the effects of resentment and a desire of exasperating. But, indeed, what I feel on my own account is half lost in what I feel for the public. When I see, that all petitions and complaints of grievances are so odious to government, that even the mere pipe which conveys them becomes obnoxious, I am at a loss to know how peace and union are to be maintained or restored between the different parts of the empire. Grievances cannot be redressed unless they are known; and they cannot be known but through complaints and petitions. If these are deemed affronts, and the messengers punished as offenders, who will henceforth send petitions?

And who will deliver them? It has been thought a dangerous thing in any state to stop up the vent of griefs. Wise governments have therefore generally received petitions with some indulgence, even when but slightly founded. Those, who think themselves injured by their rulers, are sometimes, by a mild and prudent answer, convinced of their error. But where complaining is a crime, hope becomes despair. . . .

THE BOSTON TEA PARTY

Franklin's humiliation at the Cockpit took place as news of the Boston Tea Party reached England. He explained his disapproval of the destruction of the tea four days after the Cockpit scene.

. . . I am truly concern'd as I believe all considerate Men are with you, that there should seem to any a Necessity for carrying Matters to such Extremity, as, in a Dispute about Publick Rights, to destroy private Property. This (notwithstanding the Blame justly due to those who obstructed the Return of the Tea) it is impossible to justify with People so prejudiced in favour of the Power of Parliament to tax America, as most are in this Country. — As the India Company however are not our Adversaries, and the offensive Measure of sending their Teas did not take its Rise with them, but was an Expedient of the Ministry to serve them and yet avoid a Repeal of the old Act, I cannot but wish & hope that before any compulsive Measures are thought of here, our General Court will have shewn a Disposition to repair the Damage and make Compensation

---

Writings, VI, 179; from a letter to the Committee of Correspondence in Massachusetts, February 2, 1774.

to the Company. This all our Friends here wish with me; and that if War is finally to be made upon us, which some threaten, an Act of violent Injustice on our part, unrectified may not give a colourable Pretence for it. . . .

A FINAL PLEA

TO PRESERVE THE BRITISH EMPIRE

The Coercive Acts passed by Parliament in the Spring of 1774 impelled Franklin to a defense of colonial rights and a blistering attack on the foolishness and brutality of the measures, but when he received news of the firm, orderly response in America, especially the calling of the First Continental Congress, he expressed for the last time a hope that Britain and her colonies might live together in peace and prosperity.

. . . The Coolness, Temper, & Firmness of the American Proceedings; the Unanimity of all the Colonies, in the same Sentiments of their Rights, & of the Injustice offered to Boston; and the Patience with which those Injuries are at Present borne, without the least Appearance of Submission; have a good deal surprized and disappointed our Enemies, and the Tone of Publick Conversation, which has been violently against us, begins evidently to turne; so that I make no doubt that before the meeting of Parliament it will be as general in our Favour. All who know well the State of things here, agree, that if the Non Consumption Agreement should become general, and be firmly adhered to, this Ministry must be ruined, and our Friends succeed

---

Writings, VI, 238–239; from a letter to Thomas Cushing, September 3, 1774.

them, from whom we may hope a great Constitutional Charter to be confirmed by King, Lords, & Commons, whereby our Liberties shall be recognized and established, as the only sure Foundation of that Union so necessary for our Common welfare. . . .

SOME GOOD WHIG PRINCIPLES

The date and origin of this memorandum, the most unqualified statement about suffrage among Franklin's papers, are obscure; it seems to have been written at the peak of his disgust with the English Parliament, and may very well have been drawn in consultation with some of his radical Whig friends (Richard Price or Joseph Priestley, for example) who sought earnestly to widen the franchise in Great Britain. The possibility remains that Franklin is not even a part author of the statement.

Declaration of those rights of the Commonalty of Great Britain, *without which they cannot be* free.
It is declared,
First, That the government of this realm, and the making of laws for the same, ought to be lodged in the hands of King, Lords of Parliament, and Representatives of *the whole body* of the freemen of this realm.
Secondly, That *every man* of the commonalty (excepting infants, insane persons, and criminals) is, of common right, and by the laws of God, *a freeman,* and entitled to the free enjoyment of *liberty.*

Writings, X, 130–131; from a printed paper endorsed by Franklin and probably written shortly before his departure from England, perhaps in 1774.

Thirdly, That liberty, or freedom, consists in having *an actual share* in the appointment of those who frame the laws, and who are to be the guardians of every man's life, property, and peace; for the *all* of one man is as dear to him as the *all* of another; and the poor man has an *equal* right, but *more* need, to have representatives in the legislature than the rich one.

Fourthly, That they who have *no* voice nor vote in the electing of representatives, *do not enjoy* liberty; but are absolutely *enslaved* to those who *have* votes, and to their representatives; for to be enslaved is to have governors whom *other men have set over us,* and be subject to laws *made by the representatives of others,* without having had representatives of our own to give consent in *our* behalf.

Fifthly, That *a very great majority* of the commonalty of this realm are denied the privilege of voting for representatives in Parliament; and, consequently, they are enslaved to a *small number,* who do now enjoy the privilege exclusively to themselves; but who, it may be presumed, are far from wishing to continue in the exclusive possession of a privilege, by which their fellow-subjects are deprived of *common right,* of *justice,* of *liberty;* and which, if not communicated to all, must speedily cause *the certain overthrow of our happy constitution,* and enslave us *all.*

And, sixthly and lastly, We also say and do assert, that it is *the right* of the commonalty of this realm to elect a *new* House of Commons once in *every year,* according to the ancient and sacred laws of the land; because, whenever a Parliament continues in being for *a longer term,* very great numbers of the commonalty, who have arrived at years of manhood since the last election, and *therefore* have a right to be actually represented in the House of Commons, are then *unjustly deprived* of that right.

ON CORRUPTION IN ENGLAND

A month before Franklin left England he wrote of his extreme disgust with public life there.

. . . When I consider the extream Corruption prevalent among all Orders of Men in this old rotten State, and the glorious publick Virtue so predominant in our rising Country, I cannot but apprehend more Mischief than Benefit from a closer Union. I fear they will drag us after them in all the plundering Wars, which their desperate Circumstances, Injustice, and Rapacity, may prompt them to undertake; and their wide-wasting Prodigality and Profusion is a Gulph that will swallow up every Aid we may distress ourselves to afford them.

Here Numberless and needless Places, enormous Salaries, Pensions, Perquisites, Bribes, groundless Quarrels, foolish Expeditions, false Accounts or no Accounts, Contracts and Jobbs, devour all Revenue, and produce continual Necessity in the Midst of natural Plenty. I apprehend, therefore, that to unite us intimately will only be to corrupt and poison us also. . . .

GREAT BRITAIN AND EUROPE AT THE BEGINNING OF THE AMERICAN REVOLUTION

Throughout the quarrel between Great Britain and her colonies Franklin often reminded Englishmen of the catastrophe loss of the colonies would be in British relations with the nations of

---

Writings, VI, 311–312; from a letter to Joseph Galloway, February 25, 1775.
Writings, VII, 82–86; from a manuscript probably drafted early in 1775.

Europe. In one of his last efforts to persuade Britain of the folly of waging war on the colonies Franklin wrote a satirical "Dialogue" dramatizing the glee of England's enemies at the impending struggle.

A DIALOGUE BETWEEN BRITAIN, FRANCE, SPAIN, HOLLAND, SAXONY AND AMERICA

Britain. Sister of Spain, I have a Favour to ask of you. My Subjects in America are disobedient, and I am about to chastize them; I beg you will not furnish them with any Arms or Ammunition.

Spain. Have you forgotten, then, that when my Subjects in the Low Countries rebelled against me, you not only furnish'd them with military Stores, but join'd them with an Army and a Fleet? I wonder how you can have the Impudence to ask such a Favour of me, or the Folly to expect it!

Britain. You, my dear Sister of France, will surely not refuse me this Favour.

France. Did you not assist my Rebel Hugenots with a Fleet and an Army at Rochelle? And have you not lately aided privately and sneakingly my Rebel Subjects in Corsica? And do you not at this Instant keep their Chief, pension'd, and ready to head a fresh Revolt there, whenever you can find or make an Opportunity? Dear Sister, you must be a little silly!

Britain. Honest Holland! You see it is remembered that I was once your Friend; you will therefore be mine on this Occasion. I know, indeed, you are accustom'd to smuggle with these Rebels of mine. I will wink at that; sell 'em as much Tea as you please, to enervate the Rascals, since they will not take it of me; but for God's sake don't supply them with any Arms!

Holland. 'T is true you assisted me against Philip, my Tyrant of Spain, but have I not assisted you against one of your Tyrants;[1] and enabled you to expell him? Surely that Accompt, as we Merchants say, is *ballanced,* and I am nothing in your Debt. I have indeed some Complaints against *you,* for endeavouring to starve me by your *Navigation Acts;* but, being peaceably dispos'd, I do not quarrel with you for that, I shall only go on quietly with my own Business. Trade is my Profession: 'tis all I have to subsist on. And, let me tell you, I shall make no scruple (on the prospect of a good Market for that Commodity) even to send my ships to Hell and supply the Devil with Brimstone. For you must know, I can insure in London against the Burning of my Sails.

America to Britain. Why, you old bloodthirsty Bully! You who have been everywhere vaunting your own Prowess, and defaming the Americans as poltroons! You who have boasted of being able to march over all their Bellies with a single Regiment! You who by Fraud have possessed yourself of their strongest Fortress, and all the arms they had stored up in it! You who have a disciplin'd Army in their Country, intrench'd to the Teeth, and provided with every thing! Do *you* run about begging all Europe not to supply those poor People with a little Powder and Shot? Do you mean, then, to fall upon them naked and unarm'd, and butcher them in cold Blood? Is this your Courage? Is this your Magnanimity?

Britain. Oh! you wicked−Whig−Presbyterian−Serpent! Have you the Impudence to appear before me after all your Disobedience? Surrender immediately all your Liberties and Properties into my Hands, or I will cut you to Pieces. Was it for this that I planted your country at so great an Expence? That I protected you in your Infancy, and defended you against all your Enemies?

---

[1]James 2d.

America. I shall not surrender my Liberty and Property, but with my Life. It is not true, that my Country was planted at your expence. Your own Records refute that Falshood to your Face. Nor did you ever afford me a Man or a Shilling to defend me against the Indians, the only Enemies I had upon my own Account. But, when you have quarrell'd with all Europe, and drawn me with you into all your Broils, then you value yourself upon protecting me from the Enemies you have made for me. I have no natural Cause of Difference with Spain, France, or Holland, and yet by turns I have join'd with you in Wars against them all. You would not suffer me to make or keep a separate Peace with any of them, tho' I might easily have done it to great Advantage. Does your protecting me in those Wars give you a Right to fleece me? If so, as I fought for you, as well as you for me, it gives me a proportionable Right to fleece you. What think you of an American Law to make a Monopoly of you and your Commerce, as you have done by your Laws of me and mine? Content yourself with that Monopoly if you are Wise, and learn Justice if you would be respected!

Britain. You impudent b——h! Am not I your Mother Country? Is that not a sufficient Title to your Respect and Obedience?

Saxony. Mother country! Hah, hah, he! What Respect have *you* the front to claim as a Mother Country? You know that *I* am *your* Mother Country, and yet you pay me none. Nay, it is but the other day, that you hired Ruffians[2] to rob me on the Highway,[3] and burn my House![4] For shame! Hide your Face and hold your Tongue. If you continue this Conduct, you will make yourself the Contempt of Europe!

---

[2]Prussians.
[3]They enter'd and rais'd Contributions in Saxony.
[4]And they burnt the fine Suburbs of Dresden, the Capital of Saxony.

Britain. O Lord! Where are my friends?

France, Spain, Holland, and Saxony, all together. Friends! Believe us, you have none, nor ever will have any, 'till you mend your Manners. How can we, who are your Neighbours, have any regard for you, or expect any Equity from you, should your Power increase, when we see how basely and unjustly you have us'd both your *own Mother and your own Children?*

PART THREE

Revolutionist in America

1775–1776

BRITISH VICES AND AMERICAN VIRTUES

When Franklin reached Philadelphia in May 1775 he was elected immediately a member of the Pennsylvania delegation to the Continental Congress. Shortly after news of the Battle of Bunker Hill reached him, Franklin wrote a friend in England of the spirit which infused America.

The Congress met at a time when all minds were so exasperated by the perfidy of General Gage, and his attack on the country people, that propositions of attempting an accommodation were not much relished; and it has been with difficulty that we have carried another humble petition to the crown, to give Britain one more chance, one opportunity more, of recovering the friendship of the colonies; which, however, I think she has not sense enough to embrace, and so I conclude she has lost them for ever.

She has begun to burn our seaport towns; secure, I suppose, that we shall never be able to return the outrage in kind. She may doubtless destroy them all; but, if she wishes to recover our commerce, are these the probable means? She must certainly be distracted; for no tradesman out of Bedlam ever thought of encreasing the number of his customers, by knocking them on the head; or of en-

---

Writings, VI, 408–409; from a letter to Joseph Priestley, July 7, 1775.

abling them to pay their debts, by burning their houses. If she wishes to have us subjects, and that we should submit to her as our compound sovereign, she is now giving us such miserable specimens of her government, that we shall ever detest and avoid it, as a complication of robbery, murder, famine, fire, and pestilence. . . .

. . . We have not yet applied to any foreign power for assistance, nor offered our commerce for their friendship. Perhaps we never may; yet it is natural to think of it, if we are pressed. We have now an army on our establishment, which still holds yours besieged. My time was never more fully employed. In the morning at six, I am at the Committee of Safety, appointed by the Assembly to put the province in a state of defence; which committee holds till near nine, when I am at the Congress, and that sits till after four in the afternoon. Both these bodies proceed with the greatest unanimity, and their meetings are well attended. It will scarce be credited in Britain, that men can be as diligent with us from zeal for the public good, as with you for thousands per annum. Such is the difference between uncorrupted new states, and corrupted old ones.

Great frugality and great industry are now become fashionable here. Gentlemen, who used to entertain with two or three courses, pride themselves now in treating with simple beef and pudding. By these means, and the stoppage of our consumptive trade with Britain, we shall be better able to pay our voluntary taxes for the support of our troops. . . .

ARTICLES OF CONFEDERATION
AND PERPETUAL UNION

As the author of the Albany Plan of Union and the person most intimately acquainted with the connections among the colonies through his printing business and his services as postmaster general and as agent in London, Franklin was the logical person to propose the plan of union for the now nearly-independent colonies. Though Congress was not yet ready to adopt articles of union, Franklin's plan served as a point of departure for the many proposals made after the Declaration of Independence. Bracketed words indicate changes made on the floor of Congress.

ART. I.

The Name of this Confederacy shall henceforth be THE UNITED COLONIES OF NORTH AMERICA.

ART. II.

The said United Colonies hereby severally enter into a firm League of Friendship with each other, binding [on] themselves and their Posterity, for [their common] Defence against their Enemies, for the Security of their Liberties and Properties, the Safety of their Persons and Families, and their mutual and general Welfare.

ART. III.

That each Colony shall enjoy and retain as much as it may think fit of its own present Laws, Customs, Rights, Privileges, and peculiar jurisdictions within its own Limits; and may amend its own Constitution, as shall seem best to its own Assembly or Convention.

ART. IV.

That for the more convenient Management of general Interests, Delegates shall be annually elected in each Col-

---

Writings, VI, 420–425; read in Congress July 21, 1775.

ony, to meet in General Congress at such Time and Place as shall be agreed on in the next preceding Congress. Only, where particular Circumstances do not make a Duration necessary, it is understood to be a Rule, that each succeeding Congress be held in a different Colony, till the whole Number be gone through; and so in perpetual Rotation; and that accordingly the next [Congress] after the present shall be held at Annapolis, in Maryland.

ART. V.

That the Power and Duty of the Congress shall extend to the Determining on War and Peace; the entring into Alliances, [sending and receiving ambassadors] (the reconciliation with Great Britain); the settling all Disputes and Differences between Colony and Colony, [about Limits or any other cause,] if such should arise; and the Planting of new Colonies; when proper. The Congress shall also make such general [ordinances] as, tho' necessary to the General Welfare, particular Assemblies cannot be competent to, viz. [those that may relate to our general] Commerce, or general Currency; the establishment of Posts; [and] the Regulation of [our common] Forces. The Congress shall also have the appointment of all General Officers, civil and military, appertaining to the general Confederacy, such as General Treasurer, Secretary, &c.

ART. VI.

All Charges of Wars, and all other general Expences [to be] incurr'd for the common Welfare, shall be defray'd out of a common Treasury, which is to be supply'd by each Colony in proportion to its Number of Male Polls between 16 and 60 Years of Age; the Taxes for paying that Proportion [are] to be laid and levied by [the] Laws of each Colony.

ART. VII.

The Number of Delegates to be elected and sent to the Congress by each Colony shall be regulated, from time to time, by the Number of [such] Polls return'd; so as that one Delegate be allowed for every 5000 Polls. And the Delegates are to bring with them to every Congress an authenticated return of the number of Polls in their respective Provinces, [which is] to be [triennially / annually] taken for the Purposes above mentioned.

ART. VIII.

At every Meeting of the Congress, one half of the Members return'd, exclusive of Proxies, be necessary to make a Quorum; and each Delegate at the Congress shall have a Vote in all Cases, and, if necessarily absent, shall be allow'd to appoint [any other Delegate from the same Colony to be his] Proxy, who may vote for him.

ART. IX.

An executive Council shall be appointed by the Congress [out of their own Body,] consisting of 12 Persons; of whom, in the first appointment, [one third, viz.] (four,) shall be for one Year, (four) for two Years, and (four) for three Years; and as the said terms expire, the Vacancies shall be filled by appointments for three Years; whereby one Third of the Members will be changed annually. And each Person who has served the said Term [of three Years] as Counsellor, shall have a Respite of three Years, before he can be elected again. This Council, [of whom two thirds shall be a Quorum] in the Recess of Congress, is to execute what shall have been enjoin'd thereby; [to] manage the general [Continental] Business and Interests; to receive applications from foreign Countries; [to] prepare Matters for the Consideration of the Congress; to fill up, [*pro tempore*,] [continental] offices, that fall vacant; and to draw on the General Treasurer for such Monies as may be necessary for general Services, and appropriated by the Congress to such Services.

ART. X.

No Colony shall engage in an offensive War with any Nation of Indians without the Consent of the Congress, or great Council above mentioned, who are first to consider the Justice and Necessity of such War.

ART. XI.

A perpetual Alliance, offensive and defensive, is to be entred into as soon as may be with the Six Nations; their Limits to be ascertain'd and secur'd to them; their Land not to be encroach'd on, nor any private [or Colony] Purchases made of them hereafter to be held good; nor any [Contract for Lands] to be made, but between the Great Council [of the Indians] at Onondaga and the General Congress. The Boundaries and Lands of all the other Indians shall also be [ascertain'd and] secur'd to them [in the same manner,] and Persons appointed to reside among them in proper Districts; who shall take care to prevent Injustice in the Trade with them; [and be enabled at our general Expence,] by occasional small supplies, to relieve their personal Wants and Distresses. And all Purchases from them shall be by the Congress, for the General Advantage and Benefit of the United Colonies.

ART. XII.

As all new Institutions may have Imperfections, which only Time and Experience can discover, it is agreed, that the General Congress, from time [to time,] shall propose such amendments of the Constitution as may be found necessary; which, being approv'd by a Majority of the Colony Assemblies, shall be equally binding with the rest of the Articles of this Confederation.

ART. XIII.

Any and every Colony from Great Britain [upon the continent of North America,] not at present engag'd in our Association, may, upon application [and joining the said Association,] be receiv'd into the Confederation, viz. [Ireland,] the West India Islands, Quebec, St. John's, Nova Scotia, Bermudas, and the East and West Floridas; and shall [thereupon] be entitled to all the advantages of our Union, mutual Assistance, and Commerce.

These Articles shall be propos'd to the several Provincial Conventions or Assemblies, to be by them consider'd; and if approved, they are advis'd to impower their Delegates to agree to and ratify the same in the ensuing Congress. After which the Union thereby establish'd is to continue firm, till the Terms of Reconciliation proposed in the Petition of the last Congress to the King are agreed to; till the Acts since made, restraining the American Commerce [and Fisheries,] are repeal'd; till Reparation is made for the Injury done to Boston, by shutting up its Port, for the Burning of Charlestown, and for the Expence of this unjust War; and till all the British Troops are withdrawn from America. On the Arrival of these Events, the Colonies return to their former Connection and Friendship with Britain: But on Failure thereof, this Confederation is to be perpetual.

Read Before Congress July 21, 1775.

FIRST PROPOSALS FOR PEACE

WITH GREAT BRITAIN

Independence had not been declared three months before Franklin turned to proposals for peace. Appointed by Congress a member of a commission to treat with the British commander Lord Howe, Franklin sketched the minimum conditions that would maintain American independence, and explained the "motives" for his proposals.

There shall be a perpetual peace between Great Britain and the United States of America, on the following conditions.

Great Britain shall renounce and disclaim all pretence of right or authority to govern in any of the United States of America.

To prevent those occasions of misunderstanding, which are apt to arise where the territories of different powers border on each other, through the bad conduct of frontier inhabitants on both sides, Britain shall cede to the United States the provinces or colonies of Quebec, St. John's,

---

Writings, VI, 452–454; drawn for use in conferences with Lord Howe, September 1776.

Nova Scotia, Bermuda, East and West Florida, and the Bahama Islands, with all their adjoining and intermediate territories now claimed by her.

In return for this cession, the United States shall pay to Great Britain the sum of   sterling, in annual payments; that is to say,   per annum, for and during the term of   years.

And shall, moreover, grant a free trade to all British subjects throughout the United States and the ceded colonies, and shall guaranty to Great Britain the possession of her islands in the West Indies.

MOTIVES FOR PROPOSING
A PEACE AT THIS TIME.

1. The having such propositions in charge will, by the law of nations, be some protection to the commissioners or ambassadors, if they should be taken.

2. As the news of our declared independence will tend to unite in Britain all parties against us, so our offering peace, with commerce and payments of money, will tend to divide them again. For peace is as necessary to them as to us; our commerce is wanted by their merchants and manufacturers, who will therefore incline to the accommodation, even though the monopoly is not continued, since it can be easily made to appear their *share* of our growing trade will soon be greater than the *whole* has been heretofore. Then, for the landed interest, who wish an alleviation of taxes, it is demonstrable by figures, that, if we should agree to pay, suppose ten millions in one hundred years, viz. one hundred thousand pounds per annum for that term, it would, being faithfully employed as a sinking fund, more than pay off all their present national debt. It is, besides, a prevailing opinion in England, that they must in the nature of things

sooner or later lose the colonies, and many think they had better be without the government of them; so that the proposition will, on that account, have more supporters and fewer opposers.

3. As the having such propositions to make, or any powers to treat of peace, will furnish a pretence for B. F.'s going to England, where he has many friends and acquaintance, particularly among the best writers and ablest speakers in both Houses of Parliament, he thinks he shall be able when there, if the terms are not accepted, to work up such a division of sentiments in the nation, as greatly to weaken its exertions against the United States, and lessen its credit in foreign countries.

4. The knowledge of there being powers given to the commissioners to treat with England, may have some effect in facilitating and expediting the proposed treaty with France.

5. It is worth our while to offer such a sum for the countries to be ceded, since the vacant lands will in time sell for a great part of what we shall give, if not more; and, if we are to obtain them by conquest, after perhaps a long war, they will probably cost us more than that sum. It is absolutely necessary for us to have them for our own security; and, though the sum may seem large to the present generation, in less than half the term it will be to the whole United States a mere trifle.

PART FOUR

Minister to France

1776-1785

COMPARISON OF GREAT BRITAIN AND THE UNITED STATES

Soon after reaching France in December 1776 Franklin put his practiced pen to use propagandizing the cause of the new United States. One of his first efforts must have been especially congenial for him; he scorned British frivolity and corruption and praised American frugality and industry in an attempt to establish American credit in Europe.

In the Affair of Borrowing Money, a Man's Credit depends on some, or all, of the following Particulars.
1. His known Conduct with regard to former Loans, in the Punctuality with which he discharg'd them.
2. His Industry in his Business.
3. His frugality in his Expences.
4. The Solidity of his Funds, his Estate being good, and free of prior Debts, whence his undoubted Ability of paying.
5. His well-founded Prospects of greater future Ability, by the Improvement of his Estate in Value, and by Aids from others.

Writings, VII, 1-8; written early in 1777 and widely distributed to establish American credit in Europe.

6. His known Prudence in Managing his general Affairs, and the Advantage they will probably receive from the present Loan he desires.

7. His known Virtue and honest Character, manifested by his voluntary Discharge of Debts, which he could not otherwise have been oblig'd to pay. The same Circumstances, that give a private Man credit, ought to have, and will have, their Weight with Lenders of Money to *publick Bodies* or to Nations. If then we consider and compare Britain and America in those several Lights, upon the Question, "To which is it safest to lend Money?" we shall find, . . .

. . . *With Regard to Industry in Business;* Every Man in America is employ'd; the greatest Number in cultivating their own Lands, the rest in Handicrafts, Navigation, and Commerce. An idle man there is a rarity; Idleness and Inutility is a character of Disgrace. In England the Quantity of that Character is immense; Fashion has spread it far and wide. Hence the Embarassment of private Fortunes, and the daily Bankruptcies, arising from the universal fondness for Appearance and expensive Pleasures; and hence, in some Degree, the Mismanagement of their publick Business: For Habits of Business, and Ability in it, are acquired only by Practice; and, where universal Dissipation and the perpetual Pursuit of Amusement are the Mode, the Youths who are educated in it can rarely afterwards acquire that patient Attention and close Application to Affairs, which are so necessary to a statesman charg'd with the Care of national Welfare. Hence their frequent Errors in Policy, and hence the Weariness at Publick Councils, and the Backwardness in going to them, the constant Unwillingness to engage in any Measure that requires Thought and Consideration, and the readiness for postponing every new Proposition; which postponing is therefore the only Part of Business that they come to be expert in, an Expertness produced necessarily by so much daily Practice. Whereas, in America, men bred to close Employment in their private Affairs attend with habitual Ease to those of the publick when engag'd in them, and nothing fails through Negligence.

With regard to Frugality in Expences; the Manner of Living in America is in general more simple and less Expensive than in England. Plain Tables, plain Clothing, plain Furniture in Houses, few Carriages of Pleasure. In America an expensive Appearance hurts Credit, and is therefore avoided; in England it is often put on with a View of gaining Credit, and continued to Ruin. In *publick* Affairs, the Difference is still greater. In England Salaries of Officers and Emoluments of office are Enormous. . . .

In America, Salaries, where indispensable, are extreamly low; but much of publick Business is done gratis. The Honour of serving the Publick ably and faithfully is deemed sufficient. *Public Spirit* really exists there, and has great Effects. In England it is universally deemed a NonEntity, and whoever pretends to it is laugh'd at as a fool, or suspected as a Knave. The Committees of Congress, which form the Board of War, the Board of Treasury, the Naval Board, the Committee for Accounts, the Board of Foreign Transactions for procuring Arms, Ammunition, Clothing etc., all attend the Business of their respective Functions without any Salary or Emolument whatever, tho' they spend in it much more of their Time, than any Lord of Treasury or Admiralty in England can afford from his Amusements. . . .

. . . *With Regard to Prudence in General Affairs, and the Advantages they expect from the Loan desired.* The Americans are Cultivators of Land; those engag'd in Fishery and Commerce are a small Number, compar'd with the Body of the People. They have ever conducted their several Governments with Wisdom, avoiding Wars and vain, expensive Projects, delighting only in their peaceable Occupations, which must, considering the Extent of their yet uncultivated Territory, find them Employment still for Ages. Whereas England, ever unquiet, ambitious, avaricious, imprudent, and quarrelsome, is half her Time engag'd in some War, or other, always at an expence infinitely greater than the advantages proposed if it could be obtained. . . .

Indeed, there is scarce a Nation in Europe, against which she has not made War on some frivolous Pretext or other, and by this means has imprudently accumulated a Debt, that has brought her on the Verge of bankrupcy. But the most indiscrete of all her Wars is the present against America, with whom she might for ages have preserv'd her profitable connection by only a just and equitable Conduct. She is now acting like a mad Shop-keeper, who should attempt, by beating those that pass his Door, to make them come in and be his Customers. America cannot submit to such Treatment, without being first ruined, and, being ruined, her Custom will be worth nothing. England, to bring this to pass, is increasing her Debt, and ruining herself effectually. America, on the other Hand, aims only at establishing her Liberty, and that Freedom of Commerce which will be advantageous to all Europe; while the Abolishing of the Monopoly which she has hitherto labour'd under, will be an Advantage sufficiently ample to repay the Debt, she may contract to accomplish it. . . .

. . . On the whole it appears, that, from the general Industry, Frugality, Ability, Prudence, and Virtue of America, she is a much safer Debtor than Britain: To say nothing of the Satisfaction generous Minds must have in reflecting, that by Loans to America they are opposing Tyranny, and aiding the Cause of Liberty, which is the Cause of all Mankind.

FRANKLIN'S CANDID VIEW

OF HIS MISSION IN FRANCE

Franklin's friend, the Austrian physician and scientist, Jan Ingenhousz, had written him deploring the warfare in America and asking what efforts might be made to restore peace. Franklin replied defending the justice of the American cause and her need to fight resolutely for independence.

I long laboured in England, with great zeal and sincerity, to prevent the breach that has happened, and which is now so wide, that no endeavours of mine can possibly heal it. You know the treatment I met with from that imprudent court; but I keep a separate account of private injuries, which I may forgive; and I do not think it right to mix them with public affairs. Indeed, there is no occasion for their aid to whet my resentment against a nation, that has burnt our defenceless towns in the midst of winter, has excited the savages to assassinate our innocent farmers, with their wives and children, and our slaves to murder their masters!

It would therefore be deceiving you, if I suffered you to remain in the supposition you have taken up, that I am come to Europe to make peace. I am in fact ordered hither by the Congress for a very different purpose; viz. to procure those aids from European powers, for enabling us to defend our freedom and independence, which it is certainly their interest to grant; as by that means the great and rapidly growing trade of America will be open to them all, and not a monopoly to Great Britain, as heretofore; a mo-

---

Writings, VII, 47-49; from a letter to Jan Ingenhousz, April 26, 1777.

nopoly, that, if she is suffered again to possess, will be such an increase of her strength by sea, and if she can reduce us again to submission, she will have thereby so great an addition to her strength by land, as will, together, make her the most formidable power the world has yet seen; and, from her natural pride and insolence in prosperity, of all others the most intolerable.

You desire to know my Opinion of what will probably be the End of this War; and whether our new Establishments will not be thereby reduced again to Deserts. I do not, for my part, apprehend much danger of so great an Evil to us. I think we shall be able, with a little Help, to defend ourselves, our Possessions, and our Liberties so long that England will be ruined by persisting in the wicked attempt to destroy them. I must nevertheless regret that Ruin, and wish that her Injustice and Tyranny had not deserv'd it. And I sometimes flatter myself, that, old as I am, I may possibly live to see my Country settled in Peace and Prosperity, when Britain shall make no more a formidable Figure among the Powers of Europe. . . .

THE AMERICAN REVOLUTION IN EUROPE

After five months in France Franklin wrote of the hope aroused there by a revolution seeking liberty.

. . . All Europe is on our Side of the Question, as far as Applause and good Wishes can carry them. Those who live under arbitrary Power do nevertheless approve of Liberty, and wish for it; they almost despair of recovering it in Europe; they read the Translations of our separate Colony

---

Writings, VII, 55; from a letter to Samuel Cooper, May 1, 1777.

Constitutions with Rapture; and there are such Numbers everywhere, who talk of Removing to America, with their Families and Fortunes, as soon as Peace and our Independence shall be established, that 'tis generally believed we shall have a prodigious Addition of Strength, Wealth, and Arts, from the Emigrations of Europe; and 'tis thought, that, to lessen or prevent such Emigrations, the Tyrannies established there must relax, and allow more Liberty to their People. Hence 'tis a Common Observation here, that our Cause is *the Cause of all Mankind,* and that we are fighting for their Liberty in defending our own. 'Tis a glorious task assign'd us by Providence; which has, I trust, given us Spirit and Virtue equal to it, and will at last crown it with Success. . . .

THE ALLIANCE WITH FRANCE

When news of the American victory at Saratoga reached Europe in the winter of 1777–1778, Franklin and his fellow commissioners moved to conclude the alliance with France so vital to the success of the Revolution. Franklin explained its foundation and significance in three letters, one to an English friend, another to an American friend, and a third to a secret emissary of the English government seeking a reconciliation with the former colonies.

. . . Your "earnest Caution and Request, that nothing may ever persuade America to throw themselves into the Arms of France, for that Times may mend; and that an

---

Writings, VII, 102–103, 110, 124–125; from letters to David Hartley, February 12, 1778; to Thomas Cushing, February 27, 1778; and to William Pulteney, March 30, 1778.

American must always be a Stranger in France, but that Great Britain may for Ages to come be their home," marks the goodness of your Heart, your Regard for us, and Love of your Country. But when your Nation is hiring all the Cut-Throats it can collect of all Countries and Colours, to destroy us, it is hard to persuade us not to ask or accept of Aid from any Power, that may be prevail'd with to grant it; and this from the hope that tho' you now thirst for our Blood, and pursue us with Fire and Sword, you may in some future time treat us kindly. This is too much Patience to be expected of us; indeed, I think it is not in human nature.

The Americans are received and treated here in France with a Cordiality, a Respect, and Affection they never experienc'd in England when they most deserved it; and which is now (after all the Pains taken to exasperate the English against them, and render them odious as well as contemptible,) less to be expected there than ever. And I cannot see why we may not upon an Alliance, hope for a Continuance of it, at least of as much as the Swiss enjoy, with whom France has maintained a faithful Friendship for 200 Years past, and whose People appear to live here in as much Esteem as the Natives. America has been *forc'd* and *driven* into the Arms of France. She was a dutiful and virtuous Daughter. A cruel Mother-in-Law turn'd her out of Doors, defam'd her, and sought her Life. All the World knows her Innocence, and takes her part; and her Friends hope soon to see her honourably married. They can never persuade her Return and Submission to so barbarous an Enemy. In her future Prosperity, if she forgets and forgives, 'tis all that can reasonably be expected of her. I believe she will make as good and useful a Wife as she did a Daughter, that her Husband will love and honour her, and that the Family from which she was so wickedly expelled, will long regret the Loss of her.

I know not whether a Peace with us is desired in England; I rather think it is not at present, unless on the old impossible Terms of Submission and receiving Pardon. Whenever you shall be disposed to make Peace upon equal and reasonable Terms, you will find little Difficulty, if you get first an honest Ministry. The present have all along acted so deceitfully and treacherously as well as inhumanly towards the Americans, that I imagine, the absolute want of all Confidence in them, will make a Treaty at present, between them and the Congress impracticable. . . .

. . . Give me leave to congratulate you on the Success of our Negotiations here, in the completion of the Two Treaties with his Most Christian Majesty; the one of Amity and Commerce, on the Plan of that Projected in Congress, with some good additions; the Other of Alliance for Mutual Defence, in which the Most Christian King agrees to make a Common Cause with the United States, if England attempts to Obstruct the Commerce of his Subjects with them; and guarantees to the United States their Liberties, Sovereignty, and Independance, absolute and unlimited, with the Possessions they now have, or may have, at the Conclusion of the War; and the States in return guarantees to him his Possessions in the West Indies. The great Principle in both Treaties is a perfect Equality and reciprocity; no Advantages being demanded by France, or Privileges in Commerce, which the States may not grant to any and every other Nation. . . .

When I first had the honour of conversing with you on the subject of Peace, I mention'd it as my Opinion, that every Proposition, which implied our voluntarily agreeing to return to a Dependance on Britain, was not become impossible; that a Peace on equal Terms undoubtedly might be made; and that, tho' we had no particular Powers to treat of Peace with England, we had general Powers to make Treaties of Peace, Amity, and Commerce, with any State in Europe, by which I thought we might be authoriz'd to treat with Britain; who, if sincerely disposed to Peace, might save time and much Bloodshed by treating with us directly.

I also gave it as my Opinion, that, in the Treaty to be made, Britain should endeavour, by the Fairness and Generosity of the Terms she offer'd, to recover the Esteem, Confidence, and Affection of America, without which the Peace could not be so beneficial, as it was not likely to be lasting; in this I had the Pleasure to find you of my Opinion.

But I see, by the Propositions you have communicated to me, that the Ministers cannot yet divest themselves of the Idea, that the Power of Parliament over us is constitutionally absolute and unlimited; and that the Limitations they may be willing now to put to it by Treaty are so many Favours, or so many Benefits, for which we are to make Compensation.

As our Opinions in America are totally different, a Treaty on the Terms proposed appears to me utterly inpracticable, either here or there. Here we certainly cannot make it, having not the smallest Authority to make even the Declaration specified in the proposed Letter, without which, if I understood you right, treating with us cannot be commenc'd.

I sincerely wish as much for Peace as you do, and I have enough remaining of Good Will for England to wish it for her Sake as well as for our own, and for the Sake of Humanity. In the present state of things, the proper means of obtaining it, in my Opinion, are, to acknowledge the Independence of the United States, and then enter at once into a Treaty with us for a Suspension of Arms, with the usual Provisions relating to Distances; and another for establishing Peace, Friendship, and Commerce, such as France has made. This might prevent a War between you and that Kingdom, which, in the present Circumstances and Temper of the two Nations, an Accident may bring on every Day, tho' contrary to the Interest and without the previous Intention of either. Such a Treaty we might probably now make, with the Approbation of our Friends; but, if you go to War with them on account of their Friendship for us, we are bound by Ties, stronger than can be formed by any Treaty, to fight against you with them, as long as the War against them shall continue. . . .

DIPLOMACY IN PARIS

Before Franklin received appointment as sole Minister to France in March 1779, he was merely one of three American commissioners there; the others were Arthur Lee, and first Silas Deane and later John Adams. Franklin found doing business jointly inefficient, ineffective, and so far as Lee was concerned, troublesome and irritating in the extreme, as he explained to the chairman of the Continental Congress committee of foreign affairs.

. . . As to our number, whatever advantage there might be in the joint counsels of three for framing and adjusting the articles of the treaty, there can be none in managing the common business of a resident here. On the contrary, all the advantages in negotiation that result from secrecy of

---

Writings, VII, 178–179; from a letter to James Lovell, July 22, 1778.

sentiment, and uniformity in expressing it, and in common business from despatch, are lost. In a court, too, where every word is watched and weighed, if a number of Commissioners do not every one hold the same language, in giving their opinion on any public transaction, this lessens their weight; and when it may be prudent to put on, or avoid certain appearances of concern, for example, or indifference, satisfaction, or dislike, where the utmost sincerity and candor should be used, and would gain credit, if no semblance of art showed itself in the inadvertent discourse, perhaps of only one of them, the hazard is in proportion to the number. And where every one must be consulted on every particular of common business, in answering every letter, &c., and one of them is offended if the smallest thing is done without his consent, the difficulty of being often and long enough together, the different opinions, and the time consumed in debating them, the interruptions by new applicants in the time of meeting, &c. &c., occasion so much postponing and delay, that correspondence languishes, occasions are lost, and the business is always behindhand.

I have mentioned the difficulty of being often and long enough together. This is considerable, where they cannot all be accommodated in the same house; but to find three people whose tempers are so good, and who like so well one another's company, and manner of living and conversing, as to agree well themselves, though being in one house, and whose servants will not by their indiscretion quarrel with one another, and by artful misrepresentations draw their masters in to take their parts, to the disturbance of necessary harmony, these are difficulties still greater and almost insurmountable. And, in consideration of the whole, I wish Congress would separate us. . . .

PARABLE AGAINST ENGLISH PROPOSALS THAT AMERICA BREAK THE FRENCH ALLIANCE

Franklin's friend, David Hartley, at the direction of the British Ministry, sought persistently to end the war by bringing the United States back into the British Empire and to dissolve the Franco-American Alliance. Franklin always scorned such proposals by detailing England's deceitful ill-treatment of her former colonies and by affirming his faith in American capacity to prevail with French help. He concluded one rejection with what he called "a comick Farce intitled, *God-send or the Wreckers.*"

SCENE. *Mount's Bay*

[*A Ship riding at anchor in a great Storm. A Lee Shore full of Rocks, and lin'd with people, furnish'd with Axes & Carriages to cut up Wrecks, knock the Sailors on the Head, and carry off the Plunder; according to Custom.*]

1st. *Wrecker.* This Ship rides it out longer than I expected. She must have good Ground Tackle.

2 *Wrecker.* We had better send off a Boat to her, and persuade her to take a Pilot, who can afterwards run her ashore, where we can best come at her.

3 *Wrecker.* I doubt whether the boat can live in this Sea; but if there are any brave Fellows willing to hazard themselves for the good of the Public, & a double Share, let them say aye.

Several Wreckers. I, I, I, I.

[*The Boat goes off, and comes under the Ship's Stern.*]

Spokesman. So ho, the Ship, ahoa!

Captain. Hulloa.

Sp. Wou'd you have a Pilot?

Writings, VII, 228–229; from a letter to David Hartley, February 3, 1779.

Capt. No, no!

Sp. It blows hard, & you are in Danger.

Capt. I know it.

Sp. Will you buy a better Cable? We have one in the boat here.

Capt. What do you ask for it?

Sp. Cut that you have, & then we'll talk about the price of this.

Capt. I shall not do such a foolish Thing. I have liv'd in your Parish formerly, & know the Heads of ye too well to trust ye; keep off from my Cable there; I see you have a mind to cut it yourselves. If you go any nearer to it, I'll fire into you and sink you.

Sp. It is a damn'd rotten French Cable, and will part of itself in half an hour. Where will you be then, Captain? You had better take our offer.

Capt. You offer nothing, you Rogues, but Treachery and Mischief. My cable is good & strong, and will hold long enough to baulk all your Projects.

Sp. You talk unkindly, Captain, to People who came here only for your Good.

Capt. I know you come for all our *Goods*, but, by God's help, you shall have none of them; you shall not serve us as you did the Indiaman.

Sp. Come, my Lads, let's be gone. This Fellow is not so great a Fool as we took him to be.

PASSPORT FOR CAPTAIN COOK

Before leaving England, Franklin had taken part in the preparations for Captain James Cook's great voyages of discovery in the Pacific. Learning of Cook's expected return to England,

---

Writings, VII, 242–243; issued by Franklin, March 10, 1779.

Franklin wrote as a member of the universal brotherhood of science in seeking to protect him from the hazards of war.

To all Captains and Commanders of armed Ships acting by Commission from the Congress of the United States of America, now in war with Great Britain.

Gentlemen,

A ship having been fitted out from England before the Commencement of this War, to make Discoveries of new Countries in Unknown Seas, under the Conduct of that most celebrated Navigator and Discoverer Captain Cook; an Undertaking truly laudable in itself, as the Increase of Geographical Knowledge facilitates the Communication between distant Nations, in the Exchange of useful Products and Manufactures, and the Extension of Arts, whereby the common Enjoyments of human Life are multiply'd and augmented, and Science of other kinds increased to the benefit of Mankind in general; this is, therefore, most earnestly to recommend to every one of you, that, in case the said Ship, which is now expected to be soon in the European Seas on her Return, should happen to fall into your Hands, you would not consider her as an Enemy, nor suffer any Plunder to be made of the Effects contain'd in her, nor obstruct her immediate Return to England, by detaining her or sending her into any other Part of Europe or to America, but that you would treat the said Captain Cook and his People with all Civility and Kindness, affording them, as common Friends to Mankind, all the Assistance in your Power, which they may happen to stand in need of. In so doing you will not only gratify the Generosity of your own Dispositions, but there is no doubt of your obtaining the Approbation of the Congress, and your other American Owners. I have the honour to be, Gentlemen, your most obedient humble Servant.

[Given] at Passy, near Paris, this 10th day of March, 1779.

B. FRANKLIN,

Plenipotentiary from the Congress of the United States to the Court of France.

THE MORALS OF CHESS AND DIPLOMACY

Though Franklin wrote the "Morals of Chess" to amuse his friends in France, the four qualities he described as useful in the game were also the precepts of his politics and diplomacy.

. . . The Game of Chess is not merely an idle Amusement. Several very valuable qualities of the Mind, useful in the course of human Life, are to be acquir'd or strengthened by it, so as to become habits, ready on all occasions. For Life is a kind of Chess, in which we often have Points to gain, & Competitors or Adversaries to contend with; and in which there is a vast variety of good and ill Events, that are in some degree the Effects of Prudence or the want of it. By playing at Chess, then, we may learn,

I. *Foresight,* which looks a little into futurity, and considers the Consequences that may attend an action; for it is continually occurring to the Player, "If I move this piece, what will be the advantages or disadvantages of my new situation? What Use can my Adversary make of it to annoy me? What other moves can I make to support it, and to defend myself from his attacks?"

Writings, VII, 358–359; from a bagatelle probably written in June 1779.

Minister to France 313

II. *Circumspection,* which surveys the whole Chessboard, or scene of action; the relations of the several pieces and situations, the Dangers they are respectively exposed to, the several possibilities of their aiding each other, the probabilities that the Adversary may make this or that move, and attack this or the other Piece, and what different Means can be used to avoid his stroke, or turn its consequences against him.

III. *Caution,* not to make our moves too hastily. This habit is best acquired, by observing strictly the laws of the Game; such as, *If you touch a Piece, you must move it somewhere; if you set it down, you must let it stand.* And it is therefore best that these rules should be observed, as the Game becomes thereby more the image of human Life, and particularly of War; in which, if you have incautiously put yourself into a bad and dangerous position, you cannot obtain your Enemy's Leave to withdraw your Troops, and place them more securely, but you must abide all the consequences of your rashness.

And *lastly,* we learn by Chess the habit of not being discouraged by present appearances in the state of our affairs, the habit of hoping for a favourable Change, and that of persevering in the search of resources. The Game is so full of Events, there is such a variety of turns in it, the Fortune of it is so subject to sudden Vicissitudes, and one so frequently, after long contemplation, discovers the means of extricating one's self from a supposed insurmountable Difficulty, that one is encouraged to continue the Contest to the last, in hopes of Victory from our own skill, or at least of getting a stale mate, from the Negligence of our Adversary. And whoever considers, what in Chess he often sees instances of, that success is apt to produce Presumption, & its consequent Inattention, by which more is afterwards lost than was gain'd by the preceding Advantage, while misfortunes produce more care and attention, by which the loss may be recovered, will learn not to be too much discouraged by any present success of his Adversary, nor to despair of final good fortune upon every little Check he receives in the pursuit of it. . . .

WASHINGTON'S
FAME IN EUROPE AND AMERICA'S FUTURE

Franklin always greatly admired George Washington, and, in inviting him to visit Europe, prophesied on Washington's place, and America's, in history.

. . . Should peace arrive after another Campaign or two, and afford us a little Leisure, I should be happy to see your Excellency in Europe, and to accompany you, if my Age and Strength would permit, in visiting some of its ancient and most famous Kingdoms. You would, on this side of the Sea, enjoy the great Reputation you have acquir'd, pure and free from those little Shades that the Jealousy and Envy of a Man's Countrymen and Contemporaries are ever endeavouring to cast over living Merit. Here you would know, and enjoy, what Posterity will say of Washington. For 1000 Leagues have nearly the same Effect with 1000 Years. The feeble Voice of those grovelling Passions cannot extend so far either in Time or Distance. At present I enjoy that Pleasure for you, as I frequently hear the old Generals of this martial Country, (who study the Maps of America, and mark upon them all your Operations,) speak with sincere Approbation and great Applause of your con-

---

Writings, VIII, 28–29; from a letter to George Washington, March 5, 1780.

duct; and join in giving you the Character of one of the greatest Captains of the Age.

I must soon quit the Scene, but you may live to see our Country flourish, as it will amazingly and rapidly after the War is over. Like a Field of young Indian Corn, which long Fair weather and Sunshine had enfeebled and discolored, and which in that weak State, by a Thunder Gust, of violent Wind, Hail, and Rain, seem'd to be threaten'd with absolute Destruction; yet the Storm being past, it recovers fresh Verdure, shoots up with double Vigour, and delights the Eye, not of its Owner only, but of every observing Traveller. . . .

FRANKLIN AND JOHN ADAMS

ON FRANCO-AMERICAN RELATIONS

The two principal American diplomats in Europe during the American Revolution, Franklin and John Adams, soon came to differ over relations with France. In the spring and summer of 1780 Adams took a "tougher" line toward French Foreign Minister Vergennes than that implied in Franklin's customary attitude of gratefulness. Offended, Vergennes refused to have further dealings with Adams. Franklin then explained matters to the President of the Continental Congress.

. . . Mr. Adams has given Offence to the Court here, by some Sentiments and Expressions contained in several of his Letters written to the Count de Vergennes. I mention this with Reluctance, tho' perhaps it would have been my

---

Writings, VIII, 126–128; from a letter to Samuel Huntington, August 9, 1780.

Duty to acquaint you with such a Circumstance, even were it not required of me by the Minister himself. He has sent me Copies of the Correspondence, desiring I would communicate them to Congress; and I send them herewith. Mr. Adams did not show me his Letters before he sent them. I have, in a former Letter to Mr. Lovell, mentioned some of the Inconveniencies, that attend the having more than one Minister at the same Court; one of which Inconveniencies is, that they do not always hold the same Language, and that the Impressions made by one, and intended for the Service of his Constituents, may be effaced by the Discourse of the other. It is true, that Mr. Adams's proper Business is elsewhere; but, the Time not being come for that Business, and having nothing else here wherewith to employ himself, he seems to have endeavoured to supply what he may suppose my Negociations defective in. He thinks, as he tells me himself, that America has been too free in Expressions of Gratitude to France; for that she is more oblig'd to us than we to her; and that we should show Spirit in our Applications. I apprehend, that he mistakes his Ground, and that this Court is to be treated with Decency and Delicacy. The King, a young and virtuous Prince, has, I am persuaded, a Pleasure in reflecting on the generous Benevolence of the Action in assisting an oppressed People, and proposes it as a Part of the Glory of his Reign. I think it right to encrease this Pleasure by our thankful Acknowledgments, and that such an Expression of Gratitude is not only our Duty, but our Interest. A different Conduct seems to me what is not only improper and unbecoming, but what may be hurtful to us. Mr. Adams, on the other hand, who, at the same time means our Welfare and Interest as much as I, or any man, can do, seems to think a little apparent Stoutness, and greater air of Independence and Boldness in our Demands, will procure us more ample Assistance. It is for Congress to judge and regulate their Affairs accordingly

M. Vergennes, who appears much offended, told me, yesterday, that he would enter into no further Discussions with Mr. Adams, nor answer any more of his Letters. He is gone to Holland to try, as he told me, whether something might not be done to render us less dependent on France. He says, the Ideas of this Court and those of the People in America are so totally different, that it is impossible for any Minister to please both. He ought to know America better than I do, having been there lately, and he may chuse to do what he thinks will best please the People of America. But, when I consider the Expressions of Congress in many of their public Acts, and particularly in their Letter to the Chev. de la Luzerne, of the 24th of May last, I cannot but imagine, that he mistakes the Sentiments of a few for a general Opinion. It is my Intention, while I stay here, to procure what Advantages I can for our Country, by endeavouring to please this Court; and I wish I could prevent any thing being said by any of our Countrymen here, that may have a contrary Effect, and increase an Opinion lately showing itself in Paris, that we seek a Difference, and with a view of reconciling ourselves to England. Some of them have of late been very indiscreet in their Conversations. . . .

ON STATE SUPPORT FOR RELIGION

Responding to a letter from the English liberal clergyman and friend of America, Richard Price, Franklin suggested the attitude toward church and state soon to become dominant in the United States.

Writings, VIII, 153–154; from a letter to Richard Price, October 9, 1780.

318 *The Political Thought of Benjamin Franklin*

I am fully of your Opinion respecting religious Tests; but, tho' the People of Massachusetts have not in their new Constitution kept quite clear of them, yet, if we consider what that People were 100 Years ago, we must allow they have gone great Lengths in Liberality of Sentiment on religious Subjects; and we may hope for greater Degrees of Perfection, when their Constitution, some years hence, shall be revised. If Christian Preachers had continued to teach as Christ and his Apostles did, without Salaries, and as the Quakers now do, I imagine Tests would never have existed; for I think they were invented, not so much to secure Religion itself, as the Emoluments of it. When a Religion is good, I conceive that it will support itself; and, when it cannot support itself, and God does not take care to support, so that its Professors are oblig'd to call for the help of the Civil Power, it is a sign, I apprehend, of its being a bad one. . . .

SPAIN, THE UNITED STATES, AND THE MISSISSIPPI RIVER

Military reverses in 1780 made it seem imperative to many Americans to bring Spain into the war against Great Britain more actively, even at the cost of yielding to Spain control of the Mississippi River. Such control exercised to block navigation threatened American settlements in the Mississippi Valley with extinction. Sensing that this unnatural restraint would, if carried out, inflame Spanish-American relations, Franklin protested to John Jay, then the American representative in Madrid.

Writings, VIII, 143–144, 202; from letters to John Jay, October 2, 1780 and January 27, 1781.

... Spain owes us nothing; therefore, whatever Friendship she shows us in lending Money, or furnishing Cloathing, &c., tho' not equal to our Wants & Wishes, is however *tant de gagné*. Those, who have begun to assist us, are more likely to continue than to decline, and we are still so much obliged as their aids amount to. But I hope and I am confident, that Court will be wiser than to take advantage of our Distress, & insist on our making Sacrifices by an agreement, which the Circumstance of such Distress would hereafter weaken, & the very Proposition can only give disgust at Present. Poor as we are, yet, as I know we shall be rich, I would rather agree with them to buy at a great Price the whole of their Right on the Mississippi, than sell a Drop of its Waters. A Neighbour might as well ask me to sell my Street Door. . . .

. . . I was pleas'd to find by our last Dispatches from Congress that the Sentiments express'd in mine of Oct. 2 in respect to selling the River, happen'd to coincide with theirs. If your Court thinks of exacting such Sacrifices from us, & suffers the Bills drawn on you, however imprudently drawn, to go back protested, my great Opinion of Spanish Wisdom will be somewhat diminished.—For this is precisely their time to obtain and secure a firm & lasting Friendship with a near Neighbour, and not a time to obtain little Advantages with a Risque of laying Foundations for future Quarrels. . . .

FRANKLIN'S DIPLOMATIC

SERVICE: ATTACK AND VINDICATION

In 1780, spurred by the furious charges of Arthur Lee (termed by Franklin "the most malicious Enemy I ever had"), Congress came temporarily under the influence of those hostile to Franklin and to the French Alliance. In response to an implied disparagement of his services, Franklin wrote of further loans secured from France and of Louis XVI's firm friendship for America. Franklin felt misused by his country, though, and in the same letter offered his resignation.

. . . I must now beg leave to say something relating to myself; a subject with which I have not often troubled the Congress. I have passed my seventy-fifth year, and I find that the long and severe fit of the gout, which I had the last winter, has shaken me exceedingly, and I am yet far from having recovered the bodily strength I before enjoyed. I do not know that my mental faculties are impaired; perhaps I shall be the last to discover that; but I am sensible of great diminution in my activity, a quality I think particularly necessary in your minister for this court. I am afraid, therefore, that your affairs may some time or other suffer by my deficiency. I find also, that the business is too heavy for me, and too confining. The constant attendance at home, which is necessary for receiving and accepting your bills of exchange (a matter foreign to my ministerial functions), to answer letters, and perform other parts of my employment, prevents my taking the air and exercise, which my annual journeys formerly used to afford me, and which contributed much to the preservation of my health. There are many other little personal attentions, which the infirmities of age render necessary to an old man's comfort, even in some degree to the continuance of his existence, and with which business often interferes.

I have been engaged in public affairs, and enjoyed pub-

Writings, VII, 220–221, 294–295; from letters to Samuel Huntington, March 21, 1781, and to William Carmichael, August 24, 1781.

Minister to France 321

lic confidence, in some shape or other, during the long term of fifty years, and honour sufficient to satisfy any reasonable ambition; and I have no other left but that of repose, which I hope the Congress will grant me, by sending some person to supply my place. At the same time, I beg they may be assured, that it is not any the least doubt of their success in the glorious cause, nor any disgust received in their service, that induces me to decline it, but purely and simply the reasons above mentioned. And, as I cannot at present undergo the fatigues of a sea voyage (the last having been almost too much for me), and would not again expose myself to the hazard of capture and imprisonment in this time of war, I purpose to remain here at least till the peace; perhaps may be for the remainder of my life; and, if any knowledge or experience I have acquired here may be thought of use to my successor, I shall freely communicate it, and assist him with any influence I may be supposed to have, or counsel that may be desired of me. . . .

[When Congress received this letter, Franklin's friends had regained control, and in his vindication, refused the resignation and appointed him one of the commissioners for negotiating peace with England. Writing to an American representative in Spain, Franklin expressed his pleasure in these marks of confidence, and revealed the strategy of his proffered resignation.]

. . . The Congress have done me the honour to refuse accepting my Resignation, and insist on my continuing in their Service till the Peace. I must therefore buckle again to Business, and thank God that my Health & Spirits are of late improved. I fancy it may have been a double Mortification to those Enemies you have mentioned to me, that I should ask as a Favour what they hop'd to vex me by taking from me; and that I should nevertheless be continued. But these sort of Considerations should never influence our Conduct. We ought always to do what appears best to be done, without much regarding what others may think of it. I call this Continuance an Honour, & I really esteem it to be a greater than my first Appointment, when I consider that all the Interest of my Enemies, united with my own Request, were not sufficient to prevent it. . . .

ON BETRAYING FRANCE

TO SECURE PEACE WITH GREAT BRITAIN

Even after the battle of Yorktown David Hartley continued his efforts to persuade Franklin that the United States should cease fighting her former mother country so that England could defeat the real enemy, France, after which the English-speaking peoples could reunite in peace and prosperity. Franklin responded indignantly to one such proposal.

. . . It is necessary that I should be explicit with you, & tell you plainly, that I never had such an Idea; and I believe there is not a Man in America, a few *English Tories* excepted, that would not spurn at the Thought of deserting a noble and generous Friend, for the sake of a Truce with an unjust and cruel Enemy.

I have again read over your Conciliatory Bill, with the Manuscript Propositions that accompany it, and am concerned to find, that one cannot give Vent to a simple Wish for Peace, a mere Sentiment of Humanity, without having it

---

Writings, VIII, 358–361; 381–382; from letters to David Hartley, January 15 and February 16, 1782.

Minister to France 323

interpreted as *a Disposition to submit to any base Conditions* that may be offered us, rather than continue the War: For on no other Supposition could you propose to us a Truce of ten years, during which we are to engage not to assist France, while you continue the War with her. A Truce too wherein nothing is to be mentioned that may weaken your Pretensions to Dominion over us, which you may therefore resume at the End of the Term, or at Pleasure; when we should have so covered ourselves with Infamy, by our Treachery to our first Friend, as that no other Nation can ever after be disposed to assist us, [however cruelly you might think fit to treat us.] Believe me, my dear Friend, America has too much understanding, and is too sensible of the Value of the World's good Opinion, to forfeit it all by such Perfidy. The Congress will never instruct their Commissioners to obtain a Peace on such ignominious Terms; and tho' there can be but few Things in which I should venture to disobey their Orders, yet if it were possible for them to give me such an Order as this, I should certainly refuse to act, I should instantly renounce their Commission, and banish myself for ever from so infamous a Country.

We are a little ambitious too of your Esteem; and, as I think we have acquired some Share of it by our Manner of making War with you, I trust we shall not hazard the Loss of it by consenting meanly to a dishonourable Peace. . . .

[Hartley wrote back that he never had proposed that the United States betray France; he had only spoken in general terms about such an act. Franklin replied with an analogy suggesting why he had mistaken Hartley's intent.]

. . . I thought, as I suppose an honest woman would think, if a gallant should entertain her with suppositions of cases, in which infidelity to her husband would be justifiable. Would not she naturally imagine, seeing no other foundation or motive for such conversation, that, if he could once get her to admit the general principle, his intended next step would be to persuade her, that such a case actually existed? Thus, knowing your dislike of France, and your strong desire of recovering America to England, I was impressed with the idea, that such an infidelity on our part would not be disagreeable to you; and that you were therefore aiming to lessen in my mind the horror I conceived at the idea of it. But we will finish here by mutually agreeing, that neither you were capable of proposing, nor I of acting on, such principles. . . .

BRITISH BARBARITY

DURING THE AMERICAN REVOLUTION

Franklin wrote repeatedly during the Revolution of Britain's inhumanity in conducting the war. He scorned particularly her use of Hessian mercenaries, her ill-treatment of prisoners of war, and her incitement of Indians on the frontier to rapine and murder. To publicize this last he wrote a "Supplement to the Boston *Independent Chronicle*," which he printed at Passy on his private press in the format of that newspaper. The first part of the hoax appeared to be a letter from an Indian trader conveying "pelts," actually scalps, while the second part (reprinted here) purported to be a letter from John Paul Jones to the British Ambassador to Holland who had accused Jones of piracy. George III, Franklin wrote John Adams, was "full as black a Tyrant" as the "Muley Ishmael" pictured in the letter from Jones, and he hoped that if the "newspaper" were "republish'd in England it might make them a little asham'd of themselves."

Writings, VIII, 437–447; first printed in April 1782.

TO SIR JOSEPH YORK, AMBASSADOR FROM THE KING OF ENGLAND TO THE STATES-GENERAL OF THE UNITED PROVINCES

"*Ipswich, New England, March 7, 1781.*

"SIR,

"I have lately seen a memorial, said to have been presented by your Excellency to their High Mightinesses the from us, without our consent, in violation of our rights, and the title of *pirate*.

"A pirate is defined to be *hostis humani generis* [an enemy to all mankind]. It happens, Sir, that I am an enemy to no part of mankind, except your nation, the English; which nation at the same time comes much more within the definition, being actually an enemy to, and at war with, one whole quarter of the world, America, considerable part of Asia and Africa, a great part of Europe, and in a fair way of being at war with the rest.

"A pirate makes war for the sake of *rapine*. This is not the kind of war I am engaged in against England. Ours is a war in defence of *liberty* . . . the most just of all wars; and States-general, in which you are pleased to qualify me with from us, witout our consent, in violation of our rights, and by an armed force. Yours, therefore is a war of *rapine;* of course, a piratical war; and those who approve of it, and are engaged in it, more justly deserve the name of *pirates*, which you bestow on me. It is, indeed, a war that coincides with the general spirit of your nation. Your common people in their ale-houses sing the twenty-four songs of Robin

Hood, and applaud his deer-stealing and his robberies on
the highway: those, who have just learning enough to read,
are delighted with your histories of the pirates and of the
buccaniers; and even your scholars in the universities study
Quintus Curtius, and are taught to admire Alexander for
what they call 'his conquests in the Indies.' Severe laws
and the hangmen keep down the effects of this spirit somewhat among yourselves (though in your little Island you
have nevertheless more highway robberies than there are
in all the rest of Europe put together); but a foreign war
gives it full scope. It is then that, with infinite pleasure, it
lets itself loose to strip of their property honest merchants,
employed in the innocent and useful occupation of supplying the mutual wants of mankind. Hence, having lately no
war with your ancient enemies, rather than be without a
war, you chose to make one upon your friends. In this your
piratical war with America, the mariners of your fleets and
the owners of your privateers were animated against us by
the act of your Parliament, which repealed the law of God,
'Thou shalt not steal,' by declaring it lawful for them to rob
us of all our property that they could meet with on the
ocean. This act, too, had a retrospect, and, going beyond
bulls of pardon, declared that all the robberies you *had
committed* previous to the act should be *deemed just and
lawful.* Your soldiers, too, were promised the plunder of
our cities; and your officers were flattered with the division
of our lands. You had even the baseness to corrupt our
servants, the sailors employed by us, and encourage them
to rob their masters and bring to you the ships and goods
they were entrusted with. Is there any society of pirates
on the sea or land, who, in declaring wrong to be right, and
right wrong, have less authority than your parliament? Do
any of them more justly than your parliament deserve the
title you bestow on me?

"You will tell me that we forfeited all our estates by our refusal to pay the taxes your nation would have imposed on us without the consent of our colony parliaments. Have you then forgotten the incontestable principle, which was the foundation of Hambden's glorious lawsuit with Charles the first, that 'what an English king has no right to demand, an English subject has a right to refuse'? But you cannot so soon have forgotten the instructions of your late honorable father, who, being himself a sound Whig, taught you certainly the principles of the Revolution, and that, 'if subjects might in some cases forfeit their property, kings also might forfeit their title, and all claim to the allegiance of their subjects.' I must then suppose you well acquainted with those Whig principles; on which permit me, Sir, to ask a few questions.

"Is not protection as justly due from a king to his people, as obedience from the people to their king?

"If then a king declares his people to be out of his protection:

"If he violates and deprives them of their constitutional rights:

"If he wages war against them:

"If he plunders their merchants, ravages their coasts, burns their towns, and destroys their lives:

"If he hires foreign mercenaries to help him in their destruction:

"If he engages savages to murder their defenceless farmers, women, and children:

"If he cruelly forces such of his subjects as fall into his hands, to bear arms against their country, and become executioners of their friends and brethren:

"If he sells others of them into bondage, in Africa and the East Indies:

"If he excites domestic insurrections among their servants, and encourages servants to murder their masters: —

"Does not so atrocious a conduct towards his subjects dissolve their allegiance?

"If not, please to say how or by what means it can possibly be dissolved?

"All this horrible wickedness and barbarity has been and daily is practised by the King, *your master,* (as you call him in your memorial,) upon the Americans, whom he is still pleased to claim as his subjects.

"During these six years past, he has destroyed not less than forty thousand of those subjects, by battles on land or sea, or by starving them, or poisoning them to death, in the unwholesome air, with the unwholesome food of his prisons. And he has wasted the lives of at least an equal number of his own soldiers and sailors: many of whom have been *forced* into this odious service, and *dragged* from their families and friends, by the outrageous violence of his illegal pressgangs. You are a gentleman of letters, and have read history: do you recollect any instance of any tyrant, since the beginning of the world, who, in the course of so few years, had done so much mischief, by murdering so many of his own people? Let us view one of the worst and blackest of them, Nero. He put to death a few of his courtiers, placemen, and pensioners, and among the rest his *tutor.* Had George the Third done the same, and no more, his crime, though detestable, as an act of lawless power, might have been as useful to his nation, as that of Nero was hurtful to Rome; considering the different characters and merits of the sufferers. Nero indeed wished that the people of Rome had but one neck, that he might behead them all by one stroke; but this was a simple wish. George is carrying the wish as fast as he can into execution; and, by continuing in his present course a few years longer, will have destroyed more of the British people than Nero could have found inhabitants in Rome. Hence the expression of Milton, in speaking of Charles the First, that he was 'Nerone Neronior,' is still more applicable to George the third. Like Nero, and all other tyrants, while they lived, he indeed has his flatterers, his addressers, his applauders. Pensions, places, and hopes of preferment can bribe even bishops to approve his conduct: but when those fulsome, purchased addresses and panegyrics are sunk and lost in oblivion or contempt, impartial history will step forth, speak honest truth, and rank him among public calamities. The only difference will be, that plagues, pestilences, and famines are of this world, and arise from the nature of things; but voluntary malice, mischief, and murder, are from hell; and this King will, therefore, stand foremost in the list of diabolical, bloody, and execrable tyrants. His base-bought parliaments too, who sell him their souls, and extort from the people the money with which they aid his destructive purposes, as they share his guilt, will share his infamy,—parliaments, who, to please him, have repeatedly, by different votes year after year, dipped their hands in human blood, insomuch that methinks I see it dried and caked so thick upon them, that, if they could wash it off in the Thames, which flows under their windows, the whole river would run red to the ocean.

"One is provoked by enormous wickedness: but one is ashamed and humiliated at the view of human baseness. It afflicts me, therefore, to see a gentleman of Sir Joseph York's education and talents, for the sake of a red riband and a paltry stipend, mean enough to style such a monster *his master*, wear his livery, and hold himself ready at his command even to cut the throats of fellow subjects. This makes it impossible for me to end my letter with the civility of a compliment, and obliges me to subscribe myself simply,

"JOHN PAUL JONES,
"Whom you are pleased to style a *pirate.*"

HUMAN DEPRAVITY IN WAR

In the midst of frustrating efforts to restore peace between Great Britain and the United States, Franklin received a letter from his friend, the liberal clergyman and scientist Joseph Priestley, filled with the pleasures of his work in the laboratory. Franklin then bewailed the black mark war put on the character of mankind.

. . . I should rejoice much, if I could once more recover the Leisure to search with you into the Works of Nature; I mean the *inanimate,* not the *animate* or moral part of them, the more I discover'd of the former, the more I admir'd them; the more I know of the latter, the more I am disgusted with them. Men I find to be a Sort of Beings very badly constructed, as they are generally more easily provok'd than reconcil'd, more disposed to do Mischief to each other than to make Reparation, much more easily deceiv'd than undeceiv'd, and having more Pride and even Pleasure in killing than in begetting one another; for without a Blush they assemble in great armies at NoonDay to destroy, and when they have kill'd as many as they can, they exaggerate the Number to augment the fancied Glory; but they creep into Corners, or cover themselves with the Darkness of night, when they mean to beget, as being asham'd of a virtuous Action. A virtuous Action it would be, and a vicious one the killing of them, if the Species were really worth producing or preserving; but of this I begin to doubt.

I know you have no such Doubts, because, in your zeal for their welfare, you are taking a great deal of pains to save their Souls. Perhaps as you grow older, you may look upon this as a hopeless Project, or an idle Amusement,

---

Writings, VIII, 451–453; from a letter to Joseph Priestley, June 7, 1782.

repent of having murdered in mephitic air so many honest, harmless mice, and wish that to prevent mischief, you had used Boys and Girls instead of them. In what Light we are viewed by superior Beings, may be gathered from a Piece of late West India News, which possibly has not yet reached you. A young Angel of Distinction being sent down to this world on some Business, for the first time, had an old courier-spirit assigned him as a Guide. They arriv'd over the Seas of Martinico, in the middle of the long Day of obstinate Fight between the Fleets of Rodney and De Grasse. When, thro' the Clouds of smoke, he saw the Fire of the Guns, the Decks covered with mangled Limbs, and Bodies dead or dying; the ships sinking, burning, or blown into the Air; and the Quantity of Pain, Misery, and Destruction, the Crews yet alive were thus with so much Eagerness dealing round to one another; he turn'd angrily to his Guide, and said, "You blundering Blockhead, you are ignorant of your Business; you undertook to conduct me to the Earth, and you have brought me into Hell!" "No, Sir," says the Guide, "I have made no mistake; this is really the Earth, and these are men. Devils never treat one another in this cruel manner; they have more Sense, and more of what Men (vainly) call *Humanity*."

ON RECONCILIATION BETWEEN

GREAT BRITAIN AND THE UNITED STATES

In the spring of 1782, Lord Shelburne replaced Lord North at the head of the British Ministry, signifying the failure of Britain's

---

Writings, VIII, 471–472, 470; paper prepared for a conference held on April 18, 1782.

war against the former colonies. When Shelburne's emissaries began to consult Franklin on peace terms, he kept a journal of the proceedings (ended soon after one of Franklin's fellow peace commissioners, John Jay, arrived in Paris, June 23, 1782) in which he inserted this paper given to Richard Oswald early in the negotiations.

"To make a Peace durable, what may give Occasion for future Wars should if practicable be removed.
"The Territory of the United States and that of Canada, by long extended Frontiers, touch each other.
"The Settlers on the Frontiers of the American Provinces are generally the most disorderly of the People, who, being far removed from the Eye and Controll of their respective Governments, are more bold in committing Offences against Neighbours, and are for ever occasioning Complaints and furnishing Matter for fresh Differences between their States.
"By the late Debates in Parliament, and publick Writings, it appears, that Britain desires a *Reconciliation* with the Americans. It is a sweet Word. It means much more than a mere Peace, and what is heartily to be wish'd for. Nations make a Peace whenever they are both weary of making War. But, if one of them has made War upon the other unjustly, and has wantonly and unnecessarily done it great Injuries, and refuses Reparation, though there may, for the present, be Peace, the Resentment of those Injuries will remain, and will break out again in Vengeance when Occasions offer. These Occasions will be watch'd for by one side, fear'd by the other, and the Peace will never be secure; nor can any Cordiality subsist between them.
"Many Houses and Villages have been burnt in America by the English and their Allies, the Indians. I do not know that the Americans will insist on reparation; perhaps they may. But would it not be better for England to offer it?

Minister to France 333

Nothing could have a greater Tendency to conciliate, and much of the future Commerce and returning Intercourse between the two Countries may depend on the Reconciliation. Would not the advantage of Reconciliation by such means be greater than the Expence?

"If then a Way can be proposed, which may tend to efface the Memory of Injuries, at the same time that it takes away the Occasions of fresh Quarrel and Mischief, will it not be worth considering, especially if it can be done, not only without Expence, but be a means of saving?

"Britain possesses Canada. Her chief Advantage from that Possession consists in the Trade for Peltry. Her Expences in governing and defending that Settlement must be considerable. It might be humiliating to her to give it up on the Demand of America. Perhaps America will not demand it; some of her political Rulers may consider the fear of such a Neighbour, as a means of keeping 13 States more united among themselves, and more attentive to Military Discipline. But on the Minds of the People in general would it not have an excellent Effect, if Britain should voluntarily offer to give up this Province; tho' on these Conditions, that she shall in all times coming have and enjoy the Right of Free Trade thither, unincumbred with any Duties whatsoever; that so much of the vacant Lands there shall be sold, as will raise a Sum sufficient to pay for the Houses burnt by the British Troops and their Indians; and also to indemnify the Royalists for the Confiscation of their Estates? . . .

[Franklin at the same time stated to Oswald the realistic advantages to England of ceding Canada to the United States.]

I then touch'd upon the Affair of Canada, and as in a former Conversation he had mention'd his Opinion, that the giving up of that Country to the English at the last Peace had been a politic Act in France, for that it had weaken'd the Ties between England and her Colonies, and that he himself had predicted from it the late Revolution, I spoke of the Occasions of future Quarrels that might be produc'd by her continuing to hold it; hinting at the same time but not expressing too plainly that such a Situation, to us so dangerous, would necessarily oblige us to cultivate and strengthen our Union with France.

PROGRESS, PROSPERITY, AND PEACE

While Franklin talked war and diplomacy in Paris, he received a letter from Sir Joseph Banks, President of the Royal Society, about his important botanical experiments. Struck with Banks's work for the improvement of mankind, Franklin wrote of his own irrepressible hopes for a better future.

. . . Be assured, that I long earnestly for a Return of those peaceful Times, when I could sit down in sweet Society with my English philosophic Friends, communicating to each other new Discoveries, and proposing Improvements of old ones; all tending to extend the Power of Man over Matter, avert or diminish the Evils he is subject to, or augment the Number of his Enjoyments. Much more happy should I be thus employ'd in your most desirable Company, than in that of all the Grandees of the Earth projecting Plans of Mischief, however necessary they may be supposed for obtaining greater Good.

I am glad to learn by the D^r that your great Work goes on. I admire your Magnanimity in the Undertaking, and the Perseverance with which you have prosecuted it.

Writings, VIII, 592–593; IX, 74; from letters to Sir Joseph Banks, September 9, 1782 and July 27, 1783.

I join with you most perfectly in the charming Wish you so well express, "that such Measures may be taken by both Parties as may tend to the Elevation of both, rather than the Destruction of either." If any thing has happened endangering one of them, my Comfort is, that I endeavour'd earnestly to prevent it, and gave honest, faithful Advice, which, if it had been regarded, would have been effectual. And still, if proper Means are us'd to produce, not only a Peace, but what is much more interesting, a thorough Reconciliation, a few Years may heal the Wounds that have been made in our Happiness, and produce a Degree of Prosperity of which at present we can hardly form a Conception. . . .

[After the peace treaty, Franklin wrote again to Banks.]

. . . I join with you most cordially in rejoicing at the return of Peace. I hope it will be lasting, and that Mankind will at length, as they call themselves reasonable Creatures, have Reason and Sense enough to settle their Differences without cutting Throats; for, in my opinion, *there never was a good War, or a bad Peace.* What vast additions to the Conveniences and Comforts of Living might Mankind have acquired, if the Money spent in Wars had been employed in Works of public utility! What an extension of Agriculture, even to the Tops of our Mountains: what Rivers rendered navigable, or joined by Canals: what Bridges, Aqueducts, new Roads, and other public Works, Edifices, and Improvements, rendering England a compleat Paradise, might have been obtained by spending those Millions in doing good, which in the last War have been spent in doing Mischief; in bringing Misery into thousands of Families, and destroying the Lives of so many thousands of working people, who might have performed the useful labour! . . .

INFORMATION TO THOSE WHO WOULD REMOVE TO AMERICA

Franklin received thousands of inquiries from Europeans who wanted to go to America. Some sought an honest opportunity to rise through hard work while other hoped to get-rich-quick through speculation or special privilege. Franklin replied to them generally and at the same time described the social philosophy of the new United States.

Many Persons in Europe, having directly or by Letters, express'd to the Writer of this, who is well acquainted with North America, their Desire of transporting and establishing themselves in that Country; but who appear to have formed, thro' Ignorance, mistaken Ideas and Expectations of what is to be obtained there; he thinks it may be useful, and prevent inconvenient, expensive, and fruitless Removals and Voyages of improper Persons, if he gives some clearer and truer Notions of that part of the World, than appear to have hitherto prevailed.

He finds it is imagined by Numbers, that the Inhabitants of North America are rich, capable of rewarding, and dispos'd to reward, all sorts of Ingeniuty; that they are at the same time ignorant of all the Sciences, and, consequently, that Strangers, possessing Talents in the Belles-Lettres, fine Arts, &c., must be highly esteemed, and so well paid, as to become easily rich themselves; that there are also abundance of profitable Offices to be disposed of, which the Natives are not qualified to fill; and that, having few Persons of Family among them, Strangers of Birth must be greatly respected, and of course easily obtain the best of

---

Writings, VIII, 603-614; probably written in September 1782.

those Offices, which will make all their Fortunes; that the Governments too, to encourage Emigrations from Europe, not only pay the Expence of personal Transportation, but give Lands gratis to Strangers, with Negroes to work for them, Utensils of Husbandry, and Stocks of Cattle. These are all wild Imaginations; and those who go to America with Expectations founded upon them will surely find themselves disappointed.

The Truth is, that though there are in that Country few People so miserable as the Poor of Europe, there are also very few that in Europe would be called rich; it is rather a general happy Mediocrity that prevails. There are few great Proprietors of the Soil, and few Tenants; most People cultivate their own Lands, or follow some Handicraft or Merchandise; very few rich enough to live idly upon their Rents or Incomes, or to pay the high Prices given in Europe for Paintings, Statues, Architecture, and the other Works of Art, that are more curious than useful. Hence the natural Geniuses, that have arisen in America with such Talents, have uniformly quitted that Country for Europe, where they can be more suitably rewarded. It is true, that Letters and Mathematical Knowledge are in Esteem there, but they are at the same time more common than is apprehended; there being already existing nine Colleges or Universities, viz. four in New England, and one in each of the Provinces of New York, New Jersey, Pensilvania, Maryland, and Virginia, all furnish'd with learned Professors; besides a number of smaller Academies; these educate many of their Youth in the Languages, and those Sciences that qualify men for the Professions of Divinity, Law, or Physick. Strangers indeed are by no means excluded from exercising those Professions; and the quick Increase of Inhabitants everywhere gives them a Chance of Employ, which they have in common with the Natives. Of civil Offices, or Employments, there are few; no superfluous Ones, as in Europe; and it is a Rule establish'd in some of the States, that no Office should be so profitable as to make it desirable. The 36th Article of the Constitution of Pennsilvania, runs expressly in these Words; "As every Freeman, to preserve his Independence, (if he has not a sufficient Estate) ought to have some Profession, Calling, Trade, or Farm, whereby he may honestly subsist, there can be no Necessity for, nor Use in, establishing Offices of Profit; the usual Effects of which are Dependance and Servility, unbecoming Freemen, in the Possessors and Expectants; Faction, Contention, Corruption, and Disorder among the People. Wherefore, whenever an Office, thro' Increase of Fees or otherwise, becomes so profitable, as to occasion many to apply for it, the Profits ought to be lessened by the Legislature."

These Ideas prevailing more or less in all the United States, it cannot be worth any Man's while, who has a means of Living at home, to expatriate himself, in hopes of obtaining a profitable civil Office in America; and, as to military Offices, they are at an End with the War, the Armies being disbanded. Much less is it adviseable for a Person to go thither, who has no other Quality to recommend him but his Birth. In Europe it has indeed its Value; but it is a Commodity that cannot be carried to a worse Market than that of America, where people do not inquire concerning a Stranger, *What is he?* but, *What can he do?* If he has any useful Art, he is welcome; and if he exercises it, and behaves well, he will be respected by all that know him; but a mere Man of Quality, who, on that Account, wants to live upon the Public, by some Office or Salary, will be despis'd and disregarded. The Husbandman is in honor there, and even the Mechanic, because their Employments are useful. The People have a saying, that God Almighty is himself a Mechanic, the greatest in the Univers; and he is respected and admired more for the Variety,

Ingenuity, and Utility of his Handyworks, than for the Antiquity of his Family. They are pleas'd with the Observation of a Negro, and frequently mention it, that *Boccarorra* (meaning the White men) *make de black man workee, make de Horse workee, make de Ox workee, make ebery ting workee; only de Hog. He, de hog, no workee; he eat, he drink, he walk about, he go to sleep when he please, he libb like a Gentleman.* According to these Opinions of the Americans, one of them would think himself more oblig'd to a Genealogist, who could prove for him that his Ancestors and Relations for ten Generations had been Ploughmen, Smiths, Carpenters, Turners, Weavers, Tanners, or even Shoemakers, and consequently that they were useful Members of Society; than if he could only prove that they were Gentlemen, doing nothing of Value, but living idly on the Labour of others, mere *fruges consumere nati,*[1] and otherwise *good for nothing,* till by their Death their Estates, like the Carcass of the Negro's Gentleman-Hog, come to be *cut up.*

With regard to Encouragements for Strangers from Government, they are really only what are derived from good Laws and Liberty. Strangers are welcome, because there is room enough for them all, and therefore the old Inhabitants are not jealous of them; the Laws protect them sufficiently, so that they have no need of the Patronage of Great Men; and every one will enjoy securely the Profits of his Industry. But, if he does not bring a Fortune with him, he must work and be industrious to live. One or two Years' residence gives him all the Rights of a Citizen; but the government does not at present, whatever it may have done in former times, hire People to become Settlers, by Paying their Passages, giving Land, Negroes, Utensils,

---

[1] " . . . . . . born
Merely to eat up the corn."—Watts.

Stock, or any other kind of Emolument whatsoever. In short, America is the Land of Labour, and by no means what the English call *Lubberland,* and the French *Pays de Cocagne,* where the streets are said to be pav'd with half-peck Loaves, the Houses til'd with Pancakes, and where the Fowls fly about ready roasted, crying, *Come eat me!*

Who then are the kind of Persons to whom an Emigration to America may be advantageous? And what are the Advantages they may reasonably expect?

Land being cheap in that Country, from the vast Forests still void of Inhabitants, and not likely to be occupied in an Age to come, insomuch that the Propriety of an hundred Acres of fertile Soil full of Wood may be obtained near the Frontiers, in many Places, for Eight or Ten Guineas, hearty young Labouring Men, who understand the Husbandry of Corn and Cattle, which is nearly the same in that Country as in Europe, may easily establish themselves there. A little Money sav'd of the good Wages they receive there, while they work for others, enables them to buy the Land and begin their Plantation, in which they are assisted by the Good-Will of their Neighbours, and some Credit. Multitudes of poor People from England, Ireland, Scotland, and Germany, have by this means in a few years become wealthy Farmers, who, in their own Countries, where all the Lands are fully occupied, and the Wages of Labour low, could never have emerged from the poor Condition wherein they were born.

From the salubrity of the Air, the healthiness of the Climate, the plenty of good Provisions, and the Encouragement to early Marriages by the certainty of Subsistence in cultivating the Earth, the Increase of Inhabitants by natural Generation is very rapid in America, and becomes still more so by the Accession of Strangers; hence there is a continual Demand for more Artisans of all the necessary and useful kinds, to supply those Cultivators of the Earth with

Houses, and with Furniture and Utensils of the grosser sorts, which cannot so well be brought from Europe. Tolerably good Workmen in any of those mechanic Arts are sure to find Employ, and to be well paid for their Work, there being no Restraints preventing Strangers from exercising any Art they understand, nor any Permission necessary. If they are poor, they begin first as Servants or Journeymen; and if they are sober, industrious, and frugal, they soon become Masters, establish themselves in Business, marry, raise Families, and become respectable Citizens.

Also, Persons of moderate Fortunes and Capitals, who, having a Number of Children to provide for, are desirous of bringing them up to Industry, and to secure Estates for their Posterity, have Opportunities of doing it in America, which Europe does not afford. There they may be taught and practise profitable mechanic Arts, without incurring Disgrace on that Account, but on the contrary acquiring Respect by such Abilities. There small Capitals laid out in Lands, which daily become more valuable by the Increase of People, afford a solid Prospect of ample Fortunes thereafter for those Children. The Writer of this has known several Instances of large Tracts of Land, bought, on what was then the Frontier of Pensilvania, for Ten Pounds per hundred Acres, which after 20 years, when the Settlements had been extended far beyond them, sold readily, without any Improvement made upon them, for three Pounds per Acre. The Acre in America is the same with the English Acre, or the Acre of Normandy.

Those, who desire to understand the State of Government in America, would do well to read the Constitutions of the several States, and the Articles of Confederation that bind the whole together for general Purposes, under the Direction of one Assembly, called the Congress. These Constitutions have been printed, by order of Congress, in America; two Editions of them have also been printed in

London; and a good Translation of them into French has lately been published at Paris.

Several of the Princes of Europe having of late years, from an Opinion of Advantage to arise by producing all Commodities and Manufactures within their own Dominions, so as to diminish or render useless their Importations, have endeavoured to entice Workmen from other Countries by high Salaries, Privileges, &c. Many Persons, pretending to be skilled in various great Manufactures, imagining that America must be in Want of them, and that the Congress would probably be dispos'd to imitate the Princes above mentioned, have proposed to go over, on Condition of having their Passages paid, Lands given, Salaries appointed, exclusive Privileges for Terms of years, &c. Such Persons, on reading the Articles of Confederation, will find, that the Congress have no Power committed to them, or Money put into their Hands, for such purposes; and that if any such Encouragement is given, it must be by the Government of some separate State. This, however, has rarely been done in America; and, when it has been done, it has rarely succeeded, so as to establish a Manufacture, which the Country was not yet so ripe for as to encourage private Persons to set it up; Labour being generally too dear there, and Hands difficult to be kept together, every one desiring to be a Master, and the Cheapness of Lands inclining many to leave Trades for Agriculture. Some indeed have met with Success, and are carried on to Advantage; but they are generally such as require only a few Hands, or wherein great Part of the Work is performed by Machines. Things that are bulky, and of so small Value as not well to bear the Expence of Freight, may often be made cheaper in the Country than they can be imported; and the Manufacture of such Things will be profitable wherever there is a sufficient Demand. The Farmers in America produce indeed a good deal of

Wool and Flax; and none is exported, it is all work'd up; but it is in the Way of domestic Manufacture, for the Use of the Family. The buying up Quantities of Wool and Flax, with the Design to employ Spinners, Weavers, &c., and form great Establishments, producing Quantities of Linen and Woollen Goods for Sale, has been several times attempted in different Provinces; but those Projects have generally failed, goods of equal Value being imported cheaper. And when the Governments have been solicited to support such Schemes by Encouragements, in Money, or by imposing Duties on Importation of such Goods, it has been generally refused, on this Principle, that, if the Country is ripe for the Manufacture, it may be carried on by private Persons to Advantage; and if not, it is a Folly to think of forcing Nature. Great Establishments of Manufacture require great Numbers of Poor to do the Work for small Wages; these Poor are to be found in Europe, but will not be found in America, till the Lands are all taken up and cultivated, and the Excess of People, who cannot get Land, want Employment. The Manufacture of Silk, they say, is natural in France, as that of Cloth in England, because each Country produces in Plenty the first Material; but if England will have a Manufacture of Silk as well as that of Cloth, and France one of Cloth as well as that of Silk, these unnatural Operations must be supported by mutual Prohibitions, or high Duties on the Importation of each other's Goods; by which means the Workmen are enabled to tax the home Consumer by greater Prices, while the higher Wages they receive makes them neither happier nor richer, since they only drink more and work less. Therefore the Governments in America do nothing to encourage such Projects. The People, by this Means, are not impos'd on, either by the Merchant or Mechanic. If the Merchant demands too much Profit on imported Shoes, they buy of the Shoemaker; and if he asks too high a Price, they take them of the Merchant; thus the two Professions are checks on each other. The Shoemaker, however, has, on the whole, a considerable Profit upon his Labour in America, beyond what he had in Europe, as he can add to his Price a Sum nearly equal to all the Expences of Freight and Commission, Risque or Insurance, &c., necessarily charged by the Merchant. And the Case is the same with the Workmen in every other Mechanic Art. Hence it is, that Artisans generally live better and more easily in America than in Europe; and such as are good Economists make a comfortable Provision for Age, and for their Children. Such may, therefore, remove with Advantage to America.

In the long-settled Countries of Europe, all Arts, Trades, Professions, Farms, &c., are so full, that it is difficult for a poor Man, who has Children, to place them where they may gain, or learn to gain, a decent Livelihood. The Artisans, who fear creating future Rivals in Business, refuse to take Apprentices, but upon Conditions of Money, Maintenance, or the like, which the Parents are unable to comply with. Hence the Youth are dragg'd up in Ignorance of every gainful Art, and oblig'd to become Soldiers, or Servants, or Thieves, for a Subsistence. In America, the rapid Increase of Inhabitants takes away that Fear of Rivalship, and Artisans willingly receive Apprentices from the hope of Profit by their Labour, during the Remainder of the Time stipulated, after they shall be instructed. Hence it is easy for poor Families to get their Children instructed; for the Artisans are so desirous of Apprentices, that many of them will even give Money to the Parents, to have Boys from Ten to Fifteen Years of Age bound Apprentices to them till the Age of Twenty-one; and many poor Parents have, by that means, on their Arrival in the Country, raised Money enough to buy Land sufficient to establish themselves, and to subsist the rest of their Family by Agriculture. These Contracts for Apprentices are made before a Magistrate, who regulates the Agreement according to Reason and Justice, and, having in view the Formation of a future useful Citizen, obliges the Master to engage by a written Indenture, not only that, during the time of Service stipulated, the Apprentice shall be duly provided with Meat, Drink, Apparel, washing, and Lodging, and, at its Expiration, with a compleat new Suit of Cloaths, but also that he shall be taught to read, write, and cast Accompts; and that he shall be well instructed in the Art or Profession of his Master, or some other, by which he may afterwards gain a Livelihood, and be able in his turn to raise a Family. A Copy of this Indenture is given to the Apprentice or his Friends, and the Magistrate keeps a Record of it, to which recourse may be had, in case of Failure by the Master in any Point of Performance. This desire among the Masters, to have more Hands employ'd in working for them, induces them to pay the Passages of young Persons, of both Sexes, who, on their Arrival, agree to serve them one, two, three, or four Years; those, who have already learnt a Trade, agreeing for a shorter Term, in proportion to their Skill, and the consequent immediate Value of their Service; and those, who have none, agreeing for a longer Term, in consideration of being taught an Art their Poverty would not permit them to acquire in their own Country.

The almost general Mediocrity of Fortune that prevails in America obliging its People to follow some Business for subsistence, those Vices, that arise usually from Idleness, are in a great measure prevented. Industry and constant Employment are great preservatives of the Morals and Virtue of a Nation. Hence bad Examples to Youth are more rare in America, which must be a comfortable Consideration to Parents. To this may be truly added, that serious Religion, under its various Denominations, is not only tolerated, but respected and practised. Atheism is unknown there; Infidelity rare and secret; so that persons may live to a great Age in that Country, without having their Piety shocked by meeting with either an Atheist or an Infidel. And the Divine Being seems to have manifested his Approbation of the mutual Forbearance and Kindness with which the different Sects treat each other, by the remarkable Prosperity with which He has been pleased to favour the whole Country.

THE ART OF DIPLOMACY

In signing the preliminary peace treaty with England the American commissioners violated their instructions to confer with French ministers at every step of their negotiations. Though Franklin felt keenly the need to cooperate fully with France and probably would have done so had he been the only American commissioner, he agreed with his colleagues, John Jay and John Adams, that to secure vital American interests which offered no injury to France, some steps might be taken in secret. French Foreign Minister Vergennes understood this but nevertheless chided Franklin for neglecting the instructions. Franklin replied with a diplomatic masterpiece—and at the same time asked for another loan to which Vergennes agreed within a week.

. . . Nothing has been agreed in the preliminaries contrary to the interests of France; and no peace is to take place between us and England, till you have concluded yours. Your observation is, however, apparently just, that, in not consulting you before they were signed, we have been guilty of neglecting a point of *bienséance*. But, as this

---

Writings, VIII, 642–643; from a letter to Comte de Vergennes, December 17, 1782.

was not from want of respect for the King, whom we all love and honour, we hope it will be excused, and that the great work, which has hitherto been so happily conducted, is so nearly brought to perfection, and is so glorious to his reign, will not be ruined by a single indiscretion of ours. And certainly the whole edifice sinks to the ground immediately, if you refuse on that account to give us any further assistance. . . .

. . . It is not possible for any one to be more sensible than I am, of what I and every American owe to the King, for the many and great benefits and favours he has bestowed upon us. All my letters to America are proofs of this; all tending to make the same impressions on the minds of my countrymen, that I felt in my own. And I believe, that no Prince was ever more beloved and respected by his own subjects, than the King is by the people of the United States. *The English, I just now learn, flatter themselves they have already divided us.* I hope this little misunderstanding will therefore be kept a secret, and that they will find themselves totally mistaken. With great and sincere respect, I am, Sir, &c.

B. FRANKLIN.

PROPOSALS TO MAKE WARS

LESS LIKELY AND LESS DESTRUCTIVE

While negotiating for peace Franklin drew two humanitarian papers, one denying that privateering was profitable and pointing

---

Writings, IX, 4-7; from a paper communicated to Richard Oswald, January 14, 1783.

out the evils of European management of the "Sugar Islands" in the West Indies, and the other seeking to exempt useful occupations from the ravages of war.

It is for the interest of humanity in general, that the occasions of war, and the inducements to it, should be diminished.

If rapine is abolished, one of the encouragements to war is taken away, and peace therefore more likely to continue and be lasting.

The practice of robbing merchants on the high seas, a remnant of the ancient piracy, though it may be accidentally beneficial to particular persons, is far from being profitable to all engaged in it, or to the nation that authorizes it. In the beginning of a war, some rich ships, not upon their guard, are surprised and taken. This encourages the first adventurers to fit out more armed vessels, and many others to do the same. But the enemy at the same time become more careful, arm their merchant ships better, and render them not so easy to be taken; they go also more under protection of convoys; thus, while the privateers to take them are multiplied, the vessels subject to be taken, and the chances of profit, are diminished, so that many cruises are made, wherein the expenses overgo the gains; and, as is the case in other lotteries, though particulars have got prizes, the mass of adventurers are losers, the whole expense of fitting out all the privateers, during a war, being much greater than the whole amount of goods taken. Then there is the national loss of all the labour of so many men during the time they have been employed in robbing; who, besides, spend what they get in riot, drunkenness, and debauchery, lose their habits of industry, are rarely fit for any sober business after a peace, and serve only to increase the number of highwaymen and house-breakers. Even the undertakers, who have been fortunate, are by sudden wealth led into expensive living, the habit of which continues when the means of supporting it ceases, and finally ruins them; a just punishment for their having wantonly and unfeelingly ruined many honest, innocent traders and their families, whose subsistence was employed in serving the common interests of mankind.

Should it be agreed and become a part of the law of nations, that the cultivators of the earth are not to be molested or interrupted in their peaceable and useful employment, the inhabitants of the sugar islands would perhaps come under the protection of such a regulation, which would be a great advantage to the nations who at present hold those islands, since the cost of sugar to the consumer in those nations consists not merely in the price he pays for it by the pound, but in the accumulated charge of all the taxes he pays in every war, to fit out fleets and maintain troops for the defence of the islands that raise the sugar, and the ships that bring it home. But the expense of treasure is not all. A celebrated philosophical writer remarks, that, when he considered the wars made in Africa, for prisoners to raise sugars in America, the numbers slain in those wars, the numbers that, being crowded in ships, perish in the transportation, and the numbers that die under the severities of slavery, he could scarce look on a morsel of sugar without conceiving it spotted with human blood. If he had considered also the blood of one another, which the white nations shed in fighting for those islands, he would have imagined his sugar not as spotted only, but as thoroughly dyed red. On these accounts I am persuaded, that the subjects of the Emperor of Germany, and the Empress of Russia, who have no sugar islands, consume sugar cheaper at Vienna, and Moscow, with all the charge of transporting it after its arrival in Europe, than the citizens of London or of Paris. And I sincerely believe, that if

France and England were to decide, by throwing dice, which should have the whole of their sugar islands, the loser in the throw would be the gainer. The future expense of defending them would be saved; the sugars would be bought cheaper by all Europe, if the inhabitants might make it without interruption, and, whoever imported the sugar, the same revenue might be raised by duties at the customhouses of the nation that consumed it. And, on the whole, I conceive it would be better for the nations now possessing sugar colonies to give up their claim to them, let them govern themselves, and put them under the protection of all the powers of Europe as neutral countries, open to the commerce of all, the profits of the present monopolies being by no means equivalent to the expense of maintaining them.

Article.

If war should hereafter arise between Great Britain and the United States, which God forbid, the merchants of either country then residing in the other shall be allowed to remain nine months to collect their debts, and settle their affairs, and may depart freely, carrying off all their effects without molestation or hindrance. And all fishermen, all cultivators of the earth, and all artisans or manufacturers unarmed, and inhabiting unfortified towns, villages, or places, who labour for the common subsistence and benefit of mankind, and peaceably follow their respective employments, shall be allowed to continue the same, and shall not be molested by the armed force of the enemy in whose power by the events of the war they may happen to fall; but, if any thing is necessary to be taken from them, for the use of such armed force, the same shall be paid for at a reasonable price. And all merchants or traders with their unarmed vessels, employed in commerce, exchanging the products of different places, and thereby rendering the necessaries, conveniences, and comforts of human life more easy to obtain, and more general, shall be allowed to pass freely, unmolested. And neither of the powers, parties to this treaty, shall grant or issue any commission to any private armed vessels, empowering them to take or destroy such trading ships, or interrupt such commerce.

THE ADVANTAGES OF FREE TRADE

As Franklin sought agreements to revive American commerce after the Revolution, he advised statesmen on both sides of the Atlantic on the benefits of free trade.

. . . In general I would only observe that commerce, consisting in a mutual exchange of the necessities and conveniences of life, the more free and unrestrained it is, the more it flourishes; and the happier are all the nations concerned in it. Most of the restraints put upon it in different countries seem to have been the projects of particulars for their private interest, under pretence of public good. . . .

. . . I have seen so much Embarrassment and so little Advantage in all the Restraining and Compulsive Systems, that I feel myself strongly inclin'd to believe, that a State, which leaves all her Ports open to all the World upon equal Terms, will, by that means, have foreign Commodities cheaper, sell its own Productions dearer, and be on

---

Writings, IX, 19, 63; from letters to Comte de Vergennes, March 16, 1783, and to Robert R. Livingston, July 22, 1783.

the whole the most prosperous. I have heard some Merchants say, that there is 10 per cent Difference between *Will you buy?* and *Will you sell?* When Foreigners bring us their Goods, they want to part with them speedily, that they may purchase their Cargoes and despatch their Ships, which are at constant Charges in our Ports; we have then the Advantage of their *Will you buy?* And when they demand our Produce, we have the Advantage of their *Will you sell?* And the concurring Demands of a Number also contribute to raise our Prices. Thus both those Questions are in our favour at home, against us abroad. . . .

DISPUTE WITH JOHN ADAMS

OVER GRATITUDE TOWARD FRANCE

John Adams shared neither Franklin's trust in France and her ministers nor his gratitude toward them. Franklin wrote the American Secretary for Foreign Affairs justifying the independent course pursued by the American commissioners during the peace negotiations, but at the same time repudiating Adams's hostility toward France.

. . . Nothing was stipulated to [France's] Prejudice, and none of the Stipulations were to have Force, but by a subsequent Act of their own. I suppose, indeed, that they have not complain'd of it, or you would have sent us a Copy of the Complaint, that we might have answer'd it. I long since satisfi'd Comte de V. about it here. We did what appear'd to all of us best at the Time, and, if we have done wrong, the Congress will do right, after hearing us, to

---

Writings, IX, 60-62; from a letter to Robert R. Livingston, July 22, 1783.

Minister to France 353

censure us. Their Nomination of Five Persons to the Service seems to mark, that they had some Dependence on our joint Judgment, since one alone could have made a Treaty by Direction of the French Ministry as well as twenty. . . .

[Franklin then explained why he harbored no suspicion of French misconduct, and turned to Adams.]

. . . I ought not, however, to conceal from you, that one of my Colleagues is of a very different Opinion from me in these Matters. He thinks the French Minister one of the greatest Enemies of our Country, that he would have straitned our Boundaries, to prevent the Growth of our People; contracted our Fishery, to obstruct the Increase of our Seamen; and retained the Royalists among us, to keep us divided; that he privately opposes all our Negociations with foreign Courts, and afforded us, during the War, the Assistance we receiv'd, only to keep it alive, that we might be so much the more weaken'd by it; that to think of Gratitude to France is the greatest of Follies, and that to be influenc'd by it would ruin us. He makes no Secret of his having these Opinions, expresses them publicly, sometimes in presence of the English Ministers, and speaks of hundreds of Instances which he could produce in Proof of them. None of which however, have yet appear'd to me, unless the Conversations and Letter above-mentioned are reckoned such.

If I were not convinc'd of the real Inability of this Court to furnish the further Supplys we ask'd, I should suspect these Discourses of a Person in his Station might have influenced the Refusal; but I think they have gone no farther than to occasion a Suspicion, that we have a considerable Party of Antigallicans in America, who are not Tories, and consequently to produce some doubts of the Continuance of our Friendship. As such Doubts may hereafter have a bad Effect, I think we cannot take too much care to remove them; and it is, therefore, I write this, to put you on your guard, (believing it my duty, tho' I know that I hazard by it a mortal Enmity), and to caution you respecting the Insinuations of this Gentleman against this Court, and the Instances he supposes of their ill will to us, which I take to be as imaginary as I know his Fancies to be, that Count de V. and myself are continually plotting against him, and employing the News-Writers of Europe to depreciate his Character, &c. But as Shakespear says, "Trifles light as Air," &c. I am persuaded, however, that he means well for his Country, is always an honest Man, often a wise one, but sometimes, and in some things, absolutely out of his senses. . . .

THE FOUNDATIONS

OF AMERICAN FOREIGN POLICY

Franklin remained in France nearly two years after signing the definitive peace treaty with Great Britain in September 1783. During that time he wrote frequently of what he thought should be the guideposts of United States policy in Europe, the dangers America faced there, and the things she should do for her own preservation and honor.

. . . With respect to the British Court, we should, I think, be constantly upon our Guard, and impress strongly upon our Minds, that, tho' it has made Peace with us, it is not in

---

Writings, IX, 131–132, 210, 213; from letters to Thomas Mifflin, December 15, 1783, to Samuel Mather, May 12, 1784, and to Charles Thomson, May 13, 1784.

truth reconcil'd either to us, or to its loss of us, but still flatters itself with Hopes, that some Change in the Affairs of Europe, or some Disunion among ourselves, may afford them an Opportunity of Recovering their Dominion, punishing those who have most offended, and securing our future Dependence. It is easy to see by the general Turn of the Ministerial Newspapers (light things, indeed, as Straws and Feathers, but like them they show which way the Wind blows), and by the malignant Improvement their Ministers make, in all the Foreign Courts, of every little Accident or Dissension among us, the Riot of a few Soldiers at Philadelphia, the Resolves of some Town Meetings, the Reluctance to pay Taxes, &c., all which are exaggerated, to represent our Government as so many Anarchies, of which the People themselves are weary, and the Congress as having lost its Influence, being no longer respected; I say it is easy to see from this Conduct, that they bear us no good Will, and that they wish the Reality of what they are pleas'd to imagine. They have, too, a numerous Royal Progeny to provide for, some of whom are educated in the military Line. In these Circumstances we cannot be too careful to preserve the Friendships we have acquired abroad, and the Union we have established at home, to secure our Credit by a punctual Discharge of our Obligations of every kind, and our Reputation by the wisdom of our Councils: Since we know not how soon we may have a fresh Occasion for Friends, for Credit, and for Reputation.

The extravagant Misrepresentations of our Political State in foreign Countries, made it appear necessary to give them better Information, which I thought could not be more effectually and authentically done, than by publishing a Translation into French, now the most general Language in Europe, of the Book of Constitutions, which had been printed by Order of Congress. This I accordingly got well done, and presented two Copies, handsomely bound, to every foreign Minister here, one for himself, the other more elegant for his Sovereign. It has been well taken, and has afforded Matter of Surprise to many, who had conceived mean Ideas of the State of Civilization in America, and could not have expected so much political Knowledge and Sagacity had existed in our Wildernesses. And from all Parts I have the satisfaction to hear, that our Constitutions in general are much admired. I am persuaded, that this Step will not only tend to promote the Emigration to our Country of substantial People from all Parts of Europe, by the numerous Copies I shall disperse, but will facilitate our future Treaties with foreign Courts, who could not before know what kind of Government and People they had to treat with. . . .

. . . This powerful monarchy [France] continues its friendship for the United States. It is a friendship of the utmost importance to our security, and should be carefully cultivated. Britain has not yet well digested the loss of its dominion over us, and has still at times some flattering hopes of recovering it. Accidents may increase those hopes, and encourage dangerous attempts. A breach between us and France would infallibly bring the English again upon our backs; and yet we have some wild heads among our countrymen, who are endeavouring to weaken that connexion! . . .

. . . A few years of Peace, will improve, will restore and encrease our strength; but our future safety will depend on our union and our virtue. Britain will be long watching for advantages, to recover what she has lost. If we do not convince the world, that we are a Nation to be depended on for fidelity in Treaties; if we appear negligent in paying our Debts, and ungrateful to those who have served and befriended us; our reputation, and all the strength it is capable of procuring, will be lost, and fresh attacks upon us will be encouraged and promoted by better prospects of success. Let us therefore beware of being lulled into a dangerous security; and of being both enervated and impoverished by luxury; of being weakened by internal contentions and divisions; of being shamefully extravagant in contracting private debts, while we are backward in discharging honorably those of the public; of neglect in military exercises and discipline, and in providing stores of arms and munitions of war, to be ready on occasion; for all these are circumstances that give confidence to enemies, and diffidence to friends; and the expenses required to prevent a war are much lighter than those that will, if not prevented, be absolutely necessary to maintain it. . . .

THE OBLIGATION TO PAY TAXES

When Franklin learned of the resistance of many Americans to paying taxes for the public good levied by bodies in which they had representation, he wrote of the obligation citizens owed a just government.

. . . The Remissness of our People in Paying Taxes is highly blameable; the Unwillingness to pay them is still more so. I see, in some Resolutions of Town Meetings, a Remonstrance against giving Congress a Power to take, as they call it, the People's Money out of their Pockets, tho' only to pay the Interest and Principal of Debts duly contracted. They seem to mistake the Point. Money, justly due from the People, is their Creditors' Money, and no longer

---

Writings, IX, 138; from a letter to Robert Morris, December 25, 1783.

the Money of the People, who, if they withold it, should be compell'd to pay by some Law.

All Property, indeed, except the Savage's temporary Cabin, his Bow, his Matchcoat, and other little Acquisitions, absolutely necessary for his Subsistence, seems to me to be the Creature of public Convention. Hence the Public has the Right of Regulating Descents, and all other Conveyances of Property, and even of limiting the Quantity and the Uses of it. All the Property that is necessary to a Man, for the Conservation of the Individual and the Propagation of the Species, is his natural Right, which none can justly deprive him of: But all Property superfluous to such purposes is the Property of the Publick, who, by their Laws, have created it, and who may therefore by other Laws dispose of it, whenever the Welfare of the Publick shall demand such Disposition. He that does not like civil Society on these Terms, let him retire and live among Savages. He can have no right to the benefits of Society, who will not pay his Club towards the Support of it. . . .

ON

HEREDITARY SOCIETIES AND THE EAGLE

AS AN AMERICAN SYMBOL

At the end of the Revolution certain American officers proposed to form the Society of the Cincinnati to be composed of officers who had served in the war, membership in which would descend to their sons exclusively. Sensing the aristocratic dangers in the scheme and believing it contradicted the principles of

---

Writings, IX, 161–167; from a letter to Sarah Franklin Bache, January 26, 1784.

republican government, Franklin wrote disdainfully of the society to his daughter.

. . . I only wonder that, when the united Wisdom of our Nation had, in the Articles of Confederation, manifested their Dislike of establishing Ranks of Nobility, by Authority either of the Congress or of any particular State, a Number of private Persons should think proper to distinguish themselves and their Posterity, from their fellow Citizens, and form an Order of *hereditary Knights,* in direct Opposition to the solemnly declared Sense of their Country! I imagine it must be likewise contrary to the Good Sense of most of those drawn into it by the Persuasion of its Projectors, who have been too much struck with the Ribbands and Crosses they have seen among them hanging to the Buttonholes of Foreign Officers. And I suppose those, who disapprove of it, have not hitherto given it much Opposition, from a Principle somewhat like that of your good Mother, relating to punctilious Persons, who are always exacting little Observances of Respect; that, *"if People can be pleased with small Matters, it is a pity but they should have them."*

In this View, perhaps, I should not myself, if my Advice had been ask'd, have objected to their wearing their Ribband and Badge according to their Fancy, tho' I certainly should to the entailing it as an Honour on their Posterity. For Honour, worthily obtain'd (as for Example that of our Officers), is in its Nature a *personal* Thing, and incommunicable to any but those who had some Share in obtaining it. Thus among the Chinese, the most ancient, and from long Experience the wisest of Nations, honour does not *descend,* but *ascends.* If a man from his Learning, his Wisdom, or his Valour, is promoted by the Emperor to the Rank of Mandarin, his Parents are immediately entitled to all the same Ceremonies of Respect from the People, that are establish'd as due to the Mandarin himself; on the supposition that it must have been owing to the Education, Instruction, and good Example afforded him by his Parents, that he was rendered capable of serving the Publick.

This *ascending* Honour is therefore useful to the State, as it encourages Parents to give their Children a good and virtuous Education. But the *descending Honour,* to Posterity who could have no Share in obtaining it, is not only groundless and absurd, but often hurtful to that Posterity, since it is apt to make them proud, disdaining to be employ'd in useful Arts, and thence falling into Poverty, and all the Meannesses, Servility, and Wretchedness attending it; which is the present case with much of what is called the *Noblesse* in Europe. Or if, to keep up the Dignity of the Family, Estates are entailed entire on the Eldest male heir, another Pest to Industry and Improvement of the Country is introduc'd, which will be followed by all the odious mixture of pride and Beggary, and idleness, that have half depopulated and *decultivated* Spain; occasioning continual Extinction of Families by the Discouragements of Marriage and neglect in the improvement of estates.

I wish, therefore, that the Cincinnati, if they must go on with their Project, would direct the Badges of their Order to be worn by their Parents, instead of handing them down to their Children. It would be a good Precedent, and might have good Effects. It would also be a kind of Obedience to the Fourth Commandment, in which God enjoins us to *honour* our Father and Mother, but has nowhere directed us to honour our Children. And certainly no mode of honouring those immediate Authors of our Being can be more effectual, than that of doing praiseworthy Actions, which reflect Honour on those who gave us our Education; or more becoming, than that of manifesting, by some public Expression or Token, that it is to their Instruction and Example we ascribe the Merit of those Actions. . . .

[Franklin then commented on the emblem of the Society which included in its symbolism a bald eagle.]

. . . Others object to the *Bald Eagel* as looking too much like a *Dindon,* or Turkey. For my own part, I wish the Bald Eagle had not been chosen as the Representative of our Country; he is a Bird of bad moral Character; he does not get his living honestly; you may have seen him perch'd on some dead Tree, near the River where, too lazy to fish for himself, he watches the Labour of the Fishing-Hawk; and, when that diligent Bird has at length taken a Fish, and is bearing it to his Nest for the support of his Mate and young ones, the Bald Eagle pursues him, and takes it from him. With all this Injustice he is never in good Case; but, like those among Men who live by Sharping and Robbing, he is generally poor, and often very lousy. Besides, he is a rank Coward; the little *KingBird,* not bigger than a Sparrow, attacks him boldly and drives him out of the District. He is therefore by no means a proper emblem for the brave and honest Cincinnati of America, who have driven all the *Kingbirds* from our Country; though exactly fit for that Order of Knights, which the French call *Chevaliers d'Industrie.*

I am, on this account, not displeas'd that the Figure is not known as a Bald Eagle, but looks more like a Turk'y. For in Truth, the Turk'y is in comparison a much more respectable Bird, and withal a true original Native of America. Eagles have been found in all Countries, but the Turk'y was peculiar to ours; the first of the Species seen in Europe being brought to France by the Jesuits from Canada, and serv'd up at the Wedding Table of Charles the Ninth. He is, though a little vain and silly, it is true, but not the worse emblem for that, a Bird of Courage, and would not hesitate to attack a Grenadier of the British Guards, who should presume to invade his Farm Yard with a *red* Coat on. . . .

ON DUELING

Franklin abhorred dueling which in his view had no more place in an enlightened age than feudalism and other vestiges of a dark and bloody past.

. . . It is astonishing that the murderous Practice of Duelling, which you so justly condemn, should continue so long in vogue. Formerly, when Duels were used to determine Lawsuits, from an Opinion that Providence would in every Instance favour Truth and Right with Victory, they were excusable. At present, they decide nothing. A Man says something, which another tells him is a Lie. They fight; but, whichever is killed, the Point in dispute remains unsettled. To this purpose they have a pleasant little Story here. A Gentleman in a Coffee-house desired another to sit farther from him. "Why so?" "Because, Sir, you stink." "That is an Affront, and you must fight me." "I will fight you, if you insist upon it; but I do not see how that will mend the Matter. For if you kill me, I shall stink too; and if I kill you, [you] will stink, if possible, worse than you do at present." How can such miserable Sinners as we are entertain so much Pride, as to conceit that every Offence against our imagined Honour merits *Death?* These petty Princes in their own Opinion would call that Sovereign a Tyrant, who should put one of them to death for a little uncivil Language, tho' pointed at his sacred

---

Writings, IX, 237; from a letter to Thomas Percival, July 17, 1784.

Person; yet every one of them makes himself Judge in his own Cause, condemns the offender without a Jury, and undertakes himself to be the Executioner. . . .

SELFISH INTERESTS,

COMMERCE, NECESSITIES, AND LUXURIES

Franklin never ceased, in one sense, to be Poor Richard, counseling mankind to be of good will, to attend to the skills that improved everyday life, and to shun luxury and the vices it encouraged and perpetuated.

. . . It is wonderful how preposterously the affairs of this world are managed. Naturally one would imagine, that the interest of a few individuals should give way to general interest; but individuals manage their affairs with so much more application, industry, and address, than the public do theirs, that general interest most commonly gives way to particular. We assemble parliaments and councils, to have the benefit of their collected wisdom; but we necessarily have, at the same time, the inconvenience of their collected passions, prejudices, and private interests. By the help of these, artful men overpower their wisdom, and dupe its possessors; and if we may judge by the acts, *arrêts*, and edicts, all the world over, for regulating commerce, an assembly of great men is the greatest fool upon earth. . . .

. . . I have not, indeed yet thought of a Remedy for Luxury I am not sure, that in a great State it is capable of a Remedy. Nor that the Evil is in itself always so great as it

---

Writings, IX, 241–248; from a letter to Benjamin Vaughan, July 26, 1784.

is represented. Suppose we include in the Definition of Luxury all unnecessary Expence, and then let us consider whether Laws to prevent such Expence are possible to be executed in a great Country, and whether, if they could be executed, our People generally would be happier, or even richer. Is not the Hope of one day being able to purchase and enjoy Luxuries a great Spur to Labour and Industry? May not Luxury, therefore, produce more than it consumes, if without such a Spur People would be, as they are naturally enough inclined to be, lazy and indolent? To this purpose I remember a Circumstance. The Skipper of a Shallop, employed between Cape May and Philadelphia, had done us some small Service, for which he refused Pay. My Wife, understanding that he had a Daughter, sent her as a Present a new-fashioned Cap. Three Years After, this Skipper being at my House with an old Farmer of Cape May, his Passenger, he mentioned the Cap, and how much his Daughter had been pleased with it. "But," says he, "it proved a dear Cap to our Congregation." "How so?" "When my Daughter appeared in it at Meeting, it was so much admired, that all the Girls resolved to get such Caps from Philadelphia; and my Wife and I computed, that the whole could not have cost less than a hundred Pound." "True," says the Farmer, "but you do not tell all the Story. I think the Cap was nevertheless an Advantage to us, for it was the first thing that put our Girls upon Knitting worsted Mittens for Sale at Philadelphia, that they might have wherewithal to buy Caps and Ribbands there; and you know that that Industry has continued, and is likely to continue and increase to a much greater Value, and answer better Purposes." Upon the whole, I was more reconciled to this little Piece of Luxury, since not only the Girls were made happier by having fine Caps, but the Philadelphians by the Supply of warm Mittens.

In our Commercial Towns upon the Seacoast, Fortunes

will occasionally be made. Some of those who grow rich will be prudent, live within Bounds, and preserve what they have gained for their Posterity; others, fond of showing their Wealth, will be extravagant and ruin themselves. Laws cannot prevent this; and perhaps it is not always an evil to the Publick. A Shilling spent idly by a Fool, may be picked up by a Wiser Person, who knows better what to do with it. It is therefore not lost. A vain, silly Fellow builds, a fine House, furnishes it richly, lives in it expensively, and in few years ruins himself; but the Masons, Carpenters, Smiths, and other honest Tradesmen have been by his Employ assisted in maintaining and raising their Families; the Farmer has been paid for his labour, and encouraged, and the Estate is now in better Hands. In some Cases, indeed, certain Modes of Luxury may be a publick Evil, in the same Manner as it is a Private one. If there be a Nation, for Instance, that exports its Beef and Linnen, to pay for its Importation of Claret and Porter, while a great Part of its People live upon Potatoes, and wear no Shirts, wherein does it differ from the Sot, who lets his Family starve, and sells his Clothes to buy Drink? Our American Commerce is, I confess, a little in this way. We sell our Victuals to your Islands for Rum and Sugar; the substantial Necessaries of Life for Superfluities. But we have Plenty, and live well nevertheless, tho' by being soberer, we might be richer. . . .

. . . The vast Quantity of Forest Lands we have yet to clear, and put in order for Cultivation, will for a long time keep the Body of our Nation laborious and frugal. Forming an Opinion of our People and their Manners by what is seen among the Inhabitants of the Seaports, is judging from an improper Sample. The People of the Trading Towns may be rich and luxurious, while the Country possesses all the Virtues, that tend to private Happiness and publick Prosperity. Those Towns are not much regarded by the Country; they are hardly considered as an essential Part of the States; and the Experience of the last War has shown, that their being in the Possession of the Enemy did not necessarily draw on the Subjection of the Country, which bravely continued to maintain its Freedom and Independence notwithstanding.

It has been computed by some Political Arithmetician, that, if every Man and Woman would work for four Hours each Day on something useful, that Labour would produce sufficient to procure all the Necessaries and Comforts of Life, Want and Misery would be banished out of the World, and the rest of the 24 hours might be Leisure and Pleasure.

What occasions then so much Want and Misery? It is the Employment of Men and Women in Works, that produce neither the Necessaries nor Conveniences of Life, who, with those who do nothing, consume the Necessaries raised by the Laborious. To explain this.

The first Elements of Wealth are obtained by Labour, from the Earth and Waters. I have Land, and raise Corn. With this, if I feed a Family that does nothing, my Corn will be consum'd, and at the end of the Year I shall be no richer than I was at the beginning. But if, while I feed them, I employ them, some in Spinning, others in hewing Timber and sawing Boards, others in making Bricks, &c. for Building, the Value of my Corn will be arrested and remain with me, and at the end of the Year we may all be better clothed and better lodged. And if, instead of employing a Man I feed in making Bricks, I employ him in fiddling for me, the Corn he eats is gone, and no Part of his Manufacture remains to augment the Wealth and Convenience of the family; I shall therefore be the poorer for this fiddling Man, unless the rest of my Family work more, or eat less, to make up the Deficiency he occasions.

Look round the World and see the Millions employ'd in doing nothing, or in something that amounts to nothing, when the Necessaries and Conveniences of Life are in question. What is the Bulk of Commerce, for which we fight and destroy each other, but the Toil of Millions for Superfluities, to the great Hazard and Loss of many Lives by the constant Dangers of the Sea? How much labour is spent in Building and fitting great Ships, to go to China and Arabia for Tea and Coffee, to the West Indies for Sugar, to America for Tobacco! These things cannot be called the Necessaries of Life, for our Ancestors lived very comfortably without them.

A Question may be asked; Could all these People, now employed in raising, making, or carrying Superfluities, be subsisted by raising Necessaries? I think they might. The World is large, and a great Part of it still uncultivated. Many hundred Millions of Acres in Asia, Africa, and America are still Forest, and a great Deal even in Europe. On 100 Acres of this Forest a Man might become a substantial Farmer, and 100,000 Men, employed in clearing each his 100 Acres, would hardly brighten a Spot big enough to be Visible from the Moon, unless with Herschell's Telescope; so vast are the Regions still in Wood unimproved.

'Tis however, some Comfort to reflect, that, upon the whole, the Quantity of Industry and Prudence among Mankind exceeds the Quantity of Idleness and Folly. Hence the Increase of good Buildings, Farms cultivated, and populous Cities filled with Wealth, all over Europe, which a few Ages since were only to be found on the Coasts of the Mediterranean; and this, notwithstanding the mad Wars continually raging, by which are often destroyed in one year the Works of many Years' Peace. So that we may hope the Luxury of a few Merchants on the Seacoast will not be the Ruin of America.

One reflection more, and I will end this long, rambling Letter. Almost all the Parts of our Bodies require some Expence. The Feet demand Shoes; the Legs, Stockings; the rest of the Body, Clothing; and the Belly, a good deal of Victuals. *Our* Eyes, tho' exceedingly useful, ask, when reasonable, only the cheap Assistance of Spectacles, which could not much impair our Finances. But *the Eyes of other People* are the Eyes that ruin us. If all but myself were blind, I should want neither fine Clothes, fine Houses, nor fine Furniture. . . .

REMARKS CONCERNING

THE SAVAGES OF NORTH AMERICA

In seeking to improve the *conduct* of people, Franklin over and over again satirized the self-righteousness of the white race and especially of Christians by comparing their supposed "civilization" and refined habits with that of other peoples who boasted less but who in fact acted more humanely. He made the point in speaking of the customs of the North American Indians.

Savages we call them, because their Manners differ from ours, which we think the Perfection of Civility; they think the same of theirs.

Perhaps, if we could examine the Manners of different Nations with Impartiality, we should find no People so rude, as to be without any Rules of Politeness; nor any so polite, as not to have some Remains of Rudeness.

The Indian Men, when young, are Hunters and War-

Writings, X, 97–105; printed in England in 1784 and probably written that year or shortly before.

riors; when old, Counsellors; for all their Government is by Counsel of the Sages; there is no Force, there are no Prisons, no Officers to compel Obedience, or inflict Punishment. Hence they generally study Oratory, the best Speaker having the most Influence. The Indian Women till the Ground, dress the Food, nurse and bring up the Children, and preserve and hand down to Posterity the Memory of public Transactions. These Employments of Men and Women are accounted natural and honourable. Having few artificial Wants, they have abundance of Leisure for Improvement by Conversation. Our laborious Manner of Life, compared with theirs, they esteem slavish and base; and the Learning, on which we value ourselves, they regard as frivolous and useless. An Instance of this occurred at the Treaty of Lancaster, in Pennsylvania, *anno* 1744, between the Government of Virginia and the Six Nations. After the principal Business was settled, the Commissioners from Virginia acquainted the Indians by a Speech, that there was at Williamsburg a College, with a Fund for Educating Indian youth; and that, if the Six Nations would send down half a dozen of their young Lads to that College, the Government would take care that they should be well provided for, and instructed in all the Learning of the White People. It is one of the Indian Rules of Politeness not to answer a public Proposition the same day that it is made; they think it would be treating it as a light matter, and that they show it Respect by taking time to consider it, as of a Matter important. They therefore deferr'd their Answer till the Day following; when their Speaker began, by expressing their deep Sense of the kindness of the Virginia Government, in making them that Offer; "for we know," says he, "that you highly esteem the kind of Learning taught in those Colleges, and that the Maintenance of our young Men, while with you, would be very expensive to you. We are convinc'd, therefore, that you mean to do us Good by your Proposal; and we thank you heartily. But you, who are wise, must know that different Nations have different Conceptions of things; and you will therefore not take it amiss, if our Ideas of this kind of Education happen not to be the same with yours. We have had some Experience of it; Several of our young People were formerly brought up at the Colleges of the Northern Provinces; they were instructed in all your Sciences; but, when they came back to us, they were bad Runners, ignorant of every means of living in the Woods, unable to bear either Cold or Hunger, knew neither how to build a Cabin, take a Deer, or kill an Enemy, spoke our Language imperfectly, were therefore neither fit for Hunters, Warriors, nor Counsellors; they were totally good for nothing. We are however not the less oblig'd by your kind Offer, tho' we decline accepting it; and, to show our grateful Sense of it, if the Gentlemen of Virginia will send us a Dozen of their Sons, we will take great Care of their Education, instruct them in all we know, and make *Men* of them."

Having frequent Occasions to hold public Councils, they have acquired great Order and Decency in conducting them. The old Men sit in the foremost Ranks, the Warriors in the next, and the Women and Children in the hindmost. The Business of the Women is to take exact Notice of what passes, imprint it in their Memories (for they have no Writing), and communicate it to their Children. They are the Records of the Council, and they preserve Traditions of the Stipulations in Treaties 100 Years back; which, when we compare with our Writings, we always find exact. He that would speak, rises. The rest observe a profound Silence. When he has finish'd and sits down, they leave him 5 or 6 Minutes to recollect, that, if he has omitted any thing he intended to say, or has any thing to add, he may rise again and deliver it. To interrupt another, even in common Conversation, is reckon'd highly indecent. How different this is from the conduct of a polite British House of Commons, where scarce a day passes without some Confusion, that makes the Speaker hoarse in calling *to Order;* and how different from the Mode of Conversation in many polite Companies of Europe, where, if you do not deliver your Sentence with great Rapidity, you are cut off in the middle of it by the Impatient Loquacity of those you converse with, and never suffer'd to finish it!

The Politeness of these Savages in Conversation is indeed carried to Excess, since it does not permit them to contradict or deny the Truth of what is asserted in their Presence. By this means they indeed avoid Disputes; but then it becomes difficult to know their Minds, or what Impression you make upon them. The Missionaries who have attempted to convert them to Christianity, all complain of this as one of the great Difficulties of their Mission. The Indians hear with Patience the Truths of the Gospel explain'd to them, and give their usual Tokens of Assent and Approbation; you would think they were convinc'd. No such matter. It is mere Civility.

A Swedish Minister, having assembled the chiefs of the Susquehanah Indians, made a Sermon to them, acquainting them with the principal historical Facts on which our Religion is founded; such as the Fall of our first Parents by eating an Apple, the coming of Christ to repair the Mischief, his Miracles and Suffering, &c. When he had finished, an Indian Orator stood up to thank him. "What you have told us," says he, "is all very good. It is indeed bad to eat Apples. It is better to make them all into Cyder. We are much oblig'd by your kindness in coming so far, to tell us these Things which you have heard from your Mothers. In return, I will tell you some of those we have heard from ours. In the Beginning, our Fathers had only the Flesh of Animals to subsist on; and if their Hunting was unsuccessful, they were starving. Two of our young Hunters, having kill'd a Deer, made a Fire in the Woods to broil some Part of it. When they were about to satisfy their Hunger, they beheld a beautiful young Woman descend from the Clouds, and seat herself on that Hill, which you see yonder among the blue Mountains. They said to each other, it is a Spirit that has smelt our broiling Venison, and wishes to eat of it; let us offer some to her. They presented her with the Tongue; she was pleas'd with the Taste of it, and said, 'Your kindness shall be rewarded; come to this Place after thirteen Moons, and you shall find something that will be of great Benefit in nourishing you and your Children to the latest Generations.' They did so, and, to their Surprise, found Plants they had never seen before; but which, from that ancient time, have been constantly cultivated among us, to our great Advantage. Where her right Hand had touched the Ground, they found Maize; where her left hand had touch'd it, they found Kidney-Beans; and where her Backside had sat on it, they found Tobacco." The good Missionary, disgusted with this idle Tale, said, "What I delivered to you were sacred Truths; but what you tell me is mere Fable, Fiction, and Falshood." The Indian, offended, reply'd, "My brother, it seems your Friends have not done you Justice in your Education; they have not well instructed you in the Rules of common Civility. You saw that we, who understood and practise those Rules, believ'd all your stories; why do you refuse to believe ours?" . . .

NOTE.—*It is remarkable that in all Ages and Countries Hospitality has been allow'd as the Virtue of those whom the civiliz'd were pleas'd to call Barbarians. The Greeks celebrated the Scythians for it. The Saracens possess'd it eminently, and it is to this day the reigning Virtue of the wild Arabs. St. Paul, too, in the Relation of his Voyage and Shipwreck on the Island of Melita says the Barbarous*

People shewed us no little kindness; for they kindled a fire, and received us every one, because of the present Rain, and because of the Cold. —F.

CRIME AND PUNISHMENT

In response to a request for his opinion of a book on criminal law in England, Franklin set down his thoughts on the origins and encouragements of crime there, and on the wisdom of making punishments proportional to the offense.

. . . Superfluous Property is the Creature of Society. Simple and mild Laws were sufficient to guard the Property that was merely necessary. The Savage's Bow, his Hatchet, and his Coat of Skins, were sufficiently secured, without Law, by the Fear of personal Resentment and Retaliation. When, by virtue of the first Laws, Part of the Society accumulated Wealth and grew powerful, they enacted others more severe, and would protect their Property at the Expence of Humanity. This was abusing their Power, and commencing a Tyranny. If a Savage, before he enter'd into Society, had been told, "Your Neighbour by this Means may become Owner of 100 deer; but if your Brother, or your Son, or yourself, having no Deer of your own, and being hungry, should kill one, an infamous Death must be the consequence;" he would probably have preferr'd his Liberty, and his common Right of killing any Deer, to all the Advantages of Society that might be propos'd to him. . . .

. . . I see, in the last Newspaper from London, that a

Writings, IX, 293–296; from a letter to Benjamin Vaughan, March 14, 1785.

Woman is capitally convicted at the Old Bailey, for privately stealing out of a Shop some Gauze, value 14 Shillings and threepence; is there any Proportion between the Injury done by a Theft, value $14/3$, and the Punishment of a human Creature, by Death, on a Gibbet? Might not that Woman, by her Labour, have made the Reparation ordain'd by God, in paying fourfold? Is not all Punishment inflicted beyond the Merit of the Offence, so much Punishment of Innocence? In this light, how vast is the annual Quantity of not only *injured*, but *suffering* Innocence, in almost all the civilized states of Europe!

But it seems to have been thought, that this kind of Innocence may be punished by way of *preventing* Crimes. I have read, indeed, of a cruel Turk in Barbary, who, whenever he bought a new Christian Slave, ordered him immediately to be hung up by the Legs, and to receive an 100 Blows of a Cudgel on the Soles of his Feet, that the severe Sense of the Punishment, and Fear of incurring it thereafter, might prevent the Faults that should merit it. Our Author himself would hardly approve entirely of this Turk's Conduct in the Government of Slaves; and yet he appears to recommend something like it for the government of English Subjects, when he applauds the Reply of Judge Burnet to the convict Horse-stealer, who, being ask'd what he had to say why Judgment of Death should not pass against him, and answering, that it was hard to hang a Man for *only* stealing a Horse, was told by the judge, "Man, thou art not to be hang'd *only* for stealing, but that Horses may not be stolen."

The man's Answer, if candidly examined, will I imagine appear reasonable, as founded on the Eternal Principle of Justice and Equity, that Punishments should be proportion'd to Offences; and the judge's Reply brutal and unreasonable, . . .

It is said by those who know Europe generally, that

there are more Thefts committed and punish'd annually in England, than in all the other Nations put together. If this be so, there must be a Cause or Causes for such Depravity in your common People. May not one be the Deficiency of Justice and Morality in our national Government, manifested in our oppressive Conduct to Subjects, and unjust wars on our Neighbours? View the long-persisted in, unjust monopolizing Treatment of Ireland at length acknowledged! View the plundering Government exercis'd by your Merchants in the Indies; the confiscating War made upon the American Colonies; and, to say nothing of those upon France and Spain, view the late War upon Holland, which was seen by impartial Europe in no other Light than that of a War of Rapine and Pillage; the Hopes of an immense and easy Prey being its only apparent, and probably its true and real Motive and Encouragement.

Justice is as strictly due between neighbour Nations as between neighbour Citizens. A Highwayman is as much a Robber when he plunders in a Gang, as when single; and a Nation that makes an unjust War, is only a *great Gang*. . . .

THE LEGITIMATE

POWERS OF ELECTED ASSEMBLIES

In one of his last letters written in France, Franklin explained American government under the Articles of Confederation.

. . . Our Constitution seems not to be well understood with you. If the Congress were a permanent Body, there

---

Writings, IX, 336-337; from a letter to George Whateley, May 23, 1785.

would be more Reason in being jealous of giving it Powers. But its Members are chosen annually, cannot be chosen more than three Years successively, nor more than three Years in seven; and any of them may be recall'd at any time, whenever their Constituents shall be dissatisfied with their Conduct. They are of the People, and return again to mix with the People, having no more durable preëminence than the different Grains of Sand in an Hourglass. Such an Assembly cannot easily become dangerous to Liberty. They are the Servants of the People, sent together to do the People's Business, and promote the public Welfare; their Powers must be sufficient, or their Duties cannot be performed. They have no profitable Appointments, but a mere Payment of daily Wages, such as are scarcely equivalent to their Expences; so that, having no Chance for great Places, and enormous Salaries or Pensions, as in some countries, there is no triguing or bribing for Elections. . . .

AMERICAN LOYALTY

TO THE ANCIENT ENGLISH LIBERTIES

Franklin responded to a plea for justice for Americans who had fought for England during the Revolution by remarking that they inappropriately called themselves "Loyalists."

. . . The name *loyalist* was improperly assumed by these people. *Royalists* they may perhaps be called. But the true *loyalists* were the people of America, against whom they acted. No people were ever known more truly loyal, and

---

Writings, IX, 350; from a letter to Francis Maseres, June 26, 1785.

universally so, to their sovereigns. The Protestant succession in the House of Hanover was their idol. Not a Jacobite was to be found from one end of the Colonies to the other. They were affectionate to the people of England, zealous and forward to assist in her wars, by voluntary contributions of men and money, even beyond their proportion. The King and Parliament had frequently acknowledged this by public messages, resolutions, and reimbursements. But they were equally fond of what they esteemed their rights; and, if they resisted when those were attacked, it was a resistance in favour of a British constitution, which every Englishman might share in enjoying, who should come to live among them; it was resisting arbitrary impositions, that were contrary to common right and to their fundamental constitutions, and to constant ancient usage. It was indeed a resistance in favour of the liberties of England, which might have been endangered by success in the attempt against ours; and therefore a great man in your Parliament did not scruple to declare, he *rejoiced that America had resisted.* I, for the same reason, may add this very resistance to the other instances of their loyalty. . . .

PART FIVE

Sage at Home

1785-1790

THE PROGRESS OF GOVERNMENT AND PROSPERITY IN THE UNITED STATES

Franklin returned to Philadelphia in July 1785. After a few months of intense enjoyment at being home, he wrote a friend in England of the state of public affairs and of his own nearly unanimous election as President of Pennsylvania.

. . . You seem desirous of knowing what Progress we make here in improving our Governments. We are, I think, in the right Road of Improvement, for we are making Experiments. I do not oppose all that seem wrong, for the Multitude are more effectually set right by Experience, than kept from going wrong by Reasoning with them. And I think we are daily more and more enlightened; so that I have no doubt of our obtaining in a few Years as much public Felicity, as good Government is capable of affording.

Your NewsPapers are fill'd with fictitious Accounts of Anarchy, Confusion, Distresses, and Miseries, we are

---

Writings, IX, 489-490, 548; from letters to Jonathan Shipley, February 24, 1786, and to William Hunter, November 24, 1786.

suppos'd to be involv'd in, as Consequences of the Revolution; and the few remaining Friends of the old Government among us take pains to magnify every little Inconvenience a Change in the Course of Commerce may have occasion'd. . . . I can assure you, that the great Body of our Nation find themselves happy in the Change, and have not the smallest Inclination to return to the Domination of Britain. There could not be a stronger Proof of the general Approbation of the Measures, that promoted the Change, and of the Change itself, than has been given by the Assembly and Council of this State, in the nearly unanimous Choice for their Governor, of one who had been so much concern'd in those Measures; the Assembly being themselves the unbrib'd Choice of the People, and therefore may be truly suppos'd of the same Sentiments. I say nearly unanimous, because, of between 70 and 80 Votes, there were only my own and one other in the negative. . . .

[A few months later Franklin wrote glowingly to another friend.]

. . . Your newspapers, to please honest *John Bull,* paint our situation here in frightful colours, as if we were very miserable since we broke our connexion with him. But I will give you some remarks by which you may form your own judgment. Our husbandmen, who are the bulk of the nation, have had plentiful crops, their produce sells at high prices and for ready, hard money; wheat, for instance, at 8s., and 8s. 6d. per bushel. Our working-people are all employed and get high wages, are well fed and well clad. Our estates in houses are trebled in value by the rising of rents since the Revolution. Buildings in Philadelphia increase amazingly, besides small towns rising in every quarter of the country. The laws govern, justice is well administered, and property as secure as in any country on the globe. Our wilderness lands are daily buying up by new settlers, and our settlements extend rapidly to the westward. European goods were never so cheaply afforded us, as since Britain has no longer the monopoly of supplying us. In short, all among us may be happy, who have happy dispositions; such being necessary to happiness even in Paradise.

I speak these things of Pennsylvania, with which I am most acquainted. As to the other States, when I read in all the papers of the extravagant rejoicings every 4th of July, the day on which was signed the Declaration of Independence, I am convinced, that none of them are discontented with the Revolution. . . .

THE INTERNAL STATE OF AMERICA

The letters immediately above show that in writing his friends in Europe Franklin resisted stoutly the idea that the new United States was sliding toward anarchy, chaos, and poverty. He summarized his optimism in an essay probably written for publication but which seems not to have been printed in Franklin's lifetime.

There is a Tradition, that, in the Planting of New England, the first Settlers met with many Difficulties and Hardships as is generally the Case when a civilized People attempt establishing themselves in a wilderness Country. Being piously dispos'd, they sought Relief from Heaven, by laying their Wants and Distresses before the Lord, in frequent set Days of Fasting and Prayer. Constant Meditation and Discourse on these Subjects kept their

---

Writings, X, 116–122; from a draft probably written late in 1786.

Minds gloomy and discontented; and, like the Children of Israel, there were many dispos'd to return to that Egypt, which Persecution had induc'd them to abandon. At length, when it was proposed in the Assembly to proclaim another Fast, a Farmer of plain Sense rose, and remark'd, that the Inconveniencies they suffer'd, and concerning which they had so often weary'd Heaven with their Complaints, were not so great as they might have expected, and were diminishing every day, as the Colony strengthen'd; that the Earth began to reward their Labour, and to furnish liberally for their Subsistence; that the Seas and Rivers were full of Fish, the Air sweet, the Climate healthy; and, above all, that they were there in the full Enjoyment of Liberty, civil and religious. He therefore thought, that reflecting and conversing on these Subjects would be more comfortable, as tending more to make them contented with their Situation; and that it would be more becoming the Gratitude they ow'd to the Divine Being, if, instead of a Fast, they should proclaim a Thanksgiving. His Advice was taken; and from that day to this they have, in every Year, observ'd Circumstances of public Felicity sufficient to furnish Employment for a *Thanksgiving Day;* which is therefore constantly ordered and religiously observed.

I see in the Public Papers of different States frequent Complaints of *hard Times, deadness of Trade, scarcity of Money,* &c. It is not my Intention to assert or maintain, that these Complaints are intirely without Foundation. There can be no Country or Nation existing, in which there will not be some People so circumstanced, as to find it hard to gain a Livelihood; people who are not in the way of any profitable Trade, and with whom Money is scarce, because they have nothing to give in Exchange for it; and it is always in the Power of a small Number to make a great Clamour. But let us take a cool View of the general

State of our Affairs, and perhaps the Prospect will appear less gloomy than has been imagined.

The great Business of the Continent is Agriculture. For one Artisan, or Merchant, I suppose, we have at least 100 Farmers, by far the greatest part Cultivators of their own fertile Lands, from whence many of them draw, not only the Food necessary for their Subsistance, but the Materials of their Clothing, so as to have little Occasion for foreign Supplies; while they have a Surplus of Productions to dispose of, whereby Wealth is gradually accumulated. Such has been the Goodness of Divine Providence to these Regions, and so favourable the Climate, that, since the three or four Years of Hardship in the first Settlement of our Fathers here, a Famine or Scarcity has never been heard of among us; on the contrary, tho' some Years may have been more, and others less plentiful, there has always been Provision enough for ourselves, and a Quantity to spare for Exportation. And altho' the Crops of last year were generally good, never was the Farmer better paid for the Part he can spare Commerce, as the published Price-Currents abundantly testify. The Lands he possesses are also continually rising in Value with the Increase of Population; and, on the whole, he is enabled to give such good Wages to those who work for him, that all who are acquainted with the old World must agree, that in no Part of it are the labouring Poor so well fed, well cloth'd, well lodg'd, and well paid, as in the United States of America.

If we enter the Cities, we find, that, since the Revolution, the Owners of Houses and Lots of Ground have had their Interest vastly augmented in Value; Rents have risen to an astonishing Height, and thence Encouragement to encrease Building, which gives Employment to an abundance of Workmen, as does also the encreas'd Luxury and Splendor of Living of the Inhabitants, thus made richer.

These Workmen all demand and obtain much higher Wages than any other Part of the World would afford them, and are paid in ready Money. This Rank of People therefore do not, or ought not, to complain of hard Times; and they make a very considerable part of the City Inhabitants.

At the Distance I live from our American Fisheries, I cannot speak of them with any Certainty; but I have not heard, that the Labour of the valuable Race of Men employ'd in them is worse paid, or that they meet with less Success, than before the Revolution. The Whalemen indeed have been depriv'd of one Market for their Oil; but another, I hear, is opening for them, which it is hoped may be equally advantageous; and the Demand is constantly encreasing for their Spermaceti Candles, which therefore bear a much higher Price than formerly.

There remain the Merchants and Shopkeepers. Of these, tho' they make but a small Part of the whole Nation, the Number is considerable, too great indeed for the Business they are emply'd in: For the Consumption of Goods in every Country, has its Limits; the Faculties of the People, that is, their Ability to buy and pay, being equal only to a certain Quantity of Merchandize. If Merchants calculate amiss on this Proportion, and import too much, they will of course find the Sale dull for the Overplus, and some of them will say, that Trade languishes. They should, and doubtless will, grow wiser by Experience, and import less. If too many Artificers in Town, and Farmers from the Country, flattering themselves with the Idea of leading easier Lives, turn Shopkeepers, the whole natural Quantity of Business divided among them all may afford too small a Share for each, and occasion Complaints, that Trading is dead; these may also suppose, that it is owing to Scarcity of Money, while, in fact, it is not so much from the Fewness of Buyers, as from the excessive Number of Sellers, that the Mischief arises; and, if every Shop-keeping

Farmer and Mechanic would return to the Use of his Plough and working-Tools, there would remain of Widows, and other Women, Shopkeepers sufficient for that Business, which might then afford them a comfortable Maintenance.

Whoever has travelled thro' the various Parts of Europe, and observed how small is the Proportion of People in Affluence or easy Circumstances there, compar'd with those in Poverty and Misery; the few rich and haughty Landlords, the multitude of poor, abject, and rack'd Tenants, and the half-paid and half-starv'd ragged Labourers; and views here the happy Mediocrity, that so generally prevails throughout these States, where the Cultivator works for himself, and supports his Family in decent Plenty, will, methinks, see abundant Reason to bless Divine Providence for the evident and great Difference in our Favour, and be convinc'd, that no Nation that is known to us enjoys a greater Share of human Felicity.

It is true, that in some of the States there are Parties and Discords; but let us look back, and ask if we were ever without them? Such will exist wherever there is Liberty; and perhaps they help to preserve it. By the Collision of different Sentiments, Sparks of Truth are struck out, and political Light is obtained. The different Factions, which at present divide us, aim all at the Publick Good; the Differences are only about the various Modes of promoting it. Things, Actions, Measures, and Objects of all kinds, present themselves to the Minds of Men in such a Variety of Lights, that it is not possible we should all think alike at the same time on every Subject, when hardly the same Man retains at all times the same Ideas of it. Parties are therefore the common Lot of Humanity; and ours are by no means more mischievous or less beneficial than those of other Countries, Nations, and Ages, enjoying in the same Degree the great Blessing of Political Liberty.

Some indeed among us are not so much griev'd for the present State of our Affairs, as apprehensive for the future. The Growth of Luxury alarms them, and they think we are from that alone in the high Road to Ruin. They observe, that no Revenue is sufficient without Economy, and that the most plentiful Income of a whole People from the natural Productions of their Country may be dissipated in vain and needless Expences, and Poverty be introduced in the place of Affluence. This may be possible. It however rarely happens; for there seems to be in every Nation a greater Proportion of Industry and Frugality, which tend to enrich, than of Idleness and Prodigality, which occasion Poverty; so that upon the whole there is a continual Accumulation. Reflect what Spain, Gaul, Germany, and Britain were in the Time of the Romans, inhabited by People little richer than our Savages, and consider the Wealth they at present possess, in numerous well-built Cities, improv'd Farms, rich Moveables, Magazines stor'd with valuable Manufactures, to say nothing of Plate, Jewels, and ready Money; and all this, notwithstanding their bad, wasteful, plundering Governments, and their mad, destructive Wars; and yet Luxury and Extravagant Living have never suffered much Restraint in those Countries. Then consider the great proportion of industrious frugal Farmers inhabiting the interior Part of these American States, and of whom the Body of our Nation consists; and judge whether it is probable the Luxury of our Seaports can be sufficient to ruin such a Country. If the Importation of foreign Luxuries could ruin a People, we should probably have been ruin'd long ago; for the British Nation claim'd a right, and practis'd it, of importing among us, not only the Superfluities of their own Production, but those of every Nation under Heaven; we bought and consum'd them, and yet we flourish'd and grew rich. At present, our independent Governments may do what we could not then do, discourage by heavy Duties, or prevent by Prohibitions, such importations, and thereby grow richer; if, indeed, which may admit of Dispute, the Desire of adorning ourselves with fine cloaths, possessing fine Furniture, with good Houses, &c., is not, by strongly inciting to Labour and Industry, the occasion of producing a greater Value, than is consum'd in the Gratification of that Desire.

The Agriculture and Fisheries of the United States are the great Sources of our encreasing Wealth. He that puts a Seed into the Earth is recompens'd, perhaps, by receiving twenty out of it; and he who draws a Fish out of our Waters, draws up a Piece of Silver.

Let us (and there is no Doubt but we shall) be attentive to these, and then the Power of Rivals, with all their restraining and prohibiting Acts, cannot much hurt us. We are Sons of the Earth and Seas, and, like Antaeus, if, in wrestling with Hercules, we now and then receive a Fall, the Touch of our Parents will communicate to us fresh Strength and Ability to renew the contest. Be quiet and thankful.

SPEECHES

AT THE CONSTITUTIONAL CONVENTION

Franklin experienced a propitious revival of good health during the summer of 1787; he was able, as a member of the Pennsylvania delegation, to attend every session of the Constitutional Convention. As had been his habit throughout life, he did not speak long or often, but rather made strategic suggestions and

---

Max Farrand, ed., *The Records of the Federal Convention of* 1787 (4 vols., New Haven, Yale University Press, 1937), I, 82–85, 197–199, 450–452, 523, 546; II, 120, 204–205, 236–237, 249, 641–643; from actions taken June 2–September 17, 1787, as indicated.

sought constructive compromises. He submitted his own ideas on government without making a long or tenacious defense of them. Many, in fact, were rejected by the Convention. Because it pained him to stand, his few speeches were read by his colleague James Wilson. His final speech, reprinted here in full as the last entry, bespeaks his principal contribution at the Constitutional Convention: he sought to persuade his co-workers that compromise, a sense of fallibility, and a willingness to trust men in the management of their own affairs were the requisites of free, republican government.

His major contributions to the proceedings of the Convention, speeches, parts of speeches, or motions, are reprinted here under the dates on which they were made.

On June 2 he opposed paying salaries to officials of the federal government.

. . . In this particular of salaries to the Executive branch I happen to differ; and as my opinion may appear new and chimerical, it is only from a persuasion that it is right, and from a sense of duty that I hazard it. The Committee will judge of my reasons when they have heard them, and their judgment may possibly change mine.—I think I see inconveniences in the appointment of salaries; I see none in refusing them, but on the contrary, great advantages.

Sir, there are two passions which have a powerful influence on the affairs of men. These are ambition and avarice; the love of power, and the love of money. Separately each of these has great force in prompting men to action; but when united in view of the same object, they have in many minds the most violent effects. Place before the eyes of such men a post of *honour* that shall at the same time be a place of *profit,* and they will move heaven and earth to obtain it. The vast number of such places it is that renders the British Government so tempestuous. The struggles for them are the true sources of all those factions which are perpetually dividing the Nation, distracting its councils, hurrying sometimes into fruitless & mischievous wars, and often compelling a submission to dishonorable terms of peace.

And of what kind are the men that will strive for this profitable pre-eminence, through all the bustle of cabal, the heat of contention, the infinite mutual abuse of parties, tearing to pieces the best of characters? It will not be the wise and moderate, the lovers of peace and good order, the men fittest for the trust. It will be the bold and the violent, the men of strong passions and indefatigable activity in their selfish pursuits. These will thrust themselves into your Government and be your rulers. And these too will be mistaken in the expected happiness of their situation: For their vanquished competitors of the same spirit, and from the same motives will perpetually be endeavouring to distress their administration, thwart their measures, and render them odious to the people.

Besides these evils, Sir, tho' we may set out in the beginning with moderate salaries, we shall find that such will not be of long continuance. Reasons will never be wanting for proposed augmentations. And there will always be a party for giving more to the rulers, that the rulers may be able in return to give more to them.—Hence as all history informs us, there has been in every State & Kingdom a constant kind of warfare between the Governing & Governed: the one striving to obtain more for its support, and the other to pay less. And this has alone occasioned great convulsions, actual civil wars, ending either in dethroning of the Princes or enslaving of the people. Generally indeed the ruling power carries its point, the revenues of princes constantly increasing, and we see that they are never satisfied, but always in want of more. The more the people are discontented with the oppression of taxes; the greater need the prince has of money to distribute among his partizans and pay the troops that are to suppress all resistance, and enable him to plunder at pleasure. There is scarce a king in a hundred who would not, if he could, follow the example of Pharoah, get first all the peoples money, then all their lands, and then make them and their children servants forever. It will be said, that we don't propose to establish Kings. I know it. But there is a natural inclination in mankind to Kingly Government. It sometimes relieves them from Aristocratic domination. They had rather have one tyrant than five hundred. It gives more of the appearance of equality among Citizens, and that they like. I am apprehensive therefore, perhaps too apprehensive, that the Government of these States, may in future times, end in a Monarchy. But this Catastrophe I think may be long delayed, if in our proposed system we do not sow the seeds of contention, faction & tumult, by making our posts of honor, places of profit. If we do, I fear that tho' we do employ at first a number, and not a single person, the number will in time be set aside, it will only nourish the fetus of a King, as the honorable gentleman from Virginia very aptly expressed it, and a King will the sooner be set over us.

It may be imagined by some that this is an Utopian Idea, and that we can never find men to serve us in the Executive department, without paying them well for their services. I conceive this to be a mistake. Some existing facts present themselves to me, which incline me to a contrary opinion. The high Sheriff of a County in England is an honorable office, but it is not a profitable one. It is rather expensive and therefore not sought for. But yet, it is executed and well executed, and usually by some of the principal Gentlemen of the County. In France the office of Counsellor or Member of their Judiciary Parliaments is more honorable. It is therefore purchased at a high price: There are indeed fees on the law proceedings, which are divided among them, but these fees do not amount to more than three per Cent on the sum paid for the place. Therefore as legal interest is there at five per Ct. they in fact pay two per Ct. for being allowed to do the Judiciary business of the Nation, which is at the same time entirely exempt from the burden of paying them any salaries for their services. I do not however mean to recommend this as an eligible mode for our Judiciary department. I only bring the instance to shew that the pleasure of doing good & serving their Country and the respect such conduct entitles them to, are sufficient motives with some minds to give up a great portion of their time to the Public, without the mean inducement of pecuniary satisfaction.

Another instance is that of a respectable Society who have made the experiment, and practiced it with success more than an hundred years. I mean the Quakers. It is an established rule with them, that they are not to go to law; but in their controversies they must apply to their monthly, quarterly and yearly meetings. Committees of these sit with patience to hear the parties, and spend much time in composing their differences. In doing this they are supported by a sense of duty, and the respect paid to usefulness. It is honorable to be so employed, but it was never made profitable by salaries, fees, or perquisites. And indeed in all cases of public service the less the profit the greater the honor.

To bring the matter nearer home, have we not seen the great and most important of our officers, that of General of our armies executed for eight years together without the smallest salary, by a Patriot whom I will not now offend by any other praise; and this through fatigues and distresses in common with the other brave men his military friends & companions, and the constant anxieties peculiar to his station? And shall we doubt finding three or four men in all the U. States, with public spirit enough to bear sitting in peaceful Council for perhaps an equal term, merely to preside over our civil concerns, and see that our laws are duly executed. Sir, I have a better opinion of our country. I think we shall never be without a sufficient number of wise and good men to undertake and execute well and faithfully the Office in question.

Sir, The saving of the salaries that may at first be proposed is not an object with me. The subsequent mischiefs of proposing them are what I apprehend. And therefore it is that I move the amendment. If it is not seconded or accepted I must be contented with the satisfaction of having delivered my opinion frankly and done my duty.

[On June 11 Franklin spoke on the need for calm tempers in facing the complex question of representation.]

It has given me a great pleasure to observe that till this point, the proportion of representation, came before us, our debates were carried on with great coolness & temper. If any thing of a contrary kind, has on this occasion appeared, I hope it will not be repeated; for we are sent here to *consult* not to *contend*, with each other; and declarations of a fixed opinion, and of determined resolution, never to change it, neither enlighten nor conceive us. Positiveness and warmth on one side, naturally beget their like on the other; and tend to create and augment discord & division in a great concern, wherein harmony & Union are extremely necessary to give weight to our Councils, and render them effectual in promoting & securing the common good.

I must own that I was originally of opinion it would be better if every member of Congress, or our national Council, were to consider himself rather as a representative of the whole, than as an Agent for the interests of a particular State; in which case the proportion of members for each State would be of less consequence, & it would not be very material whether they voted by States or individually. But as I find this is not to be expected, I now think the number of Representatives should bear some proportion to the number of the Represented; and that the decisions shd. be by the majority of members, not by the majority of States. This is objected to from an apprehension that the greater States would then swallow up the smaller. I do not at present clearly see what advantage the greater States could propose to themselves by swallowing the smaller, and therefore do not apprehend they would attempt it. I recollect that in the beginning of this Century, when the Union was proposed of the two Kingdoms, England & Scotland, the Scotch Patriots were full of fears, that unless they had an equal number of Representatives in Parliament, they should be ruined by the superiority of the English. They finally agreed however that the different proportions of importance in the Union, of the two Nations should be attended to, whereby they were to have only forty members in the House of Commons, and only sixteen in the House of Lords; A very great inferiority of numbers! And yet to this day I do not recollect that any thing has been done in the Parliament of Great Britain to the prejudice of Scotland; and whoever looks over the lists of public officers, Civil & military of that nation will find I believe that the North Britons enjoy at least their full proportion of emolument.

But, Sir, in the present mode of voting by States, it is equally in the power of the lesser States to swallow up the greater; and this is mathematically demonstrable. Suppose for example, that 7 smaller States had each 3 members in the House, and the 6 larger to have one with another 6 members; and that upon a question, two members of each smaller State should be in affirmative and one in the Negative, they will make

Affirmatives . . . . 14. . . . Negatives   7
And that all the larger States should
    be unanimously
in the negative, they would
    make . . . . Negatives   36
                                          In all . . .   43

It is then apparent that the 14 carry the question against the 43. and the minority overpowers the majority, contrary to the common practice of Assemblies in all Countries and Ages.

The greater States Sir are naturally as unwilling to have their property left in the disposition of the smaller, as the smaller are to have theirs in the disposition of the greater. An honorable gentleman has, to avoid this difficulty, hinted a proposition of equalizing the States. It appears to me an equitable one, and I should, for my own part, not be against such a measure, if it might be found practicable. Formerly, indeed, when almost every province had a different Constitution, some with greater others with fewer privileges, it was of importance to the borderers when their boundaries were contested, whether by running the division lines, they were placed on one side or the other. At present when such differences are done away, it is less material. The Interest of a State is made up of the interests of its individual members. If they are not injured, the State is not injured. Small States are more easily well & happily governed than large ones. If therefore in such an equal division, it should be found necessary to diminish Pennsylvania, I should not be averse to the giving a part of it to N. Jersey, and another to Delaware. But there would probably be considerable difficulties in adjusting such a division; and however equally made at first, it would be continually varying by the augumentation of inhabitants in some States, and their more fixed proportion in others; and thence frequent occasion for new divisions. . . .

[On June 28, when it seemed the Convention might break up during acrimonious debate over the mode of representation in the legislature, Franklin made his famous proposal that the sessions of the Convention be opened with prayer.]

The small progress we have made after 4 or five weeks close attendance & continual reasonings with each other — our different sentiments on almost every question, several of the last producing as many noes as ays, is methinks a melancholy proof of the imperfection of the Human Understanding. We indeed seem to feel our own want of political wisdom, since we have been running about in search of it. We have gone back to ancient history for models of Government, and examined the different forms of those Republics which having been formed with the seeds of their own dissolution now no longer exist. And we have viewed Modern States all round Europe, but find none of their Constitutions suitable to our circumstances.

In this situation of this Assembly, groping as it were in the dark to find political truth, and scarce able to distinguish it when presented to us, how has it happened, Sir, that we have not hitherto once thought of humbly applying to the Father of lights to illuminate our understandings? In the beginning of the Contest with G. Britain, when we were sensible of danger we had daily prayer in this room for the divine protection. — Our prayers, Sir, were heard, and they were graciously answered. All of us who were engaged in the struggle must have observed frequent instances of a Superintending providence in our favor. To that kind providence we owe this happy opportunity of consulting in peace on the means of establishing our future national felicity. And have we now forgotten that powerful friend? or do we imagine that we no longer need his assistance? I have lived, Sir, a long time, and the longer I live, the more convincing proofs I see of this truth—*that God governs in the affairs of men.* And if a sparrow cannot fall to the ground without his notice, is it probable that an empire can rise without his aid? We have been assured, Sir, in the sacred writings, that "except the Lord build the House they labour in vain that build it." I firmly believe this; and I also believe that without his concurring aid we shall succeed in this political building no better than the Builders of Babel: We shall be divided by our little partial local interests; our projects will be confounded, and we ourselves shall become a reproach and bye word down to future ages. And what is worse, mankind may hereafter from this unfortunate instance, despair of establishing Governments by Human Wisdom and leave it to chance, war and conquest.

I therefore beg leave to move—that henceforth prayers imploring the assistance of Heaven, and its blessings on our deliberations, be held in this Assembly every morning before we proceed to business, and that one or more of the Clergy of this City be requested to officiate in that service——

[On July 3 the Convention records note Franklin's part in arranging what has come to be called "The Great Compromise." At the conclusion of the debate in the committee appointed to resolve the representation question, Franklin made the crucial proposal.]

These remarks gave rise to a motion of Dr. Franklin, which after some modification was agreed to, and made the basis of the following report of the committee.

The committee to whom was referred the eighth resolution, reported from the committee of the whole house, and so much of the seventh as had not been decided on, submit the following report:

That the subsequent propositions be recommended to the convention, on condition that both shall be generally adopted.

That in the first branch of the legislature, each of the states now in the union, be allowed one member for every 40,000 inhabitants, of the description reported in the seventh resolution of the committee of the whole house

That each state, not containing that number, shall be allowed one member.

That all bills for raising or apportioning money, and for fixing salaries of the officers of government of the United States, shall originate in the first branch of the legislature, and shall not be altered or amended by the second branch; and that no money shall be drawn from the public treasury, but in pursuance of appropriations to be originated in the first branch.

That in the second branch of the legislature, *each state shall have an equal vote.*

[In defending this compromise, on July 6 Franklin explained why the House of Representatives should have special power over money bills.]

. . . Docr. Franklin did not mean to go into a justification of the Report; but as it had been asked what would be the use of restraining the 2d. branch from medling with money bills, he could not but remark that it was always of importance that the people should know who had disposed of their money, & how it had been disposed of. It was a maxim that those who feel, can best judge. This end would, he thought, be best attained, if money affairs were to be confined to the immediate representatives of the people. This was his inducement to concur in the report. As to the danger or difficulty that might arise from a negative in the 2d. where the people wd. not be proportionally represented, it might easily be got over by declaring that there should be no such Negative: or if that will not do, by declaring that there shall be no branch at all. . . .

[On July 26, during debate on the executive department, Franklin explained why he thought it no disgrace to forbid the re-election of the President.]

. . . It seems to have been imagined by some that the returning to the mass of the people was degrading the magistrate. This he thought was contrary to republican principles. In free Governments the rulers are the servants, and the people their superiors & sovereigns. For the former therefore to return among the latter was not to *degrade* but to *promote* them—and it would be imposing an unreasonable burden on them, to keep them always in a State of servitude, and not allow them to become again one of the Masters. . . .

[On August 7, Franklin spoke of the need in a republican government to make as many citizens as possible feel a sense of public responsibility. The best way to do this was to give them a voice in the government.]

. . . It is of great consequence that we shd. not depress the virtue & public spirit of our common people; of which they displayed a great deal during the war, and which contributed principally to the favorable issue of it. He related the honorable refusal of the American seamen who were carried in great numbers into the British Prisons during the war, to redeem themselves from misery or to seek their fortunes, by entering on board the Ships of the Enemies to their Country; contrasting their patriotism with a contemporary instance in which the British seamen made prisoners by the Americans, readily entered on the ships of the latter on being promised a share of the prizes that might be made out of their own Country. This proceeded he said, from the different manner in which the common people were treated in America & G. Britain. He did not think that the elected had any right in any case to narrow the privileges of the electors. He quoted as arbitrary the British Statute setting forth the danger of tumultuous meetings, and under that pretext, narrowing the right of suffrage to persons having freeholds of a certain value; observing that this Statute was soon followed by another under the succeeding Parliamt. subjecting the people who had no votes to peculiar labors & hardships. He was persuaded also that such a restriction as was proposed would give great uneasiness in the populous States. The sons of a substantial farmer, not being themselves freeholders, would not be pleased at being disfranchised, and there are a great many persons of that description. . . .

[On August 9 Franklin spoke, as he had done again and again throughout his life, in favor of encouraging "meritorious strangers" to immigrate to America. He therefore opposed making a long term of residence in the United States a naturalization requirement.]

. . . Docr. Franklin was not agst. a reasonable time, but should be very sorry to see any thing like illiberality inserted in the Constitution. The people in Europe are friendly to this Country. Even in the Country with which we have been lately at war, We have now & had during the war, a great many friends not only among the people at large but in both Houses of Parliament. In every other Country in Europe all the people are our friends. We found in the Course of the Revolution, that many strangers served us faithfully — and that many natives took part agst. their Country. When foreigners after looking about for some other Country in which they can obtain more happiness, give a preference to ours, it is a proof of attachment which ought to excite our confidence & affection. . . .

[On August 10 Franklin opposed a property qualification for voters.]

. . . Doctr Franklin expressed his dislike of every thing that tended to debase the spirit of the common people. If honesty was often the companion of wealth, and if poverty was exposed to peculiar temptation, it was not less true that the possession of property increased the desire of more property — Some of the greatest rogues he was ever acquainted with, were the richest rogues. We should remember the character which the Scripture requires in Rulers, that they should be men hating covetousness — This Constitution will be much read and attended to in Europe, and if it should betray a great partiality to the rich — will not only hurt us in the esteem of the most liberal and enlightened men there, but discourage the common people from removing to this Country. . . .

[On September 17, according to a plan prearranged by the supporters of the Constitution, Franklin, as the most respected delegate on the floor, made a final plea for unanimous approval.]

. . . I confess that there are several parts of this constitution which I do not at present approve, but I am not sure I shall never approve them: For having lived long, I have experienced many instances of being obliged by better information or fuller consideration, to change opinions even on important subjects, which I once thought right, but found to be otherwise. It is therefore that the older I grow, the more apt I am to doubt my own judgment, and to pay more respect to the judgment of others. Most men indeed as well as most sects in Religion, think themselves in possession of all truth, and that whereever others differ from them it is so far error. Steele, a Protestant in a Dedication tells the Pope, that the only difference between our Churches in their opinions of the certainty of their doctrines is, the Church of Rome is infallible and the Church of England is never in the wrong. But though many private persons think almost as highly of their own infallibility as of that of their sect, few express it so naturally as a certain french lady, who in a dispute with her sister, said "I don't know how it happens, Sister but I meet with no body but myself, that's always in the right" — *Il n'y a que moi qui a toujours raison."*

In these sentiments, Sir, I agree to this Constitution with all its faults, if they are such; because I think a general Government necessary for us, and there is no form of Government but what may be a blessing to the people if well administered, and believe farther that this is likely to be well administered for a course of years, and can only end in Despotism, as other forms have done before it, when the people shall become so corrupted as to need despotic Government, being incapable of any other. I doubt too whether any other Convention we can obtain may be able to make a better Constitution. For when you assemble a number of men to have the advantage of their joint wisdom, you inevitably assemble with those men, all their prejudices, their passions, their errors of opinion, their local interests, and their selfish views. From such an Assembly can a perfect production be expected? It therefore astonishes me, Sir, to find this system approaching so near to perfection as it does; and I think it will astonish our enemies, who are waiting with confidence to hear that our councils are confounded like those of the Builders of Babel; and that our States are on the point of separation, only to meet hereafter for the purpose of cutting one another's throats. Thus I consent, Sir, to this Constitution because I expect no better, and because I am not sure, that it is not the best. The opinions I have had of its errors, I sacrifice to the public good— I have never whispered a syllable of them abroad— Within these walls they were born, and here they shall die— If every one of us in returning to our Constituents were to report the objections he has had to it, and endeavor to gain partizans in support of them, we might prevent its being generally received, and thereby lose all the salutary effects & great advantages resulting naturally in our favor among foreign Nations as well as among ourselves, from our real or apparent unanimity. Much of the strength & efficiency of any Government in procuring and securing happiness to the people, depends on opinion, on the general opinion of the goodness of the Government, as well as of the wisdom and integrity of its Governors. I hope therefore that for our own sakes as a part of the people, and for the sake of posterity, we shall act heartily and unanimously in recommending this Constitution (if approved by Congress & confirmed by the Conventions) wherever our influence may extend, and turn our future thoughts & endeavors to the means of having it well administered.

On the whole, Sir, I cannot help expressing a wish that every member of the Convention who may still have objections to it, would with me, on this occasion doubt a little of his own infallibility—and to make manifest our unanimity, put his name to this instrument. . . .

Sage at Home 403

THE CONSTITUTIONAL CONVENTION
AND THE FOOLISHNESS OF WAR

Franklin's largest and longest correspondence was with his sister, Jane Mecom, a Boston housewife whose often sorrowful life Franklin did his best to make easier. They corresponded ordinarily about family matters, but at the end of the Constitutional Convention he wrote her of its work and commented on her distaste for war.

. . . The Convention finish'd the 17th Instant. I attended the Business of it 5 Hours in every Day from the Beginning, which is something more than four Months. You may judge from thence, that my Health continues; some tell me I look better, and they suppose the daily Exercise of going and returning from the Statehouse has done me good. You will see the Constitution we have propos'd in the Papers. The Forming of it so as to accommodate all the different Interests and Views was a difficult Task; and perhaps, after all, it may not be received with the same Unanimity in the different States, that the Convention have given the Example of in delivering it out for their Consideration. We have, however, done our best, and it must take its chance.

I agree with you perfectly in your disapprobation of war. Abstracted from the inhumanity of it, I think it wrong in point of human prudence; for, whatever advantage one nation would obtain from another, whether it be part of their territory, the liberty of commerce with them, free passage on their rivers, &c. &c., it would be much cheaper to purchase such advantage with ready money than to pay the expense of acquiring it by war. An army is a devouring

Writings, IX, 612–613; from a letter to Jane Mecom, September 20, 1787.

monster, and, when you have raised it, you have, in order to subsist it, not only the fair charges of pay, clothing, provisions, arms, and ammunition, with numberless other contingent and just charges to answer and satisfy, but you have all the additional knavish charges of the numerous tribe of contractors to defray, with those of every other dealer who furnishes the articles wanted for your army, and takes advantage of that want to demand exorbitant prices. It seems to me, that, if statesmen had a little more arithmetic, or were more accustomed to calculation, wars would be much less frequent. I am confident, that Canada might have been purchased from France for a tenth part of the money England spent in the conquest of it. And if, instead of fighting with us for the power of taxing us, she had kept us in good humour by allowing us to dispose of our own money, and now and then giving us a little of hers, by way of donation to colleges, or hospitals, or for cutting canals, or fortifying ports, she might have easily drawn from us much more by our occasional voluntary grants and contributions, than ever she could by taxes. Sensible people will give a bucket or two of water to a dry pump, that they may afterwards, get from it all they have occasion for. Her ministry were deficient in that little point of common sense. And so they spent one hundred millions of her money, and after all lost what they contended for. . . .

ON THE ABUSE OF THE PRESS

As an editor and as a politician Franklin believed the press had an obligation to improve the habits of its readers and to promote public tranquillity, even if this meant at times refusing to publish

---

Writings, IX, 639–642; letter to the editors of *The Pennsylvania Gazette*, March 30, 1788.

irresponsible or scurrilous pieces. During the heat of the ratification debates he addressed a letter to the editors of the paper he had published for twenty years, pleading for moderation, and, in a favorite device, assuming the role of an outside observer of the events he meant to satirize.

I lately heard a remark, that on examination of *The Pennsylvania Gazette* for fifty years, from its commencement, it appeared, that, during that long period, scarce one libellous piece had ever appeared in it. This generally chaste conduct of your paper is much to its reputation; for it has long been the opinion of sober, judicious people, that nothing is more likely to endanger the liberty of the press, than the abuse of that liberty, by employing it in personal accusation, detraction, and calumny. The excesses some of our papers have been guilty of in this particular, have set this State in a bad light abroad, as appears by the following letter, which I wish you to publish, not merely to show your own disapprobation of the practice, but as a caution to others of the profession throughout the United States. For I have seen a European newspaper, in which the editor, who had been charged with frequently calumniating the Americans, justifies himself by saying, "that he had published nothing disgraceful to us, which he had not taken from our own printed papers." I am, &c.

A. B.

"*New York, March* 30, 1788.
" DEAR FRIEND,
"My Gout has at length left me, after five Months' painful Confinement. It afforded me, however, the Leisure to read, or hear read, all the Packets of your various Newspapers, which you so kindly sent for my Amusement.
"Mrs. W. has partaken of it; she likes to read the Adver-

tisements; but she remarks some kind of Inconsistency in the announcing so many Diversions for almost every Evening of the Week, and such Quantities to be sold of expensive Superfluities, Fineries, and Luxuries *just imported,* in a Country, that at the same time fills its Papers with Complaints of *Hard Times,* and Want of Money. I tell her, that such Complaints are common to all Times and all Countries, and were made even in Solomon's Time; when, as we are told, Silver was as plenty in Jerusalem as the Stones in the Street; and yet, even then, there were People who grumbled, so as to incur this Censure from that knowing Prince. '*Say not thou that the former Times were better than these; for thou dost not enquire rightly concerning that matter.*'

"But the Inconsistence that strikes me the most is, that between the Name of your City, Philadelphia, *(Brotherly Love,)* and the Spirit of Rancour, Malice, and *Hatred* that breathes in its NewsPapers. For I learn from those Papers, that your State is divided into Parties, that each Party ascribes all the public Operations of the other to vicious Motives; that they do not even suspect one another of the smallest Degree of Honesty; that the antifederalists are such, merely from the Fear of losing Power, Places, or Emoluments, which they have in Possession or in Expectation; that the Federalists are a set of *Conspirators,* who aim at establishing a Tyranny over the Persons and Property of their Countrymen, and to live in Splendor on the Plunder of the People. I learn, too, that your Justices of the Peace, tho' chosen by their Neighbours, make a villainous Trade of their Office, and promote Discord to augment Fees, and fleece their Electors; and that this would not be mended by placing the Choice in the Executive Council, who, with interested or party Views, are continually making as improper Appointments; witness a '*petty Fidler,*

Sycophant, and Scoundrel,' appointed Judge of the Admiralty; 'an old Woman and Fomenter of Sedition' to be another of the Judges, and 'a Jeffries' Chief Justice, &c. &c.; with 'two Harpies' the Comptroller and Naval Officers, to prey upon the Merchants and deprive them of their Property by Force of Arms, &c.

"I am inform'd also by these Papers, that your General Assembly, tho' the annual choice of the People, shows no Regard to their Rights, but from sinister Views or Ignorance makes Laws in direct Violation of the Constitution, to divest the Inhabitants of their Property and give it to Strangers and Intruders; and that the Council, either fearing the Resentment of their Constituents, or plotting to enslave them, had projected to disarm them, and given Orders for that purpose; and finally, that your President, the unanimous joint choice of the Council and Assembly, is 'an old Rogue,' who gave his Assent to the federal Constitution merely to avoid refunding Money he had purloin'd from the United States.

"There is, indeed, a good deal of manifest *Inconsistency* in all this, and yet a Stranger, seeing it in your own Prints, tho' he does not believe it all, may probably believe enough of it to conclude, that Pennsylvania is peopled by a Set of the most unprincipled, wicked, rascally, and quarrelsome Scoundrels upon the Face of the Globe. I have sometimes, indeed, suspected, that those Papers are the Manufacture of foreign Enemies among you, who write with a view of disgracing your Country, and making you appear contemptible and detestable all the World over; but then I wonder at the Indiscretion of your Printers in publishing such Writings! There is, however, one of your *Inconsistencies* that consoles me a little which is, that tho' *living*, you give one another the characters of Devils; *dead*, you are all Angels! It is delightful, when any of you die, to

408 *The Political Thought of Benjamin Franklin*

read what good Husbands, good Fathers, good Friends, good Citizens, and good Christians you were, concluding with a Scrap of Poetry that places you, with certainty, every one in Heaven. So that I think Pennsylvania a good country *to dye in,* though a very bad one to *live in.*"

A COMPARISON

OF THE CONDUCT OF THE ANCIENT JEWS

AND OF THE ANTI-FEDERALISTS

IN THE UNITED STATES OF AMERICA

Though Franklin favored the new Constitution he took no direct part in the debates over its ratification other than this satire comparing the quarrelsome conduct of the antifederalists to the ancient Jews who opposed the divine ordinances of the Israelite nation.

A zealous Advocate for the propos'd Federal Constitution, in a certain public Assembly, said, that "the Repugnance of a great part of Mankind to good Government was such, that he believed, that, if an angel from Heaven was to bring down a Constitution form'd there for our Use, it would nevertheless meet with violent Opposition." He was reprov'd for the suppos'd Extravagance of the Sentiment; and he did not justify it. Probably it might not have immediately occur'd to him, that the Experiment had been

---

Writings, IX, 698–703; written for newspaper publication, probably in the winter or spring of 1788.

Sage at Home 409

try'd, and that the Event was recorded in the most faithful of all Histories, the Holy Bible; otherwise he might, as it seems to me, have supported his Opinion by that unexceptionable Authority.

The Supreme Being had been pleased to nourish up a single Family, by continued Acts of his attentive Providence, till it became a great People; and, having rescued them from Bondage by many Miracles, performed by his Servant Moses, he personally deliver'd to that chosen Servant, in the presence of the whole Nation, a Constitution and Code of Laws for their Observance; accompanied and sanction'd with Promises of great Rewards, and Threats of severe Punishments, as the Consequence of their Obedience or Disobedience.

This Constitution, tho' the Deity himself was to be at its Head (and it is therefore call'd by Political Writers a *Theocracy*), could not be carried into Execution but by the Means of his Ministers; Aaron and his Sons were therefore commission'd to be, with Moses, the first establish'd Ministry of the new Government.

One would have thought, that this Appointment of Men, who had distinguish'd themselves in procuring the Liberty of their Nation, and had hazarded their Lives in openly opposing the Will of a powerful Monarch, who would have retain'd that Nation in Slavery, might have been an Appointment acceptable to a grateful People; and that a Constitution fram'd for them by the Deity himself might, on that Account, have been secure of a universal welcome Reception. Yet there were in every one of the *thirteen Tribes* some discontented, restless Spirits, who were continually exciting them to reject the propos'd new Government, and this from various Motives.

Many still retained an Affection for Egypt, the Land of their Nativity; and these, whenever they felt any Inconvenience or Hardship, tho' the natural and unavoidable Effect of their Change of Situation, exclaim'd against their Leaders as the Authors of their Trouble; and were not only for returning into Egypt, but for stoning their deliverers. Those inclin'd to idolatry were displeas'd that their *Golden Calf* was destroy'd. Many of the Chiefs thought the new Constitution might be injurious to their particular Interests, that the *profitable Places* would be *engrossed by the Families and Friends of Moses and Aaron,* and others equally well-born excluded. In Josephus and the Talmud, we learn some Particulars, not so fully narrated in the Scripture. We are there told, "That Corah was ambitious of the Priesthood, and offended that it was conferred on Aaron; and this, as he said, by the Authority of Moses only, *without the Consent of the People.* He accus'd Moses of having, by various Artifices, fraudulently obtain'd the Government, and depriv'd the People of their Liberties; and of *conspiring* with Aaron to perpetuate the Tyranny in their Family. Thus, tho' Corah's real Motive was the Supplanting of Aaron, he persuaded the People that he meant only the *Public Good;* and they, moved by his Insinuations, began to cry out; 'Let us maintain the Common Liberty of our *respective Tribes;* we have freed ourselves from the Salvery impos'd on us by the Egyptians, and shall we now suffer ourselves to be made Slaves by Moses? If we must have a Master, it were better to return to Pharaoh, who at least fed us with Bread and Onions, than to serve this new Tyrant, who by his Operations has brought us into Danger of Famine.' Then they called in question the *Reality of his Conference* with God; and objected to the *Privacy of the Meetings,* and the *preventing any of the People from being present* at the Colloquies, or even approaching the Place, as Grounds of great Suspicion. They accused Moses also of *Peculation;* as embezzling part of the Golden Spoons and the Silver Chargers, that the Princes had offer'd at the Dedication of the Altar, and the Offerings of Gold by the common People, as well as most of the Poll-Tax; and Aaron they accus'd of pocketing much of the Gold of which he pretended to have made a molten Calf. Besides *Peculation,* they charg'd Moses with *Ambition;* to gratify which Passion he had, they said, deceiv'd the People, by promising to bring them *to* a land flowing with Milk and Honey; instead of doing which, he had brought them *from* such a Land; and that he thought light of all this mischief, provided he could make himself an *absolute Prince.* That, to support the new Dignity with Splendor in his Family, the partial Poll-Tax already levied and given to Aaron was to be follow'd by a general one, which would probably be augmented from time to time, if he were suffered to go on promulgating new Laws, on pretence of new occasional Revelations of the divine Will, till their whole Fortunes were devour'd by that Aristocracy.

Moses deny'd the Charge of Peculation; and his Accusers were destitute of Proofs to support it; tho' *Facts,* if real, are in their Nature capable of Proof. "I have not," said he (with holy Confidence in the Presence of his God), "I have not taken from this People the value of an Ass, nor done them any other Injury." But his Enemies had made the Charge, and with some Success among the Populace; for no kind of Accusation is so readily made, or easily believ'd, by Knaves as the Accusation of Knavery.

In fine, no less than two hundred and fifty of the principal Men, "famous in the Congregation, Men of Renown," heading and exciting the Mob, worked them up to such a pitch of Frenzy, that they called out, "Stone 'em, stone 'em, and thereby *secure our Liberties;* and let us chuse other Captains, that may lead us back into Egypt, in case we do not succeed in reducing the Canaanites!"

On the whole, it appears, that the Israelites were a People jealous of their newly-acquired Liberty, which Jealousy was in itself no Fault; but when they suffer'd it to be work'd upon by artful Men, pretending Public Good, with nothing really in view but private Interest, they were led to oppose the Establishment of the *New Constitution,* whereby they brought upon themselves much Inconvenience and Misfortune. It appears further, from the same inestimable History, that, when after many Ages that Constitution was become old and much abus'd, and an Amendment of it was propos'd, the populace, as they had accus'd Moses of the Ambition of making himself a *Prince,* and cried out, "Stone him, stone him;" so, excited by their High Priests and SCRIBES, they exclaim'd against the Messiah, that he aim'd at becoming King of the Jews, and cry'd out, "*Crucify him, Crucify him.*" From all which we may gather, that popular Opposition to a public Measure is no Proof of its Impropriety, even tho' the Opposition be excited and headed by Men of Distinction.

To conclude, I beg I may not be understood to infer, that our General Convention was divinely inspired, when it form'd the new federal Constitution, merely because that Constitution has been unreasonably and vehemently opposed; yet I must own I have so much Faith in the general Government of the world by *Providence,* that I can hardly conceive a Transaction of such momentous Importance to the Welfare of Millions now existing, and to exist in the Posterity of a great Nation, should be suffered to pass without being in some degree influenc'd, guided, and governed by that omnipotent, omnipresent, and beneficent Ruler, in whom all inferior Spirits live, and move, and have their Being.

B. F.

Sage at Home 413

ON

THE NEW CONSTITUTION AND PROSPECTS

FOR GOVERNMENT UNDER IT

In the year following submission of the new Constitution to the people of the states, Franklin wrote to his friends about it, responding to their criticisms and prophesying optimistically about the progress of the United States under it. Reprinted here are a series of his comments under the dates on which they were made.

[To Ferdinand Grand, October 22, 1787]

. . . I send you enclos'd the propos'd new Federal Constitution for these States. I was engag'd 4 Months of the last Summer in the convention that form'd it. It is now sent by Congress to the several States for their Confirmation. If it succeeds, I do not see why you might not in Europe carry the Project of good Henry the 4th into Execution, by forming a Federal Union and One Grand Republick of all its different States and Kingdoms, by means of a like Convention, for we had many Interests to reconcile. . . .

[To Louis Le Veillard, February 17, 1788]

. . . I sent you with my last a copy of the new Constitution proposed for the United States by the late General Convention. I sent one also to our excellent friend the

---

Writings, IX, 619, 637–638, 645–646, 657–659, 665–666, 673–674; from letters as indicated below, October 1787–October 1788.

Duke de la Rochefoucauld. I attended the business of the Convention faithfully for four months. Enclosed you have the last speech I made in it. Six States have already adopted the Constitution, and there is now little doubt of its being accepted by a sufficient number to carry it into execution, if not immediately by the whole. It has, however, met with great opposition in some States, for we are at present a nation of politicians. And, though there is a general dread of giving too much power to our *governors,* I think we are more in danger from too little obedience in the *governed.*

We shall, as you suppose, have imposts on trade, and custom-houses, not because other nations have them, but because we cannot at present do without them. We want to discharge our public debt occasioned by the late war. Direct taxes are not so easily levied on the scantily settled inhabitants of our wide-extended country; and what is paid in the price of merchandise is less felt by the consumer, and less the cause of complaint. When we are out of debt we may leave our trade free, for our ordinary charges of government will not be great. . . .

[To Louis Le Veillard, April 22, 1788]

. . . It is very possible, as you suppose, that all the articles of the proposed new government will not remain unchanged after the first meeting of the Congress. I am of opinion with you, that the *two* chambers were not necessary, and I disliked some other articles that are in, and wished for some that are not in the proposed plan. I nevertheless hope it may be adopted, though I should have nothing to do with the execution of it, being determined to quit all public business with my present employment. At eighty-three one certainly has a right to *ambition* repose. . . .

[To Louis Le Veillard, June 8, 1788]

. . . Eight States have now agreed to the proposed new constitution; there remain five who have not yet discussed it; their appointed times of meeting not being yet arrived. Two are to meet this month, the rest later. One more agreeing, it will be carried into execution. Probably some will not agree at present, but time may bring them in; so that we have little doubt of it becoming general, perhaps with some corrections. . . . General Washington is the man that all our eyes are fixed on for *President,* and what little influence I may have, is devoted to him. . . .

[To Dupont de Nemours, June 9, 1788]

. . . But we must not expect, that a new government may be formed, as a game of chess may be played, by a skilful hand, without a fault. The players of our game are so many, their ideas so different, their prejudices so strong and so various, and their particular interests, independent of the general, seeming so opposite, that not a move can be made that is not contested; the numerous objections confound the understanding; the wisest must agree to some unreasonable things, that reasonable ones of more consequence may be obtained; and thus chance has its share in many of the determinations, so that the play is more like *tric-trac* with a box of dice. . . .

[To the Duc de la Rochefoucauld, October 22, 1788]

. . . Our public Affairs begin to wear a more quiet Aspect. The Disputes about the Faculty of the new Constitution are subsided. The first Congress will probably mend the principal ones, & future Congress the rest. That which you mention did not pass unnoticed in the Convention. Many, if I remember right, were for making the President incapable of being chosen after the first four Years; but a Majority were for leaving the Election free to chuse whom they pleas'd; and it was alledged that such Incapability might tend to make the President less attentive to the duties of his Office, and to the Interests of the People, than he would be if a second Choice depended on their good Opinion of them. We are making Experiments in Politicks; what Knowledge we shall gain by them will be more certain, tho' perhaps we may hazard too much in that Mode of acquiring it. . . .

[To Louis Le Veillard, October 24, 1788]

. . . Our affairs mend daily and are getting into good order very fast. Never was any measure so thoroughly discussed as our proposed new Constitution. Many objections were made to it in the public papers, and answers to these objections. Much party heat there was, and some violent personal abuse. I kept out of the dispute, and wrote only one little paper on the occasion which I enclose. You seem to me to be so apprehensive about our President's being perpetual. Neither he nor we have any such intention. What danger there may be of such an event we are all aware of, and shall take care effectually to prevent it. The choice is from four years to four years; the appointments will be small; thus we may change our President if we don't like his conduct, and he will have less inducement to struggle for a new election. As to the two chambers, I am of your opinion that one alone would be better; but, my dear friend, nothing in human affairs and schemes is perfect; and perhaps that is the case of our opinions. . . .

ON ABUSES OF FREEDOM OF THE PRESS

Franklin never believed that liberty of the press permitted publication of irresponsible, damaging charges of all kinds against public and private persons. The printer himself, Franklin asserted, should exclude scandalous pieces, or lacking that, the public should "by any explicit law mark [the] extent and limits" of freedom of the press. He explained the evils he meant to combat in a supposed description of the "powers" of the "court" from conviction in which there was no appeal, the press.

POWER OF THIS COURT.

It may receive and promulgate accusations of all kinds, against all persons and characters among the citizens of the State, and even against all inferior courts; and may judge, sentence, and condemn to infamy, not only private individuals, but public bodies, &c., with or without inquiry or hearing, *at the court's discretion.*

IN WHOSE FAVOUR AND FOR WHOSE EMOLUMENT THIS COURT IS ESTABLISHED.

In favour of about one citizen in five hundred, who, by education or practice in scribbling, has acquired a tolerable style as to grammar and construction, so as to bear printing; or who is possessed of a press and a few types. This five hundredth part of the citizens have the privilege of accusing and abusing the other four hundred and ninety-nine parts at their pleasure; or they may hire out their pens and press to others for that purpose.

Writings, X, 36–40; written for publication in *The Federal Gazette,* September 12, 1789.

PRACTICE OF THE COURT.

It is not governed by any of the rules of common courts of law. The accused is allowed no grand jury to judge of the truth of the accusation before it is publicly made, nor is the Name of the Accuser made known to him, nor has he an Opportunity of confronting the Witnesses against him; for they are kept in the dark, as in the Spanish Court of Inquisition. Nor is there any petty Jury of his Peers, sworn to try the Truth of the Charges. The Proceedings are also sometimes so rapid, that an honest, good Citizen may find himself suddenly and unexpectedly accus'd, and in the same Morning judg'd and condemn'd, and sentence pronounc'd against him, that he is a *Rogue* and a *Villain*. Yet, if an officer of this court receives the slightest check for misconduct in this his office, he claims immediately the rights of a free citizen by the constitution, and demands to know his accuser, to confront the witnesses, and to have a fair trial by a jury of his peers.

THE FOUNDATION OF ITS AUTHORITY.

It is said to be founded on an Article of the Constitution of the State, which establishes *the Liberty of the Press;* a Liberty which every Pennsylvanian would fight and die for; tho' few of us, I believe, have distinct Ideas of its Nature and Extent. It seems indeed somewhat like the *Liberty of the Press* that Felons have, by the Common Law of England, before Conviction, that is, to be *press'd* to death or hanged. If by the *Liberty of the Press* were understood merely the Liberty of discussing the Propriety of Public Measures and political opinions, let us have as much of it as you please: But if it means the Liberty of affronting, calumniating, and defaming one another, I, for my part, own myself willing to part with my Share of it when our Legislators shall please so to alter the Law, and shall cheerfully consent to exchange my *Liberty* of Abusing others for the *Privilege* of not being abus'd myself.

BY WHOM THIS
COURT IS COMMISSIONED OR CONSTITUTED.

It is not by any Commission from the Supreme Executive Council, who might previously judge of the Abilities, Integrity, Knowledge, &c. of the Persons to be appointed to this great Trust, of deciding upon the Characters and good Fame of the Citizens; for this Court is above that Council, and may *accuse, judge,* and *condemn* it, at pleasure. Nor is it hereditary, as in the Court of *dernier Resort,* in the Peerage of England. But any Man who can procure Pen, Ink, and Paper, with a Press, and a huge pair of BLACKING Balls, may commissionate himself; and his court is immediately established in the plenary Possession and exercise of its rights. For, if you make the least complaint of the *judge's* conduct, he daubs his blacking balls in your face wherever he meets you; and, besides tearing your private character to flitters, marks you out for the odium of the public, as an *enemy to the liberty of the press.*

OF THE NATURAL SUPPORT OF THESE COURTS.

Their support is founded in the depravity of such minds, as have not been mended by religion, nor improved by good education;

> "There is a Lust in Man no charm can tame,
> Of loudly publishing his Neighbour's Shame."

Hence;

> "On Eagle's Wings immortal Scandals fly,
> While virtuous Actions are but born and die."
>   DRYDEN.

Whoever feels pain in hearing a good character of his neighbour, will feel a pleasure in the reverse. And of those who, despairing to rise into distinction by their virtues, are happy if others can be depressed to a level with themselves, there are a num'>er sufficient in every great town to maintain one of these courts by their subscriptions. A shrewd observer once said, that, in walking the streets in a slippery morning, one might see where the good-natured people lived by the ashes thrown on the ice before their doors; probably he would have formed a different conjecture of the temper of those whom he might find engaged in such a subscription.

OF THE CHECKS PROPER TO BE ESTABLISHED AGAINST THE ABUSE OF POWER IN THESE COURTS.

Hitherto there are none. But since so much has been written and published on the federal Constitution, and the necessity of checks in all other parts of good government has been so clearly and learnedly explained, I find myself so far enlightened as to suspect some check may be proper in this part also; but I have been at a loss to imagine any that may not be construed an infringement of the sacred *liberty of the press*. At length, however, I think I have found one that, instead of diminishing general liberty, shall augment it; which is, by restoring to the people a species of liberty, of which they have been deprived by our laws, I mean the *liberty of the cudgel*. In the rude state of society prior to the existence of laws, if one man gave another ill language, the affronted person would return it by a box on the ear, and, if repeated, by a good drubbing; and this without offending against any law. But now the right of making such returns is denied, and they are punished as breaches of the peace; while the right of abusing seems to remain in full force, the laws made against it being rendered ineffectual by the *liberty of the press*.

Sage at Home 421

My proposal then is, to leave the liberty of the press untouched, to be exercised in its full extent, force, and vigor; but to permit the *liberty of the cudgel* to go with it *pari passu*. Thus, my fellow-citizens, if an imprudent writer attacks your reputation, dearer to you perhaps than your life, and puts his name to the charge, you may go to him as openly and break his head. If he conceals himself behind the printer, and you can nevertheless discover who he is, you may in like manner way-lay him in the night, attack him behind, and give him a good drubbing. Thus far goes my project as to *private* resentment and retribution. But if the public should ever happen to be affronted, *as it ought to be*, with the conduct of such writers, I would not advise proceeding immediately to these extremities; but that we should in moderation content ourselves with tarring and feathering, and tossing them in a blanket.

If, however, it should be thought that this proposal of mine may disturb the public peace, I would then humbly recommend to our legislators to take up the consideration of both liberties, that of the *press*, and that of the *cudgel*, and by an explicit law mark their extent and limits; and, at the same time that they secure the person of a citizen from *assaults*, they would likewise provide for the security of his *reputation*.

A UNICAMERAL LEGISLATURE

AND EXTENSION OF THE SUFFRAGE

In 1789 Pennsylvania moved to replace her 1776 constitution with its unicameral legislature chosen annually in elections in which all taxpayers could vote. One of the new proposals ex-

---

Writings, X, 56–60; from "Queries and Remarks Respecting Alteration in the Constitution of Pennsylvania," probably written in November 1789.

plained in the newspapers called for a bicameral legislature with an upper house elected for four years by persons possessing an estate of at least £1,000. The upper house, the proposer declared, "should represent property." Franklin took strong exception to the plan and defended the 1776 constitution he had helped draft.

. . . May not the Wisdom brought to the Legislature by each Member be as effectual a Barrier against the Impulses of Passion, &c., when the Members are united in one Body, as when they are divided? If one Part of the Legislature may controul the Operations of the other, may not the Impulses of Passion, the Combinations of Interest, the Intrigues of Faction, the Haste of Folly, or the Spirit of Encroachment in one of those Bodies obstruct the good proposed by the other, and frustrate its Advantages to the Public? Have we not experienced in this Colony, when a Province under the Government of the Proprietors, the Mischiefs of a second Branch existing in the Proprietary Family, countenanced and aided by an Aristocratic Council? How many Delays and what great Expences were occasioned in carrying on the public Business; and what a Train of Mischiefs, even to the preventing of the Defence of the Province during several Years, when distressed by an Indian war, by the iniquitous Demand that the Proprietary Property should be exempt from Taxation! The Wisdom of a few Members in one single Legislative Body, may it not frequently stifle bad Motions in their Infancy, and so prevent their being adopted? whereas, if those wise Men, in case of a double Legislature, should happen to be in that Branch wherein the Motion did not arise, may it not, after being adopted by the other, occasion lengthy Disputes and Contentions between the two Bodies, expensive to the Public, obstructing the public Business, and promoting Factions among the People, many

Tempers naturally adhering obstinately to Measures they have once publicly adopted? Have we not seen, in one of our neighbouring States, a bad Measure, adopted by one Branch of the Legislature, for Want of the Assistance of some more intelligent Members who had been packed into the other, occasion many Debates, conducted with much Asperity, which could not be settled but by an expensive general Appeal to the People? And have we not seen, in another neighbouring State, a similar Difference between the two Branches, occasioning long Debates and Contentions, whereby the State was prevented for many Months enjoying the Advantage of having Senators in the Congress of the United States? And has our present Legislative in one Assembly committed any Errors of Importance, which they have not remedied, or may not easily remedy; more easily, probably, than if divided into two Branches? And if the Wisdom brought by the Members to the Assembly is divided into two Branches, may it not be too weak in each to support a good Measure, or obstruct a bad one? The Division of the Legislature into two or three Branches in England, was it the Product of Wisdom, or the Effect of Necessity, arising from the preëxisting Prevalence of an odious Feudal System? which Government, notwithstanding this Division is now become in Fact an absolute Monarchy; since the King, by bribing the Representatives with the People's Money, carries, by his Ministers, all the Measures that please him; which is equivalent to governing without a Parliament, and renders the Machine of Government much more complex and expensive, and, from its being more complex, more easily put out of Order. Has not the famous political Fable of the Snake, with two Heads and one Body, some useful Instruction contained in it? She was going to a Brook to drink, and in her Way was to pass thro' a Hedge, a Twig of which opposed her direct Course; one Head chose to go on the right side of the

Twig, the other on the left; so that time was spent in the Contest, and, before the Decision was completed, the poor Snake died with thirst. . . .

[Franklin then turned to the proposed franchise limitation.]

. . . Several Questions may arise upon this Proposition. 1st. What is the Proportion of Freemen possessing Lands and Houses of one thousand Pounds' value, compared to that of Freemen whose Possessions are inferior? Are they as one to ten? Are they even as one to twenty? I should doubt whether they are as one to fifty. If this minority is to chuse a Body expressly to controul that which is to be chosen by the great Majority of the Freemen, what have this great Majority done to forfeit so great a Portion of their Right in Elections? Why is this Power of Controul, contrary to the spirit of all Democracies, to be vested in a Minority, instead of a Majority? Then is it intended, or is it not, that the Rich should have a Vote in the Choice of Members for the lower House, while those of inferior Property are deprived of the Right of voting for Members of the upper House? And why should the upper House, chosen by a Minority, have equal Power with the lower chosen by a Majority? Is it supposed that Wisdom is the necessary concomitant of Riches, and that one Man worth a thousand Pounds must have as much Wisdom as Twenty who have each only 999; and why is Property to be represented at all? Suppose one of our Indian Nations should now agree to form a civil Society; each Individual would bring into the Stock of the Society little more Property than his Gun and his Blanket, for at present he has no other. We know, that, when one of them has attempted to keep a few Swine, he has not been able to maintain a

Property in them, his neighbours thinking they have a Right to kill and eat them whenever they want Provision, it being one of their Maxims that hunting is free for all; the accumulation therefore of Property in such a Society, and its Security to Individuals in every Society, must be an Effect of the Protection afforded to it by the joint Strength of the Society, in the Execution of its Laws. Private Property therefore is a Creature of Society, and is subject to the Calls of that Society, whenever its Necessities shall require it, even to its last Farthing; its Contributions therefore to the public Exigencies are not to be considered as conferring a Benefit on the Publick, entitling the Contributors to the Distinctions of Honour and Power, but as the Return of an Obligation previously received, or the Payment of a just Debt. The Combinations of Civil Society are not like those of a Set of Merchants, who club their Property in different Proportions for Building and Freighting a Ship, and may therefore have some Right to vote in the Disposition of the Voyage in a greater or less Degree according to their respective Contributions; but the important ends of Civil Society, and the personal Securities of Life and Liberty, these remain the same in every Member of the society; and the poorest continues to have an equal Claim to them with the most opulent, whatever Difference Time, Chance, or Industry may occasion in their Circumstances. On these Considerations, I am sorry to see the Signs this Paper I have been considering affords, of a Disposition among some of our People to commence an Aristocracy, by giving the Rich a predominancy in Government, a Choice peculiar to themselves in one half the Legislature to be proudly called the UPPER House, and the other Branch, chosen by the Majority of the People, degraded by the Denomination of the LOWER; and giving to this upper House a Permanency of four Years, and but two to the lower. . . .

EDUCATION FOR EMANCIPATED SLAVES

In his last public office Franklin served as President of The Pennsylvania Society Promoting the Abolition of Slavery, and the Relief of Free Negroes Unlawfully Held in Bondage. Seeking to promote the welfare as well as the freedom of Negroes, Franklin signed the following appeal.

It is with peculiar satisfaction we assure the friends of humanity, that, in prosecuting the design of our association, our endeavours have proved successful, far beyond our most sanguine expectations.

Encouraged by this success, and by the daily progress of that luminous and benign spirit of liberty, which is diffusing itself throughout the world, and humbly hoping for the continuance of the divine blessing on our labours, we have ventured to make an important addition to our original plan, and do therefore earnestly solicit the support and assistance of all who can feel the tender emotions of sympathy and compassion, or relish the exalted pleasure of beneficence.

Slavery is such an atrocious debasement of human nature, that its very extirpation, if not performed with solicitous care, may sometimes open a source of serious evils.

The unhappy man, who has long been treated as a brute animal, too frequently sinks beneath the common standard of the human species. The galling chains, that bind his body, do also fetter his intellectual faculties, and impair the social affections of his heart. Accustomed to move like a mere machine, by the will of a master, reflection is suspended; he has not the power of choice; and reason and conscience have but little influence over his conduct, because he is chiefly governed by the passion of fear. He

---

Writings, X, 66–68; from an Address dated November 9, 1789.

is poor and friendless; perhaps worn out by extreme labour, age, and disease.

Under such circumstances, freedom may often prove a misfortune to himself, and prejudicial to society.

Attention to emancipated black people, it is therefore to be hoped, will become a branch of our national policy; but, as far as we contribute to promote this emancipation, so far that attention is evidently a serious duty incumbent on us, and which we mean to discharge to the best of our judgment and abilities.

To instruct, to advise, to qualify those, who have been restored to freedom, for the exercise and enjoyment of civil liberty, to promote in them habits of industry, to furnish them with employments suited to their age, sex, talents, and other circumstances, and to procure their children an education calculated for their future situation in life; these are the great outlines of the annexed plan, which we have adopted, and which we conceive will essentially promote the public good, and the happiness of these our hitherto too much neglected fellow-creatures.

A plan so extensive cannot be carried into execution without considerable pecuniary resources, beyond the present ordinary funds of the Society. We hope much from the generosity of enlightened and benevolent freemen, and will gratefully receive any donations or subscriptions for this purpose. . . .

ON THE FRENCH REVOLUTION

Enfeebled and near death, Franklin heard the news of the beginning of The French Revolution with mixed reactions; he regretted the disorder and the danger posed to many of his

---

Writings, X, 68–69, 72; from letters to Jean-Baptiste LeRoy, November 13, 1789, and to David Hartley, December 4, 1789.

friends (including Louis XVI), but he rejoiced in the expected spread of liberty.

. . . Great part of the news we have had from Paris, for near a year past, has been very afflicting. I sincerely wish and pray it may all end well and happy, both for the King and the nation. The voice of *Philosophy* I apprehend can hardly be heard among those tumults. If any thing material in that way had occurred, I am persuaded you would have acquainted me with it. . . .

. . . The Convulsions in France are attended with some disagreable Circumstances; but if by the Struggle she obtains and secures for the Nation its future Liberty, and a good Constitution, a few Years' Enjoyment of those Blessings will amply repair all the Damages their Acquisition may have occasioned. God grant, that not only the Love of Liberty, but a thorough Knowledge of the Rights of Man, may pervade all the Nations of the Earth, so that a Philosopher may set his Foot anywhere on its Surface, and say, "This is my Country." . . .

THE EVILS OF THE SLAVE TRADE

On February 12, 1790, the Pennsylvania Abolition Society petitioned Congress to restrain the slave trade to the limit of its powers. A Representative from Georgia, James Jackson, denounced the petition and defended slavery and the slave trade in a speech reported in the newspapers. Franklin read the speech and roused himself, in the last month of his life, to write a lively, slashing hoax, mocking the language and sentiments of Jackson's speech.

Writings, X, 87–91; essay dated March 23, 1790, and printed in *The Federal Gazette.*

Reading last night in your excellent Paper the speech of Mr. Jackson in Congress against their meddling with the Affair of Slavery, or attempting to mend the Condition of the Slaves, it put me in mind of a similar One made about 100 Years since by Sidi Mehemet Ibrahim, a member of the Divan of Algiers, which may be seen in Martin's Account of his Consulship, anno 1687. It was against granting the Petition of the Sect called *Erika*, or Purists, who pray'd for the Abolition of Piracy and Slavery as being unjust. Mr. Jackson does not quote it; perhaps he has not seen it. If, therefore, some of its Reasonings are to be found in his eloquent Speech, it may only show that men's Interests and Intellects operate and are operated on with surprising similarity in all Countries and Climates, when under similar Circumstances. The African's Speech, as translated, is as follows.

"*Allah Bismillah, &c. God is great,
and Mahomet is his Prophet.*

"Have these *Erika* considered the Consequences of granting their Petition? If we cease our Cruises against the Christians, how shall we be furnished with the Commodities their Countries produce, and which are so necessary for us? If we forbear to make Slaves of their People, who in this hot Climate are to cultivate our Lands? Who are to perform the common Labours of our City, and in our Families? Must we not then be our own Slaves? And is there not more Compassion and more Favour due to us as Mussulmen, than to these Christian Dogs? We have now above 50,000 Slaves in and near Algiers. This Number, if not kept up by fresh Supplies, will soon diminish, and be gradually annihilated. If we then cease taking and plundering the Infidel Ships, and making Slaves of the Seamen and Passengers, our Lands will become of no Value for want of Cultivation; the Rents of Houses in the City will sink one half; and the Revenues of Government arising from its Share of Prizes be totally destroy'd! And for what? To gratify the whims of a whimsical Sect, who would have us, not only forbear making more Slaves, but even to manumit those we have.

"But who is to indemnify their Masters for the Loss? Will the State do it? Is our Treasury sufficient? Will the *Erika* do it? Can they do it? Or would they, to do what they think Justice to the Slaves, do a greater Injustice to the Owners? And if we set our Slaves free, what is to be done with them? Few of them will return to their Countries; they know too well the greater Hardships they must there be subject to; they will not embrace our holy Religion; they will not adopt our Manners; our People will not pollute themselves by intermarrying with them. Must we maintain them as Beggars in our Streets, or suffer our Properties to be the Prey of their Pillage? For Men long accustom'd to Slavery will not work for a Livelihood when not compell'd. And what is there so pitiable in their present Condition? Were they not Slaves in their own Countries?

"Are not Spain, Portugal, France, and the Italian states govern'd by Despots, who hold all their Subjects in Slavery, without Exception? Even England treats its Sailors as Slaves; for they are, whenever the Government pleases, seiz'd, and confin'd in Ships of War, condemn'd not only to work, but to fight, for small Wages, or a mere Subsistence, not better than our Slaves are allow'd by us. Is their Condition then made worse by their falling into our Hands? No; they have only exchanged one Slavery for another, and I may say a better; for here they are brought into a Land where the Sun of Islamism gives forth its Light, and shines in full Splendor, and they have an Opportunity of making themselves acquainted with the true Doctrine, and thereby saving their immortal Souls. Those who re-

Sage at Home 431

main at home have not that Happiness. Sending the Slaves home then would be sending them out of Light into Darkness.

"I repeat the Question, What is to be done with them? I have heard it suggested, that they may be planted in the Wilderness, where there is plenty of Land for them to subsist on, and where they may flourish as a free State; but they are, I doubt, too little dispos'd to labour without Compulsion, as well as too ignorant to establish a good government, and the wild Arabs would soon molest and destroy or again enslave them. While serving us, we take care to provide them with every thing, and they are treated with Humanity. The Labourers in their own Country are, as I am well informed, worse fed, lodged, and cloathed. The Condition of most of them is therefore already mended, and requires no further Improvement. Here their Lives are in Safety. They are not liable to be impress'd for Soldiers, and forc'd to cut one another's Christian Throats, as in the Wars of their own Countries. If some of the religious mad Bigots, who now teaze us with their silly Petitions, have in a Fit of blind Zeal freed their Slaves, it was not Generosity, it was not Humanity, that mov'd them to the Action; it was from the conscious Burthen of a Load of Sins, and Hope, from the supposed Merits of so good a Work, to be excus'd Damnation.

"How grossly are they mistaken in imagining Slavery to be disallow'd by the Alcoran! Are not the two Precepts, to quote no more, '*Masters, treat your Slaves with kindness; Slaves, serve your Masters with Cheerfulness and Fidelity,*' clear Proofs to the contrary? Nor can the Plundering of Infidels be in that sacred Book forbidden, since it is well known from it, that God has given the World, and all that it contains, to his faithful Mussulmen, who are to enjoy it of Right as fast as they conquer it. Let us then hear no more of this detestable Proposition, the Manumission of Christian Slaves, the Adoption of which would, by depreciating our Lands and Houses, and thereby depriving so many good Citizens of their Properties, create universal Discontent, and provoke Insurrections, to the endangering of Government and producing general Confusion. I have therefore no doubt, but this wise Council will prefer the Comfort and Happiness of a whole Nation of true Believers to the Whim of a few *Erika*, and dismiss their Petition."

The Result was, as Martin tells us, that the Divan came to this Resolution; "The Doctrine, that Plundering and Enslaving the Christians is unjust, is at best *problematical;* but that it is the Interest of this State to continue the Practice, is clear; therefore let the Petition be rejected."

And it was rejected accordingly.

And since like Motives are apt to produce in the Minds of Men like Opinions and Resolutions, may we not, Mr. Brown, venture to predict, from this Account, that the Petitions to the Parliament of England for abolishing the slave-Trade, to say nothing of other Legislatures, and the Debates upon them, will have a similar Conclusion? I am, Sir, your constant Reader and humble Servant,

HISTORICUS.

Analytical Table of Contents

I. PRINCIPLES OF GOVERNMENT
A. *Suffrage and Political Obligation*
   Franklin's Political Principles, 1756   *134*
   The Right to Vote, 1770   *233*
   Some Good Whig Principles, 1774   *280*
   The Obligation to Pay Taxes, 1783   *354*
   Speech on Public Responsibility, 1787   *398*
   Speech Opposing Property Qualifications for Voters, 1787   *400*
   The New Constitution and Prospects for Government Under It, 1788   *413*
   A Unicameral Legislature and Extension of the Suffrage, 1789   *421*
B. *Rights of Legislatures*
   The Rights of a Colonial Assembly, 1755   *111*
   Franklin's Political Principles, 1756   *134*
   Conversation . . . on Legislation for the Colonies, 1757   *141*
   Causes of American Discontents before 1768   *209*
   The Legitimate Powers of Elected Assemblies, 1785   *375*
   The House of Representatives and Money Bills, 1787   *397*
   A Unicameral Legislature and the Extension of Suffrage, 1789   *413*
C. *Union and Federation*
   The Albany Plan of Union, 1754   *83*
   Reasons and Motives for the Albany Plan of Union, 1754   *88*
   Royal Government Better Than Proprietary Rule, 1764   *162*
   An Examination Before the House of Commons, 1766   *182*
   On a Common Parliament for the British Empire, 1766   *192*
   The Seeds of Total Disunion between Great Britain and America, 1771   *239*
   Advice to the Colonies: Union, Moderation, and Firmness, 1773   *251*
   Rules by which a Great Empire May be Reduced to a Small One, 1773   *254*
   An Edict by the King of Prussia, 1773   *264*

Defense of Franklin's Career as Agent, 1774   275
A Final Plea to Preserve the British Empire, 1774   279
Articles of Confederation and Perpetual Union, 1775   288
First Proposals for Peace with Great Britain, 1776   294
A Comparison of . . . the Ancient Jews and of the Antifederalists, 1788   408
The New Constitution and Prospects for Government Under It, 1788   413

D. *Public Office and Public Trust*
The Character of Andrew Hamilton, 1741   35
Popular Support and Resisting the Proprietors, 1756   138
The Vices of British Government and the Virtues of William Pitt, 1758   144
On Office-holding, 1770   237
Defense of Franklin's Career . . . and Loss of His Offices, 1774   275
Franklin's Diplomatic Service, 1781   320
Speech Opposing Salaries for Public Officials, 1787   388
Speech Opposing Re-eligibility of the President, 1787   398

E. *Resistance to Oppression*
. . . The Place of the Colonies in the British Empire, 1754   97
Popular Support and Resisting the Proprietors, 1756   138
On Passage of the Stamp Act, 1765   169
Repeal of the Stamp Act, 1766   171
An Examination Before the House of Commons, 1766   182
America and British Politics, 1767   202
Causes of the American Discontents before 1768   209
Riots in London over "Wilkes and Liberty," 1768   224
A Strategy for Resisting British Oppression, 1769   229
The Boston Tea Party, 1774   278
American Loyalty to the Ancient English Liberties, 1785   376

F. *The Uses of Moderation and Compromise*
Advice to the Colonies: Union, Moderation, and Firmness, 1773   251
Speech Pleading for Calm Tempers, 1787   392
Speech Proposing Prayer at the Constitutional Convention, 1787   395

Motion Proposing "the Great Compromise," 1787   *396*
Final Speech at the Constitutional Convention, 1787   *400*
On the Abuse of the Press, 1788   *404*
A Comparison of . . . the Ancient Jews and of the Antifederalists, 1788   *408*
G. *Parties, Faction, and Corruption*
Franklin's Political Principles, 1756   *134*
Friends and Foes of America in England, 1759   *146*
America and British Politics, 1767   *202*
Corruption in Parliamentary Elections, 1768   *217*
An Evil Parliament and a Good King, 1770   *235*
Rules by Which A Great Empire May Be Reduced to a Small One, 1773   *251*
On Corruption in England, 1775   *282*
British Vices and American Virtues, 1775   *287*
Selfish Interests, Commerce, Necessities, and Luxuries, 1784   *363*
A Comparison of the . . . Ancient Jews and of the Antifederalists, 1788   *408*

II. CIVIL AND HUMAN RIGHTS
A. *Hereditary Privilege*
An Evil Parliament and a Good King, 1770   *235*
British Barbarity during the American Revolution, 1782   *324*
On Hereditary Societies and the Eagle as an American Symbol, 1784   *358*
B. *Freedom of the Press*
An Editorial, 1723   *7*
An Apology for Printers, 1731   *20*
Freedom of the Press, 1740   *33*
On the Abuse of the Press, 1788   *404*
On Abuses of Freedom of the Press, 1789   *417*
C. *Freedom of Religion*
Natural Religion and Freedom of Thought, 1735   *27*
A Parable Against Persecution, 1755   *109*
Toleration in Old England and New England, 1772   *245*
D. *Religion and Society*
Silence Dogood, Number 9, 1722   *3*
The Social Value of a Religion of Good Works, 1753   *80*

436 *The Political Thought of Benjamin Franklin*

    The Social Value of Religion, 1757 *142*
    On State Support for Religion, 1780 *317*
E. *Emigration*
    Criminals and Citizenship, 1751 *60*
    Observations Concerning the Increase of Mankind, 1751 *62*
    Poverty and the Effects of German Immigration to Pennsylvania, 1753 *72*
    The Natural Right of Emigration, 1773 *270*
    The American Revolution in Europe, 1777 *302*
    Information to Those Who Would Remove to America, 1782 *336*
    Speech on Naturalization, 1787 *399*
F. *American Indians*
    The Evils of the Indian Trade, 1753 *82*
    The Barbarism and Injustice of "White Savages," 1764 *158*
    Remarks Concerning the Savages of North America, 1784 *368*
G. *Slavery*
    Education for Emancipated Slaves, 1789 *426*
    The Evils of the Slave Trade, 1790 *428*
H. *Reason, Liberty, and Progress*
    Speech of Miss Polly Baker, 1747 *39*
    Humility and the Search for Truth, 1755 *109*
    The American Revolution in Europe, 1777 *302*
    Passport for Captain Cook, 1779 *310*
    Washington's Fame in Europe and America's Future, 1780 *314*
    Progress, Prosperity, and Peace, 1782 *334*
    Proposals to Make Wars Less Likely and Less Destructive, 1783 *347*
    On the French Revolution, 1789 *427*

III. POLITICAL ECONOMY
A. *Money and Credit*
    The Nature and Necessity of a Paper-Currency, 1729 *14*
    The Uses of Paper Currency, 1767 *193*
    Comparison of Great Britain and the United States, 1777 *297*

B. *Trade and Commerce*
   The Foolishness of British Commercial Restrictions, 1764   167
   Positions to Be Examined, Concerning National Wealth, 1769   226
   Information to Those Who Would Remove to America, 1782   336
   Proposals to Make Wars Less Likely and Less Destructive, 1783   347
   The Advantages of Free Trade, 1783   351
   Selfish Interests, Commerce, Necessities, and Luxuries, 1784   363
   The Internal State of America, 1786   381
C. *Demography*
   Observations Concerning the Increase of Mankind, 1751   62
   Poverty and the Effects of German Immigration to Pennsylvania, 1753   72
   The Interest of Great Britain Considered . . . , 1760   150
   The Internal State of America, 1786   381
D. *Problems of Poverty*
   Poverty and the Effects of German Immigration in Pennsylvania, 1753   72
   On the Labouring Poor, 1768   219
   The Farmers of Great Britain and New England Compared, 1772   244
   Crime and Punishment, 1785   373

IV. THE GOOD SOCIETY
A. *The Need for Virtue*
   Silence Dogood, Number 3, 1722   2
   On Titles of Honor, 1723   9
   The Busy-Body, Number 3, 1729   12
   Junto Queries, 1732   24
   Advice to a Young Tradesman, 1748   51
   A Rebuke to Cowards and Idlers, 1756   133
   The Farmers of Great Britain and New England Compared, 1772   244

British Vices and American Virtues, 1775   287
On Dueling, 1784   362
Selfish Interests, Commerce, Necessities, and Luxuries, 1784   363
Remarks Concerning the Savages of North America, 1784   368
B. *Civic Improvement*
On Lawful Process, 1742   37
The Evils of Taverns, 1745   37
Education and the Public Good, 1749   54
Hospitals, Charity, and the Public Good, 1751   57
Crime and Punishment, 1785   373
C. *Colonization*
Plan for Establishing English Colonies in the Ohio Valley, 1754   105
The Interest of Great Britain Considered, 1760   150

V. INTERNATIONAL RELATIONS
A. *Great Britain as a World Power*
Observations Concerning the Increase of Mankind, 1751   62
The Interest of Great Britain Considered, 1760   150
Great Britain and Europe at the Beginning of the American Revolution, 1775   282
Franklin's Candid View of His Mission in France, 1777   301
On Reconciliation between Great Britain and the United States, 1782   331
B. *The Art of Diplomacy*
Diplomacy in Paris, 1778   307
The Morals of Chess and Diplomacy, 1779   312
Franklin and John Adams on Franco-American Relations, 1780   315
The Art of Diplomacy, 1782   346
Dispute with John Adams over Gratitude toward France, 1783   352
C. *Armed Force and War*
Plain Truth, 1747   43
Proposals for a Volunteer and Republican Military Force, 1747   46

A Militia Act Protecting Conscientious Objectors, 1755   *126*
British Barbarity during the American Revolution, 1782   *324*
Human Depravity in War, 1782   *330*
Proposals to Make Wars Less Likely and Less Destructive, 1783   *347*
. . . The Foolishness of War, 1787   *403*

D. *The Blessings of Peace*
First Proposals for Peace with Great Britain, 1776   *294*
On Reconciliation between Great Britain and the United States, 1782   *331*
Progress, Prosperity, and Peace, 1782   *334*

E. *American National Interest*
Franklin's Candid View of His Mission to France, 1777   *301*
The Alliance with France, 1778   *303*
Parable against Breaking the French Alliance, 1779   *309*
Spain, the United States, and the Mississippi River, 1780   *318*
On Betraying France to Secure Peace with Great Britain, 1782   *322*
The Foundations of American Foreign Policy, 1783   *354*

VI. NATIONAL DESTINY

A. *The Nature of the British Empire*
Observations Concerning the Increase of Mankind, 1751   *62*
. . . The Place of the Colonies in the British Empire, 1754   *83*
The Future of the British Empire in North America, 1760   *149*
An Examination before the House of Commons, 1766   *182*
On a Common Parliament for the British Empire, 1766   *192*
The Nature of the British Empire, 1767   *197*
The British Constitution, 1768   *216*
Fables on the Mother Country and Her Colonies, 1770   *232*
A Realistic Appraisal of the British Empire, 1771   *241*
Rules by Which a Great Empire May Be Reduced to a Small One, 1773   *254*
An Edict by the King of Prussia, 1773   *264*

On Reconciliation between Great Britain and the United
States, 1782 *331*
American Loyalty to the Ancient English Liberties,
1785 *376*
B. **American National Destiny**
British Vices and American Virtues, 1775 *287*
First Proposals for Peace with Great Britain, 1776 *294*
The American Revolution in Europe, 1777 *302*
Washington's Fame in Europe and America's Future,
1780 *314*
Information for Those Who Would Remove to America,
1782 *336*
On Hereditary Societies and the Eagle as an American Symbol, 1784 *358*
The Internal State of America, 1786 *381*
On the New Constitution and Prospects for Government
Under It, 1788 *413*

Index

Abraham and the Stranger, parable on toleration, 109–111
Academy of Philadelphia, founding of, 54
Adams, John
  on constitutional government, lii
  commissioner in Paris, 307
  goes to Holland, 317
  "gratitude" to France, 315, 352–354
  insists on secrecy at preliminary treaty, 346
  "out of his Senses," 354
  Vergennes declares *persona non grata*, 315–317
Adams, Samuel
  on right of rebellion, liii
  suspicious of France, xlv
Addison, Joseph, *The Spectator*, S. Dogood in tradition of, 2
Africa, "darkening" America, 71
Agency, in Great Britain, defense of conduct of, 276
Agriculture
  base of U.S. economy, 383
  war should not obstruct, 350
Albany Plan of Union
  base for Articles of Confederation, 288–289
  defense of, 88–97
  powers of Assemblies under, xl
  proposal, xxxix
  provisions of, 83–88
  purpose, to unite against France, 83
  Shirley's alternative answered, xl, 97–105
America
  accepts sovereignty of King, 200–201, 215, 243
  advised to remain loyal to King, 236
  to appear pacified, and assert rights carefully (*See also* A Realistic Appraisal . . .), 241–244
  allegiance to Crown depends on rights as Englishmen, 216
  British politics affects, 202–203
  cause needs popularizing, 202–203
  contaminated by Britain's corruption, 180–181, 282
  cooperation with Britain reviewed, 183
  corn diet in, scorned, 175–176, defended, 180
  "darkened" by Africans, 71

442 *Index*

disobedience of, satirized, 283–286
Dissenters in, 246
established religion Presbyterian, 247
growth and development foreseen, 63
has Dissenter friends in Britain, 253
interested in rights, not independence, 174–175
in future of Britain, 62–71
morale in, after Bunker Hill, 287–288
"Mother Country" and, 285
not settled at Britain's expense, 285
punitive measures against, satirized, 232–233
refusal of British goods, 214
riots over Stamp Act, 171
"Scotch" religion in, 177–178
seeds of liberty in, 201–202
Stamp Act as punishment for, 170
Stamp Act repeal will decrease excesses in, 189–190
total guilt of, for Stamp Act riots, 180
(*See also* Assemblies, United States)
American Weekly Mercury, The, 12n.
Andrews, Jedidiah, in religious controversy, 27
Anglicans, 246
Apprentice system, in U.S. compared with Europe, 344–345
Articles of Confederation
changes in, in Congress, 288–294
powers of Congress in, xli
(*See also* The Legitimate Powers of Elected Assemblies, 375–376)
Assemblies, colonial
claim powers over crown officials (*See* Causes of American Discontents, 211–213 and The Seeds of a "Total Disunion," 239–241)
claim to privileges of House of Commons rejected, 145
final plea for rights, 279–280
impossibility of uniting with Parliament, 192–193
King is legislator for, 140
powers of, and Smith-Moore case, 147–148
powers of, to tax, 98–102
prefer voting money to being taxed, 209–211
reactions to Quartering Act, 198–199
resist alien governors, judges, 211–213
rights of, to raise money for crown, 188–189
role of, xl
satiric advice on rights of, 261–262
Assembly, Pennsylvania
FRANKLIN inconsistent in libel case against, xxxiv
kept ignorant of proprietary instructions, 122, 126
proprietary power over, 135–137
Quaker problems in, 126–127
right of, to tax proprietary estate denied, defended (*See* The Rights of a Colonial Assembly), 111–126
Association, 1747
Penn disturbed at formation of, 46
Plain Truth brings about, 43
Atrocities
at Martinique engagement, 331
British Barbarity . . . , 324–329
British to offer reparations for, 332–333
listed (*See* British Vices and American Virtues), 287–288

Index 443

made war inevitable, 301–302
Autobiography
  Art of Virtue in, xxix
  describes responsible citizenship, xliv–xlv
  Granville interview described in, 140n.
  on Association, 1747, 43
  on freedom of Press, xxxiii
  on support for churches, xxxiv
  on United Party for Virtue, 18–19
  on Whitefield, 33

Babcock, Joshua, letter to, 223n.
Bache, Sarah Franklin, letter to, 359
Banks, Sir Joseph
  letter of, answered, 334
  rejoices at Peace, 335
Beckford, William, 218
Birth rate, religion and, in America, 69
Blackbirds, anecdote, interference with religion, 73
Board of Trade
  decides fate of Albany Plan, 88
  restricts paper currency (See The Uses of Paper Currency), 193–197
Bonhomme Richard, xxx
Boston Tea Party
  disapproval of, 278
  East India Co. not responsible for, 278–279
Breintnall, Joseph, and "Busy-Body," 12
Bribery, Parliament seat anecdote, 218
British Constitution, The, and Parliamentary Sovereignty, 216–217
British Empire
  advantages of Union to, 252–253; ambitions of FRANKLIN for, in America, xxxviii–xxxix, 62–63, 201, 270

answer to Kames on Union of (See The Nature of the British Empire), 197–202
  common Parliament for, 192–192
  final plea for saving, 279–280
  importance of Canada to, xxxix, 150
  interest in "whole" of, 276–277
  trade restrictions threaten (See The Foolishness of British Commercial Restrictions), 167–169
  (See also Great Britain)
Bunker Hill, 287–288
Burke, Edmund, xlii
"Busy-Body, The," No. 3, 12–14
  genesis of, 12
  on virtue, 13
Button industry, danger to, of trade policy, 168–169

Calhoun, John C., liv
Camden, Charles Pratt, 1st Earl, xlii
Canada
  Britain should cede to U.S., xlviii, 332–333
  importance of, to Britain, xxxix, 150
  increase of British goods in, 153–154
  pamphlet war over retaining (See The Interest of Great Britain Considered . . .), 150–158)
  peopling of, 157
  trade with, 333–334
Canada Pamphlet (See The Interest of Great Britain . . . , 150–158)
Carlisle, Pa., Indian treaty at, 82
Carmichael, William, letter to, 320n.
Cato, on virtue, 13
Chess (See Morals of Chess)
China, 359–60

444 Index

Christianity
  good works vs. doctrine (See The Social Value of a Religion of Good Works), 80–82
  perversion of, in Indian reprisal, 159–160
Churchill, Winston, xlix
Cincinnati, Society of
  anti-republican, 358–359
  descending vs. ascending honor, 359–360
  native turkey symbol of, 361
Civic achievements, xxx–xxxi
Climate, in U.S., 340
Cockpit, humiliation at, 275–276, 278
Coercive Acts, and final plea for coexistence, 279–280
Collinson, Peter, letters to, 72n., 138n., 166n.
Colonial union
  failure to achieve, 154–156
  Parliament need not fear, 230
  with Britain, 237
  (See also Articles of Confederation . . . , 288–294)
Commerce (See Trade and Commerce)
Congress
  makes changes in Articles of Confederation, 289–294
  orders constitutions translated and distributed in Europe, 355–356
  powers of, explained, 375–376
  petitioned to limit slave trade, 428
  powers of, explained, 375–376
  representation debate, 1, 392–393, 395–396
  result is "Great Compromise," 1, 396–397
  two chambers not necessary, 416
  will mend faults in Constitution, 415–416

Constitution, U.S.
  adoption certain, 414
  Congress will mend faults in, 415–416
  experiment in politics, 416
  explained, 375–376
  final plea for, even with faults, 1–li, 400–401
  good government under, foreseen, 413
  great opposition to, 414
  similar one proposed for France, 413
  will improve steadily, 416
Constitutional Convention
  divine inspiration vs. Providence at, 412
  FRANKLIN at, 1–liii, 387–402
  contributions to, ideas rejected, 388
  personal report on, 403–404
Constitution, ratification campaign for (See A Comparison of Ancient Jews and Anti-Federalists), 408–412
  press asked to cooperate in, 404–405
  skilful politicking required for, 415
Constitutions, U.S. and state
  available in Europe, 341–342;
  translated into French, distributed, 355–356
Continental Congress, First, 279–80
Convict transportation
  America resents, 213
  Edict of the King of Prussia, 268
  satires on (See Criminals and Citizenship), 60–62
Cook, Capt. James, 310–312
Cool Thoughts . . . , excerpts from, 162–167
Cooper, Samuel, letters to, 229n., 235n., 302n.
Corn, Indian, 175–176, 178, 180

Courts, satire on (*See* On Lawful Process), 37
Cows and farmer, fable, 232
Creation, Indian version of, 371
Credit (*See* Advice to a Young Tradesman), 51–54
Crime, punishment as deterrent to, 373–375
Crown
 American resistance to loyalty to, 377
 officers of, create disunion (*See* The Seeds of a "Total Disunion" . . .), 239–241
 satiric advice on, 256–257, 261 (*See also* George III)
Cummings, Archibald, 33–34
Cushing, Thomas, letters to, 241*n*., 251*n*., 277, 279*n*., 303*n*.
Customs (*See* Taxes)

Deane, Silas, 307
Declaration of Independence
 fervently celebrated, 381
 followed by peace proposals, 294
 FRANKLIN enthusiasm for, xliv
 tale about FRANKLIN part in, vii
Defense, colonial, satiric advice on, 258, 262–264
Defoe, Daniel, *Essay on Projects*, influence, xxx
deGrasse, Marquis, at Martinique, 331
Deist, unidentified, ridicule by, disapproved, 142–144
Demography
 emigration and, 270–274
 essay on, 62–71
Dialogue between Britain, France, 282–286
Dialogue between X, Y, and Z
 defends Militia Act, 127
 extracts from, 130–133
Diplomacy
 FRANKLIN's, attacked, vindicated, 319–322
 guideposts for policy in Europe, 354–357
 morals of chess applied to, 312–314
Dissenters
 become Presbyterians, Quakers, etc., 247–248
 defended on intolerance, 246–247
 do not want a bishop in America, 246, 250
 in Britain, pro-American, 253
 treatment of, in Old and New England compared, 249–250
Dryden, John, quoted, 419
Dueling, 362
Dupont de Nemours, 226–227, 415

Eagle and cat, fable, 232
 compared with turkey as symbol, 361–362
East India Co., 254, 278
Edict by the King of Prussia, An, 264–269
Education, 54
Electricity, study of, 109
Emigration
 as sign of support for Revolution, 302–303
 demography of (*See* Natural Right of), 270–274
 effect on population, 69–70
 proposed bill limits, 270
 to U.S., advice on (*See* Information to Those Who Would Remove to America), 336–346
 (*See also* Demography, Immigration)
England (*See* Great Britain)
Episcopalians, 248, 250
Europe
 emigration from, 303
 relations with, if Britain loses colonies, 282–283
 supports American Revolution, 302

446 *Index*

Evans, Cadwallader, letter to, 192n.
Eyes of Other People, parable on luxury, 368

Fasts, Thanksgiving instead of, 381–382
Father Abraham, as FRANKLIN *persona*, 51
Federal Gazette, The, anti-slavery hoax in, 428n.
Fishing
  in Newfoundland, xlviii
  in 1785 in U.S., 384
  war should not obstruct, 350
France
  Adams' hostility to, 315–317, 352–354
  aid from, 301–302
  Albany Plan to cope with threat from, 83
  alliance with defended, 319
  America driven to arms of, 303–307
  America will not betray, 309–310, 322–324
  Canada must not be restored to, xxxix, 148, 150
  depopulated by war and protestant expulsion, 69
  diplomacy problems with three Commissioners, 307–308
  friendship for and need of, xlv, 356
  further loans secured, 319–320
  in satiric dialogue, 283, 286
  Ohio settlement to check, 105–109
  proposed treaty with, 296
  U.S. propaganda begins in, 297
  U.S. ties with, 333–334
  vis-à-vis Britain in U.S. policy, xlix
  voice of philosophy drowned in Revolution, 428
  (*See also* Louis XVI)
Franklin, Benjamin
  accepts doctrine of free trade, xlvi
  accepts doctrine of seditious libel, xxxiii
  accepts "manifest destiny," xlvii–xlviii
  admiration for G. Whitefield, liv
  agent for Massachusetts, 229
  ambitions for British Empire in America, xxxviii–xxxix, xliii, 62–63, 201, 270
  and Albany Plan, xxxix, 83, 97
  and Quaker pacifists, xxxv–xxxvi, 126, 134
  and Stamp Act, 169–192
  appearance before House of Commons, 182–191
  as demographer, 62–71
  as Whig, xxix, xlii, 4, 280
  at Federal Convention, xli, 1–liii, 387–402
  and Great Compromise, 1, 396–397
  awareness of role, 138
  Bonhomme Richard, xxx
  civic leader, xxx–xxxi, 57
  confidence in France, xlv–xlvi
  contempt for Commons, Ministry, xliii, 280
  defends D. Hall, xxxiii
  defends unicameral legislature, 421–424
  diplomatic service attacked, vindicated, 319–322
  disenchantment in English mission, xlii–xliii, 280, 282
  early influences, xxvii–xxviii, xxx, xli, xlvi, 2
  early political life, xxxi, 379–380
  enthusiasm for Declaration of Independence, xliv
  forms Junto, xxxii, 24–25
  inconsistent in Assembly libel case, xxxiv
  in religious controversy, 27
  joins Pitt, Camden, xlii

Index 447

juror, 37–38
on Britain-France balance, xlix, 333–334
on British government, 144–145
on Christianity, 80
on injustice to Indians, xlix, 158–161
on post-office job, 237–238
loss of, 275–276
on role of government, xxx–xxxii, lii–liii
on social value, toleration, usefulness, of religion, xxxiii–xxxv, 142–4
on War, xlvii, 330, 334, 403–404
peace correspondence with Hartley, 303–305, 309, 322–324
political thought expressed by career, xxvii, liv
Poor Richard *persona*, xxx, 51
popularity in Britain as motive for peace talks, 296
recommends royal government for Pennsylvania, xxxviii
represents Pennsylvania Assembly *vs.* Penn, xxxvii
returns to Pennsylvania, 158
Franklin, James
jailed in freedom of press issue, 3
printer of *New England Courant*, 1
released from jail, 7
uses FRANKLIN's name, 7
Franklin, Josiah, xxviii
Freedom of the Press (*See* Press, freedom of)
Free Trade
must be postponed, 414
necessity of, xlvi–xlvii
(*See also* Trade and Commerce)
Frugality (*See* Industry and Frugality)

Gage, Thomas, "perfidy" of, 287
Galloway, Joseph, letters to, 144, 191n., 202n., 217n., 224n., 282n.
Gazetteer, The, letter to, 170n.
General Advertiser, The, "Polly Baker" published in, 39n.
Genesis, apocryphal chapter hoax, 109–111
George III
and Whig principles, 327
continued loyalty to, urged, 230–231, 243
dilemma of, 251
enlistment of, against Parliament (*See* An Evil Parliament and a Good King), 235–237
Nerone Neronior, 329
on paying salaries of officials of, 243–244
prime mover of repression, xliii
(*See also* Crown)
Gentleman's Magazine, The, essay in, 216n.
Germans
in demography essay, 63, 71
industry and frugality of, 72, 79
may outnumber Americans, 78
not "patriotic," 78
"Palatine boors," 71
pouring into America deplored, 72, 76–77, 274
scorn assimilation, 77–78
"God-send or the Wreckers," 309–310
Gordon, Thomas, quoted, 4
Government
role of, xxxi–xxxii, liii
social purpose of, lii–liii
Grand, Ferdinand, proposed Constitution sent to, 413
Granville, John Carteret, 1st Earl of, xlii, 141–142
Great Britain
America in future of (*See* Observations concerning the Increase of Mankind), 62–71
American cooperation reviewed, 183

attempt to divide France and U.S., 347
Canada as market for goods of, 153–155
colonies welcome union with, if represented, 102–105
colonies as frontier of, 153
colonies not united, no threat to, 154–156
condition of poor in, 219–224
conditions and motives for peace, 1776 (*See* First Proposals . . .), 294–296
corruption of, 179–180
crime rate highest in Europe, 374–375
disapproves Albany Plan, 84
Dissenters in, pro-American, 253
effect on America of politics in, 202–203
effect of possible victory of, 301–302
emigration will not depopulate, 272
FRANKLIN'S acquaintance with politics in, 144–148
frivolous pretexts for wars of, 300
future jeopardized by trade restrictions, 167–169
importance to, of room in America, 70–71
intolerance of Dissenters in, 249–250
limited acceptance of colonial claims (*See* A Realistic Appraisal . . .), 241–244
loss of colonies and relations with Europe, 282-283
mercantile system of, 226–229
ministry change and peace overtures, 331–332
misinformed about U.S., 379–381
"mother country" in satiric dialogue, 285–286
must retain Canada (*See* The Canada Pamphlet), 150–158
peace overtures unacceptable, 322–324
Pitt to deliver from low estate, 143–144
prospective ruin regretted, 302
punitive measures satirized, 232–233
reception of petitions by, 277
secret move for reconciliation rejected, 305–307
to be watched, after Peace, 354–355
true reconciliation with, hoped for, 335
union with would corrupt America (*See* British Vices and American Virtues), 287–288
usefulness to, of union with America, 252–253
vis-à-vis France, in U.S. policy, xlix
war threat eases attitude America, 251
(*See also* Atrocities, British Empire)
Great Compromise, 1, 396–97
Guadaloupe, less important than Canada, 150, 157–158
Guinea, depopulated by slave export, 70

Halifax, George Montagu Dunk, 2d Earl of, 146
Hall, David, defended in libel suit, xxxiii
Hamilton, Andrew, as model political leader, 35–37
Hardwicke, Philip Yorke, 1st Earl of, 145–146
Hartley, David, 303–305, 309, 322–324
Hat manufacture, in "Edict" satire, 267–268
Hemphill, Samuel, 27
Hemphill-Andrews controversy (*See* Natural Religion and

Freedom of Thought), 27–33
Hessians, use of, scorned, 324
History
  Observations on Reading, 18–19
  uses of study of, 55–56
Hoax, predilection for, vii
  Against English Proposals, 309–310
  An Edict by the King of Prussia, 264–269
  Letter of J. P. Jones, 325–329
  Parable Against Persecution, 109–111
  Polly Baker, 39–43
  Remarks concerning Savages, 368–373
  Silence Dogood, 2–3, 3–6
  Slave Trade, meddling with, 429–432
  "Supplement" to *Independent Chronicle*, 324
  (*See also* Parable, Satire)
Holland
  Adams seeks loan from, 317
  in dialogue, 283–284
  resents Navigation Acts, 284
Honesty (*See* Virtue)
Horace, *Ode* quoted, 12
Hospitality, a "barbarian" virtue, 372–373
House of Commons
  American claims to privileges of, rejected, 145
  contempt for, xliii
  "Examination" before, 181–189
  (*See also* Parliament)
House of Representatives, 397–398
Howe, William, 5th Viscount, 294
Huey, Joseph, letter on religion to, 80n.
Hughes, John, letter to, 169n.
Human Depravity in War, 330–331
Humility and the Search for Truth, 109
Hunter, William, letter to, 379n.
Huntington, Samuel, letters to, 315, 320n.
Hutchinson Letters, "affair" of, 275–278
Hypocrisy, political, religious, S. Dogood defines, 4–6

Immigration
  encouragement of, 399–400
  German compared to English (*See* Poverty and the Effects of German Immigration . . .), 72–79
  on residence requirement for naturalization, 399
  (*See also* Demography, Emigration)
Independence (*See* Declaration of Independence)
Independent Chronicle, The (Boston), "Supplement" to, hoax, 324
Industry and frugality
  as religious duty, effect on birth rate, 69
  exceeds extravagance, in U.S., 367–368, 386–387
  fashionable after Bunker Hill, 288
  of German immigrants, 72, 79
  necessary in new U.S., 339–341
  Stamp Act can be fought with, 169
  way to wealth (*See* Advice to a Young Tradesman), 51–54
  western settlement will stimulate, 365–366
  will help repeal oppressive acts, 230, 231
Indians
  activity in frontier defense against, 133
  assistance to Britain in war, 333
  bloody reprisals against (*See* The Barbarism and Injustice

of "White Savages"), 158–161
crime and punishment among, compared with Britain, 373–375
difficulty of "civilizing," 73–74
injustice to, deplored, xlix
plans with, to resist French, 82, 83
plea for compassion for, 158–161
prefer nomadic life, 74–76
satire on, as "savages" (See Remarks concerning the Savages of North America), 368–373
usefulness in Ohio Valley project, 107
Indian Trade
Albany Plan and, 91–92
Alcohol and (See The Evils of the Indian Trade), 82–83
Ingenhousz, Jan, letter to, 301
Instructions, proprietary, 122, 126
Ireland
conditions in, compared with New England, 244–245
taxation in, 188
Iron manufacture, in "Edict" satire, 266–267
Israelites, ancient, compared to antifederalists, 408–412

Jackson, James, 428–432
Jay, John
arrival in Paris, 332
insists on secrecy at preliminary treaty, 346
letter to, on Spain, 318–319
Jefferson, Thomas
and Declaration of Independence, xliv
republican idealism of, li, liii
Johnson, Samuel, letter to, 56–57
Jones, John Paul
and *Bonhomme Richard*, xxx
purported letter on atrocities, 324–329

Judiciary, dissatisfaction with tenure laws governing, 212–213
Junto Queries, origin and design of, 24–25

Kames, Henry Home, Lord, letter to, 149
writes on union of British Empire, 197–200
Keimer, Samuel, 12
Kinnersley, Ebenezer, 33

Labor
basic economics of, 228
necessary for wealth, 366–367
supply in America, 63–65
in U.S., 1785, 383–384
Lancaster, Pa., reprisals of Indians near, 158
Land purchase, and paper currency, 15
Laud, Archbishop, 271
Lawyers, satire on, 37
Lee, Arthur
commissioner in France, 307
suspicious of France, xlc
undermines FRANKLIN, 319–320
Legal profession, 16
Legislature, unicameral, lii, 416, 421–424
LeRoy, Jean-Baptiste, letter to, 427n.
Lining, John, letter to, 109n.
Lion and mastiff, fable, 233
Livingston, Robert R., letter to, 352
Locke, John, xxxii, xxxvii
London, riots over Wilkes campaign, 224–226
London Chronicle, The, letters in, 97, 169n., 204n., 209n.
London Packet, The, letter in, 245n.
Louis XVI, 320, 347
Lovell, James, letter to, 307
"Loyalist," misnomer for "royalist" (See American Loyalty to the

Ancient English Liberties), 376–377
Luxury
 danger from, 364–365, 386–387
 defined, 363–368
 spur to trade, 364–365

Madison, James
 at Constitutional Convention, li
 "Memorial and Remonstrance," xxxv
"Manifest destiny," xlvii–xlviii
Mansfield, William Murray, Lord, 162
Manufactures
 America as market for, 65–66, 154–155
 blessings from, to poor, 222–223
 in America, 65, 155
 in new U.S., 333–334
 satiric advice on, 266–268
Marriages, in America, 64–65, 66
Martinique, parable of angel at, 331
Maseres, Francis, letter to, 376n.
Massachusetts
 advice to, 231, 251–254
 non-importation in, 229
 1773 petition rejected, 251
 progress in religious liberty, 315–317
 satire on "theocracy" in, 1
 solution of religious tax problem in, 248
 wishes to enforce and collect duties, 240
Mather, Cotton, *Essays to do Good*, xxx
 and "Silence Dogood," 1
Mather, Samuel, letter to, 354n.
Mecom, Jane, 403
 letters to, 237
Medical care (*See* Hospitals, Charity, and the Public Good), 57–59

Mifflin, letter to, 354n.
Mississippi River, navigation of, xlviii, 318–319
Militia, (*See* Proposals for a Voluntary Police Force, 1747), 46–51
Militia Act
 disallowed, 127
 Quakers and, 126–133, 134, 137
Mill, John Stuart, xxxiv
Milton, *Paradise Lost*, quoted, 79
Money bills, 397–398
Moore, William (*See* Smith-Moore case)
Morality, teaching of history and, 55
Morals of chess, applied to diplomacy, 312–314
Morris, Robert, letter to, 357n.
Morris, Robert Hunter, in tax dispute (*See* The Rights of a Colonial Assembly), 111–126
Moses, in parable of ancient Jews, 408–412

Natural rights
 and the British constitution, xxxix, xxxvii
 Locke on, xxix
Navigation Acts, 284
Navy, British, smuggling by officers of, 208
Negroes, in demography essay, 66, 71
 education of, 426–427
 (*See also* Slavery)
New England, conditions in, compared with Britain, 244–245
New-England Courant, The, 1, 3
Newfoundland, fishing in, xlviii
Non-importation, will help repeal oppressive acts (*See* A Strategy for Resisting . . .), 229
Norris, Isaac, letter to, 144n.
North, Frederick, Lord, xlii
Ohio Valley (*See* Plan for Estab-

452 *Index*

lishing English Colonies . . .), 105–109
reprisals for Indian uprising in, 158
On Hereditary Societies, 358–362
Oswald Richard
    paper on war sent to, 347n.
    Shelburne gives paper on peace to, 332

Paine, Thomas, liv
Paper currency
    as cause of gold and silver outflow, 193–194
    intrinsic value of, 194–195
    money and credit and, 14–18
    space advantage of, 196–197
    value of, rests on credit, 195
Parables
    Against Persecution, xxxiv–xxxv, 109–111
    angel at Martinique, 331
    blackbirds, 73
    cows and farmer, 232
    eagle and cat, 232
    eyes of other people, 368
    gentleman-hog, 339
    Indian version of Creation, 371–372
    infidelity of honest woman, 323–324
    lion and mastiff, 233
    man, son, and ass, 23–24
    Morals of Chess, 312–314
    (*See also* Hoax, Satire)
Paris, Ferdinand J., 145, 147
Paris, Treaty of (*See* Treaty of Paris)
Parliament
    Acts of, models for "Edict," 268–269
    annual elections recommended, 281
    assumes right of taxation, 234
    colonies will not surrender to, 215
    desirability of colonial representation, 199
    did not subsidize colonization, 200
    disgust with, 280
    enlisting King against (*See* an Evil Parliament and a Good King), 235–237
    has no sovereignty over colonies, 200–201
    history of bribery (*See* Corruption in Parliamentary Elections), 217–219
    immobilized during Wilkes campaign, 225
    invites disaster (*See* The Seeds of Total Disaster), 239–241
    needs to learn civility, 231
    no uniting with colonies (*See* On a Common Parliament for the British Empire), 192–193
    proposes emigration limitation, 270
    quiet resistance to, urged, 243
    reasons for decreased respect for, 183–184
    rejects colonial claim for privileges of, 145
    underestimates colonial spirit, 230
    Wilkes campaign for, 224
    (*See also* House of Commons)
Peace
    Adams makes negotiation difficult, 353–354
    aphorism on, 335
    as betrayal of France, 322–324
    benefits to accrue from, 356–357
    Britain must make overtures (*See* On Reconciliation), 331–334
    Conciliatory Bill unacceptable, 322–323
    conditions for, 1776, 294–295
    definitive treaty signed, 354
    farce on English overtures, 309–310

Index 453

motives for, 295–296
moves rejected, 305–307
not the object of French mission, 301
parable of honest woman's infidelity, 323–324
secret steps in (See The Art of Diplomacy), 346–347
yearning for (See Progress, Prosperity, and Peace), 334–335
(See also Hartley, David, Treaty of Paris)
Penn, Thomas
alarmed at FRANKLIN's influence, xxxvi, 47
as absentee landlord, xxxvi
disapproves of Association, 1747, 46
insists on tax exemption, xxxvi, 111–126
long quarrel with Pennsylvania Assembly, xxxvii–xxxviii (See The Rights of a Colonial Assembly), 111–126
Penn, William, No Cross, no Crown, parodied in Titles of Honor, 9–10
Pennsylvania
FRANKLIN elected president, 379–380
press abuses, 404–408
royal government for, xxxvii, and hindsight irony of, xli–xlii
sick of dispute with Penn, 162
voluntary militia for, 43
unicameral legislature of 1776 Constitution defended, 421–424
(See also Assembly, Pa.)
Pennsylvania Abolition Society, petition to Congress, 428
Pennsylvania Chronicle, The, letter in, 193n.
Pennsylvania Gazette, The
editorial policy explained, 20–24
essays and letters in, 27n., 33n.,

35n., 60, 62, 126n., 404n.
founding of, 12
satire on reputation of, for decency, 405–408
Pennsylvania Hospital, founding of (See Hospitals, Charity, and the Public Good), 57–59
Pennsylvania Journal, The, essay in, 134n.
Percival, Thomas, letter to, 263n.
Petitions, necessity of, 277–278
Petty, Sir William, on paper currency and inflation, 15
Physiocrats, doctrines of (See Positions to Be Examined . . .), 226–229
Pilgrim's Progress, influence, xxviii
Piracy, 325–329
Pitt, William, xlii, 144
Plain Truth
appeal to Quakers, xxxvi
secures FRANKLIN's influence, 43
sparks Association, 1747, 43
Political beginnings, FRANKLIN's, xxxi
Political discord and liberty, assessed in U.S., 385
Political thought, FRANKLIN's, expressed in career, xxvii, liv
Polly Baker (See Speech of Miss Polly Baker, The), 39–43
Pontiac, reprisals for uprising of, 158
Poor, the
blessings to, from trade policies, 222–223
incitement of, deplored, 220
live on public revenue, 222–223
natural indolence of, 221
taxation for, generous, 220–221
useless to raise wages of, 223–224
(See also Poverty)
Poor Richard, xxx, 51
Poor Richard's Almanack, 1742, 37n.
Postmaster General, Deputy

454 Index

defense of conduct in and possible loss of, 237–239
dismissal from, 276
Post Office
and smuggling, 207
flourishes under FRANKLIN, 238
Poverty
and religion, 73
amount of, compared to wealth, in U.S., 385
Pownall, Thomas, 88
Prayer, proposed at Constitutional Convention, 1, 395–396
Prerogative, royal
Assembly dispute over, 145–146, 147
satiric advice on, 259–260
Presbyterians
established religion in America, 247
in religious controversy (See Natural Religion and Freedom of Thought), 27–33
lose members to Quakers and Baptists, 247
President, office of, re-eligibility for, 398, 416
Press
as "ideal" court of judicature, 417–421
obligations of, satire on, 405–408
Press, freedom of
parable on, 23–24
(See also Apology for Printers, 20–24; defense of D. Hall, xxxiii; J. Franklin and, 7–9; religious controversy and, 33–35)
Price, Richard, letter to, 317–318
Priestley, Joseph, correspondence with, 287n., 330–331
Privateering, profit from, questionable, 348–349
Privy Council, disallows Militia Act, 127
Proposals Relating to the Education of Youth . . . (See Education and the Public Good), 54–57
Proprietors, proprietary interest
and FRANKLIN, mutual contempt, (See Popular Support and Resisting . . .), 138–139
dispute over taxing estate of, 111–112, 134–135
give £5000 in lieu of tax, 124
militia and, 137–138
paper currency and, 17
Pennsylvania government not functioning under (See Royal Government Better than Proprietary Rule), 162–167
power of Assembly and, 135–137
quarrel over prerogative, 145, 147
(See also Assembly, Pa.)
Providence, at Constitutional Convention, 412
Prussia, King of, Edict by, 264–269
Public Advertiser, The
letter for, not published, 270n.
letters in, 170n., 232n., 233n., 254n.
Pulteney, William, letter to, 303n.
Puritan ethic, early influence, xxvii–xxviii
Puritans, flight and immigration of, 271–272

Quakers
Assembly powers and, 135–137
manage without salaries, 391
Militia Act protects, 126–133
pacifism of, xxxv–xxxvi
Plain Truth as appeal to, xxxvi
problems of, in Pennsylvania Assembly, 126–127
taxes and, 134–135
Quartering
as example of problems of unified Parliament, 199

Index 455

limited victory over Act, called "rebellion," 198–199
satiric advice on, 256

Rattlesnakes (criminals), satire on, 60–62
Reconciliation (*See* Peace)
Reparations, for atrocities, 332–333
Religion
American, scorned as "Scottish," 175–177
birth rate and, 69
blackbird anecdote on interference with, 73
freedom of the press and, 33–35
German immigration and, 73
not theology, xxxiv, liii–liv, 80–82
not to be ridiculed, xxxv, 142–144
state support not needed for, 317–318
utility of, xxxv
value of, social, xxxiii
(*See also* Christianity, Dissenters, Presbyterians, Religious freedom, Witchcraft)
Religious freedom
background of Anglican intolerance and oppression (*See* Toleration on Old and New England), 245–251
controversy over (*See* Natural Religion and Freedom of Thought), 27–33
Lockean concept of, xxxv
Massachusetts progress in, 317–318
motive for emigration (*See* Natural Right of Emigration), 270–274
Parable against Persecution, 109–111
in U.S., 345–346
Revolution, American

effect on European emigration, 303
support for, in Europe, 302
theoretical foundations, xxxviii
Revolution, French, voice of philosophy drowned in, 428
Revolution of 1688, Whig ideas from, xlii
Rochefoucauld, François Duc de la, 414–415
Rodney, George Bridge, 1st Baron, at Martinique, 331
Roosevelt, Franklin D., 1
Ross, John, letter to, 224n.
Rossiter, Clinton, cited, xxix
Royal government, Pennsylvania petitions for, 162–167
Royalists, justice for, 376

Salaries
not to pay, a Utopian idea, 390–391
Quakers serve without, 391
Washington served without, 391
Saratoga, victory at, and French alliance, 303
Satire, fondness for, distrusted, vii
Abuse of the Press, 404–408
Conduct of Ancient Jews . . . , 408–412
Criminals and Citizenship, 60–62
Dialogue . . . , 282–286
Editorial, 7–9
Hospitality a "barbarian" virtue, 372–373
Indian Version of Creation, 371–372
Lawful Process, 37
Laziness, 73–74
political and social uses of, 1
Rules by Which . . . , 254–269
Titles of Honor, 9–11
(*See also* Hoax, Parable)
Savages, satire on Indians as, 368–373
Saxony, in satiric dialogue, 285

Scientific spirit, in war, 330, 334
Scotland, Scots
   American resemblance to, scorned, 177–178
   conditions in, compared with New England, 244–245
   sends convicts to America, 213
Seditious libel, doctrine of, accepted, xxxiii.
Settlement, western, Albany Plan and, 92
   many families ready for, 108
   will promote industry and frugality, 365–366
   (See also Ohio Valley)
Shelburne, William P. Lansdowne, Lord, 331–332
Shipley, Jonathan, letter to, 379n.
Shirley, William, answer to plan of union of, xl, 97–105
Silence Dogood
   No. 3, 2–3
   No. 9, 3–6
   source of nom de plume, 1
Slavery
   in America, 66
   meddling with, hoax, 429–432
   petition for limiting trade, 428
Slaves, emancipated, national policy on, urged, 426–427
Smith, Adam, free trade doctrine of, xlvi
Smith, William (See Smith-Moore case)
Smith-Moore case
   and power of colonial assemblies, 147–148
   Pennsylvania Assembly loses, 145
Smuggling, universality of, 204–209
Society for Propagating the Gospel, 247
Sovereignty of King, not of Parliament, accepted, 200–201
   and consideration for subjects, 210

Spain
   depopulation of, 70
   effect of hereditary honor in, 360
   in satiric dialogue, 283, 286
   unnecessary to court, 318–319
Spangenberg, Augustus, and Moravians, rebuked, 133
Speech of Miss Polly Baker, The, satire on law and policies, 39–43
Stamp Act
   America's total guilt for riots, 180
   campaign for repeal of, 169, 171
   can be fought with industry and frugality, 170
   FRANKLIN's attempt to prevent passage, 170
   possible effect of, on commerce, 188–189
   provoked by claims to independence, 170
   repeal of, will decrease further excesses, 171
   reverberates in daily life, 187–188
   Repeal of the Stamp Act, 171–182
   Examination before the House of Commons, 187–191
   (See also On Passage of the Stamp Act)
Suffrage
   extension of, urged, 424–425
   property qualification for, 400
   taxation and, 233–235
   Whig principles on, 280–281
   wide franchise asked, 398–399, 421–425
Sugar, real value of, and unreal taxes on, 349–350
Supreme Court, free press as, 417–421
Sweden, temporarily depopulated by war, 69–70

Tartar priest, on civilizing nomads,

Index 457

73–74
Taxation, Taxes
Albany Plan and, 93–94
as right of colonial assemblies, 111–126
at the expense of trade, 166–167, 168
collection costly, promotes disunion, 240–241
compared with Ireland, 188
external (duty) and internal (stamp) differentiated, 185–186
for poor, generous, 220–221
House of Commons questions FRANKLIN on, 181–190
internal, requires representation, 186
levied by representatives (See The Obligation to Pay Taxes), 357–358
Parliament assumes right of, 234
present amount of, 1766, 182
Quaker-Proprietor dispute over, 134–135
religious problems of, 247–248
repealed except for tea, 241
representation and, 217
1754 statement on, 97–102
requisition preferred to, 209–211
satiric advice on, 258, 260–261, 265–266
smuggling and, 204–209
suffrage and, 233–235
time to end dispute about, 203
Tea
East India Co. near monopoly on, 254
tax on not repealed, 241
(See also Boston Tea Party)
Test oaths (religious), 318
Thanksgiving Day, proclaimed, 382
Thomson, Charles, letters to, 169n., 354n.
Thrift (See Advice to a Young Tradesman), 51–54
Tippling Houses, excessive number of (See The Evils of Taverns), 37–39
Titles of Honor, satire on, 9–11
Toleration, religious (See Religion, freedom of)
Townshend, George, 1st Marquis, xlii
Townshend Acts, resistance to (See Causes of the American Discontents . . .), 209–215
Trade and Commerce
Advantages of Free Trade, The, 351–352
America feels exploited, 214
British will monopolize, if victorious, 302–303
in U.S. in 1785, 384
paper currency and, 16
physiocrat doctrine on, 227, 228
British restrictions on, 101–102
role of luxuries in, 364–365
satiric advice on, 258, 268
Stamp Act and, 188-189
war should not obstruct, 350
Trade balance, gold and silver outflow and, 193–194
Treaty of Paris, 1763, influence of Canada Pamphlet at, 150–151
1783, hope for blessings from, 335
(See also Peace)
Trenchard, John, quoted, 4
Turkey, compared with eagle as symbol, 361–362

Unicameral legislature, defended, lii, 416, 421–424
United Party for Virtue, 18–19
United States
advantages and opportunities in, 341
advice to immigrants to (See Information to those Who . . .), 336–346

agriculture base of economy of, 383
apprentice system in, 344–345
climate salubrious in, 340
conditions for peace with, 1776, 294–295
Constitution available in Europe, 341–342
domestic manufactures in, 343–344
educational facilities, 337
England misinformed about (*See* The Progress of Government and Prosperity . . .), 379–381
false impressions about corrected, 336–337
flourishing future predicted, 315
industry and frugality in, 297, 339–340
good credit risk, 300
guideposts to policy of, in Europe (*See* Foundations of American Foreign Policy), 354–357
immoral eagle symbol of, 361–362
justice of cause (*See* Candid View of Mission in France), 301–302
no desire to return to British domination, 380
optimism about future of (*See* The Internal State of America, 1786), 381–387
patience with "mother country" ended, 304–305
political discord and liberty in, 385
powers of elected assemblies in, 375–376
propaganda for, in France (*See* Comparison of Great Britain and U.S.), 297–300
realistic look at, 382
religious freedom in, 345–346
treaties with France, 305
will not betray France, 322–324

Vaughan, Benjamin, letters to, 363n., 373n.
Veillard, le, Louis, 413
letters to, 414, 415
Vergennes, Charles Gravier, Comte de
accepts apology, makes loan, 346
names Adams *persona non grata*, 315–317
satisfied with peace negotiations, 352
Virginia, 250
Virtue, personal
Advice to a Young Tradesman, 51–54
at Constitutional Convention, liv
Autobiography on, xxix
"Busy-Body" on, 12–14
Cato on, xxxi, 13
civic responsibility and, xxvii–xxviii
education of youth and, 54–57
government and, xxix, liv
international affairs and, 1
Locke on, xxxii
makes U.S. a good credit risk, 300
parliamentary elections, lack of, 218–219
Poor Richard on, xxix, 51
smuggling and, 204
United Party for, 19

Walpole, Sir Robert, anecdote about, 180
War
Albany Plan and military matters, 100
aphorism on, xlvii
atrocities made inevitable, 301
demography and, 70
diminishing inducements to (*See*

Proposals to Make Wars Less
Likely . . .), 347–351
human depravity in, 330–331
measures against, 43–45
purchase cheaper than fighting,
403–404
scientific spirit in, 330, 334
uselessness, waste of, xlvii
Washington, George
candidate for president, 415
served without salary, 391
invited to Europe after the war,
314
reputation foreseen, 315
Wealth, national
foundations of (See Positions to
be Examined . . .), 226–229
as natural resources plus labor,
366–367
Wealth, private, amount of, in
U.S., 385
Wedderburn, Alexander, attack of,
at Cockpit, 275–276
Whatley, George, letter to, 375n.
Whigs
cause equated with Dissenters,
246
constitutionalism, xxxix
development from 1688, xlii
George III and principles of, 327
hope of preserving principles of,
xlii
on suffrage, 280-281
support John Wilkes, 224
Whitefield, George
admiration for, liv
Autobiography on, 33
in religious controversy, 33
"White Savages," essay on barbarism of, 158–161
Wilkes, John
campaign for Parliament, 224
ingratitude of supporters, 225
military inclined to support, 226
Wilson, James, 388
Wilson, Woodrow, 1
Witchcraft, 177
Wool manufacture, in "Edict" satire, 267

Zenger, John Peter, 35